M000318215

THE AFFECT OF DIFFERENCE

The Affect of Difference

REPRESENTATIONS OF
RACE IN EAST ASIAN EMPIRE

EDITED BY
CHRISTOPHER P. HANSCOM
AND DENNIS WASHBURN

University of Hawai'i Press ◈ Honolulu

Printed in the United States of America

21 20 19 18 17 16 6 5 4 3 2 1

Library of Congress Cataloging-in-Publication Data

Names: Hanscom, Christopher P., editor. | Washburn, Dennis C., editor.
Title: The affect of difference : representations of race in East Asian empire / edited by Christopher P. Hanscom and Dennis Washburn.
Description: Honolulu : University of Hawaiʻi Press, [2016] | Includes bibliographical references and index.
Identifiers: LCCN 2015044543 | ISBN 9780824852801 cloth : alk. paper
Subjects: LCSH: Race awareness—Japan—Colonies. | Japan—Colonies—Asia—Race relations. | Ethnology—Japan—Colonies. | East Asians—Race identity.
Classification: LCC DS518.45 .A34 2016 | DDC 305.800952—dc23 LC record available at http://lccn.loc.gov/2015044543

University of Hawaiʻi Press books are printed on acid-free paper and meet the guidelines for permanence and durability of the Council on Library Resources.

CONTENTS

ACKNOWLEDGMENTS

This book grew out of a series of workshops, talks, and colloquia held at Dartmouth College and the University of California, Los Angeles, between 2009 and 2013. Bringing a project such as this to completion was made possible only through the help and support of many individuals and institutions. The editors are grateful first and foremost to all of the contributors, whose hard work, patience, and good humor have made our task truly a labor of love. We benefited tremendously as well from the advice and expertise of colleagues who participated in the workshops and colloquia out of which this volume took shape: Ann Stoler, Leo Ching, Tak Fujitani, Jinhee Lee, Louise Young, Alan Tansman, and Thomas Lamarre. Finally, we express our deepest appreciation to the Dean of Faculty Office at Dartmouth for the generous support it provided us through its Venture Fund and a Dartmouth Conference grant. Support from the UCLA International Institute and the Cultures in Transnational Perspective Mellon Postdoctoral Program in the Humanities at UCLA made possible our 2011 workshop on Visual Representations of Race under Japanese Empire. The Japan Foundation, the Korea Foundation (through a grant from the Northeast Asia Council of the Association for Asian Studies), and the Modern Language Association provided additional funding, without which we could not have seen this project through to completion.

Introduction

Representations of Race in East Asian Empire

This volume addresses the question of how representations of race and the particular affects they produce shed light on imperial formations in East Asia in the twentieth century. In general, studies of empire in modern East Asia follow what might be termed a standard nationalist account that emphasizes the role of nation building in overthrowing colonial rule. This historiography views racial ideologies as an external imposition following a West to East vector and thus tends to elide race as both a descriptive and an analytical category. *The Affect of Difference* challenges this master narrative by avoiding a simplistic periodization of empire or colonization as something that is over and done with and by using the particular case of Japanese empire to establish a comparative framework for studying the lingering impacts of imperial formations globally. Further, by interrogating received notions of the history of Japanese imperialism without deferring to European cases as the perceived origin of both practices and theories of empire, the chapters that follow defamiliarize long-held assumptions regarding both imperial structures of domination and the knowledge that naturalizes them—those "schemes of intelligibility that govern, and leave unaddressed and unquestionable, racial constitution and (mis)recognition."[1]

By focusing the study of Japanese empire on a consideration of the affects created in the production and representation of racial difference, this volume also inflects empire studies in the direction of the everyday, drawing attention to the subtle, often unseen ways in which imperial or racist sentiments may operate beyond the reach of our methodologies. Although almost all of the chapters deal with cases from the late nineteenth century to the end of World War II, taken together they reveal the multiple layers of imperial and colonial control that existed before and continued after the Japanese imperial project. Japan's Asian empire was rapidly established atop Qing, Chosŏn, and European colonial structures only to be displaced, following its defeat in 1945, by the expansion of American power that occurred within the Cold War geopolitical order. This complex history of imperial formations is best engaged by thinking in terms of East Asian empire rather than concentrating simply on Japan as a singular model. Moreover, if we are to avoid eliding the moral and political implications of the connections between race and empire, we must recognize that the impact of colonial cultures on the emotional and ideological structures of everyday life—among metropolitan, colonial, and diasporic populations—has a long duration that continues to the present day.

Imperial Formations and Strategies of Differential Inclusion

One of the key concepts organizing this volume is that of imperial formations, which the contributors have drawn upon and extended in various ways. We have borrowed this term from the work of Ann Stoler, who uses it to refer to particular relations of force that "harbor those mutant, rather than simply hybrid, political forms that endure beyond the formal exclusions that legislate against equal opportunity, commensurate dignities, and equal rights." Stoler's preference for the term "imperial formations" over the more commonly used "empire" arises out of her effort to shift the emphasis of historical analysis away from "fixed forms of sovereignty and its denials to *gradated forms* of sovereignty." Unlike empires, imperial formations are processes of becoming that decimate, displace, and (re)claim. Most important, they are specifically "racialized relations of allocations and appropriations"[2] that occupy multiple tenses, creating effects that exceed the tidy limits of a particular imperial period or the ideological boundaries of the nation-state. As Stoler puts it, such formations "saturate the subsoil of people's lives and persist, sometimes subjacently, over a longer durée."[3]

Because this volume focuses on imperial formations rather than a more static conception of empire defined by imposed geographical borders and institutions of control, it is best described as an archaeology of the racialized subsoil of East Asia, through which we unearth the operation of sentiments, particularly in the realms of cultural production and identity formation in everyday life. It is an archaeology that asks: How can looking at the production of an affect of racial difference shed light on other historical studies of empire?

The special relevance of this volume for comparative studies of race and empire both globally and within East Asia arises in part from the common concerns that run through all the chapters. First among these, clearly, is the subject of race and racism, concepts that operated in the late nineteenth and early twentieth centuries in direct relation to the production of imperial subjectivity. Some of the contributors deal with examples of "scientific" racism, in which biology and anthropometrics play the role of differentiating and arranging subject populations according to phenotypical differences. Others take up instances that correspond to what Etienne Balibar has termed neo-racism, an ideology characterized by a reliance on cultural or linguistic markers to identify racial others. For Balibar, the new racism is a product not of the age of imperialism but decolonization:

> It is a racism whose dominant theme is not biological heredity but the insurmountability of cultural differences, a racism which, at first sight, does not postulate the superiority of certain groups or peoples in relation to others but "only" the harmfulness of abolishing frontiers, the incompatibility of life-styles and traditions.[4]

Although neo-racism names more recent iterations of racial ideology, Balibar's term has special significance for the case of Japanese empire, which held fast to the belief that cultural difference was innate while proclaiming, among the various justifications used to legitimate its ambitions, that the imposition of a new regional order was an act of liberation in the service of decolonizing East and Southeast Asia.

Expanding on the notion of neo-racism, the case of Japan's relationship with East Asia might best be described by what Michael Hardt and Antonio Negri refer to as imperial racism, which, they argue, is based not on biological essentialism but on differences constituted by social and cultural forces:

> Biological differences have been replaced by sociological and cultural signifiers as the key representation of racial hatred and fear. In this way imperial racist theory attacks modern anti-racism from the rear, and actually co-opts and enlists its arguments. Imperial racist theory agrees that races do not constitute isolable biological units and that nature cannot be divided into different human races. It also agrees that the behavior of individuals and their abilities or aptitudes are not the result of their blood or their genes, but are due to their belonging to different historically determined cultures.[5]

Imperial racism and an apparently pluralistic modern antiracist theory thus both rest on a culturalist position that turns out to be just as essentialist as the biological one in that it conceives of contemporary racial ideologies and practices not as acts of division or exclusion but as strategies of differential inclusion—a term that Hardt and Negri borrow from the work of Gilles Deleuze and Félix Guattari.[6] While tactically different, the operations of racism here—its inscription in practices, discourse, and representation; its articulation "around stigmata of otherness"; and its organization of affects "by conferring upon them a stereotyped form"—are retained intact.[7]

Here again, the concept of a "new" racism is significant in the case of Japanese empire, which in rejecting Western impositions of biological racism was forced early on to adopt a form of racialist ideology capable of producing alterity while simultaneously inculcating the kind of subjectivity that would assure acquiescence and allegiance to Japan's imperial sovereignty. In that historically, racism has perhaps most often been defined and practiced on grounds of sentiment rather than physiology, this is also a moment of comparability between the case of modern empire in East Asia and other instances of imperial rule both past and present.

The mechanisms of inclusion and exclusion are symptoms of imperial power. Yet uncovering the connection between the imperial production of racial difference and the emergence of modern forms of subjectivity and agency presents a complex challenge—one that may be traced in part to a profound tension or dilemma within the project of constructing the modern nation that initially arose in Europe. The aspirations of bourgeois society gave rise to a sense of agency through the transformation of the medieval, feudal subject into the concept of the sovereign citizen. The sense of agency on the part of the citizen is a central element of modern subjectivity that made it possible to experience the nation as a collective imagining; an active creation of a community of individuals. This subjectivity, however, directly conflicted with the disciplinary power of the state that sought to exploit the creative agency of its citizen-subjects for its own ends. As an ideological category that acted to promote both individual identity and a sense of belonging, vice both shared obligations and obedience, the idea of the nation does not resolve this conflict but is in fact an expression of it.[8]

The dilemma of sovereignty within the modern nation-state was replicated in and coeval with the establishment of empire and of colonial institutions. In order to function, imperial sovereignty depends upon creating a sense of subjectivity (a sense of being both the subject of and subjected to imperial authority) through the process that the oxymoronic term differential inclusion, noted above, describes. This mode of subjectification is apparent in the case of the Japanese Empire, which for the most part sought to racialize populations according to linguistic or cultural associations. As a consequence, we have made the methodological choice to deemphasize the nation in our analysis of race and racism and to emphasize the political function of the everyday moods and sentiments stimulated by representations of race in a hierarchical system of imperial formations. This choice has to do not with some fundamental difference between imperial and national modes of imagining community but rather with this shared logic of inclusion and its accompanying politics of exclusion. The naturalization of differential inclusion, which is so crucial to the imagination of the nation, acts to occlude race as a descriptive and analytic category. It is this common sense that we hope to counter by restoring the affects of race and racism as both historical phenomena and analytical categories in the study of East Asian empire.

Comparative Racialization and the Intimate Politics of Assimilation

Given the parochial historical determinants that shaped the emergence of the concept of the nation-state in Asia, the reliance on nonbiological factors to configure difference is not to be understood as unique to a supposedly homogeneous East Asia. For that reason, examining the subject of race requires a comparative approach—that we think of, as Shu-mei Shih puts it, "the worldliness of race."

> We must recognize the conjuncture of time and place in each instance of racialization without losing sight of the totality produced by the colonial turn that heralded race as a structuring principle. The analytics of this turn must therefore be paired with a chronotopic analysis, and this pairing has important implications for the project of comparative racialization. Because instances of racialization are situated in specific times and places, comparison between these instances may seem random or unrelated, but *the colonial turn reveals potential and concrete relations among them.*[9]

The chapters collected here are chronotopic in the sense that Shih uses the Bakhtinian term—dealing with the specifics of colonial situations yet bound together in an analytic scope that reflects the duration of imperial time and the extensivity of imperial space. Together, the chapters work to challenge conventional definitions of empire by calling attention to the politics of comparison; to the ways in which imperial formations not only "shape how knowledge is organized, made available, retrievable and conceived" but also determine what constitutes a category and which subjects are viable as sources or objects of knowledge. In expanding the spatial and temporal scope of empire in sometimes unexpected directions, we seek to re-vision colonial history and the intimate links between colony and metropole through the conceptual lens of affect.[10]

It is our contention that the operations of affect are central to state power. The chapters in this volume may diverge in both the affects observed and in the particular roles those affects performed in the historically contingent production of racial difference, but in their practice of chronotopic analysis they share a common conceptual framework. Observing the moods and sentiments produced by representations of difference helps us understand the specific situation of Japanese empire and, at the same time, makes that situation comparable to other imperial formations.

Focusing attention on affect complicates the representational logic of both imperial and racist discourses, which see difference not just in purely biological terms but as the result of cultural, social, and historical forces, assigning characteristics to populations based on preexisting, definitive, and discriminatory categories as an ex post facto justification of the exercise of power. Against representational thinking that "submits difference to preexisting images" and privileges "stratification and identity over movement and distance,"[11] affect gives us a way to talk about inequalities that are not clear-cut and to show gradations of power or politically interested shifts in definitions of normality that are otherwise difficult to talk about or even to discern. We must ask, then, how is affect produced; how does it circulate; and how does it engender identification with certain political positions, behaviors, or actions? How are affects assigned to collectivities?

Bearing these questions in mind, the contributors approach and productively criticize a historical archive that is itself frequently prefigured or configured by categories and definitions stemming from imperial modes of knowing. Their multivalent focus on a variety of media brings to light the operation of representational thinking in diverse fields, allowing consideration of indicative or relational modes of expression that bring a broader archive of materials and practices under "empire studies." In this sense affect also complicates reading strategies, moving us beyond a reflection theory of interpretation and insisting on the need for both contextualization and interpretation of the link between expressive form and politics.

While affect serves as a unifying analytical concept in the sense that it is linked to the intentional production and circulation of meaning as an essential part of the discursive and ideological project of empire, we in no way see affect as some universal given or unified theory. In fact, we consider the diversity of the definitions of affect to be a vital element of this volume. Affects give us an investment in particular structures of meaning but cannot be simplified as a direct effect of ideological or political structures. Affect is not something that is concrete, definitive, or immediately effective on the body. It is rather a "mediation process," something organized by the discourses that structure our everyday lives that takes account of "will and attention, or moods, or orientations"—what Lawrence Grossberg has referred to as "'mattering maps', and the various culturally and phenomenological [*sic*] constituted emotional economies."[12]

An affect is something that must be present for one to invest in ideology—that is, ideology has to be affectively charged for it to constitute individual experience. Affect exists at the intersection of ideology and the experience of social, political, and everyday realities; it is through the production of affect that an easy division between the material and the discursive is complicated. To put it differently, affect makes matter (or matters) matter—it *sentimentalizes* the material but also makes that matter count *for* something. Neither mere "feelings" nor the product of ideological machinations, affect mediates the subjective experience of the social and provides a fruitful and complex category by which to approach studies of race under empire.

Whether commonsensical, literary, physiological, or scientistic, the multitude of specific affects and their accompanying theorizations reflect the polymorphous reality of affect in practice and across the diversity of situations and media that the contributors describe and analyze. That is, we are not aiming to produce a singular meaning for the term nor a singular affective function within racist strategies of empire. Rather, we are pointing to ideologically charged *readings* of affects that are imposed on colonized, subjected bodies through the everyday atmosphere created by media images and sounds; by written and spoken discourses on race; and by legal, educational, and commercial institutions.

While racialist ideologies drew justification from their purported claim to universal validity based on generalized notions of biology or culture, their propagation and suasive force could only be realized either through the application of coercive policies or through the creation of subjectivities that were concrete, specific, and local. The close attention that Japanese imperial authorities paid to personal matters such as language, dress, romance, family, hygiene, and so on exemplifies the type of dynamic intervention common to imperial formations that seek to produce difference through systems of inclusion and exclusion. This emphasis on the intimate and the everyday in seeking to produce sentiments that facilitated the assimilation of subjects into the pre- or postwar empire is a central topic of analysis throughout this volume.

The preoccupation with the intimate and the everyday in Japan's imperial formations was a defining feature of its efforts to establish the legitimacy of its own national sovereignty. As ann-elise lewallen notes, the formation of Japan as a modern nation-state was not a foreordained, geographical given, despite attempts by modernist historiography to normalize the country's present-day borders. According to this version of history, Hokkaido (formerly known as Ezo) and Okinawa have long been bracketed as "internal colonies" and are conventionally dismissed from discussions of Japan's imperial project. This historical perspective rationalizes and codifies the narrative that Hokkaido in particular is an inherent, inalienable part of Japanese territory (*koyū no ryōdo*). However, the force of this narrative begins to collapse when we take into account reports of the interrelations between Ainu women and ethnic Japanese (Wajin) men.

As lewallen's analysis shows, the sexualized subjectivity of Ainu women provides a different perspective that allows her to highlight the inextricable link between Japan's experiment with imperialism and territorial expansion and the gendering of ethnicity—that its nascent imperialism may be charted across the terrains of Ainu women's bodies. The interpellation of Ainu women as objects of sexual desire established the intimate frontiers of Japan's recasting of Ezo as a distinctly Japanese imperial zone long before its political and administrative incorporation into the Japanese nation-state. Indeed, this process of subjectification is apparent as early as the travel records of Tokugawa period surveyor Matsuura Takeshirō, which employ euphemism as a way to describe interrelations between Ainu women and Wajin men. Matsuura's observations demonstrate how, in significant ways, sexual intimacy and sexual violence are corollaries of political and physical power.

The intimacy of imperial formations was in no way limited to the erotics of personal relationships. Imperial arts and sciences often primitivized colonized subjects, turning their bodies into a mirror of the colonizers' imperialist desires. Chul Kim's chapter points out that, among various modern Japanese sciences, the discipline of physical anthropology made the body of the colonized the object of a quantifying, probing gaze and an object of dissection through camera lenses, measuring devices, and surgical instruments. Through this process, the body of the colonized became lowly, ugly, and dangerous. Above all, it was made public and visible. Loyally attendant to modern biopower, Korean naturalist and realist literature came into existence simultaneously with imperial physical anthropology's production of abject subjects. It is thus fraught with representations of degenerate bodies.

In these instances, in which imperial desire for possession is projected onto eroticized, differentiated bodies, the double message of assimilation—urging the colonized to become the same (as imperial subjects) while insisting they maintain minimally distinguishing markers—yields a never-settled process, one of ever-shifting boundaries between inclusion and exclusion that constantly defer a final becoming or belonging. The elusive project of cultural incorporation and assimilation revolved around mutually constitutive definitions of what it meant to be Japanese, Taiwanese, Korean, or Manchurian—definitions the colonial state was invested in managing but that, in practice, it could hardly control.

The instability of the process of assimilation was perhaps most clearly articulated in the essentialized discourses of Korean-ness commonly expressed through the racialized epithet *yobo*. Perceived physiognomic similarities between colonizer and colonized made it especially important to create, mark, and patrol the shifting boundaries between the diverse members of a multiethnic national community. Directing attention to colonial sensibilities figured centrally in the government-general's avowed goal to assimilate Koreans into the larger emperor-centered community. Todd A. Henry demonstrates how the use of this epithet revealed both the affective demands of assimilation directed at the colonized and Japanese settlers' aim to distance themselves from native inhabitants and thereby justify their privileges over them. Perhaps nowhere was the focus on intimacy as a means to assimilation more clearly apparent than in the particular case of Japanese colonialism in Korea.

Challenging the assimilationist initiatives of the colonial state, these discourses helped to create equally idealized notions of Japanese-ness, sensibilities the government-general could appropriate to measure the degree to which Koreans had been incorporated into the imperial community. On the other hand, inevitable encounters between Japanese settlers and the local population also produced anxious debates on the so-called *yobo*-ization of Japanese settlers. Charges of having adopted or embodied attributes of the colonized others not only suggests that some settlers had failed to remain sufficiently "Japanese" but also underscores how the project of colonial assimilation relied upon a multidirectional flow of practical sensibilities that often transgressed the carefully constructed discursive boundaries of ethnicity.

The transgressive nature of practical, everyday sensibilities is also readily apparent in the construction and assimilatory practice of forced Japanese-language education. This policy suggests just how central the management of intimacy and sentiment was to framing and enacting the material relation between colony and metropole. Japanese-language education in colonial Taiwan and Korea has been widely portrayed as a prime example of attempts to assimilate colonial populations to Japanese norms, and yet scholars have often neglected the question of what these linguistic norms were and whether or not Japanese-language fluency and the communicative encounter between colonizer and colonized actually led to or reflected the integration of metropolitan and colonial societies.

Kate McDonald addresses this issue by examining dialogues with Taiwanese aborigines that were reproduced in Japanese travel accounts of colonial Taiwan from the 1910s to the 1930s. Early Japanese visitors to Taiwan arrived with two contradictory expectations: that a shared language would eventually make a cohesive nation out of the colonial and metropolitan populations and that aborigines in Taiwan's so-called Savage Territory (Banchi) would not speak Japanese and therefore would remain outside the nation. However, encounters with Japanese-speaking aborigines, which were widely reported in travelogues, challenged these expectations. By the 1930s expectations of aboriginal incoherence had been replaced in popular representations by the expectation that although aborigines would communicate civilly in Japanese, this fluency would not alter their inherent savagery. This shift (and its attendant affects) illuminates a broader turn that took place alongside promotions of imperial Japan's multiethnic identity from linguistic nationalism toward hierarchies of linguistic aptitude that nonetheless continued to function by constituting discreet and racialized populations within the empire.

The politics of a differentially inclusive assimilation brings the specifics of the case studies presented in this volume into comparability with histories of other empires. At the same time, however, the very process of assimilation was at once so fluid and vexing that it would be misleading to view it simply as an imposition that flowed outward from the metropole toward the colonies. The desire for economic and political inclusion and the attractions of modern subjectivity are traces of the long-lasting emotional pull of imperial formations as they operated on the ground, so to speak, where their social effects were most clearly discerned in representations of selfhood, identity, and community.

Such localized, individuated desire has been a determining factor in shaping the literary-historical arc of the life and writings of Chang Hyŏkchu (1905–1997), a Korean author who eventually took Japanese citizenship. In John Whittier Treat's account, Chang's career was essentially coterminous with the Japanese imperial interregnum on the Korean peninsula, lasting from the imposition of the protectorate in the year of his birth until the defeat of Japan by the Allies on August 15, 1945. The decades after World War II were immaterial to Chang's destined literary theme, which was also the announced project of the empire: the assimilation of the Korean people into the Japanese. One person's assimilation, however, is another's collaboration, and though Chang was as prolific after the war as he was before and during it, with the collapse of the assimilatory economy established by Japan's imperial formations his readership disappeared as quickly as the utopian fantasy of an East Asia homogenized under Japanese rule.

As Chang's experience suggests, the hold that representations of colonized bodies had on conceptions of national and ethnic identities was tenuous at best and could quickly shift as political and economic regimes changed. Though he attempted to become a world author and break free of the fetters of race, his literary career illuminated and exceeded the limits of expression in a system in which language was equated with race. Given the vexing process of assimilation, then, can it be said that Japanese representations of race were really able to engender identification with imperial ideologies and policies? Were they a force able to arouse the kinds of sentiments that would facilitate the coercion and seduction of individuals and groups into an acceptance of imperial sovereignty (i.e., an acceptance of the peculiar subjectivity produced by the feeling of belonging to an empire while recognizing one's difference from the metropole)? In the case of representations of race, such imperial formations align difference with preexisting semiotic codes in a fluid process that strives to justify asymmetric power-based relations while making new categories of racial identity legible.

Representational Logic and the Affect of Difference

The modes and the policies of imperial systems make race intelligible through the representational logic of differential inclusion. The authors of this volume understand representation as basic to a racist colonial project that sought to establish race both as a baseline, a naturalized given state, and as a malleable category within which only minimal difference (of colonizer from colonized) needed to be maintained in the march toward imperial subjecthood. In the first case, representation might function as a simple reflection of the "known" world (reinforcing the knowable); in the latter case, representation might construct or figure an emerging sensibility, working to modify the boundary between inclusion and exclusion. And while it is crucial to point to moments in which such a racist politics is mirrored in concrete developments such as shifts in state boundaries or policies on language and citizenship, it is equally important to stress just how much the rationales for deciding who was to be allowed into imperial subjecthood and who was to be excluded (as un- or underqualified) relied on a shifting, amorphous hierarchy of criteria that drew not only on "hard facts" gained through empirical observation but also on affect as a key criterion that allow the boundary between inclusion and exclusion to be monitored, measured, and adjusted. Affect is a category that brings together the protean constructability of race with its representational function in a politics of imperial inclusion or exclusion.[13]

Theories about affect cannot be limited to a single generalizable model. Despite its current popularity as an analytical category, affect is not inherently equalizing nor are affects unchanging or universal. While it is possible to explore affect as a means to unsettle or displace the thought/feeling dichotomy, within which "reason" is most often privileged, sentiments are themselves susceptible to discriminatory categorization and can be privileged, for instance, as signs of cultivation, advanced sensibility, and racial superiority.[14]

Identifying affect as an object of analysis can be helpful in critiquing imperial rationality and the genealogy of reason in historical thinking and writing, but that should not blind us to the fact that such a category may itself also serve as a differentiating force in an imperial economy of ideologies and racist taxonomies.[15] Rather than privileging affect as a precognitive and prelinguistic (and hence universal) somatic response mechanism that is produced below the threshold of meaning and ideology, the chapters here understand affect as crucially linked to the *intentional* production and circulation of meaning as an essential part of the discursive and ideological project of empire.[16]

The operation of affect can also be seen as homologous to how assimilation itself works, in a way that allows for both an expanded understanding of colonial discourse and the powerful role of that discourse in the construction and categorization of subjects. Affect "arises in the midst of in-between-ness, in the capacities to act and be acted upon"—it is "integral to a body's perceptual *becoming* (always becoming otherwise . . . than what it already is)."[17] Assimilatory colonial discourse presents the colonized with a contradictory injunction, demanding that the colonized become the same—imperial subjects—while also maintaining racialized difference, thus justifying the ongoing "civilizing" role of the colonizer. Assimilation and the production of an affect of difference are thus arguably both processes of becoming other than what one already is.

Further, affect inherently points to the idea that "the capacity of a body is never defined by a body alone but is always aided and abetted by, and dovetails with, the field or context of its force relations."[18] As with a colonial discourse that binds together "a range of differences and discriminations that inform the discursive and political practices of racial and cultural hierarchization" and at the same time "produces the colonized as a social reality which is at once an 'other' and yet entirely knowable and visible,"[19] affects are hierarchical, productive, and relational, involving the power to define the capacity of a body to do or be. Yet affect also has the potential to justify a racist empire's denial of coevality to the colonized; a denial expressed as the "not yet" of the perpetually underqualified imperial subject-to-be or as an injunction against certain actions. Here, the production of an affect of difference is homologous to racist and imperial discourse in that it can both work to motivate becoming but at the same time militate against ever being.

While affects are related to undefined everyday experiences, they can reveal at the same time a collective mode of feeling that influences the social more broadly and can act as a means to bring the everyday into connection with the social-political collective. The affect-centered approach of this collection enables us to present a finely grained perspective on (and a history of) everyday life under racist empire while allowing a collective affective economy or communality to surface in the respective analysis of each chapter. Fleeting sentiments may arise from and serve as signs of the lived present, but they are also social, arising in one's encounters with another and thus sometimes able to have an impact on a wider social reality.

To grasp the ways in which race was rendered sensible—both in the broad sense of being literally available to the senses and as something knowable or commonsensical—the contributors excavate a range of cultural archives. They demonstrate how race was made visible or audible in the processes of inclusion and exclusion. From travelogues and records of speech to photographs, radio, plastic surgery, tattoos, postcards, fiction, the popular press, and film soundtracks, materials from diverse media—including, as we have seen, the human body—enable us to think through the links between the apprehension of racial difference, the formation of social and political hierarchies, and the experience of everyday life under an expanding and increasingly biopolitical realm of imperial sovereignty.

On one level all representations of alterity under Japanese empire had to reference a multiracial alterity, as Japan attempted to bring together diverse populations—whether in its colonies, in semicolonial spaces, or in the puppet state of Manchukuo—under various degrees of control. Perhaps nowhere was this effort more explicit than in the production of postcards and other mass-circulated anthropometric imagery of so-called indigenous peoples that attempted to establish and fix a taxonomy of racial groups. As Paul D. Barclay notes in his piece on race, culture, and affect in colonial Taiwan, these photographic representations are important artifacts not only because of their sheer ubiquity and explicit racial content but also because of their chronotopical sensitivity to place and time. Barclay points to the antecedent genres, sociopolitical settings, and production logistics of these images to show that they functioned, quite literally, as "race cards."

More than examples of asymmetrical power relations, mimetic imperialism, and ruthless essentialism, race cards in early twentieth-century Taiwan functioned as the "shape-shifting jokers" that W. J. T. Mitchell describes in his discussion of race as a "medium."[20] Even as they were utilized in projects to objectify and dehumanize the peoples they depicted, race cards also functioned—much like the reproduced dialogues between Japanese visitors and indigenous Taiwanese that Kate McDonald analyzes—to *counter* the discourse on savagery that legitimated the genocide of some Taiwanese. The ambivalent nature of these contested artifacts does nothing to soften the brutality of Japanese colonial rule in Taiwan, but postcolonial exposés that fail to go beyond asserting the abject nature of the men and women who sat for these photographic images have done little to mitigate the continued recirculation of race cards in Taiwan today. Despite more than a century of concerted intellectual effort to debunk various conceptions of race, it endures as a form of pseudoscientific false consciousness thanks to the lingering impact of the sentiments produced, as Barclay's work shows us, by anthropometric images.

Photographic portraiture in colonial Korea was sometimes used in ways similar to Taiwanese race cards. Portraits circulated widely there thanks to popular print culture, and within the discourse that rose up around such images, "face" developed as a keyword that carried considerable significance in the newly emerging pseudoscience of physiognomy. As Gyewon Kim argues, physiognomy—which claimed to be able to read personality traits from the individual affects and performances captured in photographs of the veridical screen of facial features—provided a veneer of authority for a way of seeing that stressed the boundaries of different races, genders, and classes. It provided a means of perceiving oneself and others through a specific set of visual criteria, concepts of representation, and modes of interaction with (and presentation of) faces that in turn assigned particular affects and (criminal, racial, and other) identities to social groups within a normative and assimilatory discourse.

As part of the process of classifying people, which expanded across the wide social spectrum in the rapidly changing urban environment of 1920s Korea, the colonial government began to archive the profile photographs of Socialists, anticolonialists, and anarchists in order to mark them as ideological criminals. As a new way of looking at others' faces, physiognomy required that people learn how to deal with communal watching, witnessing, and public encounters. This identification, differentiation, and control of the populace was authorized by the representational logic of photographic portraiture, which promised the definition of particular communities within a universal humanity knowable through its common susceptibility to the methods of empirical measurement and recording. The inherent tension of these affective functions reveals the limits and possibilities of shaping imperial subjectivities by media that circulated in the service of a politics of inclusion and exclusion.

Kari Shepherdson-Scott takes up another potent example of how mass media were used to represent racial alterity through the depiction of colonial spaces. During the 1930s the South Manchuria Railway Company (Mantetsu) advertised the "Manchuria Tour" to Japanese and foreign readers. It cast Manchuria (renamed Manchukuo, 1932–1945) as both a modern urban paradise and a wild frontier of different exotic cultures. Photographs of walled Chinese cities were crucial components in this multifaceted destination branding. These old city spaces—posited as repositories of "local color" by Mantetsu's flagship public relations magazine, *Manshū graph*—were adjacent to the new, modern South Manchuria Railway Company zones that the Japanese designed and built in major Manchurian cities. As such, images of the old cities inevitably invited comparison with the new urban spaces and contributed to narratives of difference on the continent.

The affective appeal of these narratives as they operated in an imperial economy of differential inclusion is clearly illustrated in the celebratory image reproduced on the cover of this book extolling Manchukuo's formative national slogan, "the harmony of the five races" (*gozoku kyōwa*). This image makes abundantly clear the ideological and political context within which acceptance of a sentimentalized version of shared imperial subject-hood was sought or demanded, as it codes indigenous populations and cultures as exotic commodities for tourist consumption. In the space of Mantetsu's media, the walled cities provided a tantalizing virtual space of cultural contact while also allowing the Japanese viewer to remain distant from continental racial others who were associated with dangerous figures such as "thieves." The tensions in these representations produced by conflicting emotions of desire, curiosity, anxiety at the dangerous proximity of racial others, and the alienation of distance or containment are crucial indicators of the differential affects produced by images of space and race in Mantetsu's media during this period.

When we consider how far beyond the borders of empire the multivalent affects stirred by the mediated production of an awareness of racial difference circulated, the real-world, local effects of those sentiments appear even more striking. Though Japanese migration to North and South America never involved the Japanese state attempting to claim sovereignty over the lands to which its citizens were moving, it nonetheless shared much in common with Japan's imperialist diaspora in Asia. In support of this view, Edward Mack points to the example of Japanese émigré writers in Brazil who were exposed to a level of heterogeneity that at the very least equaled that seen in Japan's colonial spaces. Yet the most striking characteristic of their representations of alterity is how little interest they evinced in *inter*racial alterity. Instead, they seemed preoccupied primarily with *intra*racial alterity. This sometimes took the form of anxiety surrounding acquired alterity (similar to the fear of *yobo*-ization that Todd Henry notes was such a powerful sentiment in colonial Korea) in which individuals were seen to have become other—marked by a variety of signs ranging from darkened skin to a complete loss of Japan's hard-won "civilization"—through exposure to alien circumstances. More frequently, however, it took the form of shock when individuals marked as racially identical betrayed an imagined racial solidarity.

The start of full-scale hostilities in China in 1937 exponentially raised the stakes for Japan's imperial project and gave greater urgency to its efforts to assimilate colonized subjects. Technologies such as radio broadcasting and sound cinema were essential to those efforts, especially at the height of the empire's expansion during the last phase of the Asia-Pacific War, when the growing demands of the war effort forced the empire to intensify inclusionary gestures to its colonial subjects and to the various ethnic groups in newly occupied territories under the banner of the Greater East Asia Co-Prosperity Sphere. In the course of studying these gestures, Ji Hee Jung poses a crucial question: Was the medium of radio, both as a technology and as a set of representational practices, effective in evoking a sense of belonging to the multiracial community at a moment when rapid imperial expansion inevitably posed a challenge to an already established discourse on the exclusive conception of nationhood?

Wartime Japanese broadcasters knew that the simple awareness of simultaneous colisteners did not automatically promote community. What was required was the establishment of strong emotional ties, or affective bonds (*jōshoteki tetsugō*). An analysis of radio scripts, broadcasting policy, NHK (Nippon Hōsō Kyōkai) publications, listeners' letters, memoirs, and newspaper articles reveals the various strategies adopted to evoke affective ties through radio: an intimate style of address, a passionate tone of announcement, and reports of around-the-empire events that invited reactions from the multiethnic audiences under the empire's purview. Despite the excitement about radio broadcasting as a powerful means of forging an affective community in Asia within the Japanese Empire, newly devised techniques of broadcasting alone could not realize the regime's great expectations so long as inclusionary gestures were perceived as merely part of a larger strategy of coercive control.

InYoung Bong's analysis of the soundtrack of the 1943 film *My Nightingale* provides further evidence of the tension between Japan's inclusionary gestures and its efforts to control indigenous populations throughout the empire via the production of racialized sound and space. As purely cinematic effects, sonic, sensory, and vocal elements render the presentation of the film's images as one of pure potential and indeterminacy, particularly in those scenes containing disjunctions between image and the sources of sound, speech acts, and subtitles. In this respect the representational logic of cinema is also homologous to the unruly logic that marked the assimilatory strategy of differential inclusion. The film's disjunctions created affective valences that extended beyond the ideological and pedagogical apparatus of its production and established a new hermeneutic space without a definite and stable center or boundaries. This analysis resonates with Kari Shepherdson-Scott's study of Mantetsu's advertising campaign by revealing the rich, unmapped cultural terrain of the Russian diaspora within Manchukuo—a diaspora whose cinematic representation both embodied and disembodied the uneasy process of simultaneously creating and containing imperial subjects.

In each of the instances noted above, representation functions in diverse ways: from self-representation (speaking for oneself) to political representation (speaking for another); from demands that the colonized speak, act, or feel as himself or herself (marking difference) to limits on that same mode of representation (legislating sameness); and from linguistic standardization and imperial language policies to censorship and the promotion of norms related to appearance. The very idea of representation itself links race to the particular emergence of the imperial subject in early twentieth-century East Asia and sheds light on strategies common to the creation and containment of subjectivity across imperial formations. As a result, because the production and perception of racial difference was not based solely on biological or morphological categories it has, perhaps among all imperial formations from the late nineteenth century, survived the longest within the nations of East Asia, which today may be considered postcolonial without necessarily being postimperial.[21]

It may seem counterintuitive to think of contemporary East Asia as continuing to live in the old chaos of Japan's imperial sun. Thus, it is important to consider how racial identities have been reinscribed on ostensibly postcolonial bodies under the postwar American imperium. The years immediately following World War II witnessed a rising fascination in Japan with the possibilities for personal and social transformation afforded by civilian applications of many wartime technologies. The practice of elective cosmetic surgery, for example, which adapted not only the methods of reconstructive surgery originally developed in response to battlefield injuries but also the anthropometric techniques developed during the colonial period, became increasingly widespread during the 1950s. Extensive discussions of new beauty practices in the popular press at the time show just how many groups throughout Japanese society surgically altered their bodies, especially their eyelids and noses.

Using articles that appeared in newsweeklies and influential women's magazines, Kim Brandt situates the 1950s boom in cosmetic surgery within a longer history of concern about the Japanese body in the context of a stratified and racialized international order. From the late nineteenth century on, rapid industrialization along with the interaction of Euro-American and Japanese imperialism helped to produce new and changing bodily ideals throughout East Asia. The beauty that many Japanese tried to achieve by means of cosmetic surgery and other practices was commonly defined in terms of a greater capacity to express interior states and qualities and to elicit affective responses in others. By seeking to remedy the inscrutability, apathy, and stupidity or even barbarity associated most notably with single-lidded eyes and "flat" faces, doctors and patients in 1950s Japan ironically contributed to reshaping and reviving earlier imperial formations—a revival that expressed a new form of subjectivity emerging out of the desire to emulate and assimilate into American norms. This "contribution" has since been emulated and replicated in turn throughout East Asia.

An equally striking instance of how the lingering effects of imperial formations have saturated the subsoil of racial consciousness in postwar Asian cultures is the life, or perhaps more properly, the long half-life, that the character Little Black Sambo enjoyed in postwar Japan. The publication, reception, and cultural history of *Chibikuro Sambo,* the Japanese translation of Helen Bannerman's (1862–1946) *Little Black Sambo* (1899), exemplifies the rhetorical hermeneutics of comparative racialization, that is, the representational logic underpinning interpretations of colonial bodies at specific times and places. *Little Black Sambo* was written at the zenith of British power by a Scotswoman stationed in India; the 1953 Iwanami translation of *Chibikuro Sambo* included illustrations an American publishing house originally commissioned in the 1920s. The specter of imperialism thus haunts *Chibikuro Sambo,* and to read the work in the context of the history of postwar Japan we must first, as William H. Bridges urges, read the traces left on the text by the imperial regimes it traversed. Western imperial writings on race created circuits of affection and a language of sentiment (textual and imagistic) that helped determine postwar receptions of Bannerman's book in a series of what Bridges calls "affective reading communities"—interpretations that took the racial difference of Sambo as a proxy for the racialized identity of the postwar Japanese themselves.

The stubborn duration of circuits of affection related to the racialized consciousness created under Japanese empire is apparent not merely in explicitly racist representations such as *Little Black Sambo.* The continuous postwar presence of the haunting figure of Lu Xun is a fascinating case in point that Angela Yiu explores in her chapter. No other twentieth-century Chinese writer has enjoyed greater status in Japan than Lu Xun. Apart from spending nearly seven years (1902–1909) studying there, his works address matters that resonate deeply in the spiritual and intellectual consciousness of East Asia, touching on issues and sentiments concomitant with the instabilities of modernity and the violence enacted by imperial authorities on bodies and psyches. Further, the lingering aura of Lu Xun in Japan is inextricably connected to the form of differential inclusion practiced by scholars and writers who created an afterlife for him in their biographies and fiction. Takeuchi Yoshimi's (1910–1977) *Rojin* (Lu Xun, 1944), Dazai Osamu's (1909–1948) *Sekibetsu* (Farewell, 1945), and Inoue Hisashi's (1934–2010) *Shanhai muun* (Shanghai moon, 1991) represent a Lu Xun that crosses national, racial, and ideological borders. These writers dig deep into their personal struggles with their relationship to the Japanese Empire, constructing a life that speaks eloquently of their own dreams and losses while making Lu Xun intelligible to Japanese readers.

The postwar transfiguration of Lu Xun is an especially poignant reminder that while affects produced by representations of racial difference are not reducible to, nor assumed to precede, the political or the ideological or the social, they are not separable from them, either. Though affect as a category for cultural analysis may seem, at first glance, like an ephemeral phenomenon—one sometimes difficult to isolate—the studies presented in this volume demonstrate its profound and impactful role in the formation and maintenance of imperial rule in East Asia. In their attention to the differential operations of specific affects produced, utilized, induced, and sustained across a wide variety of media, the contributors reveal the borders and byways of imperial sensibilities that stretch into the present day.

Notes

1. Judith Butler and Athena Athanasiou, *Dispossession: The Performative in the Political* (Cambridge: Polity, 2013), 83.

2. Ann Stoler, "Introduction," in *Imperial Debris: On Ruins and Ruination* (Durham, NC: Duke University Press, 2013), 8 (her italics). Stoler urges us to consider imperial formations as "polities of dislocation and deferral which cut through the nation-state by delimiting interior frontiers as well as exterior ones, 24."

3. Ibid., 5.

4. Etienne Balibar, "Is There a 'Neo-racism?,'" in Etienne Balibar and Immanuel Wallerstein, *Race, Nation, Class: Ambiguous Identities* (New York: Verso, 1991), 21.

5. Michael Hardt and Antonio Negri, *Empire* (Cambridge, MA: Harvard University Press, 2000), 191–192. In coining the term "imperial racism," the authors acknowledge their debt to Balibar's concept of neo-racism.

6. Ibid., 193–94.

7. Balibar, "Is There a Neo-racism?,'" 17–18.

8. For a thorough overview of conceptions of sovereignty for the nation-state and colonial sovereignty, see the relevant chapters in Hardt and Negri, *Empire,* 93–136.

9. Shu-mei Shih, "Comparative Racialization: An Introduction," *PMLA* 123, no. 5 (October 2008): 1349 (our italics).

10. We are indebted to Ann Stoler for the language of this description, which comes out of an early draft of her article "Colonial Aphasia: Race and Disabled Histories in France," *Public Culture* 23, no. 1 (2011): 121–156.

11. Lorna Burns and Brigit M. Kaiser, "Introduction: Navigating Differential Futures, Unmaking Colonial Pasts," in *Postcolonial Literatures and Deleuze: Colonial Pasts, Differential Futures,* ed. Burns and Kaiser (New York: Palgrave MacMillan, 2012), 4.

12. Lawrence Grossberg, "Affect's Future: Rediscovering the Virtual in the Actual," in *The Affect Theory Reader,* ed. Melissa Gregg and Gregory Seigworth (Durham, NC: Duke University Press, 2010), 316.

13. While we focus here on the production of affect in the representation of race, it is important to keep in mind that race and its representation can also work on affect, with categorical schemes of race "deployed by normative regimes to organize, induce, adjudicate, and sustain affect differentially." In such cases, "we have to ask which affective bonds get recognized and which ones remain foreclosed, unintelligible, misrecognized, repudiated, or censured." Butler and Athanasiou, *Dispossession,* 164–165.

14. See Sara Ahmed, *The Cultural Politics of Emotion* (New York: Routledge, 2004), 3–4.

15. Here we are thinking of "category" in Said's sense of the term, as something that stands in for (represents) an otherwise "impossibly diffuse" field, which "allows one to see new things, things seen for the first time, as versions of a previously known thing. In essence such a category is not so much a way of receiving new information as it is a method of controlling what seems to be a threat to some established view of things." Edward Said, *Orientalism* (New York: Vintage, 1978), 58–59.

16. Our caution in linking the notion of affect to the intentional production and circulation of meaning rather than focusing on the understanding of affect as a precognitive response to stimuli is prompted in part by the criticism of affect theory put forth in Ruth Leys' essay, "The Turn to Affect: A Critique," *Critical Inquiry* 37 (Spring 2011): 434–472.

17. Melissa Gregg and Gregory Seigworth, eds., "An Inventory of Shimmers," in *The Affect Theory Reader* (Durham, NC: Duke University Press, 2010), 2–3.

18. Ibid., 3. For further discussion of emotions as social and cultural practices in an "affective economy," see Ahmed, *Cultural Politics of Emotion*, 8–9.

19. Homi K. Bhabha, *The Location of Culture* (London: Routledge, 1994), 96, 101.

20. Mitchell draws his notion from the work of Raymond Williams, who defines a medium as a social practice, and of Rosalind Krauss, who sees a medium as a recursive structure that discloses patterns of internal differentiation and a history of origins, innovation and obsolescence. *Seeing through Race* (Cambridge, MA: Harvard University Press, 2012), 17–19.

21. This is not unique to East Asia. Writing on the case of France, where race is not recognized as a legal category, Ann Stoler points out that "racial formations have long marked differences by other names . . . distribute specific sentiments among social kinds, assign who are made into subjects of pity and whose cultural competencies and capital are deemed inadequate to make political claims. As such, they demand that we ask who and what are made into 'problems,' how certain narratives are made 'easy to think,' and what 'common sense' such formulations have fostered and continue to serve." Stoler, "Colonial Aphasia," 130.

"Intimate Frontiers"

Disciplining Ethnicity and Ainu Women's Sexual Subjectivity in Early Colonial Hokkaido

The ballad of "Esashi Oiwake" is one of the most popular *minyō* folk songs in Japanese contemporary memory, the object of a national competition, and central to the town of Esashi's tourist industry. Delivered in an evocative yodel of pain and simultaneous ecstasy at the release from suffering through song, this requiem is thick with affective resonances of the sexual subjectivity of Ainu women in early colonial Hokkaido.

Unending rains in Ezo and Matsumae, *Yansanoe,* these unruly waves part us, the wind blows,
We may laugh or weep yet only this evening remains, tomorrow the ship sets sail, over the waves.
A strong mountain wind at my back, the wind pushes us apart, I must be resigned;
How soon may we reunite, if indeed we may meet?
Forlorn, my tears stream; pitying the sorrow of parting, the plover cries
On the seashore, the waves break and retreat, *Yansanoe.* Boatman, the open sea is rough!
Tonight this one night, there is no end to our chatter;
Tomorrow the ship sets sail, I pray it be postponed,
No matter how I weep, inevitably he will go. Alas the wind and waves are calm.
"Weep not!" I tell myself, but my breath catches in my throat and the tears fall without ceasing
One cannot but cry, plovers on the beach.

This folk song, by an unknown composer, relays the tragic tale of an Ainu woman, a chief's daughter named Carenka, who suffers from unrequited love for the medieval warrior Minamoto no Yoshitsune. As a *minyō,* the ballad has conflicting origin stories, including two concerning Carenka. In one version, Carenka throws herself from a cliff while mourning Yoshitsune's sudden departure, cursing all ships carrying Wajin women that round the Shakotan Peninsula to a fate of capsizing and sinking. In an ironic turn that I describe below, this curse critically endangers Ainu women under early Hokkaido colonialism more so than Wajin women. In another version, Carenka is inconsolable at Yoshitsune's sudden departure and pursues him to the tip of the Shakotan Peninsula. Meanwhile, Carenka's father, Sitakabe, outraged that Carenka would desert her Ainu fiancé, cuts down his own daughter on the rock face of the promontory. When Carenka's fiancé visits the peninsula to mourn Carenka, he finds a striking red flower blooming there and fashions a reed whistle from the flower's stem. The melody that emerges from the reed whistle becomes "Esashi Oiwake."[1]

"Esashi Oiwake" evokes the grief of Ainu women and their sorrow for the loss of their ancestral land while metaphorically pointing to the intimate violence that cannot be divorced from colonial invasion. In its lyrical phrases, the beach plover's mournful cry suggests the suffering of Carenka, whose own voice has been silenced by the hostile waves. This silencing acts as a metaphor for the silencing of Ainu women in the Japanese historical archive, including the lack of textual representations of their experiences and the erasure of their subjectivity vis-à-vis the regulation of their sexuality and gendered practice in Hokkaido. Notably, contemporary Ainu women have claimed the ballad as an index of gendered colonial violence. Ainu activist Tahara Ryoko reads this lament as speaking to Ainu women's social circumstances in early colonial Hokkaido.[2] For her the ballad invokes the sexual subjectivity and everyday reality of Wajin men's sexual exploitation of Ainu women outside legally sanctioned marriages and the normalization of sexual violence as an apparatus for asserting Wajin dominance.

Yet the ballad is more than an elegy for Carenka; its affective power lies in the diverse readings that audiences have drawn from it. Contemporary Ainu claim the ballad invokes the story of Ainu dispossession. Yet the emotion of loss is not restricted to Ainu. Modern audiences now revel in the tragic beauty of melancholia bound in this ballad. The southwest Hokkaido town of Esashi has capitalized on the affective power of loss and commoditized Carenka's lament as a town symbol, as a national and even international folk song competition, and as the heart of its tourist industry. Loss is compelling as a shared affective experience because it appeals to a sense of communal grieving common to the human experience and in the case of Japan, a national embrace of melancholy. In the words of bard Aosaka Mitsuru, "Esashi Oiwake" engages this shared experience and is widely loved because it "resonates in the inner heart of Japanese. Both labor and life, the pathos of human affection—severity and beauty—are all woven into the song."[3]

One of the abiding concerns framing this inquiry into Ainu women's sexual subjectivity in early colonial Hokkaido is the use of sexual conquest to establish imperial hegemony. Sexual subjectivity refers both to women's ability to choose sexual partners and to freely exercise sexual desire and draws attention to the sexualization of Ainu women as objects of colonial conquest. Central to my argument is the proposition that Ainu women's imperial interpellation as objects of sexual desire facilitated the recasting of Hokkaido as a distinctly Japanese imperial zone long before its political and administrative colonization by the Japanese nation-state. Ainu women were key targets of this project; they constituted the intimate frontiers of Japan's first modern colonial expansion. In Ainu communities, as elsewhere across the globe, sexuality and sexual violence have long served as mediums for managing colonial populations and enacting imperial violence.

In significant ways, sexual intimacy and sexual violence are corollaries of political and physical power. Reflecting on how colonization has had different impacts on men and women, indigenous feminists Shari Huhndorf and Cheryl Suzack contend that "colonization has reordered gender relations to subordinate women."[4] In travelers' diaries in the Americas, indigenous women were portrayed as sexual objects and prostitution was promoted as a means of regulating the sexual desires of the British colonists, as feminist historian Jean Barman has documented.[5] For historical geographer Richard Phillips, imperial sexual politics were influenced by "geographies of domination (concentrations of imperial power) and resistance (with scope for agency)."[6] Edward Said once wrote that the sexual conquest of Oriental women by Western men constituted a metaphor for "the pattern of relative strength between East and West and the discourse about the Orient that it enabled."[7] These contrasts call to mind the ways in which imperial categories engage taxonomies of representation and reproduce hierarchical relations, even as they emerge from historically and geographically distinct conditions. Indeed, as Anne McClintock has written, "the gendered dynamics of colonized cultures were contorted in such ways as to alter, in turn, the irregular shapes that imperialism took in various parts of the world."[8]

As I elaborate below, Ainu women constituted the intimate frontiers of Japan's expansion into Hokkaido. Such "intimate domains" of empire are sites where relations between colonizer and colonized confound or confirm "the strictures of governance and the categories of rule."[9] By attending to Ainu women's exploitation as resources of empire in the early colonial economy, I urge that scholars reevaluate the conventional "markers" of empire and colonialism, namely chronological and geographic markers, and nurture approaches that recognize the range of terrains in which imperial power may be exercised, including the most intimate spaces. Below, I focus on sexuality as locally defined and enacted; on the impact of imperial power on gendering practice; and on the ways in which sexual acts produce, constrain, and codify racial and ethnic difference as classificatory practice. My analysis addresses two key themes. First, how might the Japanese-authored historiography be parsed to understand Ainu women's position vis-à-vis Wajin men in early imperial Hokkaido? Second, taking into account the multiple euphemisms for how Ainu women were positioned both as sexual subjects and as gendered bodies within Ainu families and in Wajin colonial society in Hokkaido, how might women's subjectivity be interpreted?

Imperial Traces in Early Colonial Hokkaido

Nineteenth-century Hokkaido has been depicted as a frontier zone, lawless and wild, with a clear division separating Ezochi,[10] or the Ainu domain, from Wajinchi, or the domain of the Wajin, or ethnic Japanese. Aside from the demanding labor performed at the fisheries, gambling, sake, and prostitution were the key pursuits of many Wajin migrant workers. The Matsumae feudal domain controlled the non-Japanese areas of Hokkaido from the fifteenth century through 1799. Anxiety over impending Russian encroachment led to control shifting hands between the Tokugawa shogun and the Matsumae feudal domain twice between 1799 and 1869, when Hokkaido came under the formal political administration of Japan. Each time control shifted, local policies toward Ainu and regulation of Ainu laborers at Wajin-run fisheries changed significantly. Few records exist to document Ainu women's experiences, but based on Japanese correspondence, it's clear that Ainu women's political status and cultural authority were gradually attenuated between the fifteenth and twentieth centuries. Women's political and reproductive wellness experienced dramatic impacts from the breakdown of family units as Ainu men were forced to leave local villages and labor in slave-like conditions under the contract fishery system (*basho ukeoisei*). According to anthropologist Rick Siddle, the Wajin men who immigrated to Hokkaido fisheries for wage labor generally represented second and third sons from impoverished Tohoku communities; these men had little hope of starting a branch family or inheriting property. In Hokkaido fisheries they were employed as overseers, translators, and sailors, receiving nearly three times the salary of Ainu laborers. Records of their behavior toward Ainu describe entrenched patterns of cruelty, and at least one account suggests these men were "outlaws, refugees, or persons denounced by their kinfolk."[11]

One of the primary causes of the last major armed warfare against Wajin invaders, the Kunasir-Menasi War (1789), is known to be the repeated threat of and actual violence against Ainu, especially the sexual assault of Ainu women.[12] Chronic exploitation of Ainu labor at the contract fisheries reached its nadir when one Ainu woman was beaten to death. This fed Ainu desperation and thus fomented the brutal uprising in 1789. In early colonial Hokkaido, the physical destruction of Ainu land was enacted alongside the violation of Ainu women's bodies. This expansive notion of empire's capacity as territorial conquest and as interior relations between "colonizer" and "colonized" is best captured by the term "intimate frontiers." In the analysis below, I focus on sexual conquest to understand its impact on Ainu women, Ainu families, and its influence on the gendering of Ainu subjectivities more broadly. Early assimilation policies that mandated gender-specific customs reforms (*kizoku*), such as compelling a switch to agriculture or sanctioning Wajin men's marriage to and exploitation of Ainu women, had lasting effects on Ainu relations with the local *kamuy* (A. spiritual beings) and shaped gender practice in ways that continue to figure among Ainu today.

The Gendering Affect(s) of Colonial Power

The pattern of Ainu women's lives that emerges from primary Japanese sources is limited. While comparatively much has been written about the generic "Ainu" figure in primary Japanese sources and early chroniclers left a wealth of journals and other official and unofficial correspondence, very little is known about the gendered experience of early Hokkaido colonialism. Ainu women themselves did not leave any text-based records because of the language gap and the fact that early colonial Ainu society was primarily an oral culture. And while Ainu possess a vast store of oral literature, retained in living memory or more recently recorded by Ainu linguists and others, these accounts do not specifically address women's experiences of Wajin colonization. Aside from brief references to Ainu warrior women in seventeenth-century Japanese documents (ca. 1669), Ainu women tended to be portrayed according to Japanese images of idealized femininity: they performed labor for husbands and children, they were patient and enduring of hardships, and they never complained.[13]

While a paucity of written documents such as diaries, letters, autobiographies, or other personalized records makes it difficult to determine women's actual sentiments, Ainu women did leave a semiotically rich archive of their embroidered resistances to Wajin men's brutality. Contemporary Ainu artist and scholar of Ainu textiles Tsuda Nobuko argues that women refined their techniques of survival in response to colonial violence. She interprets the fiercely embroidered thorns and other protective appliqued motifs in these Ainu designs during this period as women's creative responses to the horror they experienced at the hands of Wajin men.[14] For example, women empowered the guardian spirits who governed the backs of their clothing by embroidering protective motifs to protect family members. Similarly, artist-activist Cikap Mieko observed that women sewed eye-like patterns to enhance the symbolism of "watching" outward from the women's backs.[15]

One of the most prolific chroniclers of Ainu communities, Matsu'ura Takeshirō, appointed by the Tokugawa government as a surveyor of imperial expansion into Hokkaido, left some two dozen volumes including diaries and official and unofficial accounts of his interactions in Ainu villages across Hokkaido during the mid-nineteenth century. Matsu'ura is widely recognized as one of the most sympathetic Wajin observers of Ainu affairs in the nineteenth century, and thus his accounts provide one of the most candid records available from a Wajin perspective. Indeed, Matsu'ura's most damning account of Wajin colonial violence in Hokkaido, *Kinsei Ezo jinbutsushi* (The human chronicles of early modern Hokkaido) was refused publication by the shogun's Hakodate magistrate in 1858 and did not appear in print until twenty years after Matsu'ura's death in 1912.[16] While my central argument about Ainu women's sexual subjectivity being compromised rests on a limited body of primary materials, Matsu'ura's discussion of some dozen or more Ainu women being sexually violated must be recognized for its significance in the larger narrative of Hokkaido colonization. These accounts should be seen as depicting a larger pattern of sexual violence rather than as aberrations in Hokkaido colonial history. [17] Students of Japanese history must recognize these episodes as characterizing a systemic pattern of colonial exploitation, a pattern mandated under the Tokugawa government's "local wives" (*genchi tsuma*) system (1799–1855), whereby a 1799 policy mandated Wajin marriages to Ainu women, amounted to state-sanctioned sexual assault in many cases and precipitated the breakdown of Ainu families.[18]

Matsu'ura addresses twelve Ainu women in chapter headings but includes many others among the 102 persons featured in *Kinsei Ezo Jinbutsushi.* He employs terms such as "mistresses" or "concubines" to describe Wajin men and Ainu women's interrelations. Couched in conservative nineteenth-century language, he employs euphemisms to describe acts of sexual intimacy, but his meticulous diaries do provide one of the few uncensored records from this time. For example, he phrases his descriptions in veiled terms: the Wajin men "did as they pleased" (*omou mama ni suru*). Guided by Ainu taboos against sexual impropriety, Ainu women were said to "despise being forced to do things they found embarrassing" but "they had no alternative but to obey." Wajin men reportedly threatened women with and frequently resorted to physical violence to force their acquiescence. Fisheries personnel punished those who resisted: Ainu women were tied with rope and flogged, lashed to wooden beams, denied food and water, and often tortured until they relented. If women were so unfortunate as to contract syphilis or other venereal diseases from the sexual violation, as many did, they were abandoned, with no food or medicine. Women who became pregnant were forced to ingest herbal tonics that induced abortion and ultimately destroyed their reproductive capacities.[19]

Matsu'ura's documentation reveals a range of coping mechanisms, illustrating key patterns in Wajin-Ainu interrelations. In contrast to Paul Barclay's argument with regard to interethnic marriage in Taiwan, interpreting the word 妾 *mekake* (frequently translated as mistress) as "second legal wife" is unsupported by my reading of primary sources in the case of Hokkaido. Few of these relationships can be said to have constituted consensual marriage nor did these marriages convey social capital to Ainu women in early colonial Hokkaido, as Barclay argues was the case in Taiwan.[20] Indeed, many of the Ainu women's husbands had been banished to distant fisheries or labor camps, and many of the Wajin overseers and laborers were already married but had temporarily left their families in mainland Japan. For some Ainu women, being taken as a "local wife" was a death penalty. Women who became pregnant from these undesired unions were frequently forced to abort their children, as in one tragic episode involving a woman named Ihesirasi. Unaware that Ihesirasi was pregnant with her Ainu husband's child and assuming the baby to be his own, the Wajin rapist caused her untimely death by forcing her to ingest an herbal concoction to induce abortion. When Ihesirasi's husband returned and learned of his wife's fate, he hanged himself on the riverbank in grief.[21] In another case, a woman named Shutcirosi who was violated by a Wajin overseer took her own life by drinking wolfbane, a poison commonly used in hunting.[22] But not all of these encounters ended in tragedy for the Ainu women. In another notable case, a woman who had endured repeated sexual advances from one particular overseer struggled and managed to crush her would-be rapist's penis. Years later this overseer was reportedly still experiencing such excruciating pain that he was unable to work.[23]

Drawing from this variegated archive of diverse texts and interviews, this examination of the nexus between sex, gender, and ethnic relations prior to Hokkaido's political annexation in 1869 reveals how Japanese interlopers claimed hegemony initially through these intimate frontiers.[24] Japan's multicentury conversion of Hokkaido entailed myriad experiments in eugenics, assimilation, and sexual colonialism, as Ainu women's bodies were appropriated by Wajin laborers in recurring episodes of sexual violence.[25] The Japanese government today argues that Hokkaido colonization proceeded from "inherent dominion" (*koyū no ryōdo*) over Hokkaido, as seventh-century general Abe no Hirafu asserted.[26] Conventional histories link the start of Japan's imperial project with so-called external colonies, marked with the 1895 colonization of Taiwan. Yet the notion that Hokkaido and Okinawa constitute "internal colonies" stems from an ex post facto axiom naturalizing these territories as part of Japan proper, a practice cultural studies scholar Michele Mason characterizes as ranking territories under a "hierarchy of colonial authenticity."[27]

Indeed, control of Hokkaido was a primary concern of Japan's modern project: Ainu ancestral lands (Hokkaido, Sakhalin, and the Kurils) straddle the borderlands between Japan and Russia and in the nineteenth century still constituted terrains of imperialist desire.[28] Hokkaido served as a pilot project for later Asia-Pacific imperialism. Wajin transformed Hokkaido through settlement, including Wajin soldier-farmers (*tondenhei*), merchants, and settlers from deposed domains. Moreover, the Colonization Commission's attempts to establish order in and develop Hokkaido foreshadowed later colonial strategies in Taiwan, Korea, Manchuria, and beyond into the twentieth century, as this volume demonstrates.[29]

The narrative of Ainu cultural decline and gradual assimilation into Wajin society has been documented so extensively that decline and disappearance have become the dominant tropes of the latter so-called Ainu period. Conventionally, this history begins with the formal political colonization of Hokkaido in 1869, but much work remains to revise the narrative of Ainu colonization. Critically, by soft-pedaling the actual violence of such long-term and gradual strategies of occupation, especially the devastation that the sexualization of Ainu women and the local wives policy wrought on Ainu communities, earlier historiography whitewashed the reality of a prolonged Wajin colonial occupation of Ainu lands and its destructive impact on Ainu lifeways. In recent years, distinguished historians such as David Howell, Brett Walker, Kikuchi Isao, and Iwasaki Naoko have contributed to recognition that a gradual process of colonization eroded Ainu autonomy in succeeding waves of Wajin authorities.[30] Even though these policies may not have been devised with colonial intent and viewed as connected or long term, their net impact was the collapse of Ainu families and the annihilation of Ainu communities. Viewed from a twenty-first-century Ainu vantage point, early colonial contact wherein Wajin fisheries overseers exploited Ainu women as sexual objects to quench the desires of Wajin laborers was catastrophic.

Empire operates on a visceral, affective level. Intimate terrains and spaces of home are especially vulnerable to the detrimental impact of colonial occupation. Acknowledging the affective operation of empire in such intimate domains compels scholars to radically redefine the way we understand imperial processes. A focus on geopolitics, territorial conquest, and even economic and social systems cannot expose the visceral experience of empire as felt in one's body and in one's emotions. Recent survey results indicate that twentieth-century Ainu women still preferred Wajin men as spouses, even when these relationships frequently spiraled into domestic violence or other forms of abuse.[31] This preference stemmed from a widespread anxiety that children who inherited Ainu ancestry from both parents and therefore possessed "thicker blood" would more likely experience racism and bullying. Thus, for living Ainu, the settler colonial state continues to thrive, if rendered diffuse through mental internalization and normalization of state political structures.

The administration of Ainu lands gradually shifted from the less intrusive tactics used during the initial Wajin settlement claims in the 1400s, including strict demarcation between Ainu and Wajin land, and over the centuries escalated into a totalizing political colonization of Ainu territories by 1869. Drawing from Matsumae domain records and shogunate policies, we can see how Ainu women's political status and local authority was gradually attenuated between the fifteenth and twentieth centuries.[32] The shifting of Hokkaido's administration between Matsumae and the Edo shogunate meant that the breadth and severity of Ainu assimilation policies was in flux. Rather than enabling greater freedom, this fluidity had an impact on women's political and reproductive wellness due to the breakdown of family units as Ainu men were removed and compelled to labor at distant fisheries.[33]

Starting in the fifteenth century, Wajin control of Hokkaido oscillated between Matsumae domain authority (1593–1799, 1821–1855) and Tokugawa shogunate authority (1799–1821, 1855–1869) and eventually shifted to Meiji state authority (1869–1912) when Hokkaido was christened Hokkaido, or "north-sea-route," projecting Japan's desires for the Northern Territories. As customs reform (1799–1821 and 1855–1874) and eventually full-scale assimilation (1870s-onward) were introduced, intermarriage mandated between Ainu women and Wajin men became known euphemistically as the wife-mistress (*tsuma-mekake*) system. This nomenclature underscored the nonconsensual nature of these unions. Indeed, there were some exceptional examples wherein Ainu women actively sought romantic relationships with Wajin men, such as the case of Wotonna from Kotoni, who abandoned her Ainu family for a Wajin guard.[34] Exceptions notwithstanding, the intersecting colonial and patriarchal structures of this system were not designed for Ainu women's welfare but were imposed to manage Ainu women's reproductive faculties and regulate Wajin men's needs. From the present-day point of view, it may seem that Ainu women's status as subjects of the Japanese state was a foreordained destiny. Yet it is important to recall that until 1869, Ainu were a sovereign people, even if that sovereignty was vastly compromised by domainal and shogunal policies.

From 1899 colonization became an explicitly gendered process that pressed men to assimilate and relegated women to a despised domestic otherness. In Ainu families, women were encouraged by their male kin to continue *Ainupuri* (ancestral ways) in the home. From the mid-eighteenth through the twentieth century, Ainu women's comparative lack of access to public sphere communications with Wajin, aside from informal trade and business transactions, put them at a disadvantage for acquiring the Japanese language. This disadvantage actually allowed women to preserve and maintain Ainu language; everyday practices; and aesthetic traditions such as oral folklore, clothwork, and shamanic skills.[35] Ainu women's marginality and their ongoing cultural practices enabled the continuation of Ainupuri into the early twentieth century. But as primarily domestic agents in what was seen as a dependent population, Ainu women in this early period also found themselves compelled to partner with Wajin immigrants, and many had little choice but to endure marriages that amounted to extended sexual assault.

Sexual Slaves and the Contract Fishery System

The advent of the contract fisheries system (roughly 1740–1855) proved devastating for Ainu-Wajin relations and particularly for Ainu families. From the mid-eighteenth century, the Matsumae Domain leased coastal trading posts to Honshu-based merchants, and the contract fishery system emerged. One of the most significant obstacles to recruiting Wajin men for contract fisheries labor was also a determining factor in the collapse of Ainu families, that is, the requirement that Wajin workers leave their families at home. Purportedly originating in Carenka's curse against Wajin women, a legend describing the catastrophes that would befall those who attempted to enter Hokkaido kept Wajin women out of Ezochi until the de facto ban was lifted in 1855.[36] Meanwhile, Wajin officials conducted negotiations solely with Ainu men, who were held to represent entire communities, and as a result, Ainu men achieved better mastery of the Japanese language.[37]

Through the contract fisheries subcontractor, merchants pressed Ainu men into grueling corvée labor for road building, transportation, and work in the fisheries. These men were often removed from their families and sent to locations far from their home villages, although all able-bodied men and women were expected to work in the fisheries. Most Ainu women, elders, and young children remained in home communities, where they processed herring meal into fertilizer, gathered kelp, and cooked for local fishery workers. The gendered division of labor whereby the contract fishery system was organized made Ainu women vulnerable by design. Meanwhile, subcontractor merchants and other Wajin men based near Ainu communities sought out local women, claiming these women as mistresses and wives and violating those who did not easily acquiesce.[38]

In the aftermath of the Kunasir-Menasi conflict, the Tokugawa shogunate assumed direct control over Hokkaido. To make long-term residence on Hokkaido appealing to Wajin men, shogunate officials mandated the institution of local wives, under which local shogunate representatives arranged for the provision of Ainu women to Wajin fisheries managers and guards.[39] The appropriation of women's bodies and sexual subjectivity as a resource of empire further escalated when Matsumae assumed direct administration and the shogunate ordered some five hundred Wajin soldiers to be stationed around Hokkaido to seal the eastern border against Russia in 1821. The vast majority of these Wajin men are believed to have compelled Ainu women into concubinage or marriage as local wives. By 1850, thirty-six of the forty-one guards stationed in Kushiro Fishery had taken Ainu women as local wives, and Matsu'ura describes the phenomenon as widespread across Hokkaido.[40]

Shortly after codifying the local wives policy, the "mixed-blood offspring" of such unions were deemed undesirable, and Wajin men were required to obtain marriage licenses before compelling Ainu women to marry them. Although these offspring were listed as Ainu in official registries (*ninbetsucho*), they were known colloquially as Shamo seeds (*shamo tane*), meaning of ethnic Wajin paternity.[41] In 1850 in the Ishikari Fishery, the most productive salmon fishery in western Ezochi, Matsu'ura recorded thirty-three examples of Ainu women who were claimed by Wajin men: five women listed as wives, twenty-eight women listed as Wajin mistresses, and eight children born from these unions. Among these women, some twelve were already married to Ainu men, but this was irrelevant to the fisheries supervisors who nevertheless paired them with Wajin. Kaiho Yōko recounts that one Ainu man named Kūtoe was flogged so severely while trying to resist his wife's abduction by a Wajin fisheries manager that he eventually died.[42]

It is difficult to conceive that Wajin male-Ainu female relations were based on parity in social status or that they were in fact consensual. Primary sources are riddled with euphemisms. Language used to describe interactions between Ainu women and Wajin immigrants evokes structural inequalities and underscores the power differential between "primitive Ainu" and "civilized Wajin," female and male, and colonized and colonizer. Japanese historians Kaiho Yōko and Kojima Kyoko avoid terms such as "sexual violence" or "rape" in relating Ainu women's subordination to Wajin men. They prefer historical terms such as "wife-mistress" or "local wives" that correlate with Tokugawa government categories. Anglophone sources describe Ainu women's relations with Wajin as "concubines" or the more mysterious "liaisons." But drawing from Matsu'ura's graphic discussion of the brutal violence and the deadly conditions in the fisheries, these relations might more accurately be described as rape at the interpersonal level and sexual enslavement at the systemic level.

Unions with Wajin men were detrimental not only for local matrilineal networks; they were devastating for individual women and represented the unspeakable sexual violence of colonial conquest. Ainu women were raped, abused, abducted, and forced to become mistresses and wives for Wajin merchants, despite the presence of their own families and children. Often, a single Wajin man exploited multiple Ainu women, as with Ishikari overseer Enkichi, who claimed four Ainu women.[43] If former mistresses became ill with disease or died, they were easily replaced with other Ainu women. Historian Kōhei Hanasaki has argued that together with an influx of fisheries overseers and migrant workers into Hokkaido, the sexual exploitation of Ainu women both by rape and by consensual sex outside of conjugal relations increased exponentially.[44] Hanasaki is one of the few historians to use the term "rape" to describe the sexual conquest Wajin men perpetrated against Ainu women. Based on the range of Tokugawa edicts attempting to regulate Ainu-Wajin intermarriage, it should be clear that at no point were the conditions for such marriages adjusted to accommodate the needs, desires, or agency of Ainu women. Instead, Tokugawa legislation of these unions flexed to accommodate state management of women's sexuality and reproductive capacities as a resource of empire.

The impact of the local wives system extended across Ainu society. The expansion of the contract fisheries precipitated a sharp decrease in the Ainu population, primarily because women of childbearing age were separated from their spouses but also due to the spread of communicable diseases such as smallpox, measles, and venereal diseases in these population-dense locales. While many women perished as a result of sexual and physical abuse, still others attempted suicide.[45] Ainu women who contracted venereal diseases were rarely offered food or medicine by their abusers and sought refuge in or were banished to mountainous areas where they suffered in solitude or shared meager resources with relatives. Ainu women's loss of social status during this period can also be interpreted as a loss of political, reproductive (in terms of labor connected with childbirth and social reproduction), and productive (economic subsistence activities through reciprocal networks) status as well.

Demographic data are scarce for Ainu during this period. But in the Ishikari Fishery, in fewer than fifty years between the first and second periods of Tokugawa direct rule, 1807 and 1854, respectively, the Ainu population had shrunk by two-thirds, from 2,285 to 726 persons.[46] The collapse of the Ainu labor population due to a smallpox epidemic drove the management to recruit Ainu from thirteen inland villages. In the Shari and the Abashiri fisheries in eastern Hokkaido—two of the most productive fisheries on the island—exploitation of the labor force was similarly devastating, with men and women segregated to provide fisheries personnel with unhindered access to Ainu women. A population of 2,000 Ainu in 1789 had shrunk to 1,312 Ainu in 1822, and by 1859 it had collapsed to 713 persons.[47]

Venereal diseases, particularly syphilis, proved to be a central factor in the sharp Ainu population decline in the nineteenth century.[48] As theorist of ecological imperialism Alfred Crosby has argued, such venereal diseases "cripple" the ability of colonized peoples to reproduce and thus act as population control agents.[49] One case that Matsu'ura titled "Three Destitute Women" is particularly troubling. In 1857 he encountered a group of three Ainu women living in a makeshift hut of butterbur plants on the upper Uryū River. The youngest, Yaeresika, had been taken as the mistress of a Wajin watchman, and her husband had been banished to the fishery in Otaru. Despite her resistance, Yaeresika was repeatedly raped by the watchman and contracted syphilis. The watchman's passions toward her cooled immediately; he left Yaeresika to starve alone without medical treatment. Initially, Yaeresika solicited food from other Ainu at the fishery, but as her condition worsened, her flesh began to disintegrate. Desperate to escape this miserable situation, she hired a boat to take her upstream, where she attempted suicide but was stopped by fellow passengers. Eventually, she disembarked further upstream and found an elder woman named Yaekoere living in a hut fashioned from butterbur stalks. Yaekoere had been abandoned when her children were taken away to work in the fisheries. Blind in one eye and in failing health, Yaekoere had resolved to subsist on wild plants until the winter, when she would give her ailing body to the earth. A second elder woman, Hisiruwe, who had also been left alone when her sons were dragged to the fisheries, joined the two women in the hut. Together, the three women dreamed about the day they would surrender to starvation. With spirits liberated together, they would avenge their tormenters: the fisheries overseers and the watchmen.[50]

Colonial Practices: "The Gendering of Ethnicity" and "Customs Reform"

As Wajin further consolidated their hegemony in Hokkaido, Ainu were called upon to perform as assimilated Japanese. And not infrequently, Ainu women were compelled to enhance the narrative of Hokkaido as inalienable Japanese territory through intimate relations with these Wajin invaders. In particular, Ainu women who became intimately involved with or were sexually violated by Wajin were expected to transform themselves through customs reform. Pressured to reject their own ancestral ways, many Ainu feared the wrath of the *kamuy* and interpreted any illness as punishment for abandoning their time-honored customs.[51]

While ethnic identity and ideas of gender have been nurtured within Ainu society over time, the twin forces of colonization and patriarchy (vis-à-vis Confucian ideology) radically reshaped Ainu conceptions of gender and ethnicity. As noted earlier, customs reforms (1799–1821 and 1855–1874), imposed by Tokugawa leadership, differed according to gender. As an extension of the Tokugawa understanding of phenotypical and ethnic difference as mutable and embedded in manners and customs (*fūzoku*), customs reform policies encapsulated a range of behavioral modifications designed to mold the Ainu population into Wajin through modified sartorial practice and adoption of an agricultural livelihood. As Sasaki has noted, examples of "reformed" Ainu are distinguished from unreformed Ainu in several of the picture scrolls from the early Tokugawa period.[52] Ainu cooperation in complying with these objectives was neither as geographically uniform nor as efficacious across the population as earlier accounts have claimed.[53]

A brief review of customs reform policy illustrates the fluid nature of differing factions' approaches in imposing their authority on Ainu populations and the varying degree of assimilation policies. In 1799, a full century ahead of the pro-agriculture assimilation regime known as the Former Aborigines Protection Act (1899), Ainu in eastern Hokkaido underwent customs reforms. They were compelled to adopt Japanese practices, shift from meat to a grain-based diet, cut their hair and shave their beards, wear Wajin peasant clothing, and adopt Japanese language. Women were compelled to abandon facial tattoos. Ainu who "reformed" were granted a monthly subsidy, Wajin clothing, and a house and were assigned a Japanese name in the official registries.[54]

By focusing assimilation campaigns on performances of Wajin ethnicity in the public sphere and allowing the domestic practices of Ainupuri to continue, colonial administrators inadvertently facilitated the continuation of Ainu ethnicity. In general, during this early period women experienced less pressure to reform and exercised some agency in choosing which reforms to adopt. Official records included special notations such as *menoko* (A. woman) or male-female Ezo (*danjo* Ezo-jin) in some cases, signifying that women were being targeted by certain regulations.[55] Wary of engendering resistance, Tokugawa officials were cautious in mandating compliance and sought to make customs reform attractive so as to motivate rather than compel other Ainu. Both tattooing and earrings were considered morally reprehensible by Wajin standards. Tattooing, for example, was associated with criminality in Japanese society. Judging from the records that European chroniclers left through the early twentieth century, tattooing practices were not easily changed. This certainly correlates with Ainu values in which women's full tattoos, together with the *usporkut* cord worn under their clothing, ensured their husband's success in fishing and hunting and thus guaranteed food for Ainu families.[56]

With Hokkaido's political colonization by the Meiji state in 1869 and the birth of Hokkaido Prefecture, the management of Ainu and assimilation policy shifted to the Colonization Commission. Michele Mason argues that Japan's modernization must be seen as inextricably entwined with the colonial settlement of Hokkaido: "No clearer case than Hokkaido exists of the influential ideological groundwork laid out in the opening years of the Meiji era that shored up the modern processes of imperial and national myth-making."[57] Nowhere is this clearer than in the regimentation of gender relations, as regulated by local Ainu communities. Attempts to structure the everyday lives of individual Ainu were regimented by gender distinction: while men were expected to shed their ethnic subjectivity, women came to be seen as receptacles of Ainu ethnicity.

Assimilation policies served the larger objective of modernizing all subjects of the Japanese nation, first by rejecting the "validity of non-Japanese ethnicity" and second by promoting agriculture through training. Between 1869 and 1882, the Colonization Commission issued edicts proscribing the tattooing of women's faces and men wearing earrings (1871 and 1876), the immolation of women's houses after their death (1871), and Ainu hunting methods such as poisoned arrows and trip-wired bows (1875 and 1876).[58] As with their customs reform predecessors, these assimilation programs exhorted Ainu to adopt agriculture and learn the Japanese language. Despite their relative marginality working in the domestic sphere, Ainu women experienced pressure to assimilate through violence and bullying. That is, changes in language, tattooing, clothing, and subsistence foods came about in large part due to the influx of Wajin settler-pioneers who imposed their worldview and cultural logic on neighboring Ainu.

Resulting directly from these vertical (i.e., state and colonial authorities) and horizontal (i.e., communities and individuals) assimilation pressures, Ainu women chose to reject certain vestiges of physical Ainu-ness while retaining others that connected them to ancestral memory.

In 1899 the Former Aborigines Protection Act was passed, producing a dependent population and policing it by mandating the Ainu transition to an agricultural livelihood and allotting 12.25 acres of land to Ainu households.[59] For women this legislation and the policy changes it fostered had weighty implications. As the managers and primary laborers under the gendered division of labor in precolonial Ainu communities, women were expected to take on the bulk of agricultural labor. Prior to this law, women cultivated grains, including several types of millet, using swidden-style agriculture.[60] Together with their families, women were compelled to relocate to remote areas for agricultural training, and much of the paltry sum of land allocated to Ainu families was rocky and unsuitable for farming.[61] After Ainu men lost access to hunting territories, fishing was criminalized, and men resorted to cash labor work in the fisheries and as guides for surveyors. Women took on roles as the family anchor through farm labor, childrearing, and otherwise securing a livelihood. While not directly targeted at women, men's conscription in the Imperial Army to serve in the Russo-Japanese War (1905) and even matriculation in school had deep impacts on the expectations toward women in the early twentieth century.

By virtue of the uneven application of assimilation policies across Ainu society, gender emerged as a distinct social category and the primary vehicle of Ainu ethnicity. Assimilation mandates conventionally focused on external aspects of ethnicity such as livelihood and sumptuary practices, and the state appeared less interested in transforming Ainu private lives. Men were thus able to continue self-identifying as Ainu and carry on with private spiritual practices. Yet as pressures for men to enter the public sphere increased, Ainu women came to be entrusted as culture bearers in the domestic context, strengthened by their own convictions to continue the Ainupuri of their forebears.[62] Accordingly, Ainu women were painted as keepers of "traditional culture." Kojima contends that they were predisposed to conservation because of the advantage of retaining the Ainu language and the production techniques for textiles.[63] With this development, gender, which had formerly been determinate only within the domain of sex-separate labor, emerged as a locus of ethnic Ainu expression.[64] As a result of public sphere-focused assimilation policies, women's ethnicity, which had been sequestered in the domestic realm, was allowed to continue without state interference. Colonial and state authorities that focused on evaluating assimilation success by assessing shifts in the public sphere assumed that Ainu had adopted Japanese cultural mores. But in fact, by overlooking Ainu domestic spaces, colonial administrators unintentionally accommodated the continuation of Ainupuri.[65]

Certainly the local wives system and the gendering of ethnicity phenomenon had radically different impacts on Ainu women's subjectivity. That is, Ainu women's ability to enjoy affective agency, meaning their ability to exercise self-determination in sexual and social livelihood and engage in a range of self-expression within a socially gendered system, were severely influenced by colonial and patriarchal forms of gender and sexuality. Careful examination of these intimate frontiers reveals how colonial forces intersected with gender (social roles) and sexual subjectivity (ability to exercise desire freely) and demonstrates how gender and sexuality are critical loci for the operations of empire. In spite of whether feudal authorities deliberately targeted these intimate domains, the operation of empire had an irrevocable impact on women and women's agency.

Conclusion

Until 1855 Carenka's curse proved a formidable obstacle to recruiting migrant workers and fisheries overseers to work in Hokkaido and take leave of their wives and children. By mandating this spatial and emotional distance from home and dispersing these men across an unfamiliar and inhospitable landscape, wittingly or not, the contract fisheries instigated a precarious situation for Ainu women. Desperate for physical and emotional intimacy, Wajin men quelled their collective thirst by partnering with and sexually assaulting Ainu women, and when these women's husbands and partners attempted to intervene, the Wajin overseers in many cases exiled these spouses to distant fisheries. The very conditions whereby Ainu women were rendered vulnerable originated in this gendered division of colonial labor and the overseers' deliberate fracturing of Ainu families to intensify fisheries production. In an ironic twist, the ballad of Carenka and her curse on Yoshitsune's lovers imperiled Ainu women rather than Wajin women. Entangled in this tragic nexus of imperial desires and women's own sexual subjectivity, Carenka's melancholic wail still reverberates in the everyday experiences of violence, racism, and sexual exploitation across Japan. Though its origins remain subject to controversy, "Esashi Oiwake" attends to contemporary Ainu women's ambivalence toward the Japanese state, which for them is neither a postcolonial nor a past-tense occupier. These Ainu women understand the ballad as a requiem for their ancestors, elders, and those for whom settler colonialism has signified loss—loss of autonomy and loss of reproductive self-determination.

In the fall of 2008, I happened upon the song unexpectedly. The setting was a conference of minority women from across Japan, gathered to share strategies for domestic lobbying and empowerment. As the finale, each minority women's group presented a short performance. After the Zainichi Korean women's rendition of "Ariran," two young Ainu women in their twenties jumped on the stage. They wore baggy black trousers and loose-fitting shirts, plain black ski hats, and high-top tennis shoes, invoking a self-consciously hip-hop fashion. I anticipated they would break into an original rap on Ainu identity, underscoring the notion that hip-hop is global resistance music. To my surprise they launched into "Esashi Oiwake." Their attire belied this genre and its lyrics, which surged from one melancholic note to another. To my untutored ears, the ballad of "Esashi Oiwake" resonated as one extended plaintive yodel, its lyrics muddled. Their moving rendition brought the audience to its feet. They had managed to transform an elegy of Ainu women's dispossession into a site of collective empowerment; they inspired the minority women's group as youth reclaiming an ancestral legacy of colonial conquest and recasting this as a space to project an alternative future.

Hokkaido and its predecessor Ezochi have long constituted a colonial terrain. Today, the scattered debris of this colonialism continues to cast long shadows, affecting Ainu women's lived realities and conditioning their educations and career trajectories. The racial ontologies forged under Japanese imperialism, whereby Ainu continue to be subjected to discrimination, and the material and mental effects of the colonial project are everywhere present in socioeconomic conditions. Moreover, these ontologies continue to resonate deeply in affective spaces, especially in the raw emotions and psyches of Ainu youth and women who experience low self-esteem, depression, and occasionally are driven to suicide.

Ainu women were key targets of Japan's earliest colonial settlements; they constituted the intimate frontiers of Japan's expansion into Ezo, which was later recast under the name Hokkaido as a distinctly Japanese imperial zone, long before its political and administrative incorporation to the Japanese nation-state. Even in the absence of an official colonial relationship between Ezo and Edo, sexual conquest facilitated the apparatus of Wajin dominance and the exercise of imperial power. This account of Ainu women's position and interpellation in the gradual incorporation of Hokkaido as "imperial formation" urges us to rethink the formal political "markers"—both chronological and geographic—delineating imperial zones and develop models attending to the flexibility of imperial power in insinuating itself in a range of terrains, particularly, those involving less visible intimate frontiers.

Notes

1. Esashi Oiwake Kai, "Esahi Oiwake Origins," *Esashi Shōkō Kankō-ka,* accessed December 19, 2014, http://esashi-oiwake.com/origin1. See also Matsumura Takashi, *Tabakaze ni utau: Esashi Oiwake Aosaka Mitsuru* (Sapporo: Hokkaido Shimbunsha, 2006).

2. Tahara Ryoko, "Ainu no shiten kara," in "Minority Women's Perspectives into Society! Into Policy!, ed. International Movement against All Forms of Discrimination and Racism Japan Committee (Tokyo: IMADR-JC, 2003), 113.

3. Mitsuru Aosaka, "Esashi-Oiwake, Sono hito no jinsei ga kikoeru uta," *Esahi-Oiwake Kai,* accessed December 20, 2014, http://esashi-oiwake.com/.

4. Shari Hunhdorf and Cheryl Suzack, "Indigenous Feminism," in *Indigenous Women and Feminism,* ed. Cheryl Suzack et al. (Vancouver: UBC Press, 2010).

5. Jean Barman, "Indigenous Women and Feminism on the Cusp of Contact," in Suzack et al., *Indigenous Women,* 92–95.

6. Richard Phillips, *Sex, Politics and Empire: A Postcolonial Geography* (New York: Manchester University Press, 2006), 220.

7. Edward W. Said, *Orientalism* (New York: Vintage Books, 1979), 6.

8. Anne McClintock, *Imperial Leather: Race, Gender, and Sexuality in the Colonial Contest* (New York: Routledge, 1995), 6.

9. Ann Laura Stoler, ed., *Haunted by Empire* (Durham, NC: Duke University Press, 2006), 24.

10. The Japanese labeled Ainu with the term Ezo, or barbarians (蝦夷) and demarcated the areas of Hokkaido dominated by Ainu as the land of the barbarians (Ezochi), until Hokkaido's official colonization by the Meiji state in 1869.

11. Tōyama Kinshirō and Satao Muragaki, *Tōkai Santan,* 1806, Hakodate Municipal Library Collection.

12. Tahara Ryoko, "Ainu no shiten kara," 113.

13. Kyoko Kojima, "Esunishitii no Hari: 18/19 seiki no Ainu Minzoku," in *Esunishiti Jenda kara miru Nihon no Rekishi,* ed. Kuroda Hiroko and Nagano Hiroko (Tokyo: Yoshikawa Kōbunkan, 2002), 68.

14. Tsuda Nobuko, personal communication, March 2010.

15. Mieko Cikap, "I Am Ainu, Am I Not?," *AMPO Japan-Asia Quarterly Review* 18, nos. 2–3 (1986): 82.

16. The text was first published serially in the journal *Sekai* in 1912 but did not appear in monograph form until Sarashina and Yoshida's contemporary Japanese translation in 1981. Sarashina Genzō and Yoshida Yutaka, "Introduction," in *Kinsei Ezo Jinbutsushi,* ed. Matsu'ura Takeshirō (Tokyo: Nōsangyoson Bunka Kyōkai, 1981), 12.

17. My gratitude to historian David Howell for insightful feedback on the manuscript.

18. Hanzō Yamazaki, "Ezochi Torishimari Goyōkake Matsudaira Shinanoshu," 1799, in *Ezo Nikki,* Hakodate Municipal Library Collection.

19. Matsu'ura Takeshirō, *Kinsei Ezo Jinbutsushi,* in *Nihon Shomin Seikatsu Shiryō Shūsei Vol. 4: Hoppō hen,* ed. Shin'ichiro Takakura (Tokyo: San'ichi Shobō, 1969), 768–770. Materials from this text are listed as *NS4.*

20. Paul Barclay, "Cultural Brokerage and Interethnic Marriage in Colonial Taiwan: Japanese Subalterns and Their Aborigine Wives, 1895–1930," *Journal of Asian Studies* 64, no. 2 (May 2005): 323–360.

21. *NS4,* 751–752.

22. Ibid., 749.

23. Ibid., 745.

24. See Yōko Kaiho's *Kindai Hoppō-shi: Ainu Minzoku to Josei to* (Tokyo: San'ichi Shobō, 1992) and "Ainu Josei no Shinsei," in *Nihon Joseishi Saiko: Onna to Otoko no Jiku,* ed. K. Nobuko (Tokyo: Furukawa Shoten, 1995). See also Kyoko Kojima's "Dentōteki Ainu Shakai ni okeru Josei no Yakuwari," in *Kazoku to Josei no Rekishi: Kodai, Chūsei* (Tokyo: Yoshikawa Kōbunkan, 1989); "Esunishitii no Hari"; *Ainu Minzokushi no Kenkyū: Hokkaido Ainu-kan no Rekishiteki Hensen* (Tokyo: Yoshikawa Kōbunkan, 2003); and "Gender, Ethnicity, and the Ainu," in *Gender and Nation: Historical Perspectives on Japan* (conference paper, German Institute for Japanese Studies, Tokyo, 2004).

25. Kaiho, *Kindai Hoppō-shi;* Kōsuke Sugawara, *Gendai no Ainu, Minzoku Idō no Roman* (Tokyo: Genbunsha, 1978).

26. Kojima, *Ainu Minzokushi no Kenkyū,* 166.

27. Michele Mason, *Dominant Narratives of Colonial Hokkaido and Imperial Japan: Envisioning the Periphery and the Modern Nation-State* (New York: Palgrave Macmillan, 2012), 18.

28. Brett L. Walker, *The Conquest of Ainu Lands: Ecology and Culture in Japanese Expansion, 1590–1800* (Berkeley: University of California Press, 2001).

29. See Mason, *Dominant Narratives;* and Richard Siddle, *Race, Resistance and the Ainu of Japan* (New York: Routledge,1996).

30. See Walker, *Conquest of Ainu Lands;* David Howell, *Geographies of Identity in Nineteenth-Century Japan* (Berkeley: University of California Press, 2005); Naoko Iwasaki, *Nihon kinsei no Ainu shakai* (Tokyo: Azekura Shobō, 1998); and Isao Kikuchi, *Hoppōshi no naka no kinsei Nihon* (Tokyo: Azekura Shobō, 1991).

31. ann-elise lewallen, "Beyond Feminism: Indigenous Ainu Women and Narratives of Empowerment in Japan," in Suzack et al., *Indigenous Women,* 161.

32. Kojima, *Ainu Minzokushi no Kenkyū.*

33. Certainly, Ainu desired and even depended on the commodities they received in exchange for their labor and thus a "structural coercion" was built in to the Wajin-Ainu relationships at the contract fisheries. Howell, *Geographies of Identity,* 112–115. See also Walker, *Conquest of Ainu Lands* for the origins of the Ainu dependency on Wajin commodities.

34. Kaiho, *Kindai Hoppō-shi,* 183.

35. Kojima, *Ainu Minzokushi no Kenkyū,* 395–396.

36. According to legend, the presence of Wajin women would cause boats to capsize when they rounded the Shakotan Peninsula because of a curse against women's presence in this area. Kaiho, *Kindai Hoppō-shi,* 197–198. As discussed earlier, one interpretation of "Esashi Oiwake" suggests this curse originated with Carenka. Still today a small sign reading "Women Prohibited" (*nyonin kinshi*) guards the path to the shrine at Shakotan Peninsula.

37. Kojima, *Ainu Minzokushi,* 398.

38. Takeshirō Matsu'ura, *Kinsei Ezo Jinbutsushi,* trans. Sarashina Genzō and Yoshida Yutaka (Tokyo: Nōsangyoson Bunka Kyōkai, 1981).

39. In Etorof, the policy was used to promote Hokkaido as a labor destination by claiming that "Ainu women could be applied for and *utilized* by Wajin personnel as wives" (*Ijo wo sorezore nyōbo ni tsukau*). Yamazaki, "Ezochi Torishimari Goyōkake Matsudaira Shinanoshu," 1799.

40. *NS4,* 786–787.

41. Kaiho, "Ainu Josei no Shinsei," 493.

42. Kaiho, *Kindai Hoppō-shi,* 183–185.

43. Ibid., 186.

44. Kōhei Hanasaki, *Shizuka na Daichi—Matsu'ura Takeshirō to Ainu Minzoku* (Tokyo: Iwanami Shoten, 1993), 49.

45. Kaiho, *Kindai Hoppō-shi,* 186.

46. Ibid., 189.

47. Hanasaki, *Shizuka na Daichi,* 231.

48. Ryō Okuyama, *Ainu Suibōshi* (Sapporo, Hokkaido: Miyama Shobō, 1966).

49. Alfred Crosby, *Ecological Imperialism* (Cambridge: Cambridge University Press, 1986), 214.

50. *NS4,* 737–739.

51. See Kaihō, *Kindai Hoppō-shi,* 195.

52. Toshikazu Sasaki, *Ainu-shi no jidai he: Yorekisho* (Sapporo: Hokkaido Daigaku Shuppankai, 2013).

53. See Howell, *Geographies of Identity;* Shinichiro Takakura, *Ainu seisaku shi* (History of Ainu policy) (Tokyo: San'ichi Shobo, 1972); and Siddle, *Race, Resistance and the Ainu of Japan.*

54. See Kaihō, *Kindai Hoppō-shi,* 194–196.

55. See Kojima, *Ainu Minzokushi no Kenkyū,* 394–395.

56. See Kiyoko Segawa, *Ainu no Kon'in* (Ainu marriage) (Tokyo: Miraisha, 1972), 17–18.

57. Mason, *Dominant Narratives,* 18.

58. See Howell, *Geographies of Identity,* 179.

59. Yūko Baba, "A Study of Minority-Majority Relations: The Ainu and Japanese in Hokkaido," *Japan Interpreter* 13, no. 1 (1980): 68–69.

60. Sarah Strong and Yukie Chiri, *Ainu Spirits Singing: The Living World of Chiri Yukie's Ainu Shinyōshū* (Honolulu: University of Hawai'i Press, 2011), 67.

61. Ibid., 67.

62. See Kojima, *Ainu Minzokushi no Kenkyū*, 394–397.

63. See Ibid., 396.

64. I describe this shift as the "gendering of ethnicity," based on my reading of Ainu women's history in Kojima, *Ainu Minzokushi*, 395–397, and developed further in lewallen, *The Fabric of Ainu Indigeneity: Modern Ainu Identity and Gender in Colonial Japan* (Albuquerque: University of New Mexico Press and School for Advanced Research Press, 2016).

65. See lewallen, 2016.

3 ◈ PAUL D. BARCLAY

Playing the Race Card in Japanese-Governed Taiwan

Or, Anthropometric Photographs as "Shape-Shifting Jokers"

> Race is . . . a word and notion that functions as a kind of talisman filled with magic, a power recognized in the vernacular expression 'playing the race card' as a kind of shape-shifting joker that can take the place of any card that has a fixed, legible identity.
>
> —W. J. T. Mitchell, *Seeing through Race*

A century before the Internet era, anthropometric photographs of an Atayal woman named Paazeh Naheh (ca. 1880–ca. 1910) went viral. From 1903 through the 1920s, her image was propagated via several forms of mass media, including picture postcards, international exposition displays, magic lantern slides, photo albums, geography textbooks, and newspaper file photos. Her image most commonly appeared in the form of "race cards"—picture postcards that feature anthropometric photographs.[1] Figure 3.1[2] is typical.

Race cards were much more than the exemplars of asymmetrical power relations, mimetic imperialism, and ruthless essentialism they appear to be at first sight. The evidence discussed below suggests that, in early twentieth-century Taiwan, race cards functioned as what W. J. T. Mitchell has described as "shape-shifting jokers." Through the artifices of captioning, cropping, and framing, publishers created race cards that indeed dehumanized their subjects, as the literature on anthropometric photography and imperialism would predict. Nonetheless, the original photographs were not an attempt at dehumanization. They were made by ethnographers and tourism-industry photographers to counter the idea that Taiwan indigenous peoples were savages who could be killed off with impunity. The state may have had genocidal intentions, but these race cards proposed an alternative vision of the place of indigenous peoples within Japan's first formal colony.

To recuperate the ambivalent nature of these contested artifacts by reexamining the conditions surrounding their production and reception is not to soft-

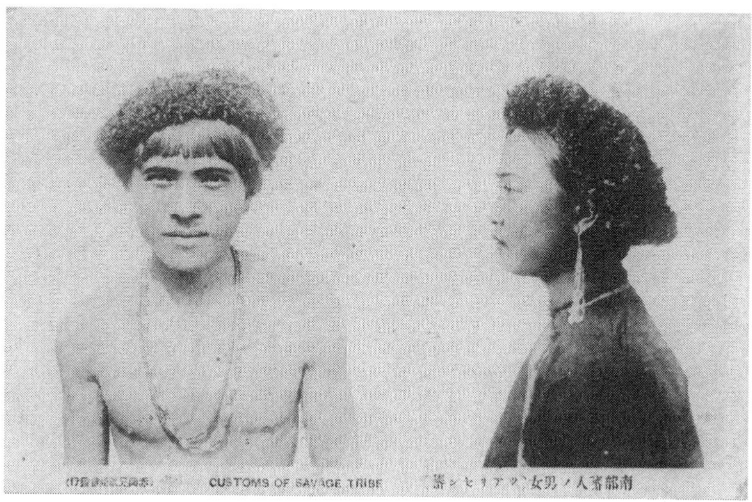

Figure 3.1. These portraits of a Tsarisen Tribe male and female appeared in numerous official publications between 1905 and 1911. Akaoka Kyōdai postcard, ca. 1920. East Asia Image Collection (Easton, PA: Lafayette College, 2012).

pedal the brutality of Japanese colonial rule in Taiwan. A number of postcolonial "exposés" of anthropology and photography have failed to go much beyond asserting the abject nature of the men and women who sat for such photos and the nefarious intentions of their producers.[3] Yet such studies have done little to mitigate the continuing revival and recirculation of race cards in Taiwan, Japan, and elsewhere. Why, despite over a century of concerted intellectual effort to debunk race as a form of pseudoscientific false consciousness and lay the invention and construction of race at the feet of discredited colonial regimes, does "race" refuse to die?

Writing in the 1990s about the history of American slavery, Ira Berlin observed that the now widely held theory that race is socially constructed has done little to change behavior. The reason for this, he believes, is that race "is not simply a social construction; it is a particular kind of social construction—a historical construction. Indeed, like other historical constructions—the most famous of course being class—*it cannot exist outside of time and place.*"[4] This argument counters the notion that "race" is essentially a scientific, systematically articulated, top-down construct that can be treated as a formal system of knowledge embedded in the "history of ideas." Following Edward Thompson's formulation of class as "a fluency which evades analysis if we attempt to stop it dead at any given moment and atomize its structure," Berlin notes that race is subjectively experienced by racializers and the racialized in the event of its historical emergence. In this view, it is much more than an externally imposed category.

While formally trained ethnologists had a role to play in the popularization, operationalization, and conceptualization of race in colonial Taiwan, they shared the field with consumers, officials, colonized subjects, and myriad stakeholders who contested, modified, imperfectly understood, or rejected their learned pronouncements. As "shape-shifting jokers," race cards gave these contests over the meaning of race a material form. In particular, a single set of anthropometric photographs taken in early 1903 assumed pride of place out of the hundreds of photographs that were available to publishers during the Meiji and Taishō eras (1868–1926).

One major reason for the impact of the 1903 photographs was timing. As armed conflict between Taiwan indigenous peoples and the Japanese state-backed camphor industry escalated at century's turn, a historical conjuncture thrust a particular set of images into the national and international limelight. The 1903 Osaka National Industrial Exposition and the Russo-Japanese War postcard boom bookended an alliance between Atayal headmen and Japanese expeditionary forces near Wulai in northern Taiwan. These two foundational moments in metropolitan mass culture provided the platforms for exhibit designers and publishers to render a handful of photographic encounters, orchestrated under the fluid political conditions of frontier diplomacy in Taiwan, into enduring and widely disseminated racial icons. The meanings attached to these photographs were varied and often contradictory but had everything to do with the historical emergence of racial categories and sentiments in Taiwan that persist to the present day. Thus, colonial Taiwan's most iconic anthropometric photographs, whose authority rested on the assumption of their timelessness and placelessness, were the very pictures of timeliness.

To capture the complexity and tenacity of race in contemporary political life, W. J. T. Mitchell has urged us to conceptualize race as a "medium," akin to a language game, rather than as an abstraction that might have a referent. For Mitchell, the medium of race provides the iconography and language for the expression of any theory, ideal, or argument that asserts the internal homogeneity and "group-ness" of particular "kinds" of human beings and their distinctiveness from similarly configured groups (races). The racial medium is a field wherein the deployment of race is often inflected with the familiar metaphor of species difference. But "race-talk and race-thinking" can also adopt the imagery and discourse of sexuality and gender to configure difference as "natural."[5]

Mitchell's analysis is salient here because, as we shall see, photographer-anthropologists, publishers, propagandists, and merchants rarely portrayed Taiwanese racial difference in strict, Linnaean terms or even in logically consistent language or iconography. Rather, race was the thread or mediating category that conjoined a mix of ethnonyms, slurs, stereotypes, and ideals into a language of difference and hierarchy.

Any analysis of race making in Japanese-governed Taiwan must make a clear distinction between *racism* and *race.* For Mitchell, racism is "what hurts." It is the practice of discrimination, genocide, exclusion, isolation, or segregation implemented against a race.[6] Indeed, Qing period resource wars (1700s–1895) along the frontier of the Han settlement on Taiwan produced a virulent racism whose institutionalization provided the terminology and raw materials for Japanese race scientists to contend with in the Meiji period and beyond.[7] That is to say, the use of imported foreign ideas involving somatological or linguistic criteria for racial classification did not produce racism in Taiwan but provided a new language game, or medium, for framing policy options that could exacerbate or mitigate preexisting forms of racism. The curious history of Paazeh's portrait supports Mitchell's contention that "*race* is the ambiguous medicine/poison, the *pharmakon*, for inflicting or alleviating the pain caused by *racism*."[8]

The formalistic, scientific model of race focuses our attention on the imperial centers where such discourses are distilled and attain their institutional inertia. To understand the genesis, meaning, and staying power of race cards in Taiwan, we must not only ask what men like Gotō Shinpei hoped to achieve by endorsing abstract notions of hierarchy and order but also identify and locate the dispersed interests, mechanisms, and micropolitical arrangements that allowed the medium of race to proliferate and sustain itself across vast social fields.[9] One particular anthropometric portrait taken in 1903 went viral and has maintained its historical momentum to this day precisely because it accommodated multiple constituencies at the "capillary" extremities of power. That is to say, Paazeh's photo recommended itself to commercially, academically, and officially inclined image makers for a number of reasons irrespective of the photographer's original purposes. At the same time, its physical form as a high-resolution, large-format photo negative lent itself to serial reproduction by parties separated by several degrees from the photograph's point of origin. In short, Paazeh's anthropometric portrait took on a life of its own.

The Face of "Savage Taiwan": Paazeh from Wulai

The portraits in figures 3.2[10] and 3.3[11] are arguably the most widely viewed set of photographs of an individual Taiwanese during the colonial period.

The sitter's name does not appear in any of the myriad reproductions of her photograph, but I have identified her as the woman referred to variously as Paazeh Naheh and Hazehe Watan in textual sources (hereafter Paazeh). Paazeh lived in or around Wulai and was known as a member of the Kusshaku (Ch. Quchi) tribe or ethnicity when these shots were taken in February 1903. She was the daughter of Watan Yūra, a "headman" who reportedly held sway over some five different settlements in the mountainous area just south of the Taipei basin in the early 1900s.[12]

Paazeh's photographer Mori Ushinosuke (1877–1926) was an interpreter, museum curator, government ethnologist, and protégé of Torii Ryūzō (1870–1953). Mori is considered by his Taiwanese and Japanese biographers to have been an indefatigable trekker adept at the Austronesian languages spoken in Taiwan's interior.[13] He was also considered a "friend" of the peoples now known as Taiwan indigenous peoples.[14] As Torii's apprentice, Mori became an ardent race scientist, committed to the arts of taxonomy as they revolved around anthropometry, comparative linguistics, and holistic studies of "culture."

Figure 3.2. Hand-colored postcard of Paazeh, ca. 1903–1907. East Asia Image Collection (Easton, PA: Lafayette College, 2012).

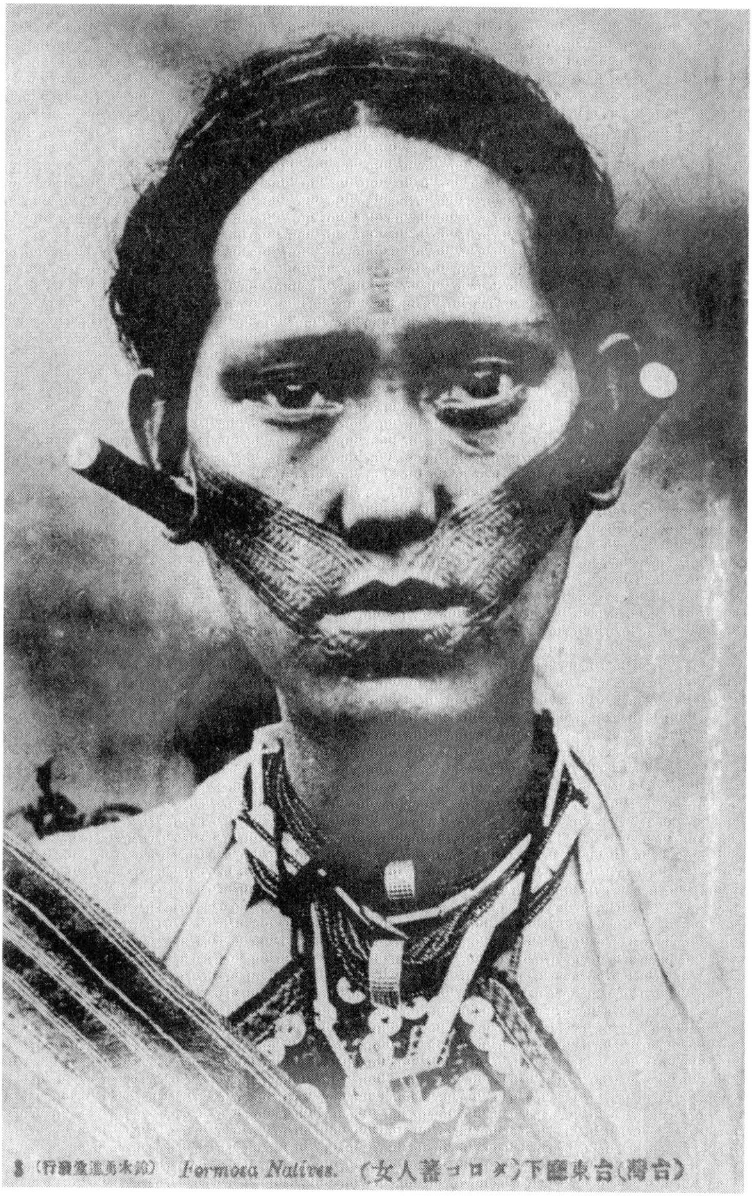

Figure 3.3. Postcard of Paazeh, ca. 1920, published by Suzuki Yūshindō. Used with permission of the National Central Library (Taiwan) (#002414438).

Paazeh and Mori first met to produce photographs in 1902. Mori then returned to Wulai to make more portraits of Paazeh and her family for the Fifth National Industrial Exposition in Osaka. Soon after her famous portraits were shot in February 1903, a larger-than-life reproduction was displayed at the Osaka exposition's Taiwan Pavilion,[15] attended by over five million visitors from throughout Japan and abroad.[16] The Japanese government sent a copy to the St. Louis Louisiana Purchase Exposition of 1904 for further display[17] to an even larger audience.[18]

As the national committee and the Taiwan Government-General put the wheels in motion to stage the Osaka expo, Japan's leaders were preparing for war against Russia. In fact, the Osaka expo was organized in part to demonstrate Japan's national strength in the face of the Russian menace.[19] The famous attack on Port Arthur in February 1904 was followed by a mass-media campaign to rally the Japanese public and secure international support. Between September 1904 and May 1906, millions of privately and officially produced picture postcards of Japanese war heroes, battleships, military triumphs, and patriotic gatherings touched off a national craze for the new medium.[20]

Catching this wave, anthropometric portraits of Paazeh appeared in at least seventeen different picture postcard designs between 1903 and the 1920s. At the time, the picture postcard was the most affordable and abundant medium for the dissemination of photographic images in Japan.[21] But the expositions and the postcard boom were just the beginning. As a file photo in newspaper rooms, consular offices, and anthropology labs, Paazeh's portrait circulated throughout the empire and migrated across the Pacific Ocean.

In September 1905, her profile was reproduced in Takekoshi Yosaburō's influential *Taiwan tōchi shi.*[22] It reappeared in George Braithwaite's 1907 English translation of Takekoshi's book as a "savage type,"[23] the same year that Ōshima Kumaji, the director of police for the Taiwan Government-General, submitted her frontal portrait in a report to U.S. Consul Julean Arnold, who then had it published by the Smithsonian Institution.[24] In 1908, Canadian travel writer Mary T. S. Schaffer picked up a print of Paazeh's photo in Wulai, which she promptly turned into a colorful glass-lantern slide to show in her lectures about travels in Asia.[25] Around the same time, Paazeh's portrait was shipped to the Philadelphia Commercial Museum with the rest of the Formosan Exhibit from St. Louis, to again be displayed with other artifacts of Taiwanese material life. Through the offices of William P. Wilson, the Philadelphia Commercial Museum's curator, the frontal shot of Paazeh appeared in an April 4, 1909, *Detroit Free Press* feature titled "Hunting Head Hunters with Live Electric Wires."[26] The same portrait was published in the June 26, 1910, *Washington Post.* It was then picked up in syndication to appear in August 1910 issues of the *Nashua Reporter* in Iowa and the *Star Gazette* of Sallisaw, Oklahoma, and probably many other small-market newspapers in the United States.[27] An etching of her profile can even be found in an article called "Surprising the Barbarians" in the magazine *Popular Electricity in Plain English.*[28]

That same year a line drawing based on Paazeh's portrait illustrated the "Taiwan" section of the Japanese Ministry of Education's elementary school geography textbook.[29] In 1912 her profile was published in a coffee-table album titled *Taiwan seiban shuzoku shashinchō* (Taiwan's aborigine tribes) in Taipei.[30] Finally, in 1915 and 1918, frontal and profile shots of Paazeh appeared in the massive photographic collection *Taiwan banzoku zufu* (Taiwan indigenous tribes pictorial), published in Taipei and Tokyo, respectively, under the byline of Mori Ushinosuke.[31] In sum, Paazeh's portrait, without an identifying name; contextualizing scenery; or clues to her social, political, and familial standing, was reproduced in Japanese- and English-language governmental, scholarly, and commercial media and displayed at expositions as a representative figure of Taiwan's most "savage" headhunters, the Atayal tribe, for over two decades.

True to the anthropometric genre, the race cards of Paazeh feature washed-out backgrounds, lack personal names in the captions, and pose their subject in frontal and profile views to facilitate comparison with other similarly posed "specimens." Based on their resemblance to so many other anthropometric images from other colonial settings, one can surmise an intention to subordinate and distance Paazeh by constructing her as a member of an inferior race, rhetorically buttressing a number of projects in imperial domination and segregation.[32] Matsuda Kyōko's pioneering book on the imperial gaze at the 1903 Osaka exposition, which mentions the anthropometric photographs analyzed in this chapter, follows this line of analysis. In Matsuda's account, dioramas, photographs, handicrafts, and other Taiwan-related articles were selected and displayed according to a classificatory system designed to make Taiwan intelligible to both its new government and Japanese home islanders (*naichijin*). As such, the anthropometric photographs concretized a taxonomy of Taiwan's ethnic groups into visually discernible races, thus enabling comparison between the Japanese Self and the Taiwanese Other along somatic lines. Matsuda refers to the objects and images gathered in the Taiwan Pavilion as "the Taiwan that could not represent itself."[33]

Hu Chia-yu argues that these displays functioned to dramatize the civilizational distance between Japan and its colonial wards while extolling the prowess of the ruling government.[34] Ka F. Wong has concentrated on implicating anthropometric photographs themselves in the domination of Taiwan indigenous peoples. According to Ka, the anthropometric images in the photographs taken by Torii Ryūzō (Mori Ushinosuke's mentor) "mirrored a legitimized racial superiority in the name of scientific representation. The aboriginal people became 'dehumanized' as 'passive objects of study.'"[35]

Common to the analyses of Matsuda, Hu, and Wong is the assumption that consumers and producers interpreted anthropometric photographs in reference to the unmarked "Japanese self" and that these images were part of a distancing and denigrating project. In this narrative, race cards become agents in the domination of the colonial Other by means of typification, boundary-drawing, and invidious comparison. Christopher Pinney refers to this interpretive tradition as "the first history of photography," wherein photography "stands at the technological, semiotic and perceptual apex of 'vision,' which itself serves as the emulative metaphor for all other ways of knowing . . . in the context of colonialism, the 'divine' power of photography comes to reflect a Western technological and epistemological prowess."[36]

Viewing these anthropometric photographs today, their racist intent and invidious effects seem obvious. With historical hindsight, we can see that the "flag followed the camera" in the areas that would come to be known as the Aborigine Territory in colonized Taiwan. But as Pinney points out, photography and cameras, while "globally disseminated," were always "locally appropriated."[37] Julia Adeney Thomas has elaborated this point and has added a temporal vector to Pinney's spatial analysis. Thomas speaks of the temptation to assign meanings and values to imagery from the past based on our necessarily visceral reactions to photographs.[38] Nonetheless, she argues, historians need to tread lightly when imputing motives and meanings to the photographers and photographs of the past, whose "ways of seeing" cannot be assumed to be similar to our own. The excavation of meaning in the historical study of photographs requires careful investigation into the discourses, debates, and institutions that gave particular photographs their impetus at the time of production.[39] Taking a cue from Thomas' work, anthropometric photographs should be analyzed as temporally specific, locally planned and executed documents. On the one hand, these photographs were creatures of conditions in the Japanese-Han-indigenous frontier in Taiwan circa 1903, the site of their production. On the other hand, their design and reception was shaped by the specific agendas of Taiwan exhibit organizers at the major expositions of the early twentieth century.

Considered as products of a locally appropriated medium with historically specific meanings, the Japanese anthropometric photographs of Taiwan indigenous peoples that reached very large audiences in the early twentieth century were not primarily attempts to locate the Japanese Self by Othering the "savages." Rather, photographers and exhibitors were countering the image of the "savage" of Qing discourse. Though the trope of savagery continued to resonate with Japanese policy-makers and appeared in Japanese mass media well into the 1910s, photographs such as Paazeh's portrait were initially created as an element of a broader ethnological offensive against the dominant discourse on savagery.

The Contrasting Logics of Savagery and Ethnicity

It would have been consistent with prevailing political and discursive winds for early twentieth-century postcard owners to have viewed Paazeh and the Atayal peoples as "animal-like" beings—subhumans who could be slaughtered by the state with impunity.[40] In December 1902, only a couple of months before Mori Ushinosuke took Paazeh's photos for the exposition, councilor Mochiji Rokusaburō, Gotō Shinpei's braintrust on "Aborigine Policy," issued his famous "opinion paper on the Aborigine problem (*Bansei mondai ni kansuru ikensho*)." In it, he argued that Taiwan's *seiban* (savage) population lacked recognizable organs of government and therefore stood outside the rules of civilized warfare and diplomacy. As Mochiji put it, "Sociologically speaking, they are indeed human beings (*jinrui*), but looked at from the viewpoint of international law, they resemble animals (*dōbutsu no gotoki mono*)."[41]

Based on Mochiji's recommendations, the Taiwan Government-General proceeded to streamline its "Aborigine Administration" under Police Bureau control and launch military assaults on tribes actively resisting the harvest of timber in their territories. As these campaigns got underway, in June 1904 parliamentarian Takekoshi Yosaburō arrived in Taiwan to write a progress report. Echoing Mochiji, Takekoshi considered the so-called *seiban* an existential threat to Japan's Empire. He wrote that the militarization of Japanese-Atayal relations "does not mean that we have no sympathy at all for the savages. It simply means that we have to think more about *our* 45,000,000 sons and daughters than about the 104,000 savages."[42] Takekoshi thus embraced *naichijin* Japanese as "sons and daughters" while banishing *seiban* from the national family. Indeed, from 1904 through the 1910s, thousands of Atayal people were indiscriminately slaughtered or impoverished by punitive trade embargoes and mechanized bombardments by combined Japanese forces of privateers, policemen, auxiliaries, and soldiers in operations that Mochiji's and Takekoshi's militant rhetoric justified.

In September 1905, Takekoshi published *Taiwan tōchi shi,* his encomium to Japanese rule based on his 1904 visit, and included a profile picture of Paazeh as a nameless Atayaru-zoku jo (Atayal tribe female) next to exemplars from each officially recognized "tribe." These portraits were interleaved with photos of Japanese military maneuvers and an imperial inspection tour of camphor forests. In this context, Paazeh's profile, as an emblem of recalcitrant Atayals, marked her and her tribe as an expendable race and as affronts to Japanese sovereignty. The rhetoric on savagery was amplified and reinforced by the captions for various contemporary postcards that identify Paazeh as a *seiban,* bellicose *seiban,* or (incorrectly) as a member of the Taroko *seiban,* the most militarily resistant subgroup of Atayal peoples.[43]

Captioning was essential for positioning anthropometric portraits within different narratives of colonial history. Elizabeth Edwards has argued that still photographs, as slices of time that freeze events, cannot narrate themselves without the help of external markers, such as text or juxtaposition with other photographs.[44] Alternative captioning for Paazeh's card indeed reveals other possibilities and uses for her portrait. For example, the caption for figure 3.2 merely refers to Paazeh as "Shinkō [administrative district], Urai-sha [place name] Woman, Taiyal Tribe," sans terminology for "savage." The ethnonym "Taiyal" (also spelled "Atayal") was a Japanese innovation, embedded in a different logic of representation than the term *seiban* (raw barbarian) or *banjin* (barbarian peoples).

The competing logics can be illustrated by reference to contemporary maps. The first is a 1905 census map of Taiwan (fig. 3.4[45]). It shares one important trait with official Qing representations of the island: lands beyond areas of rice, sugar,

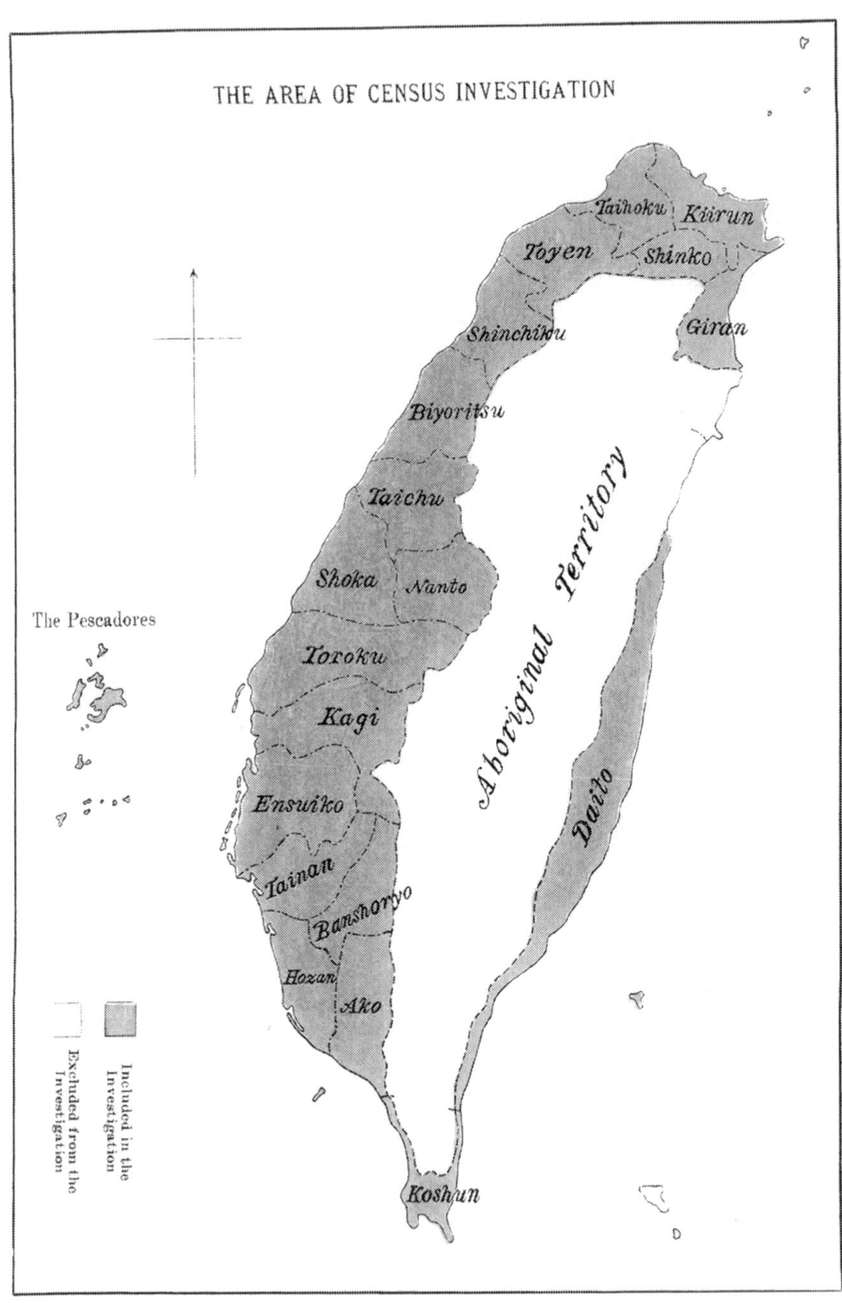

Figure 3.4. The 1905 census of Taiwan. *The Special Population Census of Formosa 1905: Report of the Committee of the Formosan Special Census Investigation* (Tokyo: Imperial Printing Bureau, 1909).

and tea cultivation were left blank as testament to the ability of Taiwanese highlanders to fend off tax collectors and census takers and remain "illegible" to the state.[46] Men like Mochiji Rokusaburō populated this white space with *seibanjin* who lacked a legal identity under international law. In the discourse on savagery, the Aborigine Territory was *terra nullius*.

The ethnographers, who were race scientists to a man, took the blank space as evidence of Qing lassitude and a lack of scientific curiosity. To bring *terra nullius* within the field of international anthropology's academic prestige system, they populated the white space with "culture zones" and "races" that were worthy of study, if not a certain kind of appreciation. Torii, Inō, and Mori shifted the *ban* (savage) category of Qing parlance over to the "Malay race" of Blumenbach's racial taxonomy. Mixing the language of species and culture freely, the anthropologists' aim was not so much to promote relativism as to put "Malays" on the map as human beings.

On April 23, 1898, Inō Kanori (1867–1925) unveiled the newly devised taxonomy with a photographic montage composed of representative "types."[47] For an audience of scholars and officials in Taiwan, Inō placed the montage on the cover of the first issue of the *Banjō kenkyūkaishi* (Journal of the Society for Research on Aborigine Conditions) on August 16, 1898.[48] It was reproduced for a general metropolitan readership on August 5, 1899, in *Taiwan meisho shashin chō* (A photo album of Taiwan's famous sites) (fig. 3.5[49]).

The "Atayal type" in figure 3.5 is captioned as the "Tattooed Face Savage" (黥面蕃) in kanji.[50] The use of *ban* 蕃 as part of the ethnic designator recalls the Qing taxonomy that put Atayals in the outer circle in *hua-yi/ka-i* ideology[51] but could also connote the bottom rung on the social Darwinistic ladder.[52] In either scheme, *ban* denoted the absence of civility, not the presence of "Atayalness." In this same caption, however, the word for "Tattooed Face Savage" is glossed in *furigana* as "Atayal." The new ethnonym redefined the "savages" in terms of unique attributes manifested in language and material culture; neither connected to nor dependent upon their relationship to a Japanese or Qing imperial center. In other words, the ethnonym "Atayal" asserted a *presence*.

Inō's montage was composed to populate a map that asserted the Atayal's ethnic presence cartographically. It configured Taiwan's ethnic groups as commensurate units resembling nation-states on a Mercator projection map (fig. 3.6[53]), suggesting ontological parity for each unit.

In contrast to the ethnological map (fig. 3.6), the montage (fig. 3.5) could not provide visual consistency across ethnic groups. Some of the photos are studio portraits; others were apparently shot in situ. Some displayed noted cultural markers, while others did little to distinguish their subjects from other Taiwanese. For example, the "Tattooed Face Savage/Atayal" (*upper right corner* in figure 3.5), in contrast to written ethnological descriptions that informed Inō's map, wears no jewelry, has no visible tattoos, and is carrying an imported weapon. Mori's Kusshaku photographs, as we shall see, would close this gap between the written and photographic ethnological record in the Japanese colonial archive.

Figure 3.5. *Taiwan's Savage Tribes.* Inō Kanori's montage illustrates his pioneering taxonomy of Taiwan indigenous peoples. By permission of the National Taiwan Library (Taipei).

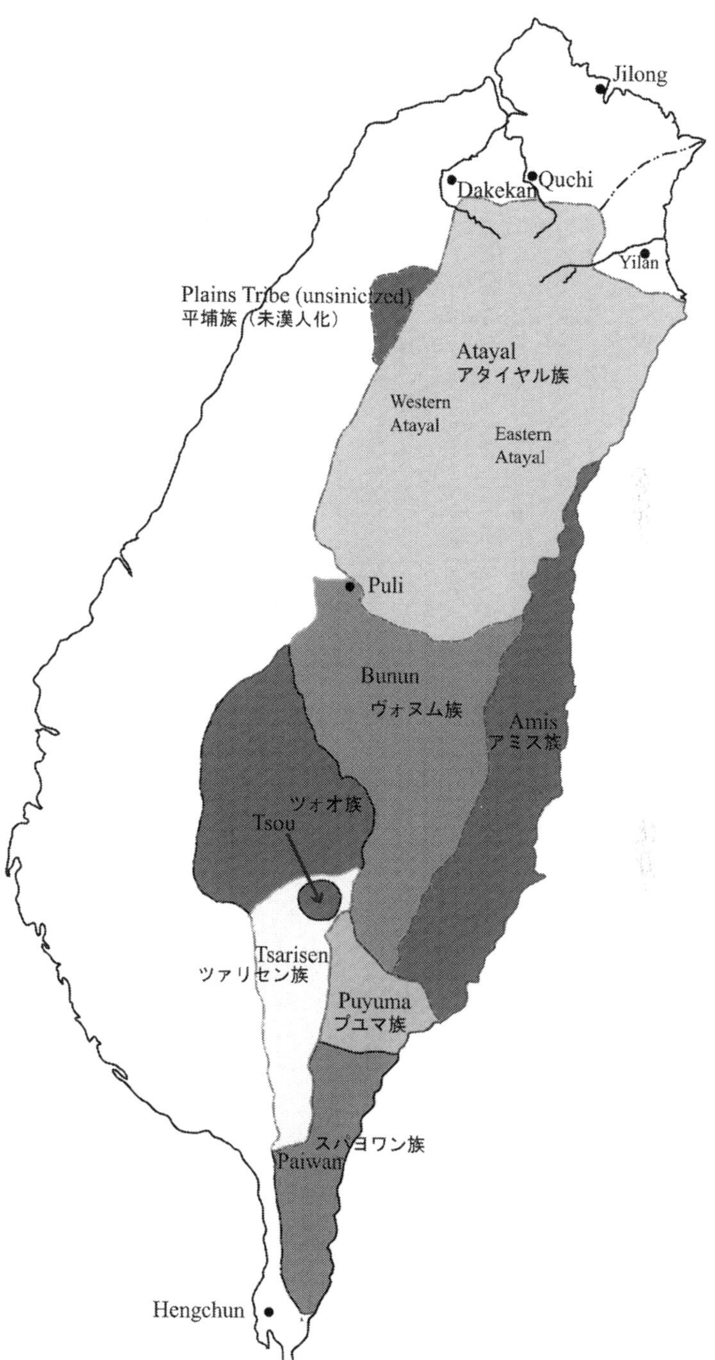

Figure 3.6. Imperial Japan's first ethnic cartography of Taiwan. Based on Inō Kanori's map in *Taiwan banjin jijo* (1900).

The Atayalization of the "Tattooed Face Savages"

A glass plate negative of Inō's Tattooed Face Savage is held at the U.S. Library of Congress as part of the Bain News Service photographs (fig. 3.7[54]), along with a portrait of two well-armed "chiefs" (fig. 3.8[55]), two photographs of headhunters with fresh heads, and a picture of a skull shelf.[56] This negative (fig. 3.7) is captioned "Typical fighting man of the headhunters, Formosa." The Japanese word for "savage" is burned on the negative. The other "chiefs" in the Bain News Service set are also referred to as savages, while the other three Bain negatives provide graphic evidence of *seiban* barbarity by displaying severed heads or skulls.[57] The term "Atayal" is not attached to any of these photographic negatives.

Other photos of the armed man from Inō's 1898 montage have been reproduced in the 1999 book *Images of Taiwan Indigenous Peoples from the Inō Kanori Archive.* One shows him seated with a rifle and a Japanese flag; the other shows him directing soldiers with weapons, again carrying a Japanese flag. The editors of this volume argue, convincingly, that he probably fought on the side of the Japanese state against Han rebels in late 1895 and 1896, as an irregular in the employ of Japanese station chiefs stationed near Kusshaku (Paazeh's home area).[58] His image was also reproduced on cabinet cards, a popular photographic medium from the 1860s through the 1890s. The cabinet-card caption refers to

Figure 3.7. *(Left) Typical Fighting Man of the Headhunters, Formosa.* From the George Grantham Bain Collection, Library of Congress.

Figure 3.8. *(Right) Savage Chiefs, Formosa.* From the George Grantham Bain Collection, Library of Congress.

him as an "armed Taiwan bandit who roams the mountains with food on his back," a description at complete odds with the photographic evidence of his service under the Japanese flag but consistent with the rhetoric of savagery that permeates the Bain News Service photos.[59]

For some reason, this particular Tattooed Face Savage's portrait faded from view as picture postcards emerged on the scene during the Russo-Japanese War. Nonetheless, the generic "armed head-hunting savage" crossed over into the picture-postcard era with official help. The Taiwan Government-General issued a set of three commemorative postcards on October 15, 1905. One featured a studio portrait of armed "headhunters," labeled "Taiwan savages" (Taiwan *banjin*) in Japanese (Fig. 3.9).[60] They are pictured in front of thick draperies on a carpeted floor, the same setting that was cropped out of the Tattooed Face Savage photo in Inō's montage.[61]

The officially sanctioned headhunter card was probably issued in a print run numbering in the tens of thousands, if not more.[62]

Studio portraits with chairs, drapes, and rugs may seem incongruent with photographs of the so-called *seiban,* a word whose very etymology suggests great distance from centers of civilization or refinement. This disconnect between the domestic settings of the portraits and the putative savagery of their human subjects was in part a function of photographic technology in colonial Taiwan circa 1900. As Ulrich Keller has pointed out regarding photographs of the Crimean War, cameras and their operators in the age of slow shutter speeds and bulky equipment were restricted to genres and compositions that could accommodate the limited mobility and agility of the apparatus.[63] The studio portraits of *seiban,* then, had less to do with the artistic intent of the photographers than with their technical constraints, which were also shaped by political conditions in upland Taiwan. The travelogues of Inō Kanori, Mori Ushinosuke, and Torii Ryūzō suggest that in situ photography was a difficult proposition in Taiwan's northern interior during the 1895–1905 period.[64] The studio portraits of this early period are in fact testaments to the jealously guarded abodes of these assembled headmen and mercenaries. As men whose economic and political status partly rested on their ability to monopolize access to prestige goods from the lowlands vis-à-vis their fellow highlanders while simultaneously restricting access to timber stands and upland traders, chiefs and headmen had every reason to keep Japanese photographers (and others) away from their settlements.[65] In fact, Inō Kanori coined the ethnonym "Atayal" based on his interpreter-assisted interviews with members of a twenty-seven-member party from the Wulai area in Taipei. The Tattooed Face Savage himself was probably among them, and Paazeh's father, Watan, was certainly present.[66]

The female Atayal in Inō's 1898 montage (fig. 3.5) also contains elements of savage imagery. Ethnic markers appear irrelevant, and evidence of borderland provenance appears prominent. She is wearing Chinese-style upper garments, not local weaves. In early Japanese photography of Atayal peoples, this type of clothing was predominant for females because anthropologists depended upon bicultural, Sino-Atayal hybrid informants, usually represented by female interpreters.[67]

臺灣總督府始政十年紀念
臺灣蕃人
Head Hunters in Formosa.
著作權登錄濟 臺灣總督府發行 小川一眞印行

Figure 3.9. Taiwan Government-General Tenth Anniversary postcard, 1905, titled *Head Hunters in Formosa.* East Asia Image Collection (Easton, PA: Lafayette College, 2012).

In contrast to the ethnically ambiguous Atayal photographs in the 1898 montage (fig. 3.5), Inō's canonical 1900 textual description of the Atayal describes them as face-tattooed peoples, richly adorned in geometrically carved earrings and accessories that included buttons, brass, shiny metal, and colored threads.[68] To harmonize the discordance between Inō's textual and cartographic representations of clear-cut, unambiguous ethnic diversity among Taiwan's non-Han population (fig. 3.6) and the motley assemblage of photographs in the 1898 montage (fig. 3.5), Inō commissioned a color painting for the Paris Universal Exposition in 1900 (fig. 3.10[69]).

The 1900 painting (fig. 3.10) adds head feathers, necklaces, hats, and earrings to each representative "savage type" to accentuate cultural differences among them, as can be seen in the comparison of figures 3.10 and 3.5.[70] The process of fabrication is even more evident in the similarly augmented illustration for the 1907 Tokyo Industrial Exhibition, also curated by Inō (fig. 3.11).[71]

In figures 3.10 and 3.11, the gun has been airbrushed out of the Atayal man's hand, large bamboo earrings have been painted in, and forehead and chin tattoos have been darkened or added. In the 1898 montage (fig. 3.5), the Bain News Service photograph (fig. 3.7), and the cabinet card, the facial tattoo on his forehead is invisible or barely visible, and the chin tattoo is obscured by shadow. The high-resolution negative stored in the Library of Congress reveals a very faint forehead tattoo with high magnification but also rules out a chest tattoo. The photos of alternative poses from the same session show no evidence of visible facial or chest tattoos. Yet the reproduction in James Davidson's 1903 book (for which Inō Kanori was the ethnological advisor) exhibits pronounced forehead, chin, and chest tattoos, apparently the result of doctoring.[72]

In the "ethnicized" 1900 and 1907 paintings (figs. 10 and 11), the female Atayal type shed her Chinese-style upper garment for an Atayal sleeveless vest, decorative chest embroidery, and a striped handwoven cape. The reornamented Atayal woman wears ethnologically correct earrings and necklaces as well. Whereas the ethnicized male Atayal model was transformed with a paintbrush or pencil, his female counterpart was removed from the 1898 photomontage and replaced by a more appropriate model in the 1900 and 1907 composite portraits.[73]

As curator for the 1900, 1903, 1904, and 1907 expositions, Inō Kanori was charged with educating the public about the non-Chinese population of Taiwan. In the course of preparing the visual component of his exhibits, Inō turned "savages" into Atayal and nondescript males into Yami and Paiwan by embellishing visual documents. As part of a larger project in census taking, mapmaking, and museum curation,[74] it would be accurate to view these fabrications as an exercise in top-down ethnogenesis.

Making Photographs in a Qing Hinterland

James C. Scott's characterization of a parallel project in British Burma suggests that Inō's difficulties were not unique. As was the case with British officials,

Figure 3.10. The painting *Countenances of the Savage Tribes* (*Fanzu xiangmao tu*) was sent to the 1900 Paris Universal Exposition. By permission of the Taiwan National University Museum of Anthropology (item #370). 臺大人類系標本藏品【370】「蕃族相貌圖」

Figure 3.11. This embellished version of Inō Kanori's 1898 montage (see fig. 3.5) appeared as the *Species of Savages in Formosa* in a 1907 exhibition guide and in a 1908 travel guide. By permission of the National Taiwan Library (Taipei).

Japanese agents in upland Taiwan found even the act of naming tribes to be fraught with problems because of the hybridity they regularly encountered (as depicted in the photographs in the 1898 montage). Of these turn-of-the-century classificatory schemes, Scott writes that "a major reason why trait-based designations of ethnic or tribal identity fail utterly to make sense of actual affiliations is precisely that hill groups themselves, as manpower systems, absorbed whomever they could. This absorptive capacity led to great cultural diversity within hill societies."[75] These multiform, ethnically diverse "manpower absorbing" societies were precisely the kind of formations Japanese officials encountered on the "savage border" circa 1900. In his study of the Nanzhuang incident of July 1902, Antonio C. Tavares observes that Saisiyat "tribes" under "chieftains" in the late Qing period were conglomerates of Han, non-Han, and hybrid actors, with hierarchies of power and wealth that ran counter to *hua-yi* norms.[76] Mori's 1902 description of Paazeh's family portrait (fig. 3.12[77]) illustrates how, like the Nanzhuang operators, Wulai headmen adopted and absorbed outsiders to create hybrid formations to the chagrin of ethnic cartographers like Inō:

Figure 3.12. Paazeh, *furthest left.* Her father, Watan Yūra, is the caped man, *center,* flanked by his Atayal-Chinese interpreters. This photograph was displayed at the 1903 Osaka Industrial and the 1904 Louisiana Purchase Expositions, in several publications, and on postcards. Mori Ushinosuke, *Taiwan banzoku zufu,* vol. 1 (Taipei: Rinji Taiwan kyūkan chōsakai, 1915), plate 23.

> Wulai settlement's paramount chief Watan Yūra's eldest daughter Paazeh and his adopted son (*yōshi*) are both about twenty years of age. This couple is the "poken," meaning that if the line of succession is maintained, they will become chiefs. . . .[78]
>
> To the right of Watan Yūra is standing a Plains Aborigine [Peipozoku] (cooked barbarian [*jukuban*]) male without tattoos. About twenty years ago, it is said that he entered this settlement/village and became a savage brave [*bantei*] . . . To the left are four wives of savages (*banjin*). They are wearing Chinese style blouses and gaiters.[79]

Unlike the Nanzhuang rebel Ri Aguai, who rebuffed Japanese attempts to reduce him to a local official or licensed merchant, leaders in Kusshaku, for a fee and other considerations, mobilized followers to assist Japanese capitalists and officials. From as early as 1896, a number of young men in Kusshaku threw their lot in with the government against adversaries the Japanese referred to as bandits (*dohi*) of Han extraction.[80] Inō Kanori's travel notes from 1898 and his 1900 ethnological report list Jiku Shōmin as his local informant for Kusshaku. Jiku came to Taiwan with the Imperial Guard in 1895. In 1896, under orders from first Governor-General Kabayama Sukenori, Jiku made his way to Kusshaku to "pacify the locals."[81] Subsequently, he married into a leading Kusshaku family to establish a beachhead for Japanese logging concerns in conjunction with camphor entrepreneur Dogura Ryūjirō. As an adopted outsider who in many respects resembled Ri Aguai, Jiku took the title Watan Karaho to reckon himself a true local chief (*toumu*).[82]

At century's turn, as image makers were depicting Taiwan's indigenous peoples alternately as savages in studio photographs and as Atayals in embellished drawings and paintings, northern Taiwan was wracked by a wave of attacks on camphor workers. This generalized resistance all but halted production by 1902, except for in a few cooperative areas near Kusshaku and in Yilan.[83] In November of that year, a contract between the Taiwan Camphor Harvesting and Development Group and the "Kusshaku tribes" was renewed. The agreement gave the acting Kusshaku headman a fifty-*sen*-per-day stipend for liaising with Japanese officials to arrange for Kusshaku guards to protect camphor workers from attacks.[84] A Japanese journalist spent the first ten days of 1903 tramping around the Kusshaku settlements. In his serialized account, he credited Mori Ushinosuke with introducing him to a coterie of figures who managed Japanese-Kusshaku relations.[85]

The networks that emerged through intermarriage, business dealings, armed conflict, and research among Japanese officials, ethnologists, merchants, and leading families from Kusshaku provided the setting for the production of Paazeh's portrait. In contrast to our earliest examples of ideal typical "head-hunting chiefs" photographed in Taipei studios, the photographs made in Kusshaku during the establishment of the guardline were shot at or near the residences of the subjects. The increased number of poses and more intricate stagecraft evident in the Kusshaku photographs suggest a heightened degree of familiarity between photographers and subjects. Rimogan (of Kusshaku) resident Marai Watan was the other Atayal exemplar to appear in the Osaka and St. Louis expositions, as portrait number 1. Marai was paired with Paazeh, who appeared as portrait number 2. Marai was in his early twenties in 1903 and was the Rimogan headman's heir apparent. The woman to his left in figure 3.13[86] was Marai's wife, Yūgai Watan.[87]

On January 28, 1903, Mori Ushinosuke himself brought Marai and Yūgai to Taipei to view a local theater production of *Ishiyama Gunki,* meet the staff of the *Taiwan Daily News,* and see the sights. According to the short write-up, the Rimogan couple "came down from the mountains to visit Kusshaku-town once or twice a year, but had never been to Taipei."[88] Since Marai's portrait from a different pose made it to the Osaka exposition, which opened on March 1, 1903, it is reasonable to assume that Mori photographed this couple just before or after their visit to the capital city in January. The portrait shown here (fig. 3.13) was shot in April 1903. It was included in a number of official publications as well as formed the basis for at least two picture postcard designs.[89] Postcards were also generated from different poses of the same couple, indicating the ideological and commercial appeal of their likenesses as rendered by Mori's camera.

Yūgai's image, in tandem with Paazeh's, underwent further transformations before becoming commodified as a race card. Her published anthropometric

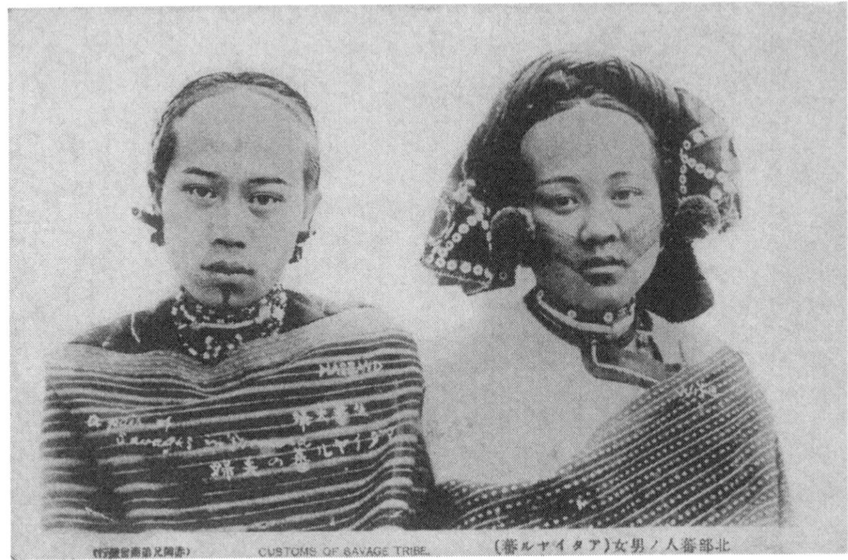

Figure 3.13. Marai and Yūgai of Rimogan, June 1903. This couple traveled to Taipei with photographer Mori Ushinosuke in January 1903 and appeared in several picture postcards and other publications in the Meiji and Taisho periods. East Asia Image Collection (Easton, PA: Lafayette College, 2012).

portrait shows her Chinese-style upper garments clearly, as indicated in figure 3.13. In figure 3.14[90] a more "authentic" Yūgai dons a cape of local design, concealing her Chinese clothing. This de-Sinicized version of Yūgai's portrait showed up in various picture postcards, in a 1932 book by ethnographer Koizumi Tetsu, in a collection of government statistics, and on the sleeve for a set of Taiwan indigenous peoples picture postcards.[91]

Due to the prominence accorded the Taiwan Pavilion, the Osaka National Industrial Exposition of 1903 has rightly been referred to as Japan's first imperial exposition. During the more than 150 days that it remained open, it drew over five million visitors.[92] The Taiwan Government-General, in anticipation of this massive undertaking, lobbied intensively for exposition space under the energetic leadership of Gotō Shinpei. For Gotō, the Ōsaka expo presented an opportunity to educate Japanese on the home islands about Taiwan's strategic importance, its potential economic benefits, and its cultural and culinary attractions. A prevailing home-islander image of Taiwan, which Gotō hoped to dispel, was that of a savage place where demonic tribes practiced cannibalism.[93] Against this backdrop, the photos of men with tattooed faces and large guns glaring at cameras in studio settings were hardly appropriate. Gotō's opportunistic aversion to savagery dovetailed with Inō Kanori's preference for "cultural" themes in evidence on the 1900 Paris Exposition painting (fig. 3.10). Thanks to Mori's new photographs from Kusshaku, Inō was able to accommodate both desiderata without recourse to another commissioned painting.

Figure 3.14. Postcard of Yūgai with "Chinese-style upper garments" concealed by her Atayal clothing (compare to fig. 3.13). East Asia Image Collection (Easton, PA: Lafayette College, 2012).

Figure 3.15. Both photographs from Mori Ushinosuke, *Taiwan banzoku zufu,* vol. 1 (Tokyo: Rinji Taiwan kyūkan chōsakai, 1918). The portrait on the *left* is cropped and enlarged from plate 23 (see fig. 3.12); the portrait on the *right* is from plate 35.

The "savage" (*left*) and "ethnicized" (*right*) portraits in figure 3.15[94] were taken near Wulai in February 1903. The "savage" portrait is an enlarged and cropped detail from figure 3.12. This group portrait shows Paazeh seated in the midst of an extended "absorptive manpower system" complete with Han interpreters wearing Atayal clothing and Atayal women wearing Chinese clothing. It appeared in a Taiwan Government-General publication of 1911, the general circulation magazine *Taiyō* in 1917, and in Mori's 1915 and 1918 ethnological picture albums, as well as in Shōwa-period picture postcards.[95] It was also picked up for syndication in the United States.[96] Also in February 1903, quite likely on the same day, Paazeh put on bamboo earrings, locally woven fabrics, necklaces, and a diamond-shaped breast cover festooned with white buttons for her anthropometric portrait (see figs. 2, 3, and 15). The differences in Paazeh's dress and ornamentation in the two portraits from February 1903 recall Inō's alterations of the 1898 montage (figs. 5, 10, and 11) discussed above.

Paazeh's Portrait as Shape-Shifting Joker

Let us imagine the blank white space in the center of the Japanese 1905 census map of Taiwan (fig. 3.4) as the screen upon which a variety of colonial ambitions, fantasies, fears, and visions were projected. If all went well, according to Mochiji's plan, the "white space" would eventually become the abode of tax-paying, imperial subjects, while recalcitrant *seibanjin* were either killed, assimilated, or scattered among the rest of the population. Takekoshi's gloss on Mochiji's policy, which presented "them" as an existential threat to "us," coupled with Mochiji's declaration that *"seiban"* had the status of "animals" under the law of nations, provides us with a frank statement of species differentiation. The captions in some picture postcards of Paazeh reproduce Mochiji's language of savagery by framing Paazeh's portrait with terms like "raw barbarian" and "bellicose barbarian." Newspaper and magazine drawings of fierce Atayal warriors in the 1895–1905 period used facial tattoos as shorthand for *"seibanjin,"* so Paazeh's portrait, so captioned, would have been associated with this reservoir of epithets.

The caption in figure 3.2, "Shinkō-chō, Wulai Atayal-zoku," resembles the placards Inō used to exhibit Marai and Paazeh as exemplary "culture-bearers" in Osaka and St. Louis. This softer portrait, with pastel tints and a clinical caption, replicates the "cultural" discourse on difference as understood by its photographer and his cohort, who considered bamboo earrings with geometric patterns, facial tattoos, hair binding, and sleeveless vests to be the distinctive features of the Atayal. Inō's, Torii's, and Mori's writings present many examples, though scattered and oblique, that suggest they lobbied for a gradualist policy that would accommodate difference within a framework of racially graded imperial hierarchy.

Moving from "species" and "culture" on Mitchell's compass of race to the "sex-gender" quadrant, we note that Paazeh's portrait also eroticized Atayal women as "maidens," "beauties," or "colonial nudes."[97] At least two picture postcards explicitly sexualize Paazeh. She is a "barbaric beauty" in one Meiji-period card, while another postcard with Paazeh's profile and Yūgai's frontal portrait is more florid, describing them in captions as: "A Southern Savage . . . and a Kusshaku woman. [They] have just come of age; they embody the renown allure and voluptuousness [of the Atayal]."[98]

From the early years of Japanese rule in Taiwan, liaisons between Japanese policemen, district officials, or interpreters and Atayal women were the subject of news stories in the Japanese press, often with a Pocahontas flavor.[99] As Faye Yuan Kleeman and Robert Tierney have noted, the figure of the sexually available Atayal woman was commonplace in Japanese literature in the colonial period. For Chief of Aborigine Affairs Ōtsu Rinpei, the assumption of sexual availability underwrote his policy of encouraging Japanese policemen to "marry" Atayal women solely for the purposes of political expedience.[100]

While picture postcards portrayed Korean, Manchu, northern Chinese, and Han Taiwanese males as belonging to a race, or races, of "coolies" with superhuman endurance and strength, such motifs do not predominate in depictions of Taiwan indigenous males. Women are frequently posed as beasts of burden, in accordance with a common imperialist trope on how "savages treat their women." However, a preponderance of Japanese picture postcards of indigenous males directly captioned them as headmen or chiefs or posed them in regal postures that suggest anything but abjection or objectification. This preference may indicate that actual chiefs, as the link between the colonial government and local society, were available or wanted to be photographed. Mori Ushinosuke himself noted that, unlike other "primitives," Taiwan indigenous peoples were unafraid of cameras.[101] Borrowing from Patricia Albers' analysis of Native American picture postcards, this motif might be referred to as the "Noble Vanquished Warrior."[102] Paazeh's portrait falls squarely within this genre.

During Mori's photo shoots in Wulai, Japanese observers remarked upon the alternating nature of the paramount chieftain position. Moreover, the fifty-*sen* stipend that was proposed for the Kusshaku headman included the proviso that it would shift in accordance with alternating leadership. The documentation associated with these portraits suggests that Marai and Yūgai were from the Rimogan family that rivaled Paazeh's Wulai clan for Kusshaku paramountcy in 1903. If there was no outright competition among Kusshaku's hereditary leaders to secure access to Japanese money, job opportunities, and protection against other Atayal groups, certainly there were assertions of rank involved to obtain Japanese backing. In late 1902 and early 1903, alliance with, or strategic subordination to, Japan's local agents offered material benefits and a leg up in intra-Atayal competition.

In a sort of comic but illustrative coda to Japanese colonial representational practices vis-à-vis Taiwanese, the American newspaper feature "Ripley's Believe It or Not" commented upon the political significance of the Atayal diamond-shaped, button-studded chest ornament in a 1945 feature titled "Button Man." This same item was the distinguishing feature of Paazeh's and Marai's famous portraits. Ostensibly, the point of the illustration was to teach American invading forces how to identify Aborigine chieftains when they occupied Taiwan. Although this cartoon makes the dubious claim that its wearer will die if a single button is removed, its assertion that the breast covering signifies political power is consonant with dozens of Japanese photographs. This design was worn by Atayal males who were either labeled as headmen or who at least struck the upright, almost defiant pose of headmen.

Anthropologist Hu Chia-yu has pointed out that this design and its buttons, in contrast to larger shell or ceramic disks, did not signify paramount rank. Nonetheless, these ornaments were considered to be precious items and consequently items of formal male Atayal dress. Was it Paazeh's or Watan Yūra's decision to display these precious items, usually found only on males, for this photograph (figs. 3 and 15)? Or did Mori fasten on to this item of material culture and request its presence in the photo? It is plausible, though conjectural, that there existed a temporary community of interests between Inō the government expert, Mori the up-and-coming protégé, and Paazeh the contender for patronage in the construction of this portrait.

In May 1903, two months after the opening of the Osaka exposition, Japanese authorities imprisoned nine Kusshaku men as hostages to secure the cooperation of Kusshaku leaders in building a cordon sanitaire to separate camphor fields and taxpaying settlements from marauding Atayal who resisted the new order. This stratagem was successful. During the years 1904 and 1905, the local knowledge, military prowess, and political agility of Kusshaku residents turned the tide for Japanese forces. Thereafter, from their Kusshaku base, the Taiwan Government- General built several hundred miles of guardline across northern Taiwan, tightening its embargo and forcing hundreds of Atayal settlements to surrender their weapons until the last Taroko tribes submitted in 1914.[103]

In December 1908, travel writer and explorer Mary T. S. Schaffer and three Canadian companions visited Wulai to get a glimpse of the world-renowned "head-hunters of Formosa." As many a visitor after her, Schaffer wrote excitedly about the prospects of meeting a savage head-taker and even purchased a postcard of a freshly taken head held by its exultant killers. But when she actually met Atayal people on the trail, she found them to be friendly and too happy to pose for photographs in exchange for silver coins. While travelers would not be found in other parts of Atayal country until well into the 1910s, Wulai had already become a place the Government-General could send foreign tourists under light escort. Included in Schaffer's collection of magic lantern slides was a color-tinted profile of Paazeh.[104]

In early 1908 the Japanese government built its first school for Atayal children in Kusshaku. Paazeh and Marai passed away around 1910, just before the Atayal school was moved to Wulai in 1911. The bulk of instruction was dedicated to field cultivation, tree felling, and other "regular employments" designed to turn the Kusshaku tribes into taxpaying subjects. Japanese-language training was the second most important pursuit.[105] By the end of Meiji, then, the people of Kusshaku and its environs were well on the road to becoming peoples who would little resemble the photographs that Mori Ushinosuke created in 1903 (see fig. 3.16[106]). Nonetheless, their portraits lived on in official publications, picture postcards, textbooks, newspapers, exposition exhibits, and museum displays as shape-shifting jokers that satisfied a variety of market niches, political positions, and local aspirations.

Conclusions

In 1903 Paazeh's portrait and the ethnological discourse that initially gave it meaning asserted an Atayal ethnic presence in the opaque interior of Taiwan as a counterweight to Qing and Japanese terminology that marked indigenous peoples as expendable *fanren/banjin* (savages). In the bargain the Japanese anthropologists who devised a substitute nomenclature based on the canons of modern race science achieved a modicum of fame and recompense as pioneers in an unexplored ethnographic treasure trove. In the face of metropolitan pressure to increase the efficiency of the camphor industry, however, the discourse on indigenous ethnic integrity proved a weak defense against guardline policies justified by the necropolitical calculus of "us or them." As military operations and trade embargoes against Atayal peoples intensified in the years leading up to World War I, publishers recaptioned Mori Ushinosuke's antiseptic portrait of the "Shinkō, Urai-sha Woman, Taiyal Tribe" with a variety of denigrating epithets to connote savage menace and exotic forbidden fruit.

Figure 3.16. The Wulai School for Indigenous Children, opened in 1911. The standing adults wear the trademark embroidered upper garments with decorative buttons, as immortalized by Mori Ushinosuke's Kusshaku portraits. The male children sport Japanese-style haircuts and imported clothing while the girls wear Atayal leggings with "Chinese-style upper garments." East Asia Image Collection (Easton, PA: Lafayette College, 2012).

At the same time, the continued reproduction of race cards like Paazeh's into the Shōwa period provided a visually consistent image of Taiwan indigenous peoples that belied the rapid changes fomented by Japanese policies. While it would be incorrect to assert that Mori's anthropometric portraits were unmediated visual documents of social life, other records of the period suggest that numerous women in northern Taiwan adorned themselves in rough conformity to Paazeh's famous portrait. In the 1910s and the 1920s, however, Japanese race cards became less and less representative of living conditions along the Xindian River and the wider Atayal culture area. During the Taishō period, the Taiwan Government-General proscribed face tattooing and head-taking while ringing the Atayal territories with trading posts for the import of Japanese-manufactured kimonos, shirts, and trousers. During the *kōminka* period of the 1930s and the 1940s, an energetic police force, with the aid of indigenous youth groups, mobilized Atayal and other indigenous peoples to speak Japanese, worship at Shintō shrines, and wear Japanese clothing in ever-greater numbers.[107] Consequently, imported clothing was the norm, and by the late 1930s, facial tattoos were no longer ubiquitous among young Atayal women in Taiwan.[108]

Despite these changes in material conditions on the ground, the Japanese government continued to propagate the image of Atayal peoples as "traditional" and culturally intact to highlight the non-Chinese status of Taiwan, to bolster Japan's credentials as a steward of indigenous peoples, and to nurture a budding ethnic tourism industry.[109] With the defeat of the Japanese military in World War II, however, the reproduction of race cards for general consumption seems to have come to a halt. Nationalist Party (KMT) legitimacy was based on the notion that Taiwan is part of China. The KMT stigmatized indigenous peoples as "mountain compatriots" and "savages" and pressed assimilation in the name of official, state-directed Han chauvinism.[110] They also demonized the Japanese as the invaders of mainland China and suppressed research into colonial history and its large documentary record.[111] It would be surprising, therefore, if a cache of Japanese-era race cards were to be located among the publications, exhibits, or ephemera from martial-law period Taiwan (1949–1987), though it is quite possible that they circulated beneath the state's radar.

After the lifting of martial law in 1987, the administrations of Li Denghui and Chen Shui-bian abandoned the KMT rhetoric of Taiwan as a Chinese space and indigenous peoples as "not-yet-Chinese." As part of a "homeland-ization" movement (*bentuhua*), leading Taiwanese politicians and their local followers mobilized state resources and the bully pulpit to support an indigenous cultural renaissance. Han intellectuals called for Nationalists to accentuate the indigenous element of Taiwan's composite identity to signal the island's distinctiveness from the mainland and to reconfigure indigenous claims to prior occupation of the island into a source of Taiwanese "subjectivity."[112] The founding of the Alliance of Taiwan Aborigines in 1984 is a commonly cited starting point for indigenous activism, which was initially concerned with issues surrounding poverty, discrimination against individual indigenous persons, and other social problems. In the late 1980s, the focus shifted toward collective rights and identity politics.[113]

A confluence of interests and coordinated political action between Han Nationalists and indigenous activists produced a number of reforms. The Wu-feng myth that characterized indigenous peoples as both savage headhunters and grateful Qing lackeys was expunged from textbooks in 1988. The official name "mountain compatriot" was changed to *yuanzhumin* (indigenous people) in 1994 and then *yuanzhuminzu* (indigenous ethnos/race). Registration laws were changed to allow indigenous peoples to use their non-Han names and reckon descent bilaterally. In 1996, the Council of Aboriginal Affairs was established at the cabinet level, greatly raising the status of indigenous issues in official and popular domains.[114]

In the wake of these changes, Paazeh's likeness has reappeared. Along with several other Mori Ushinosuke photographs, her portrait has shown up in books on Taiwan indigenous history, material culture, and society since the late 1980s. In our own century, her frontal portrait (fig. 3.3) graces the covers of three successive printings of Yang Nanjun's Chinese translation of Mori's travelogues.[115] Her profile (fig. 3.2) also illustrates the covers of two successive printings of a collection of indigenous-themed picture postcards aimed at the

照片上人物的面部刺文、竹飾穿耳等，均是

Figure 3.17. Paazeh's portrait at the Wulai Atayal Museum with author, November 29, 2014. Photograph by Roi Ariel.

youth market.[116] Paazeh models earrings on a wall of the Shung Ye Museum of Formosan Aborigines in Taipei while her wall-sized likeness fills the main stairwell in the museum of Atayal culture in Wulai, not far from the site of its creation (see fig. 3.17).

In all of the above instances, Paazeh remains anonymous. She has no name, family, or political status and remains a vehicle for Atayal facial tattoos, clothing, and bamboo earrings. In the year 2015, the gap between everyday life in Taiwan and Atayal race cards is even wider than in the 1940s. Facial tattoos are very much a thing of the past; the few remaining women who have them are considered cultural treasures. And yet, conventionalized images of face-tattooed women have become de rigueur in indigenous-area public art. The examples in figure 3.18[117] from the Nanshan Township Elementary School and figure 3.19 from the Xiulin Township Middle School are typical.

The existential threat posed to Atayal peoples by Taiwan Government-General (1895–1945) and KMT (1949–1987) official racism has subsided. Today, the notion that indigenous peoples are distinct from Han Taiwanese and that Taiwan's multiracial composition should be celebrated rather than overcome are mainstream political positions[118]—for the first time in the island's history. In light of these sea changes, race cards would appear to have outlived their usefulness. So what should we make of their rediscovery and continued proliferation?

In one guise, race cards and the icons they inspire are assertions of long-suppressed or denied ethnic pride, both homegrown and government supported.

Figure 3.18. Fence surrounding Nanshan Township Elementary School, Yilan County, November 15, 2014. Photograph by author.

Since the late 1980s, nongovernmental organizations, the central government, and county offices have dispersed funding for indigenous-language school curricula; the revival of dormant public rituals; and the manufacture of indigenous textiles, sculptures, and other items of material culture. As a result, the post-1990 affirmations of face tattooing and head-taking and the rediscovery of Atayal textiles and traditional music and dance have erased much of the public and private stigma that the Japanese and the Han have attached to Atayal culture over the past century.[119]

The consultation of colonial-era ethnological writings, illustrations, and photographs has been a crucial component in many, if not all, of these revivalist projects.[120] The Japanese-period documentary record has been critical to the authentication of "native" traditions in Taiwan partly due to the deracinating effects of Japanese and KMT policies. Perhaps more significantly, under KMT rule, 80–90 percent of Taiwan's indigenous population converted to Christianity while roughly 50 percent of Taiwan's indigenous population migrated to urban environments antithetical to the maintenance of early twentieth-century markers of ethnic distinction.[121]

Recent ethnographic research suggests that top-down cultural politics are integral to the indigenous renaissance in Taiwan. Anthropologist Michael Rudolph has noted that, as Christians, many Taiwan indigenous peoples did not

Figure 3.19. Mural on the wall of the Xiulin Middle School, Hualien County, October 28, 2014. Photograph by author.

initially identify with the revitalized symbolism, languages, and ceremonies that were being promoted by "elite traditionalists." A period of time was required for adaptation and reappropriation. Scott Simon has written extensively about the emergence of an indigenous "elite" in the 1950s in response to KMT changes in property law and rural administration. These indigenous political operators often "play the race card" to fulfill their own political ambitions and are viewed with derision by their rank-and-file constituents. Mitsuda Yayoi corroborates the general pattern: educated elites formulate and promote particular versions of indigenous ethnic identity and subsequently mobilize followers to achieve state recognition for a given interpretation of "tradition."[122]

Can the indigenous renaissance in Taiwan, therefore, be likened to top-down cultural revitalization projects in other postcolonial situations? Critical scholarship of the Indian case has suggested that cultural elites have invoked unifying symbols of Indian, Hindu, or Maharashtra continuity, cohesion, and distinctiveness to quash internal dissent in the name of national survival.[123] In Taiwan, on a much smaller scale, energized groups of indigenous activists have won official recognition for their ethnic groups to become eligible for the office holding, public funding, and political patronage that accrue with state recognition. Since 2001, the number of recognized indigenous groups in Taiwan has climbed from nine to sixteen.[124] While the motives of such leaders and their followers are mixed and complicated, these battles have occurred in an institutional framework that incentivizes the homogenization of particular ethnic identities and the accentuation of differences among them.[125] And it was precisely these two processes that Mori Ushinosuke sought to consolidate with his Kusshaku photographs of 1903.

Some would consider it irresponsible to put the Taiwan indigenous renaissance on a par with postcolonial Indian nationalism. The move to historicize putatively timeless entities such as the Atayal can undermine "indigenous claims to identity," according to this line of thought.[126] James Clifford's classic study of the courtroom travails of the Mashpee Indians, whose legal claims to rights and resources hinged on their ability to document the autochthony and continuity of their community by recourse to visible markers of culture, is a case in point.[127] To suggest that any indigenous identity has been "staged," as I have done in this chapter, can be considered an attack upon the claims to collective redress that are part and parcel of First Nations rights recovery movements.

But not all effective proponents of preservationism are indigenous peoples laboring against staggering odds to regain stolen rights or establish a modicum of dignity. In post–martial law Taiwan, Han intellectuals who have invoked indigenous "otherness" as a tool for revitalizing Taiwanese national culture or for pulling Taiwan out of China's cultural orbit are primarily interested in indigenous peoples as symbols. The symbolism of authentic, timeless, and non-Han indigenous peoples secures Taiwan's Austronesian heritage in this discourse.[128] The problem here is that the preservationist ethos encoded in Paazeh's race card can backfire by creating unreasonable expectations that have grave real-world consequences. The notion that indigenous peoples are inauthentic, or not truly indigenous, if they do not wear traditional clothing or bear other markers of ethnic difference easily recognized by outsiders is in fact a common one. This fixation on authenticity shades into the political view that visibly "assimilated" indigenous peoples should ipso facto lose rights or privileges (such as access to waterways, hunting grounds, or preferential treatment on university-entrance or civil-service exams).[129] The specter of the inauthentic (and undeserving) indigenous person is never far from the surface.

As was the case in the period of Japanese colonial rule, there are scholars today who find certain elements of indigenous cultures intrinsically valuable and of high aesthetic worth. Han anthropologists have worked in recent years to reinstate reconstructed forms of indigenous dance and song into the fabric of everyday life by promoting public performance-as-education. One critic of this movement has asked:

> Shall those young Aborigines who have been in contact with Han society for a long time identify with an image of Aborigines that has stagnated for several decades or centuries? Or shall they identify with a culture that has—as a result of inevitable historical development—interacted with other ethnic groups? And what kind of "Aborigines" shall non-Aborigines identify with? Is it possible that [Han preservationists]—in order to redress the Han's former hegemony or for reasons of political correctness—unconsciously bring all possibility for the Aborigines' pluralist cultural development to an end?[130]

In this view, the interests of curators, ethnologists, neo-primitivists, and progressive Han activists are pitted against the majority of indigenous peoples who have lived among the Han for many decades and who do not wish to turn back the clock.

Wulai-area residents Paazeh Naheh (1880?–1910?); her father, Watan Yūra; and their neighbors upstream in Rimogan—Yūgai and Marai—were historical figures who became and remain racial mascots. Yet they were not victims of imperial photographers who wielded cameras as figurative guns. In the 1870s Kusshaku was known to travelers as a contact zone for the exchange of goods and services between Han, indigenous, and foreign agents.[131] The political, economic, and linguistic skills they acquired in this late nineteenth-century milieu positioned Kusshaku residents to take advantage of new opportunities that came with the Japanese occupation while their position on the old Qing border area exposed them to new risks. In the course of mediating the claims of upriver Atayal natives with the demands of downriver Japanese newcomers, they sat for multiple sessions with photographer Mori Ushinosuke to create Meiji Japan's most well-known photographs of Taiwan indigenous peoples.

Perhaps because their strategy of alliance with agents of the new state backfired or because political leadership in Atayal societies is earned rather than inherited, their names have been lost to time. Moreover, Mori himself, and those who followed him, found nothing particularly noteworthy about these individuals. Nonetheless, generations of publishers, anthropologists, curators, historians, and consumers have found their portraits worthy of reproduction and repurposing. The continued dissemination of Paazeh's, Watan's, Yūgai's, and Marai's portraits as nameless avatars of the Atayal—as race cards—is a complex operation conducted by a host of agents with varied agendas. The point of this chapter is to suggest that the various iterations of these storied photographs make arguments about Taiwan's future and past—some benign, some hopeful, and others mendacious. With the digitization of the Taiwan Government-General archive and many other sources of colonial history, it is now possible, though still difficult, to identify and learn more about the people on the other side of Mori Ushinosuke's camera. When the multiple other sources of indigenous Taiwanese identity are taken into account, it would seem that bringing these stories to light will increase, rather than diminish, the capacity of these old photographs to further the interests of Paazeh's descendents in and around Wulai.

Notes

The author would like to thank Hu Chia-yu for sharing her extensive knowledge of Atayal material culture and providing me with key documents for this research. Thanks to Joseph Allen for generously sharing his detailed notes on the visual holdings of the Taiwan Government-General library, now housed at the National Taiwan Library. The research for this paper was made possible by an advanced research grant from the National Endowment for the Humanities, research funds from the Lafayette College Provost's Office, and a Taiwan Ministry of Foreign Affairs research fellowship. Thanks to Caroline Hui-yu Ts'ai and Huang Chih-Huei at the Institute of Taiwan History at Academia Sinica and Kishi Toshihiko at the Kyoto University Center for Integrated Area Studies for academic support and office space.

Epigraph. W. J. T. Mitchell, *Seeing through Race* (Cambridge, MA: Harvard University Press, 2012), 19.

1. For a discussion and definition of anthropometric photographs, see Cory Willmott, "The Lens of Science: Anthropometric Photography and the Chippewa, 1890–1920," *Visual Anthropology* 18 (2005): 310.

2. *[ip0743] Customs of Savage Tribe,* 2012, East Asia Image Collection, Lafayette College, Easton, PA, accessed May 31, 2013, http://digital.lafayette.edu/collections/eastasia/.

3. James P. Ryan, *Picturing Empire: Photography and the Visualization of the British Empire,* (Chicago: University of Chicago Press, 1997), 140–182; Rosalind Morris, "Introduction," in *Photographies East: The Camera and Its Histories in East and Southeast Asia,* ed. Rosalind Morris (Durham, NC: Duke University Press, 2009).

4. Ira Berlin, *Many Thousands Gone: The First Two Centuries of Slavery in North America* (Cambridge, MA: Harvard University Press, 1998), 1 (emphasis added).

5. Mitchell, *Seeing through Race,* 34–35.

6. Ibid., 17.

7. Ke Zhiming, *Fantou jia: Qing dai Taiwan zuqun zhengzhi yu shufan diquan* (Taipei, Taiwan: Zhongyang yanjiuyuan shehuixue yanjiusuo, 2001); Emma Jinhua Teng, *Taiwan's Imagined Geography: Chinese Colonial Travel Writing and Pictures, 1683–1895* (Cambridge, MA: Harvard University Press, 2004).

8. Mitchell, *Seeing through Race,* 17 (emphasis added).

9. Michel Foucault, "Two Lectures," in *Culture/Power/History: A Reader in Contemporary Social Theory,* ed. Nicholas B. Dirks, Geoff Eley, and Sherry B. Ortner (Princeton, NJ: Princeton University Press, 1994), 213.

10. *[ip1448] Shinkō, Urai-sha Woman, Taiyal Tribe,* 2012, East Asia Image Collection, Lafayette College, Easton, PA, accessed September 10, 2013, http://digital.lafayette.edu/collections/eastasia/.

11. Ibid., *[lw0384] The Barbaric Woman of Formosa,* accessed March 30, 2013.

12. The name is spelled "パァゼッヘ、ナッヘー" in "Taiwan banjin fūzoku shashin zusetu," *Tokyo jinruigakkai zasshi* 213 (December 20, 1903): 109; パーセツ in Mori Ushinosuke, "Zappō," *Tokyo jinruigakkai zasshi* 199 (October 20, 1902): 39; and ハゼヘワタン in Mori Ushinosuke, "Shōgaku chirikan ni banjin no sōga ni tsuite," *Taiwan kyōiku zasshi* 11, no. 127 (November 1, 1912): 1080.

13. Miyaoka Maoko, "Mori Ushinosuke no chosaku mokuroku oyobi jakkan no kaisetsu," *Taiwan Genjūmin kenkyū* 2 (1997): 189–199; Mori Ushinosuke, "Taiwan banzoku ni tsuite," in *Taiwan banzoku shi* (1917; repr. Taipei, Taiwan: Nanten shokyoku, 1996), 1–6; Yang Nanjun, *Maboroshi no jinruigakusha: Mori Ushinosuke,* trans. and ed. Kasahara Masaharu, Miyaoka Maoko, and Miyazaki Seiko (Tokyo: Fūkyōsha, 2005).

14. Yanagimoto Michihiko, *Meiji no Bōken kagakushatachi: Shintenchi-Taiwan ni kaketa yume* (Tokyo: Shinchōsha, 2005), 184.

15. "Taiwan banjin fūzoku," 108.

16. Itō Mamiko, *Meiji Nihon to bankoku hakurankai* (Tokyo: Yoshikawa kōbunkan, 2008), 94.

17. Isoda Masatomo, *Handbook and Catalog of Exhibits at Agriculture Building World's Fair, St. Louis 1904:* compiled and published under the direction of the Bureau of Productive Industries, Government of Formosa, Japan, (St. Louis: Woodward and Tiernan, 1904), 35–36; "Taiwan banjin fūzoku," 108–117; "Hunting Head Hunters with Live Electric Wires," *Detroit Free Press,* April 4, 1909.

18. An estimated twenty million people attended this fair, but it is uncertain how many people actually looked at Mori's photographs. Missouri Historical Society, *1904: The World's Fair, Looking Back at Looking Forward,* accessed July 28, 2013, http://www.mohistory.org/Fair/WF/HTML/Overview/.

19. Itō, *Meiji Nihon,* 119.

20. Kōgo Eriko, "Teishinshō hakkō Nichiro seneki kinen ehagaki: Sono jissō to igi," *Bijutsushi kenkyū* 41 (2003): 103–142.

21. Paul D. Barclay, "Peddling Postcards and Selling Empire: Image-Making in Taiwan under Japanese Colonial Rule," *Japanese Studies* 30, no. 1 (May 2010): 81–110.

22. Takekoshi Yosaburō, *Taiwan tōchi shi* (Tokyo: Hakubunkan, 1905).

23. Takekoshi Yosaburō, *Japanese Rule in Formosa,* trans. George Braithwaite (London: Longmans, Green, 1907), 219.

24. Julean Arnold, "The Peoples of Formosa," *Smithsonian Miscellaneous Collections* 52 (1910): plate 22.

25. Michale Lang, *An Adventurous Woman Abroad: The Selected Lantern Slides of Mary T. S. Schaffer* (Vancouver: Rocky Mountain Books, 2011), 258–263.

26. This headline refers to the colonial government's stratagem of enclosing unsubdued areas with live electric wires to keep enemy settlements from breaching the "guardline" that separated governed from nongoverned spaces in upland Taiwan.

27. Rene Bache, "War with Headhunters on Japan's Hands," *Washington Post,* June 26, 1910, 8; "To Wipe Out or Civilize? Savages of Formosa," (*Sallisaw, Oklahoma*) *Star Gazette,* August 5, 1910, 6; "To Wipe Out or Civilize? Savages of Formosa," *Nashua* (*IA*) *Reporter,* August 11, 1910, 2. Each accessed July 6, 2013, www.newspapers.com.

28. "Surprising the Barbarians of Formosa," *Popular Electricity in Plain English* 5, no. 3 (July 1912): 219, *Smithsonian Libraries,* accessed January 8, 2015, http://library.si.edu/digital-library/book/popularelectric519121chic.

29. Monbushō, ed., *Jinjō shōgaku chiri ken ni: Jidō yō* (Standard elementary school geography volume 2: For youth) (Tokyo: Monbushō, 1910), 21; Mori, "Shōgaku chirikan," 1080.

30. Narita Takeshi, *Taiwan seiban shuzoku shashinchō* (1912; repr. Taipei, Taiwan: Southern Materials Center, 1995), 31.

31. Mori Ushinosuke, *Taiwan banzoku zufu,* vol. 1 (Taipei: Rinji Taiwan kyūkan chōsakai, 1915; Tokyo: Rinji Taiwan kyūkan chōsakai, 1918), plate 35.

32. Elizabeth Edwards, "Introduction," in *Anthropology and Photography: 1860–1920,* ed. Elizabeth Edwards (New Haven, CT: Yale University Press, 1992), 6.

33. Matsuda Kyōko, *Teikoku no shisen: Hakurankai to ibunka hyōshō* (Tokyo: Yoshikawa kōbunkan, 2003), 58–73.

34. Hu Chia-yu, "Bolan huikuai yu Taiwan Yuanzhumin: Zhimin shiqi de dizhanshi zhengzhi yu 'tazhe' yixiang," *Kaogu renleixue kan,* 2005, 26–27. Thank you to Sun Xiaofei for translating this article.

35. Ka F. Wong, "Entanglements of Ethnographic Images: Torii Ryūzō's Photographic Record of Taiwan Aborigines (1896–1900)," *Japanese Studies* 24, no. 3 (December 2004): 289.

36. Christopher Pinney, "The Parallel Histories of Anthropology and Photography," in Edwards, *Anthropology and Photography,* 74, 81.

37. Christopher Pinney, "Introduction: How the Other Half . . . ," in *Photography's Other Histories,* ed. Christopher Pinney and Nicolas Peterson (Durham, NC: Duke University Press, 2003), 1–4.

38. Julia Adeney Thomas, "The Evidence of Sight," *History and Theory* 48 (December 2009): 151–168.

39. Julia Adeney Thomas, "Power Made Visible: Photography and Postwar Japan's Elusive Reality," *Journal of Asian Studies* 67, no. 2 (May 2008): 369.

40. "In the eyes of the conqueror, *savage life* is just another form of *animal life,* a horrifying experience . . . What makes the savages different from other human beings is less the color of their skin than the fear that they behave like a part of nature, that they treat nature as their undisputed master . . . The savages are, as it were, 'natural' human beings who lack the specifically human character, the specifically human reality, 'so that when European men massacred them they somehow were not aware that they had committed murder." Achille Mbembe, "Necropolitics," trans. Libby Meintjes, *Public Culture* 15, no. 1 (2003): 24.

41. Inō Kanori, ed., *Riban shikō dai ikkan* (Records of Aborigine administration vol. 1) (Taipei: Taiwan sōtokufu keisatsu honsho, 1918), 182.

42. Takekoshi, *Japanese Rule in Formosa,* 230 (emphasis added).

43. See figure 3.3 and *[lw0384] The Barbaric Woman of Formosa,* 2012, East Asia Image Collection, Lafayette College, Easton, PA, 2012, accessed March 30, 2013, http://digital.lafayette.edu/collections/eastasia/; *[lw0391] Woman of Savage,* 2012, East Asia Image Collection, Lafayette College, Easton, PA, accessed March 30, 2013, http://digital.lafayette.edu/collections/eastasia/.

44. Edwards, "Introduction," 11.

45. *The Special Population Census of Formosa 1905: Report of the Committee of the Formosan Special Census Investigation* (Tokyo: Imperial Printing Bureau, 1909).

46. Here, "illegibility" follows James C. Scott's formulation in *Seeing like a State.* "Legibility" refers to the quality of being *seen* by centrally located state bureaucrats in such a way that "legible" populations can be acted upon at a distance from an apex of routinized power. "Illegible" peoples and places existed beyond the net of census, police, and taxing organs of the state. Scott, *Seeing like a State: How Certain Schemes to Improve the Human Condition Have Failed* (New Haven, CT: Yale University Press, 1998), 2–3.

47. Hu Chia-yu, "Taiwanese Aboriginal Art and Artifacts: Entangled Images of Colonization and Modernization," in *Refracted Modernity Visual Culture and Identity in Colonial Taiwan,*

ed. Kikuchi Yūko (Honolulu: University of Hawai'i Press, 2007), 198; *Taida renlei xuexi yi neng cangpin yanjiu* (Studies on Ino's collection at department of anthropology of National Taiwan University), ed. Hu Jiayu and Yilan Cui (Taipei: Guoli Taiwan daxue chuban zhongxin, 1998), 263.

48. *Banjō kenyūkaishi* 1 (August 16, 1898): front matter. Thanks to Professor Hu Chia-yu for sending me an intact copy of this issue.

49. Ishikawa Gen'ichirō, ed., *Taiwan meisho shashinchō* (Taipei: Taiwan shōhōsha, 1899).

50. Torii Ryūzō used the terms "Yūgeiban" 有黥蕃 and "Yūgeimenban" 有黥面蕃 to designate Atayal peoples, while Inō Kanori used the term "アタヤル."

51. For an explanation of this "world-ordering" logic, see Tessa Morris-Suzuki, *Re-inventing Japan: Time, Space, Nation* (Armonk, NY: M. E. Sharpe, 1998), 15–24.

52. Matsuda Kyōko, "Inō Kanori's 'History' of Taiwan: Colonial Ethnology, the Civilizing Mission and Struggles for Survival in East Asia," trans. Paul D. Barclay, *History and Anthropology* 14, no. 2 (2003): 191.

53. This map is based on Inō Kanori and Awano Dennosuke, *Taiwan Banjin jijō* (Taipei: Taiwan sōtokufu minseibu bunshoka, 1900), n.p.

54. *Typical Head Hunter, Formosa,* George Grantham Bain Collection, Library of Congress Prints and Photographs Division, Prints and Photographs Online Catalog, Washington, DC, accessed April 3, 2013, http://www.loc.gov/pictures/item/ggb2004002272/.

55. *Tribal Chiefs, Formosa,* George Grantham Bain Collection, Library of Congress Prints and Photographs Division, Prints and Photographs Online Catalog, Washington, DC, accessed April 3, 2013, http://www.loc.gov/pictures/item/ggb2004002269/. This image was used for a postcard published by the Moriwaki Hishindō 森脇日進堂 ca. 1910. It was captioned "Savage Headmen from Yilan" with no background at all; the seated figures are put up against a white background, obscuring the studio trappings so apparent in the negative pictured here. See Chen Zhongren, ed., *Shiji rongyan: Bainian qian de Taiwan yuanzhumin tuxiang,* vol. 1 (Taipei, Taiwan: Guojia tushuguan, 2003), 17.

56. The two grisly Bain News Service photos were used to illustrate the short piece, suggesting that they had been made available to American publishers before that time. "Electricity Used to Capture Head Hunters," *Popular Mechanics,* May 1909, 444, accessed January 9, 2015, https://books.google.co.jp/books?id=mt8DAAAAMBAJ&lpg=PA444&ots=k1snqUUX5J.

57. *Head Hunting Natives and Japanese Police in Group around a Head, Head Hunters Seated with Their Head, Formosa,* and *Skull Shelf of Head Hunter, Formosa,* George Grantham Bain Collection, Library of Congress Prints and Photographs Division, Prints and Photographs Online Catalog, Washington, DC.

58. Nihon Jun'eki Taiwan Genjūmin Kenkyūkai, ed., *Inō Kanori shozō Taiwan Genjūmin shashinshū* (Photographs of Taiwan Aborigines from the Inō Kanori collections) (Taipei: Jun'eki Taiwan Genjūmin hakubutsukan, 1999), 108–111.

59. A high-resolution scan of this cabinet card and its reverse side was posted on eBay by the seller eby071 on December 14, 2010.

60. *[lw0264] Head hunters in Formosa,* 2012, East Asia Image Collection, Lafayette College, Easton, PA, accessed March 30, 2013, http://digital.lafayette.edu/collections/eastasia/.

61. The photo in Jun'eki 1999 shows him seated much as the figures in the postcard in figure 3.12.

62. On October 15, 1905, fifteen different postcards commemorating aspects of the Russo-Japanese War were put on sale. For each design, 140,000 cards were issued, for a grand total of 2.1 million postcards. I have seen at least two instances of Russo-Japanese and Taiwan Government-General postcards interleaved in albums, leading me to suspect that the avari-

cious collectors of late Meiji would have required a similarly large print run of the cards pictured in figure 3.13. See Kōgo Eriko, "Teishinshō hakkō Nichiro."

63. Ulrich Keller, "Photography, History (Dis)belief," *Visual Resources: An International Journal of Documentation* 26, no. 2 (2010): 95–111.

64. Torii Ryūzō, "Taiwan chūō sanmyaku no ōdan," in *Torii Ryūzō zenshū* 11, ed. Asahi Shinbunsha (Tokyo: Asahi Shinbun, 1976), 433–434.

65. Paul D. Barclay, "Profits as Contagion, Production as Progress: Trading Posts, Tribute, and Feasting in the History of Japanese-Formosan Relations, 1895–1917," International Symposium: Studies on Indigenous Peoples of Taiwan: Retrospect and Prospect in Japan and Taiwan, Research Institute for Languages and Cultures of Asia and Africa, Tokyo University of Foreign Studies, Tokyo, March 26–27, 2005, L1–L36.

66. Inō Kanori, "Taiwan tsūshin dai rokkai" (Sixth communique from Taiwan), *Tokyo jinruigakkai zasshi* (Journal of the Tokyo Anthropological Society) 11, no. 121 (1896): 272–278.

67. Paul D. Barclay, "The Taiwanese 'Banfu' in Imperial Japan: Bi-cultural Interpreters, Marriage Alliances, and Sexual Slavery in the Tribal Zone," Association for Asian Studies Annual Meeting, Washington, DC, April 4–7, 2002.

68. Inō Kanori and Awano Dennosuke, *Taiwan Banjin jijō* (Taipei: Taiwan sōtokufu minseibu bunshoka, 1900), 15.The authors stipulate that some Atayal wore ornaments, while others did not. The popularized versions of Inō's sketch that appeared in James Davidson, *The Island of Formosa Past and Present* (Yokohama: Japan Times Newspaper, 1903), 565; and Takekoshi, *Japanese Rule in Formosa,* 221, are less subtle, like the placards at the exhibitions and the captions for postcards.

69. Hu Jiayu and Yilan Cui, *Taida renlei xuexi,* facing 263.

70. Hu Chia-yu, "Taiwanese Aboriginal Art," 198–199.

71. Ishizaka Tonan, *Photographs of Formosa: Collected in Commemoration of the Tokyo Industrial Exhibition in 1907,* Sōtokufu Archives, Taiwan National Library, Taipei, 13. This drawing was reproduced in an early travel guide, before tourists could actually visit indigenous settlements. See Taiwan sōtokufu tetsudō bu, ed., Untitled Railway Guide (Tokyo: Eriguchi shōkai, 1908), Sōtokufu Archives, Taiwan National Library, Taipei, 57.

72. Davidson, *Island of Formosa,* 563.

73. Ishikawa, *Taiwan meisho.*

74. Benedict Anderson's discussion of nation making in the colonial setting emphasizes the role of officially produced images, displays, and icons in the dissemination of certain imaginaries of affiliation and distinction. See Anderson, *Imagined Communities* (London: Verso, 1983), 163–185.

75. Scott, *The Art of Not Being Governed: An Anarchist History of Upland Southeast Asia* (New Haven: Yale University Press, 2009), 238; 241.

76. Antonio C. Tavares, "The Japanese Colonial State and the Dissolution of the Late Imperial Frontier Economy in Taiwan, 1886–1909," *Journal of Asian Studies* 64, no. 2 (2005): 361–385.

77. Mori, *Taiwan banzoku zufu,* plate 23.

78. "Mori Ushinosuke to Tsuboi Shōgorō, 9/2/1902," *Tokyo jinruigakkai zasshi* 199 (October 20, 1902): 39.

79. "Taiwan banjin fūzoku," 111.

80. *Riban gaiyō* (A synopsis of Aboriginal policy) (Taipei: Taiwan sōtokufu minseibu banmu honsho, 1912), 51; Nihon Jun'eki, *Inō Kanori shozō,* 108–109.

81. "Jiku-shi no banjin buiku to Koore bansha no kijun," *Tokyo asahi shinbun,* November 22, 1897, 6.

82. "Hokuban daishū-chō no shukushi," *Taiwan kyōkai kaihō* 1 (1898): 102; Harada Zenshichi (原田善七), "Hokuban ko'ō kettō no zu," *Taiwan kyōkai kaihō* 6 (1899): 76–77.

83. "Banchi no fuon to seinōdaka," *Taiwan nichinichi shinpō,* October 16, 1902.

84. "Kusshaku-ban keiyaku no kōkai," *Taiwan nichinichi shinpō,* November 18, 1902.

85. Aki Satsuki (秋皐), "Kusshaku no shinnen (ni)," *Taiwan nichinichi shinpō,* January 13, 1903; Aki Satsuki, "Kusshaku no shinnen (go)," *Taiwan nichinichi shinpō,* January 18, 1903. A September 2, 1902, letter from Mori to Tsuboi refers to the "Bato Watan household" as a Rimogan household (see note 78), while a detailed journalistic account identified Batō Watan as a Rahao headman signed to mobilize twenty Kusshaku men as guards for an expedition to recover the bodies of slain camphor workers. "Shin-nōryō seiban raishō no gohō," *Taiwan nichinichi shinpō,* January 11, 1903.

86. *[ip1225] Taroko Tribe Husband and Wife,* 2012, East Asian Image Collection, Lafayette College, Easton, PA, accessed March 30, 2013, http://digital.lafayette.edu/collections/eastasia/.

87. "Seiban no raisha," *Taiwan nichinichi shinpō,* January 30, 1903; "Taiwan banjin fūzoku," 108.

88. "Seiban no raisha"; "Taiwan banjin fūzoku," 108.

89. Taiwan Government Bureau of Aborigine Affairs, ed., *Report on the Control of the Aborigines in Formosa* (Taipei: Taiwan Government General, 1911), facing 3; Ishii Shinji, *The Island of Formosa and Its Primitive Inhabitants: A Paper Read at a Joint Meeting of the China Society and the Japan Society, Held at Caxton Hall, on Thursday, February 24, 1916* (London: China Society, 1916), plate 8; Fujisaki Seinosuke, *Taiwan no banzoku* (Tokyo: Kokushi kankōkai, 1931), 248.

90. *[ip1020] (33) Aborigines Woman, Formosa,* 2012, East Asia Image Collection, Lafayette College, Easton, PA, accessed March 30, 2013, http://digital.lafayette.edu/collections/eastasia/.

91. See the postcard reproduced in Narita, *Taiwan seiban shuzoku,* 31; Koizumi Tetsu, *Bankyō fūzokuki* (Tokyo: Kensetsusha, 1932), plate 13; *[lw0522] All about the Aborigine Territories Postcard Collection,* 2012, East Asia Image Collection, Lafayette College, Easton, PA, accessed March 30, 2013, http://digital.lafayette.edu/collections/eastasia.

92. Matsuda, *Teikoku no shisen,* 15–19.

93. Kuni Takeyuki, *Hakurankai no jidai* (Tokyo: Iwata shoin, 2005), 176.

94. Mori, *Taiwan banzoku zufu,* plate 23.

95. Taiwan Government Bureau of Aborigine Affairs, *Report on the Control of the Aborigines,* facing 3; *Taiyō* 23, no. 7 (June 15, 1917); Mori, *Taiwan banzoku zufu,* plate 23; *[lw0002] 2 Kusshaku Savages of Taiyaru Tribe, Farmosa* [*sic*], 2012, East Asia Image Collection, Lafayette College, Easton, PA, accessed July 28, 2013, http://digital.lafayette.edu/collections/eastasia/.

96. "Hunting Head Hunters with Live Electric Wires," *Detroit Free Press,* April 4, 1909.

97. For Atayal nudity, see Lee Ju-ling, "Constructing an Imaginary of Taiwanese Aborigines through Postcards (1895–1945)," in *Translation, History and Arts: New Horizons in Asian Interdisciplinary Humanities Research,* ed. Meng Ji and Ukai Atsuko (London: Cambridge Scholars, 2013), 111–135.

98. This postcard's montage, and its caption, is also found in Narita, *Taiwan seiban shuzoku,* 31.

99. Araki Masayasu, ed., *Shinbun ga kataru meijishi* 2 (Tokyo: Hara shobō, 1979), 79; Kirsten Laurie Ziomek, "Subaltern Speak: Imperial Multiplicities in Japan's Empire and Postwar Colonialisms" (PhD diss., University of California, Santa Barbara, 2011), 193–219.

100. Faye Yuan Kleeman, *Under an Imperial Sun: Japanese Colonial Literature of Taiwan and the South* (Honolulu: University of Hawai'i Press, 2003), 18–25; Robert Thomas Tierney, *Tropics of Savagery: The Culture of Japanese Empire in Comparative Frame* (Berkeley: University of California Press, 2010), 58–59; Paul D. Barclay, "Cultural Brokerage and Interethnic

Marriage in Colonial Taiwan: Japanese Subalterns and Their Aborigine Wives, 1895–1930," *Journal of Asian Studies* 64, no. 2 (May 2005): 323–360.

101. Yang, *Maboroshi jinruigakusha,* 52.

102. Barclay, "Peddling Postcards."

103. Inō, *Riban shikō,* 349; Fujii Shizue, *Riju shiqi Taiwan zongdufu de lifan zhengce* (Taipei: Guoli Taiwan shifan daxue lishi yanjiusuo, 1989), 190–191. Thanks to Linda Yu for translation.

104. Lang, *Adventurous Woman,* 232–261.

105. Inō, *Riban shikō,* 849–850.

106. *[lw0410] The School of Urai Savage Tribe,* East Asia Image Collection, 2012, Lafayette College, Easton, PA, accessed July 28, 2013, http://digital.lafayette.edu/collections/eastasia/.

107. Scott Simon, *Sadyaq Balae!: L'autochthonie Formosan dans tous ses états* (Quebec City: Les Presses de L'Université Laval, 2012), 88–89. Thanks to Sharon Chen for the translation.

108. Paul D. Barclay, "Tangled Up in Red: Textiles, Trading Posts and the Emergence of Indigenous Modernity in Japanese Taiwan," in *Japanese Taiwan: Colonial Rule and Its Contested Legacy,* ed. Andrew D. Morris (London: Bloomsbury Press, 2015).

109. Barclay, "Peddling Postcards."

110. Mitsuda Yayoi, "First Case of the New Recognition System: The Survival Strategies of the Thao," in *Taiwan since Martial Law: Society, Culture, Politics, Economy,* ed. David Blundell (Taipei, Taiwan: Shung Ye Museum of Formosan Aborigines, 2012), 154–155; Michael Rudolph, *Ritual Performances as Authenticating Practices: Cultural Representations of Taiwan's Aborigines in Times of Political Change* (New Brunswick, NJ: Transaction, 2008), 106; Simon, *Sadyaq Balae!,* 82–85.

111. Huang Chih-huei, "Ethnic Diversity, Two-Layered Colonization and Modern Taiwanese Attitudes toward Japan," in Morris, *Japanese Taiwan.*

112. Rudolph, *Ritual Performances,* 1–4, 36–38; Mitsuda, "First Case," 166–167.

113. Ku Kun-hui, "Rights to Recognition: Minorities and Indigenous Politics in Emerging Taiwan Nationalism," in Blundell, *Taiwan since Martial Law,* 95, 98–99.

114. Mitsuda, "First Case," 157–159, 167; Simon, *Sadyaq Balae!,* 85; Rudolph, *Ritual Performances,* 4–5.

115. See Nanjun Yang, *Shengfan xingjiao: Senchou zhizhu de taiwan tanxian* (Taipei, Taiwan: Yuanliu, 2012). The first edition was published in 2000; the second in 2004.

116. Zhou Menggui, *Taiwan laoming xinpian* (Gaoxiong, China: Chuanmen qiye chuban, 2008). The first edition was published in 2003.

117. Similar iconography can be found on public schools in Fushan Township (near Wulai), Hanxi (Yilan Province), and Fuxing (Taoyuan Province).

118. Rudolph, *Ritual Performances,* 55; Simon, *Sadyaq Balae!,* 86–87.

119. Rudolph, *Ritual Performances,* 7.

120. Barclay, "Tangled up in Red"; Simon, *Sadyaq Balae!,* 89–90; Rudolph, *Ritual Performances,* 107–08, 117.

121. Rudolph, *Ritual Performances,* 6–7, 106; Simon, *Sadyaq Balae!,* 82–84; Ku, "Rights to Recognition," 93.

122. Rudolph, *Ritual Performances,* 114–127; Simon, *Sadyaq Balae!,* 14–16, 228–233; Mitsuda, "First Case," 169–170.

123. Shahid Amin, *Event, Metaphor, Memory: Chauri Chaura, 1922–1992* (Berkeley: University of California Press, 1995); Gyan Prakash, *Mumbai Fables* (Princeton, NJ: Princeton University Press, 2010).

124. Simon, *Sadyaq Balae!,* 28–33; *China Post,* "Gov't Officially Recognizes Two More Aboriginal Tribes," June 27, 2014, accessed January 8, 2015, http://www.chinapost.com.tw/taiwan/national/national-news/2014/06/27/411066/Govt-officially.htm.

125. Rudolph, *Ritual Performances,* 107–115; Mitsuda, "First Case," 170.

126. Arif Dirlik, *The Postcolonial Aura: Third World Criticism in the Age of Global Capitalism* (Boulder, CO: Westview Press, 1997), 227.

127. James Clifford, "Identity in Mashpee," in *The Predicament of Culture: Twentieth-Century Ethnography, Literature and Art,* ed. James Clifford (Cambridge, MA: Harvard University Press, 1988), 277–348.

128. Hsiau A-chin, *Contemporary Taiwanese Cultural Nationalism* (London: Routledge, 2000), 162–164; Rudolph, *Ritual Performances,* 55–59; Ku, "Rights to Recognition," 104, 122.

129. Simon, *Sadyaq Balae!,* 220–225.

130. Rudolph, *Ritual Performances,* 60–62.

131. Charles William Le Gendre, Douglas L. Fix, and John Shufelt, *Notes of Travel in Formosa* (Tainan: National Museum of Taiwan History, 2012), 49–53.

Assimilation's Racializing Sensibilities

Colonized Koreans as *Yobos* and the "*Yobo*-ization" of Expatriate Japanese

Seeking to engage in comparative and transnational dialogues about the place of cultural racism in projects of imperial rule, this chapter examines recurrent debates on the proper embodiment of "Japanese" sensibilities to reveal the unruly project of constructing and maintaining cultural differences among various strata of colonized Koreans and Japanese settlers within the context of capitalist production and modern power.[1] Although internal discourses tended to highlight considerable schisms between these two ethnic groups, official pronouncements of racial similarity exposed a countervailing campaign aimed at distinguishing Japan's form of rule over Korea as somehow distinct and even less repressive than that of its Euro-American counterparts. It is no coincidence that early twentieth-century arguments about the putative uniqueness of emperor-centered assimilation (J. *dōka*, K. *tonghwa*) emerged at the very moment when most European powers were moving toward a greater emphasis on ruling strategies that segregated and cordoned off colonized peoples from metropolitan settlers.[2] In contrast, government officials and media pundits liked to tout the policy, if not the practice, of assimilating colonized Koreans—an ideological project they understood as intrinsic to Japan's imagined predominance in premodern East Asia and one both commensurate and competitive with other distinctly modern forms of imperialism.[3]

Despite elaborate efforts to present assimilation as unique and superior to the imperialist powers of the day, colonial projects aimed at transforming the cultural practices of the colonized population into ones deemed adequately "Japanese" remained highly discriminatory as long as officials continually denied most Koreans the political rights and economic privileges that expatriates enjoyed. In this sense, colonized Koreans found themselves in a similarly disenfranchised position as their South Asian counterparts, whom English rulers relegated to what Dipesh Chakrabarty has called the "waiting room of history."[4] However, unlike those in the British Raj or other Euro-American empires, the racializing mechanisms of assimilating Koreans relied more heavily on the less visible criteria of cultural sensibilities than on the more dependable differences of scientific biology.[5] To capture these nuances of Japanese rule, I have coined the term "affective racism." By this term, I am referring to the insidious practices of differential incorporation that depended on ethnic proximity and the lure of cultural assimilation as the basis for temporarily, if not permanently, marking the inherently porous boundaries between model Japanese subjects and colonized Korean Others. In practice, both ethnic groups did, to varying degrees, fail to embody the highly idealized sensibilities constituting the model subject, typically conceived of as a Japanese middle-class adult male. However, even lower-class individuals who had yet to embody these sensibilities, thus becoming the objects of racialized slurs and other petty forms of colonial violence, were still perceived by ruling authorities as forming an integral and productive part of the emperor-centered community, especially during the period of wartime mobilization (1937–1945).[6] By relying on the logic of an extended family of related kin, these authorities could conveniently disavow radical differences within the Asian "race" and, instead, posit only degrees of cultural inclusion, or what Oguma Eiji has creatively called "ambivalent sameness."[7] The articulation of colonial relationships as familial had the effect of blurring hierarchical distinctions between Japanese colonizers and colonized Koreans, thereby suppressing the inherent contradictions between assimilation and discrimination. Affective racism worked to bridge that gap by enticing Koreans to gradually embody an amorphous set of cultural sensibilities often described as forming the unique "Yamato spirit." At the same time, however, the definitional ambiguity of this "Japanese" spirit tended to frustrate culturally assimilated individuals on the fringes of the imperial community when they struggled to become more fully accepted members and thereby benefit from the political rights and economic benefits associated with imperial citizenship.

I apply this understanding of affective racism to an analysis of debates surrounding the Japanese neologism *yobo* (ヨボ), a term Japanese settlers and colonialist writers appropriated from the Korean term *yŏbo* (여보). In its original linguistic context, this second-person pronoun was used by higher-ranking individuals to address their juniors or equally ranked friends. During the early twentieth century, women also came to employ *yŏbo* (in conjunction with *sŏbang-nim* 서방님, husband) as a way of hailing their male partner, although the terms *chane* (자내), *kesyŭ* (게셔), and *naŭri* (나으리) were more commonly used for this function.[8] Disregarding these local meanings, an increasingly large number of expatriate settlers redeployed the Japanese term *yobo* as a racial epithet—a rhetorical tactic they used to mark the porous cultural boundaries separating themselves as upstart colonizers from newly colonized Koreans.[9]

After Usuda Zan'un (1877–1956) had given new meanings to a term already popular by the protectorate period (1905–1910), elite Korean writers such as Sŏk Jinhyŏng (1877–1946) found a discursive space in the Japanese press (despite harsh government censorship) to criticize the widespread abuse of *yŏbo*. Colonialist responses to these critiques downplayed the discriminatory nature of Japanese rule and instead focused on the affective demands of assimilation, exhorting Koreans to "Japanize" their cultural practices according to an idealized set of sensibilities and thus discourage Japanese settlers from demeaning them as *yobos*. As Korean rebuttals to such pressures would show, however, this compromise proved a Faustian bargain.

The racist impulses of "*yobo*-izing" the colonized population were also turned against the expatriate community in accusations that the relatively large number of its lower-class members had become "Koreanized." Although contributors to this debate failed to come to any consensus on the *yobo*-ization question, the debate reveals the precarious position that working-class settlers occupied in colonial society. While their bourgeois leaders hoped that these intractable expatriates would come to act as cultural missionaries for unassimilated Koreans, they failed in most locales throughout the colony to erect a network of cultural institutions capable of imparting the idealized sensibilities of Japanese subjects. The anticolonial movement of 1919 further unbound the already beleaguered project of assimilation, leading the new administration of Governor-General Saitō Makoto (r. 1919–1927) to desperately attempt to "harmonize Japanese and Koreans" (J. *naisen yūwa*, K. *naesŏn yunghwa*). Aimed at hierarchically fusing the sensibilities of colonizer and colonized, this new strategy of "cultural rule" only led to more aggressive critiques of affective racism, which persisted in the *yobo*-izing practices of many expatriate settlers. Although continuing to work within the ideological structures of colonial rule, Korean critics boldly challenged the colonial state to a degree unprecedented before 1919, seriously questioning the racializing sensibilities the colonized population had been encouraged to embody as imperial subjects. Faulting Japanese settlers for their own immoral shortcomings, these writers sought to preserve and strengthen Korean customs, deflecting the homogenizing impulses of assimilation while facilitating their own liberal projects of "cultural nationalism."

Usuda Zan'un and the "*Yobo*-ization" of Semicolonized Koreans

Although it is uncertain when the Japanese term *yobo* was first coined, its increasingly frequent usage was clearly a product of the growing presence of settlers during the late Chosŏn period (1392–1910). With the Meiji government's forceful opening of Korean treaty ports in 1876, Japanese diplomats, businessmen, small merchants, and a considerable population of female sex workers began to reside in urban centers such as Seoul, Pusan, Inch'ŏn, Wŏnsan, P'yŏngyang, Chinnamp'o, Masan, Mokp'o, and Kunsan.[10] Although Japanese expatriates in Korea numbered only 7,500 in 1890, their country's military victory in the 1894–1895 Sino-Japanese War led to a rapid influx of new emigrants, more than doubling the settler population to nearly 16,000 by 1900. Despite these numerical increases, population turnover was commonplace, and the number of lower-class expatriates—composing as much as one-third of the settler community in Seoul, for example—remained relatively high well into the early colonial period.[11] In response, Japanese officials implemented a number of legal and ideological mechanisms to ensure a greater sense of national purpose among the growing expatriate community.[12] Despite continued problems with controlling uncooperative settlers, the era following Japan's victory in the 1904–1905 Russo-Japanese War and the ensuing protectorate period (1905–1910) witnessed another dramatic increase in the settler population, whose number grew to more than 170,000 by the time of the annexation in 1910.[13]

Among the thousands of Japanese who traveled to Korea as part of Japan's gradual colonization of the peninsula were eager journalists and other writers who took it upon themselves to chronicle Korean culture as a way to encourage future emigration and tourism as well as to legitimize the annexation. Elsewhere, I have discussed the prominent role that "popular ethnographers" such as Okita Kinjō played in the creation of semicolonized Korean culture. In his 1905 *Rimen no Kankoku* (Korea behind the mask), Okita selectively appropriated cultural fragments of native manners and customs in order to demonstrate an essentialized portrait of the colonized as lazy, unproductive, insular, and thus in need of Japanese colonial "guidance."[14] Although many of the same motifs appeared in his popular ethnographies, Usuda Zan'un, writing in the immediate wake of Okita, played an even more important role in linking these Korean traits with the equally essentializing term *yobo.* A literature major who later worked as a journalist and novelist, Usuda popularized this Japanese neologism in three ethnographies on Korean manners and customs he penned during a year-long sojourn in Seoul.[15] While drawing on the Korean word *yŏbo,* Usuda redeployed this native term of endearment as a racial epithet, much as expatriate settlers used it to denigrate the semicolonized population.

In June 1908, Usuda published his first popular ethnography, *Yoboki* (Records of Koreanness), which not only takes this racial epithet as its title but also uses it extensively throughout the text.[16] Regularly appending the *katakana* letters for the Japanese term *yobo* (ヨボ) as a gloss for the Chinese term meaning senility (*rōmō* 老耄), he employed the racial epithet *yobo* as a metonym for Korea's declining state of affairs and its "feeble-minded" people. For instance, in the opening chapter of *Yoboki*—titled "A Senile Country" (Yobokuku 老耄國)—Usuda described a typical colonial encounter between a coterie of Japanese settler men sharply dressed in black suits with an anonymous group of former Korean *yangban* smoking long pipes and dressed in "dirty" white clothing.[17]

Sympathizing with the sentiments of his brethren, Usuda denigrated these landed aristocrats as a nuisance to Japanese settlers as they traveled along Honmachi Street, the narrow east–west thoroughfare traversing the heart of Seoul's Japanese community. Offended by this cultural "intrusion" into their ethnic enclave, the expatriate men retaliated by calling them *yobo* (Hey you, Koreans!) with a rising intonation. In response, the *yangban* men uttered the Korean word *aigo* (my goodness!), an emotive expression conveying their disillusionment. They also turned back at the vulgar Japanese settlers with a threatening gaze. However, in a gesture indicative of their declining position within late Chosŏn society, they ultimately succumbed to the demands of the increasingly dominant expatriate community. Redeploying *yobo* in another linguistic context familiar to his readers, Usuda explained the retreat of these incensed yet powerless Korean men with the Japanese onomatopoeia *yobo yobo* ("[to walk] totteringly," "to hobble," "to dodder") to describe their frailty in yielding the right-of-way to the Japanese settlers, who briskly passed them as if threading a

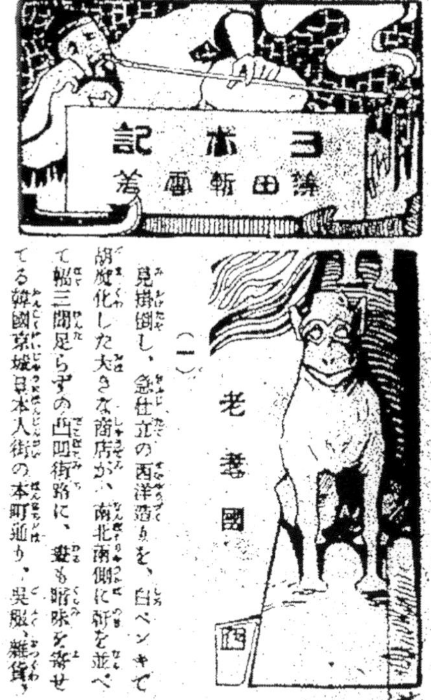

Figure 4.1. "A Senile Country," Usuda Zan'un, *Yoboki* (*Records of Koreanness*), 1908, 1.

needle. Based on this colonial encounter, he triumphantly proclaimed that the Japanese word *yobo* had become a commonly used pronoun synonymous with the inherent backwardness, weakness, and inferiority of Koreans and their "senile," near-colonized country.

In the following months leading up to Korea's annexation, Usuda provided adjectival meanings to the already popular pronoun *yobo* in two sequels he penned to *Yoboki, Ankoku naru Chōsen* (Dark Korea) and *Chōsen manga* (Korean caricatures). Published in October 1908, *Dark Korea*—a work reminiscent of other social exposés written about the squalor of domestic slums and overseas colonies, such as *In Darkest London* (1889) and *In Darkest Africa* (1890)—explores the ignominious particularities of Koreans and their customs.[18] Presented in a series of pithy vignettes, *Dark Korea* spotlights individuals and practices such as shamans and their "feeble" attempts to save the country from colonization, the "uncivilized" Korean practice of forcing young children into early marital engagements, and of course, the fallen status of *yangban* whose position he shamelessly likened to the dirt under one's fingernails.

Whatever the particular ethnographic portrait, Usuda uniformly referred to all Koreans as *yobo*s, the derogatory term he played a large part in popularizing. For example, Usuda chronicled a trip he took to an unspecified part of the countryside, a site he portrayed as the cultural epicenter of Korean "backwardness." Using this racial epithet as an adjective nearly ten times in fewer than fifteen

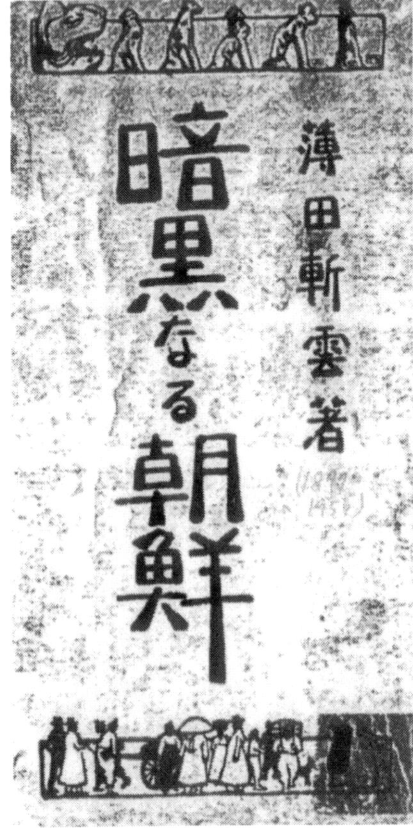

Figure 4.2. "Ignominious Particularities of Koreans and Their Customs," Usuda Zan'un, *Ankoku naru Chōsen* (Dark Korea), 1908, front cover.

pages, Usuda likened the clothing of farmers to that worn by lower-class *yobo*s living in Seoul, recoiled at the foul odor of *yobo* kimchi, and complained about the fecal odor suffusing *yobo* inns.[19]

In his final ethnography, *Chōsen manga,* a work illustrated by Torigoe Seishi, Usuda generated a series of racialized caricatures of Koreans as inherently backward Others, images that regularly found their way onto the pages of popular colonial journals such as *Chōsen oyobi manshū* (Korea and Manchuria).[20] In many of the fifty caricatures published from this text, Usuda and Torigoe employed the term *yobo* as an essentialized adjective to define virtually all Koreans and their cultural practices. For example, they used it to describe the unseemliness of native rice cakes, the short stature of Korean pimps who purveyed lower-class prostitutes, and even the purported laziness of local cattle.

In addition to qualifying the level of cultural "backwardness," they also deployed *yobo* in its other popular usage—that is, as a pronoun synonymous with Koreans themselves. In the vignette on Koreans' quarrels, for example, Usuda and Torigoe explained the tendency for native men to engage in shrill verbal confrontations, performances that attracted crowds of pipe-smoking Korean on-

Figure 4.3a. *(Left)* "Unseemly Rice Cakes," Usuda Zan'un and Torigoe Seishi, *Chōsen manga* (Korean caricatures), 1909, 47.

Figure 4.3b. *(Center)* "Lower-Class Prostitute," Usuda Zan'un and Torigoe Seishi, *Chōsen manga* (Korean caricatures), 1909, 17.

Figure 4.3c. *(Right)* "Lazy Cattle," Usuda Zan'un and Torigoe Seishi, *Chōsen manga* (Korean caricatures), 1909, 77.

lookers. However, these long-lasting quarrels, which the authors likened to catfights, only brought tired yawns to the faces of Japanese spectators who considered this reckless behavior a sign of Koreans' "stupidity" and "immorality." In another vignette on Korean sawyers, the authors explained how two pipe-smoking men leisurely conversed while cutting logs—a "languid" custom they hoped to reform by introducing a more efficient Japanese practice that required the labor of only one man.

Through these portraits of Koreans as deplorable and in need of "Japanization," Usuda provided novel meanings to the racist caricature embodied in the already popular term *yobo.* By the time of the annexation, this term thus had not only permeated the discursive space of colonial journalism but had also spread in daily interactions between colonized Koreans and Japanese settlers.

Elite Korean Critiques of *Yobo* and Assimilationist Responses by Japanese Pundits

Despite the Government-General's harsh censorship of Korean-language publications during the first decade of Japanese rule, educated elites, positioning themselves as well-assimilated native ethnographers of Korean culture, made active use of the settler press to criticize the racialized use of *yŏbo* to denote the alleged inferiority of their own colonized nation. To complain about the misuse

Figure 4.4. "Ineffective Korean Sawyers," Usuda Zan'un and Torigoe Seishi, *Chōsen manga* (Korean caricatures), 1909, 9.

of this term was, in turn, a means for Korean elites writing in Japanese to claim class solidarity with their more "polite" Japanese counterparts and to distance themselves from the vulgarity of lower-class expatriates who indiscriminately used derogatory language in their everyday interactions with their Korean counterparts.[21] Sŏk Jinhyŏng—a graduate in law from Hōsei University in Tokyo and later an instructor at Posŏng College (the forerunner of Korea University) in Seoul—was one such critic.[22] Writing in a November 1912 issue of *Chōsen oyobi manshū,* Sŏk asserted his own assimilated status by emphasizing his familiarity and knowledge of Japanese customs, the Japanese language, and the nature of the Japanese people. Given the rapid embodiment of these foreign sensibilities just years after the 1910 annexation, he found it revolting that less educated settlers continued to assail him with the racialized epithet *yobo.* This is to say nothing of lower-class Koreans whose ignorance, the patronizing Sŏk agreed, had prevented them from adequately acquiring Japanese sensibilities and thus made them easy targets of affective racism. As a native ethnographer, Sŏk conveyed to his Japanese readers the ill will that this word aroused in Koreans who, he reminded them, typically used it only as an intimate expression among friends and equally ranked colleagues. Translating its autochthonous nuances into the language of his colonizers, Sŏk equated the use of *yobo* to the Japanese expressions *o-i* (Hey, you!) or *moshi moshi* (hello, as used on the telephone, but used here as an aggressive greeting) as ways of calling lower-ranked or younger individuals. However, he argued that both uses of the word *yŏbo* among Koreans did not necessarily carry negative connotations in a society characterized by strong traditions of social hierarchy. Therefore, he expressed his resentment that expatriates had channeled these culturally specific meanings into a widely used moniker to refer to all fifteen million Koreans as a uniform lot of idiots, causing the colonized population to feel a sense of discomfort, regret, and estrangement.

Although Sŏk thus clearly bemoaned the discriminatory use of *yobo* by Japanese settlers, he did not seek to relocate the object of this racialized epithet (colonized Koreans) within an anticolonial community advocating national independence. Under a regime that had the authority to censor all publications and writing in a magazine dominated by the voices of Japanese settlers, such a position remained virtually unspeakable.[23] Instead, this critic worked from within the surprisingly loose parameters of assimilation to challenge the derogatory nature of what I am calling affective racism. In his critique, Sŏk revisited the language of the annexation treaty, which had called for the material and spiritual development of Koreans as new subjects in the imperial community.[24] Summoning his Japanese readers to make good on this official policy, he urged expatriates to desist from using the discriminatory word *yobo*—a term that had created a feeling of separation between settlers and Koreans.

If critics like Sŏk exposed the internal contradictions of affective racism under the new regime of assimilation, Japanese respondents to these Korean critiques sought to bridge this obvious gap between racist discrimination and cultural incorporation. To do so, they encouraged the colonized population to adopt the governing rationality of the colonial state and become active agents of their own assimilation, much as Sŏk had done.[25] Embodying an idealized set of sensibilities characteristic of ethnic Japanese would, these pundits argued, obviate the need for settlers to racialize them as *yobo*s in the first place. An anonymous author, presumably of Japanese ethnicity who styled himself with the nationalist pseudonym Man from the Land of the Rising Sun, adopted exactly this position in response to Sŏk's critique. Published in the same 1912 issue of *Chōsen oyobi manshū,* he urged the colonized population to rid themselves of their cultural "deficiencies" and gradually transform themselves according to a normative standard at whose endpoint stood the cultural attributes of the idealized Japanese subject. Uninterested in Sŏk's explanation of nuances specific to the Korean use of the word *yŏbo,* Man of the Land of the Rising Sun instead defended its continued misappropriation by expatriates. He disagreed with Sŏk, arguing that the Japanese term *yobo,* although not polite, was not inherently deprecating. Speaking from a position of colonial superiority, the author considered it arrogant for Koreans to expect that the more "civilized" Japanese would refer to a "less civilized" population with more polite expressions, such as *yŏng'gam* (영감) or *yangban* (양반). Koreans' discomfort with Japanese settlers' use of *yobo*—a term that could, according to this author's assimilationist logic, eventually become a polite word—thus resulted from its *contingently* pejorative associations with "filth," "shamelessness," "servility," "evasiveness," "stubbornness," "arrogance," "slyness," and "feigned allegiances," as well as a lack of transcendent "ideals," "aspirations," or "persistence." Depicting these qualifiers as the social reality of the present, the author shifted the burden to Koreans, who could avoid being criticized by simply civilizing themselves in line with government reforms aimed at both modernizing the country and assimilating its inhabitants. Through a common strategy of "colonial humanism" these self-generated efforts at more fully embodying Japanese sensibilities would, this author argued, encourage settlers to respect and love Koreans as equals, thus reducing expressions of affective racism conveyed by the pejoratively inflected term *yobo.*[26]

Given the coercive tactics of the early colonial state and the discriminatory attitudes of many expatriates toward Koreans, such liberal promises of love and respect rang hollow, whether or not the colonized population assimilated themselves to the set of sensibilities considered to characterize model Japanese subjects.[27] The continued use of discriminatory terms such as *yobo,* both in the colonial media and in everyday speech, did not diminish, in part because it allowed Japanese settlers a tactic through which to challenge the authority of the Government-General, which many believed used the policy of assimilation to undercut settlers' own privileges. Although settlers could not prevent the colonial state from abolishing their legal autonomy as extraterritorial enclaves, members of the expatriate community, particularly those of the working classes, capitalized on the racist assumptions of Japanese rule by *yobo*-izing Koreans—vulgar tactics that clearly undercut bourgeois pretensions of assimilation.[28]

Even as these expressions of discrimination continued apace, Sŏk Jinhyŏng and other concerned Koreans writing in colonial journals pressed for greater inclusion in this culturally insulated community of ethnic Japanese, if only as a way to obtain the political rights and economic power denied to them by assimilation.[29] In support of his position, Sŏk offered the example of his own child who, at the age of five, entered the Nanzan Kindergarten, an elite educational institution attended primarily by Japanese settlers. Within two years, his seven-year-old son had, he claimed, learned to speak "standard" Japanese and had also acquired outward gestures and external appearances indistinguishable from those of an expatriate child. He compared the purposeful cultivation of these Japanese sensibilities by his biologically "pure" Korean son to the mixed-blood daughter of a former Japanese train station manager, who cleaved to his Korean wife and thus became fully Koreanized.[30] Consciously avoiding the derogatory term *yobo* used by his colonialist counterparts, Sŏk qualified this child's move away from the Japanese sensibilities required for assimilation by describing her close association with Korean street urchins and the inability to speak the "national language." These lower-class sensibilities, often used by Japanese pundits to *yobo*-ize Koreans, precluded the colonized masses from acquiring the benefits of imperial citizenship—a problem Sŏk sought to remedy by calling on both Japanese and Koreans to work toward the goal of assimilation, albeit from within the unequal relations of power that colonial rule generated.

Assimilation's Racializing Reversals: Japanese Anxieties over the *Yobo*-ization of Expatriate Settlers

Insofar as it formed part of an elite settler discourse, the example of Sŏk's son clearly resonated with the official ideology of transforming Korean sensibilities along a cultural continuum at whose endpoint sat a model Japanese subject, typically described as an adult bourgeois man. However, Sŏk's discussion of the Koreanized mixed-blood offspring also demonstrates how the fluid relationship between ethnic background and cultural affinity confounded the terms and direction of assimilation, whose affectively racist character was most boldly expressed by the epithet *yobo.* At the same time, these fluidities and the colonial state's attempt to manage them also came to affect the growing population of Japanese settlers, especially those of the working classes. Many of these expatriates struggled, with limited success, to embody the sensibilities expected of them and could, therefore, be condemned for becoming *yobo*-ized. Concerns over such instances of affective "delinquency" were found, for example, in frequent complaints about the scarcity of libraries, parks, Shintō shrines, and theaters—cultural institutions seen as necessary to the cultivation of proper Japanese "taste," a key word connoting bourgeois sensibilities.[31] Even Japanese settlers in early colonial Seoul, a city that boasted many of these edifying institutions, struggled to find the same dense networks of national ideology and imperial pageantry that residents, especially those living in urban centers, were intensely subjected to during the Meiji period (1868–1912).[32]

Although it may have lacked the cultural infrastructure necessary to inculcate national virtues, the early colonial state, itself preoccupied with distracting cases of disobedient settlers, hoped that these expatriates would first reform themselves and eventually lead Koreans toward the official goal of assimilation. In the end, however, many profit-seeking settlers neglected these responsibilities in the pursuit of their own material welfare, often at the expense of even more impoverished Koreans.[33] As an ethnic minority, Japanese settlers were surrounded by a much larger population of Koreans in virtually every urban center to which the majority of expatriates emigrated.[34] Despite elaborate efforts to insulate themselves from what many writers viewed as Koreans' contaminating sensibilities, expatriates found themselves psychologically under siege by nearby Koreans. By 1925, the Korean population of Seoul not only made up over 90 percent of inhabitants in the northern half of the city, but they also constituted slightly over 35 percent of residents in the southern half of the city, where Japanese expatriates were firmly ensconced.[35]

Concerns over the physical health and spiritual well-being of the settler population emerged even before Korea was annexed in 1910, but these anxieties increased in intensity thereafter, as assimilation took root as the guiding ideology of Japanese rule.[36] A local newspaper article from May 1912 expressed such anxieties by seeking to define the essence of "Japaneseness," or the Yamato spirit, as it called it. In particular, the article seamlessly linked Shintō-inspired traditions of ritual purity to the new Japanese penchant for promoting public health, practices that he expected expatriates to convey to newly colonized Koreans as part of the Government-General's policy of assimilation. However, in defining Japanese culture as inherently hygienic, the author also recognized the possibility that some settlers might not live up to these officially sanctioned standards. Worse still, he worried that some expatriates might sully the pristine image of their community by engaging in "uncivilized" behavior, such as public urination, and thereby become assimilated to the *yobo*-like practices of "unhygienic" Koreans.[37] Such condemnations, of course, overlooked the fact that Japanese residents of Meiji cities often engaged in such "uncivilized" practices, which, in the new colonial setting, were now being racially inflected as Korean. In addition to cleanliness, other writers from the early colonial period described the sensibilities defining the Yamato spirit as including graciousness, chastity, faith, generosity, bravery, and, above all, strong feelings of loyalty.[38] These authors feared that Japanese settlers' failure to embody these attributes was a sign that they were not only struggling to meet expectations of assimilation but were themselves becoming Koreanized.

Such fears found voice in anxious discussions about the so-called *yobo*-ization of Japanese expatriates, although contributors to this debate never came to a consensus on the degree to which settlers had in fact been Koreanized, the possible causes for this phenomenon, or adequate solutions to the problem. In a 1917 article published in *Chōsen oyobi manshū*, for example, the editors of this popular colonial journal presented the incoming governor-general, Hasegawa Yoshimichi (r. 1916–1919), with a series of opinions from government officials and local notables. Of the three most important topics they discussed, one was whether the Japanese residents of Korea had acquired *yobo*-ized sensibilities.[39] The Japanese respondents to this question constituted a wide-ranging cross-section of what can best be described as the colony's few but powerful "new middle class," which included officials, teachers, journalists, lawyers, and businessmen.[40] Despite their common socioeconomic standing in colonial Korea, these individuals presented a broad range of answers that together highlighted the elusive nature of assimilation as the embodiment of a fluid and nebulous set of Japanese sensibilities, which many used to subject "delinquent" expatriates to racializing impulses. For some, such as the vice-director of the administration for Korea's former royal house, the task of evaluating settlers' degrees of *yobo*-ization was a "useless exercise" since, as he pithily wrote using the logic of social Darwinism: "From the beginning, the strong rule the weak." Other respondents, such as the chief of the Government-General's public safety division, took the matter far more seriously. Agreeing that Japanese settlers had indeed become Koreanized, he made the drastic proposal that the government return to the homeland those Japanese expatriates who had adopted "harmful" Korean customs.

Still others focused on the nature of settlers' *yobo*-ization, pathologizing the injurious effects caused by the colony's physical and human environment. For example, a contribution from an expatriate lawyer suggested the inevitability of being Koreanized to some degree by the local climate and native landscape, but he upbraided delinquent settlers for carelessly engaging in swindling and fraud, criminal activities he identified as inherently Korean. These racialized manifestations of *yobo*-ization suggested to this particular author that some settlers had, in his words, "abandoned their Yamato spirit" and could thus be considered Japanese in name only. Other contributors to the debate specified the sensibilities constituting this amorphous Japanese spirit, insisting that they nonetheless served as the standard by which to assimilate Koreans. The principal of a local high school in Seoul, for example, compared the practices of Japanese expatriates in Korea with their metropolitan counterparts in the Kansai area, suggesting that the former were considerably more lax than the latter. Another contributor to the debate bemoaned most settlers' weak spirit of self-improvement and their lack of diligence. Comparing them to successful metropole-based entrepreneurs such as Iwasaki Yatarō (1835–1885), Yasuda Zenjirō (1838–1921), and Ōkura Kihachirō (1882–1963), this contributor complained that most local businessmen set minimal goals for themselves and thus remained satisfied with relatively low levels of success.

Because these Koreanized sensibilities resulted from environmental determinism, as one government official suggested, they could only be temporarily remedied through more vigilant self-awareness. According to his argument, Korean elites who spent time living in Japan could adopt metropolitan sensibilities approximating those of their "upstanding" Japanese counterparts, but they often reverted back to a "lazy" Korean lifestyle of smoking long pipes while sitting on the enervating *ondol* (water-heated) flooring. In a similar way, Japanese settlers tended to adopt these *yobo*-like practices as a result of their sojourn in Korea and could therefore only reestablish themselves as "true" Japanese by returning to the metropole. This particular author proposed, as a long-term solution to this problem, the further Japanization of Korea(ns) by increasing the number of settlers. However, he could only offer for the short term a makeshift proposal that expatriate communities already living on the peninsula guard against their own *yobo*-ization by recalling the idealized set of Japanese sensibilities uniting them as a modern ethnic nation.

So pervasive was this racializing discourse on the Koreanization of expatriate settlers that it even extended to critiquing the practices of otherwise upstanding settlers, repositioning their cultural "inadequacies" into racialized "deficiencies" typically attributed to the colonized population. The company president of a major shipping company, for example, used this discourse to excoriate Japanese members of the Seoul Chamber of Commerce for skipping meetings and failing to pay dues, duties that most civic-minded Korean members performed according to expectations.[41] Wada Ichirō, the head of the Government-General's land survey department, spoke of the *yobo*-ization problem in a similar way. He mobilized this racialized discourse to demonstrate that high-ranking colonial officials, unlike their more egalitarian counterparts in the metropole, had adopted the strong hierarchical sensibilities of local Koreans who, Wada claimed, tended to look down on lower-ranking functionaries. Although lower-class Japanese settlers had deployed the epithet *yobo* as a way of racializing Koreans and thereby marking their distance from an assimilated status, the homogenizing discourse of *yobo* also came to judge the disparate sensibilities of the expatriate population, becoming a polemical tool to criticize any practice deemed unbecoming of "upstanding" subjects. Through these racializing reversals, settler pundits did not frame the "defects" constituting *yobo*-ness in terms of innate biological differences but attributed them to the insufficient embodiment of a diametrically opposed set of Japanese sensibilities.

"Harmonizing Japanese and Koreans": The Unbinding of Assimilation's Homogenizing Sensibilities

Just as this anxious debate on the *yobo*-ization of settlers reached an emotional yet indefinite conclusion, a broad segment of colonized Koreans rose up in protest in 1919 against their disenfranchisement and mistreatment during the first decade of Japanese rule.[42] Although the demands of the March 1st Movement to bypass assimilation through immediate independence failed, colonial officials were forced to respond to this unexpected eruption of anticolonial nationalism by allowing Koreans more opportunities for public debate and a greater, if limited, degree of political autonomy. As a result, the newly appointed governor-general, Saitō Makoto, instituted a divide-and-rule strategy to co-opt willing Korean elites who could, in turn, disseminate the colonial state's governing rationalities among the lower classes. As part of these efforts to establish a stronger basis for a colonial rule, the Government-General also modified its approach to assimilation with a new focus on "harmonizing Japanese and Koreans" (J. *naisen yūwa*), a catchphrase appearing frequently during the 1920s and the early 1930s.[43] This accommodationist approach to colonial rule was, as before, aimed at transforming the sensibilities of Koreans into idealized Japanese ones. However, the notable appearance of Koreans alongside Japanese in this amalgamated neologism disclosed a subtle change in the preexisting meaning of assimilation, which the March 1st Movement helped further unbind. Although still imbued with heavy doses of affective racism, *naisen yūwa* shifted part of the onus to transform themselves on expatriates who, even the local Japanese-language press admitted, continued to discriminate against Koreans. A concept based on the hierarchical fusion of cultural sensibilities, *naisen yūwa* also allowed native writers to capitalize on the Koreanization of settlers by insisting that these Japanese colonialists make greater efforts to understand and respect local customs without *yobo*-izing them. Although continuing to work within the ideological structures of Japanese rule, these Korean elites deployed what Michael Robinson has called "cultural nationalism" as a defensive strategy to challenge the direction of assimilation and thereby dilute its homogenizing power to "Japanize" them according to what they viewed as morally questionable standards.[44]

Just a month after the March 1st Movement erupted, the editors of *Chōsen oyobi manshū* published a short article in which they situated the highly politicized term *yobo* within the emerging context of "harmonizing Japanese and Koreans."[45] Although reiterating their difficulties in understanding why elite Koreans continued to oppose the term *yobo,* the authors of this piece grudgingly recognized that the insensitive Japanese appropriation of native words—even the otherwise polite expression *yangban,* for example—might sound insulting to Korean listeners. However, rather than calling for an end to the use of such politically sensitive words, they instead reframed the issue as a "mutual problem of feelings," calling on both ethnic groups to redouble their efforts in support of assimilation. Toward Koreans, the authors reiterated preexisting sentiments of affective racism by urging them to reform their cultural practices away from those that could be characterized as "barbaric," "dirty," "shameless," and "ignorant." As before, they called on colonized individuals to raise their level of civilization, thereby transforming themselves into upstanding subjects immune from settler abuse as *yobo*s. At the same time, the authors began to question the indiscriminate use of this racialized epithet as a pronoun to refer to *all* Koreans—particularly by lower-class settlers, women, and children—whom they singled out and urged to reflect on their own discriminatory attitudes.[46] Reiterating these same gendered and class-inflected dimensions of Japaneseness, they also called on expatriate settlers to refrain from using this abusive term toward gentlemen, intellectuals, government officials, and company employees. By showcasing individuals who did embody the amorphous sensibilities of Japanese subjects, colonialist authors attempted to deflect ongoing Korean criticisms of *yobo.* Although the discriminatory policy and practice of assimilation thus remained unchanged, the new formula of "harmonizing Japanese and Koreans" called on both ethnic groups to support this conciliatory strategy of rule following the disruptive March 1st Movement.

Even as Korean writers continued to work within these reconfigured parameters of Japanese rule, they took advantage of its ideological inconsistencies to challenge the unidirectional pretensions of assimilation through their own liberal articulations of "cultural nationalism."[47] These discursive strategies are seen in Im Iksang's essay, "My Point of View on the Harmonization of Japanese and Koreans," published by *Chōsen kōron* (Korea digest) in the fall of 1921 as part of a contest this journal sponsored for Koreans writing in Japanese. Although his age and socioeconomic status remain unclear, this resident of Kaesŏng harshly criticized the ongoing dominance of Japanese sensibilities in the new formulation of assimilating Koreans through the innocuous-sounding term *naisen yūwa.* Like his predecessors, Im did not challenge the legitimacy of this ruling strategy per se but instead questioned the unequal basis of its everyday operation. He complained, for example, that while Koreans had made considerable progress in learning the Japanese language, settlers had not only failed to learn Korean but also regularly ignored its potential usefulness. Problems of intercultural communication thus continued to dog the official goal of "harmonizing Japanese and Koreans," which Im suggested should be a bilingual (rather than a monolingual) project.

Using a titillating metaphor to describe the intimate relations between men and women, he likened the nature of interethnic relations during the early 1920s to the evanescent one-night stands between Japanese geisha and their customers, in which communication was unnecessary to enjoy the carnal pleasures of such fraternizations. Continuing these metaphorical allusions to sexual intimacy, he portrayed the ideal relationship between Japanese and Koreans as husband and wife, a bond of conjugality that would also produce a peaceful household. However, in order to imbue their relationships with what he called "spiritual kindness," Im advocated the need to transcend the imperfect medium of translation and, instead, speak one another's languages. Although he praised the governor-general for instituting a new policy whereby Japanese police officers learned basic Korean, Im pressed officials to extend this policy to expatriates by establishing Korean-language classes in Japanese schools.[48] Attributing interethnic conflicts to settlers' imprudent attitudes toward Koreans' language and manners, Im challenged the value-free connotations of *yobo* posited by most Japanese writers. Instead, he pointedly wrote of the term's *stinking* contempt (*keibetsuteki akui*) for Koreans, as commonly expressed in phrases such as "For you *yobo* [who are supposed to be compliant], you certainly are audacious!" (*Yobo no kuse ni namaiki*) and "You *yobo*s are no good!" (*Yobo wa dame*). In concluding his critique of *naisen yūwa,* Im reinvoked the official ideology of assimilation, with its dogmatic assertion that all subjects equally enjoyed the beneficent gaze of the emperor. In particular, he called on the Government-General to make good on its post-1919 promise to eliminate discrimination against Koreans, who, he lamented, remained an alien and subordinated ethnic group within the Japanese Empire.

That expatriates continued to discriminate against Koreans as *yobo*s during the early 1920s is also borne out by the literature of this period. Even short stories written by Japanese authors with strong connections to Korea made specific references to the unnerving effect of this racializing epithet. Take, for example, Nakajima Atsushi's "Landscape with Patrolman: A Sketch from 1923."[49] In this revealing story about interethnic and class relations in the colonial situation, Nakajima uses the critical viewpoint of Cho Kyoyŏng—a Korean patrolman and one of thousands of young colonized men subordinated to their Japanese overlords as "native informants." While on the train, Cho observed a quarrel between what Nakajima describes as "a shabbily dressed Japanese woman," a likely reference to a lower-class settler, and "a young student who was wearing white Korean clothes."[50] The Japanese woman berated the "assimilating" student (who had close connections to the Korean school system), with the epithet *yobo* as she tried to offer him a seat on the train. Unaware of the demeaning nature of the term, the Japanese woman claimed that by affixing the Japanese suffix *san* (mister), she had in fact paid him due respect and begged this "*Yobo*-san," as she repeated, to have a seat, to no avail.[51] Nakajima describes the ensuing confrontation, conducted in muted protest, as follows: "Realizing there was no point in arguing with this ignorant woman, the young man fell silent and glared at her." Forced to observe such deplorable scenes of discrimination, Cho quickly sensed the powerlessness of the student's nonverbal form of resistance, causing the former to feel a deep sense of disquiet. Unable to overcome his despair, the Korean patrolman was resigned to ponder the following set of disconcerting questions about the colonial situation: "Why did this young man get caught in such a quarrel? And why did this woman who protested her innocence take such pride in the fact that she was an outsider? And why did one always have to feel ashamed of who one was?"

Before he could answer, Cho reflected on yet another troubling incident involving a highly "assimilated" Korean subject and the offensive term *yobo.* The incident occurred when a Japanese teenage boy "wearing dirty clothes," a likely reference to his lower-class status within the expatriate community, assaulted the only Korean running for a position in the Seoul metropolitan assembly. Even though he spoke in fluent Japanese to his fellow assemblymen and had once served as a member of the local chamber of commerce, the settler boy interrupted the Korean representative by shouting, "Shut up, you pretentious *yobo!*" Undeterred in his efforts to capitalize on the benefits of having acquired the outward markers of an assimilated subject, the Korean assemblyman retorted, "We have all heard a most unfortunate word uttered. However, come what may, I am still one who firmly believes that all of us belong to the glorious Japanese people." In contrast to the assemblyman's optimism, patrolman Cho, once again, silently registered his indignation at the discriminatory underside of assimilation and the unlikely possibility that Koreans would ever reap the benefits of "belonging to the glorious Japanese people." Recollecting the rude teenage settler and the upstanding Korean gentleman, all this colonized patrolman could think of was the dilemma he faced in working for a repressive regime in order to financially support his wife and only child waiting for him at home.

Although reports from the early 1920s suggest that settlers such as the shabbily dressed Japanese woman and the teenage boy wearing dirty clothes failed to heed the wishes of discontented Koreans such as the young student and the Japanese-speaking assemblyman, colonized critics continued to carve out a discursive space within the colonial press to aggressively challenge the discriminatory nature of *naisen yūwa.*[52] For example, Kim Chŏngch'ŏn, a Korean youth and frequent contributor to *Chōsen kōron,* went so far as to call assimilation a "failed policy." In an article from late 1923, Kim wrote that *naisen yūwa,* although theoretically possible, was like mixing water and oil insofar as everyday interactions between individual Japanese and Koreans remained remarkably coarse. He attributed the main cause for the estranged nature of interethnic relations to Japanese settlers' own derision of Koreans, charging the colonial regime of failing to carry out its officially stated aim of improving the lives of Koreans. Rather than accept the superiority of Japanese settlers based on their economic and political power, Kim urged expatriates to reflect deeply on their own personal shortcomings, particularly those that continued to negatively affect the lives of the colonized population. The sentiments he singled out as requiring immediate reform included expatriates' shallow feelings of obligation, quickness to emotional ups and downs, penchant for flattery, tendency toward impatience, and overemphasis on outer appearances. Redirecting a critical gaze back onto Japanese settlers, Kim excoriated them for lacking a moral mind (J. *dōtokushin,* K. *todŏksim*), a Confucian-inflected term used to counter criticisms from Japanese pundits that Koreans lacked a commitment to civic morality (J. *kōtokushin,* K. *kongdŏksim*).[53] Kim concluded his liberal critique by revealing that after over twenty years of interacting with Japanese settlers he had yet to experience a case of their "true kindness." Rather than consent to the official set of sensibilities advanced by Japanese proponents of assimilation, Kim argued that expatriates needed to display greater compassion toward the colonized population if *naisen yūwa* were ever to succeed.[54]

If Kim Chŏngch'ŏn expressed some hope that settlers could set assimilation on a healthier course, Kim Il, another Korean author writing in late 1924, voiced serious doubts about whether this project could ever take root given an inherently partial colonial state's ongoing discrimination against Koreans and the *yobo*-izing practices of Japanese expatriates.[55] He underscored the emptiness of *naisen yūwa* as an oft-repeated slogan that officials had failed to implement. Not one to resort to polite euphemisms, Kim chastised the Government-General for continuing to disenfranchise Koreans, a foolish policy that he argued belied its humanitarian promises to implement a more egalitarian system of rule. To his mind, however, the discriminatory attitudes of Japanese settlers constituted a more significant obstacle to the eventual possibility of "harmonizing Japanese and Koreans."

To illustrate his point, he offered a personal anecdote of a disturbing incident he witnessed in the fall of 1924. This incident, Kim reminded his readers, coincided with the fourth anniversary of a highly symbolic event in the history of assimilation, the marriage of the Korean Prince Yi Ŭn (1897–1970) to the Japanese Princess Nashimotonomiya Masako (1901–1989).[56] While walking in the settler-populated neighborhoods of Seoul, he encountered a group of Japanese junior high school students who were bullying two Korean junior high school students for bumping into them as they walked down the narrow thoroughfare of Honmachi Street.[57] Just as Kim tried to console the tearful Korean students, one of the Japanese students aggressively approached him and said, "You idiot, are you blind?" Unwilling to countenance this insult, an incensed Kim retorted, only to be verbally attacked by the students, who invited him to a fight. Reiterating the discriminatory use of *yobo* criticized by Im three years earlier, the belligerent students exclaimed, "For you *yobo,* you certainly say audacious things. Shut up and come over here!" According to Kim, these Japanese youngsters had apparently learned this racial epithet from their schoolteachers, who casually used it in front of students to denigrate Koreans, a habit he deplored as the unfortunate reality of everyday life in the colony. Kim even went so far as to attribute the various misunderstandings continuing to vex interethnic relations to the Japanese misuse of this one word. Challenging earlier sentiments of affective racism expressed by Japanese writers, Kim argued that the true harmonization of Koreans and Japanese could only emerge if settlers avoided deep-rooted tendencies to *yobo*-ize the colonized and instead made greater efforts to understand what he called the "real Korea" and the "real Koreans"—terms used to promote their own totalizing program of "cultural nationalism." In this way, Kim used the liberal language and ideology of *naisen yūwa* to counter the discriminatory underside of assimilation. In doing so, he placed an equal burden on Japanese settlers to dispel Koreans' doubts about the seeming disadvantages of joining an imperial family whose "elder brothers" failed in their Confucian duties to lead and teach their "younger siblings" the cultural sensibilities that might have led to greater political and economic empowerment. It was this empowering function of the colonized state that cultural nationalists such as Kim hoped to eventually wrest away from Japanese officials in their own efforts to become the legitimate custodians of underclass Koreans.

Conclusion

The *yobo*-ization of Koreans by expatriates in the heart of the Japanese settlement, a scene echoing the first chapter of Usuda's 1908 *Yoboki,* was a recurring manifestation of what I have described as affective racism. As discussed above, the official ideology of assimilation prioritized the differential incorporation of Koreans, whose cultural practices settlers were entrusted to transform into those deemed appropriately "Japanese." However, these expatriates, not always reliable supporters of the colonial state or exemplary models of imperial subjects, often resorted to racializing the latter as reproachable *yobo*s—a vulgar tactic of colonial violence that Korean elites vehemently opposed in the Japanese press. As Japanese responses to these critiques suggest, even colonialists who condoned the ongoing use of *yobo* as a denigrating epithet could not afford to completely reject the colonized population. As an enticement for greater inclusion in the emperor-centered community, these pundits urged unassimilated Koreans to become active agents in transforming their cultural sensibilities to be more like their idealized Japanese counterparts. Assimilation thus served to judge Koreans according to standards that posited degrees of sameness along a continuum at whose endpoint stood a unified, but unequal, community of imperial subjects. Meanwhile, settlers continued in their blatant use of such derogatory terms as *yobo,* even toward colonized elites who had adopted "Japanese" sensibilities as desired by proponents of assimilation. Such contradictory practices suggest that some, if not many, expatriates refused to assess Koreans' cultural sensibilities according to the amorphous norms that made this insidious strategy of rule all the more potent.

To be sure, the arbitrary misuse of the term *yobo* most negatively affected colonized Koreans, but the sway of this demeaning epithet also had the effect of racializing Japanese settlers deemed similarly unassimilated. As discussed above, the considerable presence of lower-class expatriates in early colonial Korea meant that many Japanese settlers struggled to embody the bourgeois sensibilities expected of idealized subjects. That these working-class expatriates failed to insulate themselves from the allegedly "contagious" practices of nearby Korean residents—a perception expressed so anxiously by the white-collar participants of the *yobo*-ization debate—made the official project of assimilating Koreans through these "imperfect" settlers all the more difficult. In this politicized context, unsavory practices common to the lower classes of Meiji Japan—public urination, for example—became racialized characteristics of their alleged Koreanization in the colonial situation. In this racializing reversal, Japanese pundits discerned the "wayward" state of their own settlers from the same set of cultural sensibilities that "uncivilized" Koreans were being urged to abandon as part of their own incorporation into a multiethnic empire. Meanwhile, *yobo*-ized expatriates continued to use their ethnic privilege as colonizers to prevent assimilated Koreans from occupying a more significant place in this hierarchical community.

These contradictions of Japanese rule came to a head in March 1919 when thousands of Koreans joined the call for national independence as a way to escape the *yobo*-izing underside of assimilation. Rejecting their unexpected demands for sovereignty, officials instead implemented a renewed policy of assimilation aimed at "harmonizing Japanese and Koreans." This makeshift strategy called on the leaders of both ethnic groups to more fully support the Government-General's efforts to strengthen the basis of colonial rule while reminding Japanese settlers in particular of the pernicious effects of affective racism. Cognizant of the political opening created by the March 1st Movement, a new coterie of Korean critics took advantage of this opportunity to further challenge the inherent contradictions between the ongoing demands of cultural incorporation and the troubling reality of their nation's political and economic disenfranchisement. Through liberal tactics associated with cultural nationalism, these bourgeois critics urged the colonial state to institute measures that would reduce instances of affective racism, including better acquainting expatriates with Korean customs. Rejecting ethnocentric expectations that their compatriots unilaterally Japanize their sensibilities, Korean writers used the post-1919 logic of *naisen yūwa* to demand that settlers respect the positive attributes of Koreans' culture without insensitively *yobo*-izing them. In this way, they devised a defensive strategy to deflect the homogenizing impulses of assimilation and thereby establish a more habitable place for colonized Koreans within an empire that continued to relegate them to the position of second-class citizens.

As in other modern empires, questions surrounding the embodiment of cultural sensibilities—the class- and gender-specific criteria constituting the amorphous target known as the Yamato spirit—were central both to the strategies of Japanese rule and to their contestations by expatriate settlers and colonized Koreans. Affective racism is the term that captures both the most explosive, if understudied, nuances of Japanese assimilation as lived experience as well as the connections of Japanese assimilation to other imperial formations. To be sure, the somatic markers of biological race played a far less important role in colonial

Korea than in other Euro-American empires where differential incorporation could depend on such visible criteria as skin color. The racialization of a subordinate group by a more dominant group can, of course, occur in situations in which the two groups share a similar physiognomy. In fact, this phenomenon often thrives in situations of racial proximity, especially when officials sanction physiognomic similarities as an underlying justification for and a primary strategy of imperial control. In colonial Korea, for example, ideologues attempted to articulate assimilation as a unique, monoracial extension of the Japanese family—a project they actively contrasted with the allegedly rapacious policies of their Euro-American competitors. Although the frequent recurrence of affective racism belied their convictions of Pan-Asian superiority, biological similarities placed a heavy burden on Japanese officials—a burden perhaps even heavier than their Western counterparts encountered—to mark, manage, and police the less visible cultural sensibilities that functioned as the amorphous and mutable criteria used to differentially incorporate Koreans into Japan's emperor-centered community. This politicized context of racial proximity also served as the uneven terrain from which cultural nationalists waged their critiques of assimilation, calling on Japanese authorities to make good on their promise of ensuring Korean welfare.

Revealing the comparative and transnational connections animating these hidden histories of belonging may be one effective method of making visible the imperial formations that remain overshadowed by, but were also intimately connected to, those of continental Europe and North America. To provide but one concluding example of these global connections, let us return to the aforementioned Kim Il's critique of assimilation in late 1924. When Kim upbraided settlers' continued abuse of the Korean term *yŏbo,* he spoke not only of this recurring manifestation of affective racism as an impediment to the "harmonization of Japanese and Koreans." Going beyond Japan's empire in Korea, Kim also leveled his critique of Japanese rule with direct reference to the racist practices of another imperial power, the United States. As he took pains to emphasize, the U.S. Congress had recently passed legislation (the 1924 Johnson-Reed Act) to exclude Asian immigrants from entering that white-dominated nation-state.[58] To be sure, this reference, part of an official archive sanctioned by the colonial state, lent needed support to an ideology aimed at portraying colonial Korea as an integrated part of a Pan-Asian community and one distinct from the xenophobic practices of its Euro-American counterparts. However, on another level, Kim's comparative framing of Japanese assimilation in colonial Korea reveals the "circuits of knowledge production that traversed imperial borders."[59]

Although critical scholars of colonial studies have increasingly invoked this important point, they have not always pursued it with the same vigor in regions such as East Asia, where the United States (and the Soviet Union) has dominated postwar history. Nor have scholars of East Asia (myself included) made the efforts necessary to reintegrate "area studies" into global processes that linked the modern world, including imperialism. Given these conditions, the time has finally come to more fully examine the uneven "grids of intelligibility" informing scholarly traditions that have concealed important connections between the Japanese Empire and its Euro-American counterparts. Only with such knowledge can the pressing issues of East Asia's postcolonial present be understood in all their transnational and racialized complicities.

Notes

1. On cultural racism in contemporary France, see Etienne Balibar, "Is There Neo-racism?," in *Race, Nation, Class: Ambiguous Identities*, Etienne Balibar and Immanuel Wallerstein (London: Verso, 1991). For its connection to modern imperialism, see Ann Laura Stoler, *Carnal Knowledge and Imperial Power* (Berkeley: University of California Press, 2002).

2. On the French case, see, for example, Raymond F. Betts, *Assimilation and Association in French Colonial Theory, 1890–1914* (Lincoln: University of Nebraska Press, 2005).

3. For studies addressing these complex connections, see Jun Uchida, *Brokers of Empire: Japanese Settler Colonialism in Korea, 1876–1945* (Cambridge, MA: Harvard University Press, 2011); Mark E. Caprio, *Japanese Assimilation Policies in Colonial Korea, 1910–1945* (Seattle: University of Washington Press, 2009); Nicole Leah Cohen, "Children of Empire: Growing up Japanese in Colonial Korea, 1876–1945" (PhD diss., Columbia University, 2006); and Helen Jeesung Lee, "Popular Media and the Racialization of Koreans under Occupation" (PhD diss., University of California, Irvine, 2003).

4. Dipesh Chakrabarty, *Provincializing Europe: Postcolonial Thought and Historical Difference* (Princeton, NJ: Princeton University Press, 2000).

5. See Ann Laura Stoler, "Racial Histories and Their Regimes of Truth," *Political Power and Social Theory* 11 (1997): 183–206.

6. Takashi Fujitani has described this early phenomenon as "vulgar racism," which he distinguishes from the emergence of "polite racism" during the Asia-Pacific War. See his *Race under Fire: Koreans as Japanese and Japanese as Americans in WWII* (Berkeley: University of California Press, 2011). A shorter version appears as "Right to Kill, Right to Make Live: Koreans as Japanese and Japanese as Americans during WWII," *Representations* 99 (Summer 2007): 13–39.

7. Oguma Eiji, *Tan'itsu minzoku shinwa no kigen: "Nihonjin" no jigazōno keifu* (The origins of the myth of ethnic homogeneity: The genealogy of "Japanese" self-images) (Tokyo: Shin'yōsha, 1995), 376–379, 387–388.

8. Hwang Munhwan, "Chosŏn sidae ŏngan charyo ŭi pubukan hoch'ing kwa hwagye" (Address terms and speech levels between spouses in vernacular letters from the Chosŏn period), *Changsŏgak* 17 (June 2007): 121–139. In the postcolonial era (1945–present), the term *yŏbo* also came to be used as a term of endearment between couples alongside derogatory usages to refer to sex workers.

9. For a study of class distinctions in the colonial encounter of Japanese literary expressions, see Helen J. S. Lee, "Writing Colonial Relations of Everyday Life in Senryu," *positions* 16, no. 3 (2008): 601–628.

10. Women constituted 30–40 percent of Japanese settlers until the turn of the century, after which time their presence increased to approximately 45 percent. Uchida, *Brokers of Empire*, 66.

11. Peter Duus, *The Abacus and the Sword: The Japanese Penetration of Korea, 1895–1910* (Berkeley: University of California Press, 1995), 289–292. For a breakdown of settlers by occupation as of 1906 and 1907, see ibid., 335–337. According to occupational statistics from 1910, "laborers" (6 percent), "geisha, waitresses" (2 percent), and the "unemployed" (6 percent) composed 14 percent of the settler population. If one considers the ambiguous category of "miscellaneous" workers (23 percent), the percentage of lower-class settlers rises to more than one-third of expatriate Japanese. See Uchida, *Brokers of Empire*, 67.

12. For a discussion of legal measures aimed at controlling unruly expatriate settlers, see Lee Chongmin, "Keihanzai no torishimari hōrei ni miru minshū tōsei: Chōsen no bāi o chūshin ni" (Control of the populace as seen through the legal regulation of petty crimes: The case of Korea), in *Shokuminchi teikoku nihon no hōteki kōzō* (The legal structure of imperial Japan in its colonies), ed. Asano Toyomi and Matsuda Toshihiko (Tokyo: Shinsansha, 2004), 319–352.

13. For more on the early history of Japanese emigration to Korea, see Duus, *Abacus and the Sword*, 289–323; Uchida, *Brokers of Empire*, 35–95; and Kimura Kenji, *Zaichō nihonjin no shakaishi* (A social history of Japanese settlers in Korea) (Tokyo: Miraisha, 1989), 10–66.

14. Todd A. Henry, "Sanitizing Empire: Japanese Colonial Articulations of Korean Otherness and the Construction of Early Colonial Seoul, 1905–19," *Journal of Asian Studies* 64, no. 3 (2005): 639–675.

15. The Seoul-based publishing house, Nikkan shobō, released all three texts in Korea, while its metropolitan counterpart, Hakubunkan, distributed copies in the home islands. On the latter, see Giles Richter, "Entrepreneurship and Culture: The Hakubunkan Publishing Empire in Meiji Japan," in *New Directions in the Study of Meiji Japan*, ed. Helen Hardacre and Adam L. Kern (Leiden, Netherlands: Brill, 1997), 590–602.

16. Usuda Zan'un, *Yoboki* (Records of Koreanness) (Seoul: Nikkan shobō, 1908).

17. Okita had already established this Japanese portrait of colonized Korean men (Henry, "Sanitizing Empire," 646–649). On the deplorable position of the *yangban* in Korean Nationalist discourse of the same period, see Andre Schmid, *Korea between Empires, 1895–1910* (New York: Columbia University Press, 2000), 121–129.

18. In 1893, the Japanese author Matsubara Iwagorō published a similar work titled *Saiankokuno Tōkyō* (In darkest Tokyo). Four years later, an English version appeared as *In Darkest Tokyo: Sketches of Humble Life in the Capital of Japan* (Yokohama, Japan: Eastern World Publication Office, 1897). For an exegesis of this text, see Maeda Ai, *Text and the City: Essays on Japanese Modernity* (Durham, NC: Duke University Press, 2004), 21–64.

19. Usuda Zan'un, *Ankoku naru Chōsen* (Dark Korea) (Seoul: Nikkan shobō, 1908), 100–115.

20. In 1909, this Seoul-based journal had a circulation of 15,600 in Korea (7,000 in the capital alone), 7,200 in Japan, 840 in Taiwan, and 360 in China. Barbara Brooks, "Reading the Japanese Colonial Archive: Gender and Bourgeois Civility in Korea and Manchuria before 1932," in *Gendering Modern Japanese History*, ed. Barbara Molony and Kathleen Uno (Cambridge, MA: Harvard University Press, 2005), 298. The following discussion is based on Usuda Zan'un and Torigoe Seishi, *Chōsen manga* (Korean caricatures) (Seoul: Nikkan shobō, 1909).

21. I am indebted to Michael Bourdaghs for this observation.

22. Sŏk later became a capitalist financier, founding a number of important banks and companies. Recognizing his talents, the colonial government appointed him to a number of important political positions, including the governor of the South Ch'ungch'ŏng and the South Chŏlla provinces. A full biography of Sŏk, now considered a pro-Japanese collaborator by the South Korean government, can be found at the History Liberation Campaign Center (Yŏksa Kwangbok Undong Ponbu) website, accessed August 24, 2012, www.bluecabin.com.ne.kr/split99/sjh1166.htm. The following discussion is based on Sŏk's "'Yobo' to iu go ni tsukite" (On the word *yobo*), *Chōsen oyobi manshū* (Korea and Manchuria) 63 (November 15, 1912): 14–15.

23. Kyong-hee Choi, *Beneath the Vermillion Ink: Japanese Colonial Censorship and the Making of Modern Korean Literature* (Ithaca, NY: Cornell University Press, forthcoming).

24. A translation of this treaty appears online: "Japan-Korea Annexation Treaty," accessed October 4, 2012, en.wikisource.org/wiki/Japan-Korea Annexation Treaty.

25. On this Foucault-inspired notion, see David Scott, "Colonial Governmentality," *Social Text* 43 (1995): 191–220.

26. "Yobo to yobaru koto yorokobazaru Chōsenjin ni kigosu" (Communicating with Koreans who dislike being called *yobos*), *Chōsen oyobi manshū* 63 (November 15, 1912): 2–4. For another self-defensive rationale for the continued Japanese use of *yobo* toward Koreans, see Asami Rintarō's "Chōsen no ryūkōgo" (Fashionable words in colonial Korea), *Chōsen kōron* (Korea digest) 1, no. 9 (1913): 67–68. On humanism in one colonial guise, see Gary Wilder, *The French Imperial Nation-State: Negritude and Colonial Humanism between the Two World Wars* (Chicago: University of Chicago Press, 2005).

27. Although uncommon, some concerned Japanese with close connections to Koreans, such as the P'yŏngyang-based Protestant clergyman Kurihara Yōtarō, pointed out what he called the "irony" between Koreans as new imperial subjects and the slave-like derision by their Japanese masters. For Kurihara's critique, see "Kokuminteki shirenchi toshite no Chōsen" (Korea as a place of national trials), *Shinjin* (New man) 15, no. 10 (1914): 62–63. I thank Emily Anderson for bringing this material to my attention.

28. For more on elite settler opposition to the early colonial state, see Uchida, *Brokers of Empire*, 96–139.

29. Unless otherwise noted, the following discussion is based on "Chōsenjin yori mitaru Nissen dōkakan" (A view of Japanese-Korean assimilation as seen by a Korean), *Chōsen oyobi manshū* 66 (January 1, 1913): 26–30.

30. Unlike most European contexts in which colonizing men tended to engage in intimate relations with colonized women, it was more common in colonial East Asia for Japanese women to marry Korean men, particularly well-educated ones living in cities. Between 1912 and 1918, the average number of Japanese men who married Korean women was approximately forty-five, as compared to sixty Korean men who married Japanese wives. As these statistics suggest, the total number of interethnic marriages remained relatively low at fewer than 1 in 180,000 for Koreans and just 1 in 5,000 for Japanese. "Naisenjin tsūkon no jōtai ika" (Conditions of Japanese-Korean common law marriages), *Chōsen oyobi manshū* 125 (November 1, 1917): 77–83; and Nanba Kōsei, "Tōkei ni arawareru naisen dōka no katei" (The households of Japanese-Korean assimilation as seen through statistics), *Keijō nippō* (Daily Seoul), July 16, 1919. For a more specific discussion of both cases of cross-ethnic marriages, see Tenraisei, "Naisen kekkonsha to sono katei" (Japanese-Korean marriages and their families), *Chōsen oyobi manshū* 125 (November 1, 1917): 84–87.

31. See, for example, "Shumika no setsubi" (Institutions promoting taste) and "Ika ni seba shumika shiuruka?" (What to do to promote taste?), *Chōsen oyobi manshū* 49 (March 1, 1912): 6–7, 45–58. For more on conceptions of taste in the Japanese metropole, see Jordan Sand, *House and Home in Modern Japan: Architecture, Domestic Space, and Bourgeois Culture, 1880–1930* (Cambridge, MA: Harvard University Press, 2003), 95–96, 99.

32. For a discussion of these nationalizing initiatives, see Carol Gluck, *Japan's Modern Myths: Ideology in the Late Meiji Period* (Princeton, NJ: Princeton University Press, 1985); and Takashi Fujitani, *Splendid Monarchy: Power and Pageantry in Modern Japan* (Berkeley: University of California Press, 1996).

33. One scholar estimates that more than 60 percent of Koreans living in cities (versus 40 percent living in the countryside) in the 1920s fell within the broad category of "the poor," and an equal percentage of individuals inhabiting Seoul could not even afford to pay their

taxes. Son Chŏngmok, *Ilche kangjŏmgi tosi sahoesang yŏn'gu* (Facets of urban society during the Japanese occupation period) (Seoul: Iljisa, 1996), 106.

34. Although Japanese settlers made up no more than 3 percent of the total population of colonial Korea, approximately 70 percent of them resided in cities. The Japanese population of Seoul never exceeded 30 percent and dropped to less than 17 percent during the 1940s (partly owing to the city's expansion into the surrounding areas). Pusan was the only city where the Japanese population came close to matching the Korean one. For a more detailed study on population changes, see Kim T'aehwan, "Ilche sidae ŭi tosihwa" (Urbanization during the colonial period), in *Ilche singmin t'ongch'i wa sahoe kujo ŭi pyŏnhwa* (Japanese colonial rule and changes in social structures), ed. Yi Hyŏnjae (Seongnam, South Korea: Han'guk chŏngsin munhwa yŏn'guwŏn, 1990), 251–298.

35. Korean scholars often suggest the Ch'ŏnggye Stream as dividing the city's northern and southern districts, although usually without discussing the flow of people, goods, and culture that permeated this ethnic divide. See, for example, Son, *Ilche kangjŏmgi tosi sahoesang yŏn'gu*, 360–384. For a critique of this model, see Kim Chong'gŭn, "Signmin tosi Kyŏngsŏng ijung tosiron e taehan pip'anjŏk koch'al" (A critical analysis of the theory of a divided city in colonial Seoul), *Sŏulhak yŏn'gu* (Seoul studies) 38 (February 2010): 1–68.

36. For a discussion of this issue during the late protectorate period, see "Zaichō nihonjin shakai: Shinkei chūsu o kaku" (Japanese settler society in Korea: Lack of a spiritual spine), *Keijō shimpō* (Daily Seoul), March 24, 1909; and "Zaikan hōjin to shumi" (Japanese in Korea and taste), *Chōsen* (Korea) 5 (January 1, 1910): 6–7.

37. "Seiketsu to dōka (jō)" (Cleanliness and assimilation [part 1]), *Chōsen shinbun* (Korean daily), May 14, 1912.

38. "Naisenjin no dōka (2): Shin-nihon damashi o tsukure" (Assimilating Japanese and Koreans [part 2]: Create a new Japanese spirit), *Keijō nippō*, October 17, 1916.

39. The following discussion is based on "Kanmin no koe o atsumete" (Opinions gathered from the government and the people) and "Yoboka ni tsuite" (On [the question of] *yobo*-ization), *Chōsen oyobi manshū* 115 (January 1, 1917): 60–62, 67–68. For an extended discussion on this debate, see "Chōsenkaron: Waga naichijin o imashimu" (The Koreanization thesis: A warning to our Japanese brethren), *Chōsen oyobi manshū* 130 (April 1, 1918): 2–8.

40. On the development of the new middle class in the metropole, see David R. Ambaras, "Social Knowledge, Cultural Capital, and the New Middle Class in Japan, 1895–1912," *Journal of Japanese Studies* 24, no. 1 (1998): 1–33.

41. Japanese officials frequently reprimanded lower-class Koreans, the majority of the population, for failing to pay taxes and other public dues.

42. Frank Baldwin, "Participatory Anti-imperialism: The 1919 Independence Movement," *Journal of Korean Studies* 1 (1979): 123–162.

43. On the origins and development of this slogan, see Kwŏn T'aeŏk, "1920–30 nyŏndae ilche tonghwa chŏngch'aengnon" (Policy debates on colonial assimilation during the 1920s and 1930s), in *Hanguk kŭndae sahoe wa munhwa III: 1920–1930 nyŏndae 'singminjijŏk kŭndae wa hangukin ŭi taeŭng* (Modern Korean society and culture III: Colonial modernity and Koreans' responses during the 1920s and 1930s) (Seoul: Soul taehakkyo ch'ulp'anbu, 2007), 7–17; and Ch'oe Yuri, *Ilche malgi singminji chibae chŏngch'aek yŏn'gu* (Studies on policies of rule in late colonial Korea) (Seoul: Kukhak charyowŏn, 1997), 17–27.

44. Michael Robinson, *Cultural Nationalism in Colonial Korea, 1920–25* (Seattle: University of Washington Press, 1989).

45. The author of one concerned report cited settlers' blatant use of *yobo* as the principal cause for the grievances that led to the March 1st Movement. "Chōsen seiji o ika ni isshin subekika" (How to renew Korean politics), *Chōsen oyobi manshū* 144 (June 1, 1919): 3. The following

discussion is based on "Yobo to iu kotoba" (On the word *yobo*), *Chōsen oyobi manshū* 142 (April 1, 1919): 63.

46. For another account exhorting youngsters, the lower classes, and women to undertake the mission of assimilating Koreans, see "Naichijin wa ika ni Chōsenjin ni taisen to suru ka" (How should Japanese approach Koreans?), *Chōsen oyobi manshū* 144 (June 1, 1919): 10–11.

47. The following discussion is based on Im Iksang, "Naisen yūwa ni taisuru kanken" (My point of view on the harmonization of Japanese and Koreans), *Chōsen kōron* 9, no. 10 (1921): 69–71.

48. For more on this project, see Yamada Kanto, "Nihonjin keisatsukan ni taisuru Chōsengo shōreisaku" (The policy for encouraging Japanese police officers to learn Korean), *Chōsenshi kenkyūkai ronbunshū* (Journal of the Korean History Research Association) 30 (October 2000): 123–149.

49. See Nakajima Atsushi, "Landscape with Patrolman: A Sketch from 1923," trans. Robert Tierney, 1–11, accessed October 4, 2012, ceas.uchicago.edu/japanese/R.Tierney, Nakajima%20 Landscape%20 with% 20Patrolman.pdf. This piece first appeared in 1929 in *Kyōiku zasshi,* the literary magazine of the Tokyo First Higher School. For the original Japanese text, see *Nakajima Atsushi zenshū* (The complete works of Nakajima Atsushi), vol. 2 (Tokyo: Chikuma shobō, 2001), 68–81. For a short introduction to Nakajima and his short stories related to the Japanese empire, see ceas.uchicago.edu/japanese/R.Tierney.Final%20Introduction.pdf, accessed October 4, 2012. The term *yobo* also appeared in some Korean literature of the period, including Yŏm Sangsŏp's autobiographical story "Mansejŏn" (On the eve of the uprising, 1924). For an English translation, see Sunyoung Park, *On the Eve of the Uprising and Other Stories from Colonial Korea* (Ithaca, NY: Cornell University, 2010), 5–114.

50. For more on the role played by Koreans in the Japanese colonial police force, see Chang Sin, "Chosŏn ch'ongdokbu ŭi kyŏngch'al insa wa Chosŏnin kyŏngch'al" (The Government-General's appointment of policemen and Korean officers), *Yŏksa munje yŏn'gu* (Journal of Korean historical studies) 22 (2009): 145–183; and Yi Sang'ŭi, "Ilcheha Chosŏn kyŏngch'al ŭi tŭkjing kwa imiji" (Characteristics and images of Korean police officers under Japanese rule), *Yŏksa kyoyuk* (Journal of historical education) 115 (2010): 165–198.

51. On the double-edged use of *yobo*-san and other varieties of this derogatory term, see Kwŏn Sŏkyŏng, "'Yobo' to iu besshō" (The derogatory term *yobo*), *Hokkaidō daigaku bungaku kenkyū kiyō* (Literary studies bulletin of Hokkaidō University) 132 (2010): 139–172.

52. So rampant was this discriminatory word during the 1920s that members of the newly established Dōminkai, a joint Japanese-Korean organization aimed at promoting "ethnic harmony," had to circulate thousands of handbills throughout the peninsula, calling on Japanese residents to refrain from using *yobo* as a derogatory pronoun for Koreans. Uchida, *Brokers of Empire,* 171.

53. On Japanese accusations of Koreans' lack of civic morality as regards their alleged misuse of public facilities, see Henry, "Sanitizing Empire," 657–658.

54. "Naisen dōkasaku to gojin no shuchō" (The policy of Japanese-Korean assimilation and our contention), *Chōsen kōron* 11, no. 9 (1923): 62–66. Kim also used the metaphor of relations between the members of a family to describe the ideal bonds between Japanese and Koreans.

55. The following discussion is based on Kim Il, "Zaichō naichijin no hansei o unagasu" (Urging Japanese settlers in Korea to reflect [on their behavior]), *Chōsen kōron* 12, no. 11 (1924): 84–85.

56. For more on this event, see Shinjō Michihiko, "Ōzoku o kaishita 'nihon' gainen no kashika to chūshōka: Ri Kon and Nashimotonomiya Masako to no ketsugi ni miru Chōsen tōchi" (The visualization and abstraction of the concept of "Japan" mediated by the royal family: The rule of Korea as seen through the wedding ceremony of Yi Ŭn and Nashimotonomiya Masako),

Kankoku gengo bunka kenkyū (Journal of Korean language and culture studies) 4 (June 2003): 1–25.

57. For a short story chronicling the interethnic politics of discrimination among school children in mid-1920s Korea, see Yuasa Katsuei's "Kannani," in *Kannani and Document of Flames: Two Japanese Colonial Novellas,* trans. Mark Driscoll (Durham, NC: Duke University Press, 2005), 37–98.

58. Kim, "Zaichō naichijin no hansei o unagasu," 84–85. For one institutionalized embodiment of this Pan-Asianist position, see Uchida's discussion of the Dōminkai in *Brokers of Empire,* 165–177.

59. Stoler, *Carnal Knowledge,* 210.

5 ◈ CHUL KIM

How Do Abject Bodies Respond?

Ethnographies of a Dispersed Empire

After receiving an appointment in 1915 as professor of human anatomy in the Keijō Medical College, Kubo Takeshi, a scholar with a doctorate in the same field, devoted his research efforts to the study of "racial anatomy" through analyzing the corpses of Koreans. His findings were published between 1915 and 1922 in twenty-three installments in the *Journal of the Chōsen Medical Association* under the title "Research Concerning the Racial Anatomy of Koreans." Kubo Takeshi's voluminous writings represent the earliest extant research into the physical anthropology of Koreans.[1]

This research, which seems to boast a strong scholarly tone, concluded:

> The weight of the skeletons of Koreans is heavier than that of Japanese. The muscular system of the Japanese is superior to that of Koreans. The skin and the subcutaneous fat of Koreans are comparatively larger. The digestive and respiratory organs of Koreans are considerably larger, but especially so in the case of the digestive organs. The circulatory organs and central nervous system of the Japanese are superior. This result is sensible when one considers the general living conditions and lifestyles of Koreans. The fact that Koreans are inactive owes to the weak growth of their muscular systems and the excess of subcutaneous fat. Furthermore, the fact that Koreans consume lots of food that is both coarse and difficult to digest causes me to think that their digestive organs are extremely well developed. The relative smallness of their central nervous systems and circulatory systems demonstrates that great defects exist in their intellectual faculties.[2]

I first aim to investigate how, following its adoption by the Japanese Empire, physical anthropology—which through cutting-edge science secured the animalistic image of Koreans as "sluggish in their actions, willing to eat any food whatsoever, and as having major intellectual deficiencies"—ultimately influenced colonial and imperial subjects' perception and understanding of Self and Other. In particular, with respect to the issue of race, I intend to discuss the perpetual fear and unease that existed between the Japanese colonists and the colonized people of Korea. Mechanisms of division, hierarchization, subsumption, and exclusion all served as fundamental conceptual tools in racial studies, an academic arena that sought to demonstrate the homogeneity of each race. Though it was the colonists who deployed these mechanisms, both the colonists and the colonized shared the tensions, unease, and fear thereby generated. I want to stress that this unease and fear presented a "hole" that destroyed the efforts of the ruling powers to establish a "safe society."[3]

The development of physical anthropology in Japan was used to objectify colonial Korean subjects. This racial outlook, broadly shared by both colonizers and colonized, did not so much strengthen and clarify the boundaries between Japanese and Koreans as intended as become instead a source of tension and unease that threatened to blur and efface those boundaries. In the analysis that follows I will examine the anxiety and friction produced by racist sensibilities as depicted in Yŏm Sangsŏp's novel *On the Eve of the Uprising* and Kim Saryang's novella *Pegasus.* These works of fiction not only elaborately portray the stripped-bare bodies of the colonized, continuously abjected under colonial power, but also capture the "hole" of insecurity and fear experienced by the very colonial power that observed and scrutinized those colonized.

Japanese Physical Anthropology and Koreans

Physical anthropology, which sought to determine the relative superiority of the races on the basis of physical traits such as height, skin, eye shape and color, nose and ear shape, skull size, the length and weight of bones, blood type, the size of internal organs, or the appearance of hair and pubic hair dominated Japanese anthropology after the Taishō period. Kubo Takeshi, who believed in a correlation between the size of the central nervous system or the circulatory organs and intellectual ability, presents one example of this trend. Kyoto Imperial University's Kiyono Kenji, one of prewar Japan's representative anthropologists, headed the Kiyono Anthropology Research Center, which in introducing a new statistical methodology made itself the center of Japanese anthropological research. At the same time, it was extremely influential in laying the scientific groundwork and setting the standard for anthropological research carried out by amateur natural historians such as Tsuboi Shōgorō, dubbed Japan's first anthropologist.[4]

It was not until the 1930s that Japanese research into the physical anthropology of colonized Koreans began in earnest. The efforts of Imamura Yutaka and Ueda Tsunekichi, who were both professors of anatomy at Keijō Imperial University and spearheaded research into the physical anthropology of Koreans (with help from their students), contributed greatly to the development of the discourse concerning the "specific characteristics" of Koreans and to the project of identifying how they differ from the Japanese. However, any science claiming that the differences between Koreans, Japanese, and Chinese were intrinsic and biological could not but encounter difficulties.[5] A ninety-four-page article titled "Research into the Physical Anthropology of the People of Chosŏn" was published in the *Journal of the Chōsen Medical Association* in 1934. It presented the results of a nationwide survey of body measurements of Koreans conducted between 1930 and 1932 by the anatomy research group led by Imamura and Ueda at Keijō Imperial University. The authors began the article by mentioning several problematic aspects of Kubo Takeshi's research: they noted that the Koreans Kubo measured were drawn from only a select few occupations, especially *kisaeng* (female entertainers) and soldiers, and that Kubo's survey was restricted to a few locales. They also commented that he failed to take "modern measurements" of living bodies.[6] The foregoing points demonstrate that Ueda and Imamura operated under the principle that it was better to have "more elaborate measurement and quantification of more people in more regions." This notion had not once been called into question in the whole history of physical anthropology. As a result, this extensive article was filled with innumerable data, elaborate and complex formulae, and "modern calculations" that the average person could not penetrate, all clearly meant to lend the article some sort of scientific gravitas and reliability.

In spite of this vast collection of data, the research team either failed to draw any conclusions or simply drew exceedingly bland ones, such as reiterating the fact that there were indeed "differences" in the measurements of the races. Weak results of this sort filled published articles at the time. For example, when Ueda argued in a 1935 article on the comparative measurements of Koreans and Japanese that "Kyoto skulls are very similar to those of Yongsan," "as a race, Koreans are very close to the Japanese," or "peoples with large bodies came from the Korean peninsula, crossed through Chūgoku, and established themselves in Kinki,"[7] one sees the end product of the extensive research efforts of Japanese anthropologists and anatomists since the Meiji era. For examples of such research, we can point to Kubo's work, to a survey on 2,980 Koreans conducted between 1912 and 1916 by Torii Ryūzō as part of the Chosŏn governor-general's "source material survey,"[8] or to measurements of Koreans and Manchurians taken by Ueda and the anatomy research group at Keijō Imperial University. However, the general conclusion that "no significant racial difference between the Japanese and the Koreans exists" seems to render their previous research efforts somewhat meaningless.

We should pay attention to the fact that Ueda always takes "the Japanese" as the basis of comparison when he claims that "as a race, Koreans are close to the Japanese." As is well known, the countless theories about "the native Japanese," as well as the dense research on and debates over the origins of modern Japanese people, all have the dual goal of creating a homogeneous grouping of "Japanese people" (or "the Japanese race") and proving the particularity (or even superiority) of that same group. Here, the important point is not to demonstrate whether racial difference exists between the Japanese and Korean or Chinese peoples; the point is rather this development itself—the operation of epistemological-political power in positioning someone as Other within a system of knowledge and discourse that constructed the homogeneity of the "Japanese." In other words, racism is a system of knowledge and discourse that establishes one group as the object of comparison and observation in order to construct the self-identity of another group. Through the effects of the forms of recognition and practice that arise from within this system, we have the invention of the other race. Accordingly, we should focus less on questions pertaining to the scientific validity of racial theory and more on the epistemological-political authority that forms its foundation, on the effects of such power, and on the very people who found themselves in the position of the racial Other.

Abject Bodies

One can easily see the affinities between physical anthropology and modern biopolitics, given the former's goal of observing and measuring as many human corpses as possible. Furthermore, physical anthropology functions as a modern ideology of oversight and discipline, considering its foundational belief in the existence of a reciprocal relationship between bodily traits and mental abilities and, consequently, its adoption of the body and mind as an object of control, renewal, transformation, and modification.

In a world characterized by racism with a scientific basis in physical anthropology, all social relationships are reduced to that between the viewer and the viewed. Power and authority emerge from the gaze. Camera lenses, devices for measuring human bodies, and anatomical tools take naked life and stare at it, measure it, penetrate it, probe it, and amputate it. The person who stands behind the lens remains unseen. The anatomist who stands above the dissecting table with scalpel in hand is also hidden behind a mask. Only those unsightly, disgusting, gruesome, and dangerous "abject bodies" are overtly visible. Bodies placed before a measuring device cannot speak. This goes without saying for corpses. However, even those abject bodies lined up for live measurements (usually under the auspices of the military or the police) are thought of as silent Others. Their bodies are collected, disassembled, measured, categorized, and in the end represented by the surveyors. How? And for that matter, why?

As discussed previously, anthropology, as a project that both classifies and hierarchically positions the races, generates the notion of group homogeneity within a nation-state and offers a narrative about the birth of an "us," of a "nation."[9] In order to establish such a narrative, a "them"—that is, the "barbarian" or the "uncivilized"—who stands in contrast to "us" must be discovered or invented. Tomiyama Ichirō eloquently explains how and by what necessity the Ainu—the "barbarians" of Hokkaidō—were constructed. According to him, the notion of the barbarian Ainu originated with a theory of Japanese cannibalism. In 1877 E. S. Morse, an American who strongly influenced Japanese anthropology, argued on the basis of results obtained from the excavation of a shell mound that cannibalistic practices existed in ancient Japan. In order to escape this awkward predicament, Japanese anthropology "discovered in the Ainu a stone-age people, presented 'cannibalistic races' as the 'uncivilized' other, and thereby began to construct the homogeneity of 'the Japanese.'" In other words, "'the uncivilized' of the Stone Age became objectified in the Ainu, who were thereafter branded with alterity and presented as 'uncivilized.' The Ainu, much like Stone Age remains, were seen as eternally uncivilized persons who had lost any of their own history," while "'the Japanese' were seen as the inheritors of the history of enlightenment."[10]

While the process of entrenching the Ainu in a Stone Age framework and thereby distinguishing between the Japanese race and other races followed geographical boundaries, other methodologies existed as well. For example, the *burakumin,* outcaste villagers who have endured discrimination since the Middle Ages, present a similar case. These people did not live in areas far removed from the Japanese mainland like Hokkaidō or Okinawa. Nevertheless, early Japanese anthropology categorized them as an alien race or as foreigners, thus pushing the *burakumin* outside the boundaries of "the Japanese." Sakano Tōru explains that "this categorization resulted from the process of re-organizing people under the category of 'national subject' [*kokumin*] after the end of the feudal order and the concomitant equalization of society." In other words, the real reason for differentiating outcastes was the "objection to having the people branded as 'Eta' under the previous status system included in the emerging category of 'us.'"[11]

The above examples demonstrate that the inclusions and exclusions the anthropological gaze generates do not necessarily follow geographical lines of division or colonial or imperial boundaries. To be sure, Japanese anthropology discovered many barbarian and distinct races in the colonized areas and regions subsumed into the expanding territory of the empire; however, social relationships inside the nation-state formed yet another racial boundary. Of course, this is in no way unique to Japanese anthropology. The birth of the new national people and the genesis of the displaced (*nanmin*) excluded from that group—those people who, according to Kim Hang, "assumed the role of disclosing the primitive accumulation of colonial rule, who at the root of colonial control formed the transcendental basis that made the existence of colonial domination possible"[12]—was a global phenomenon. The racial categorizations that anthropology creates are thus reflected in the emergence of the categories of the national subject and the refugee.

Who are these "displaced" that anthropology discovered or created? The most marginalized groups of society, including *kisaeng* (female entertainers or courtesans), vagrants, criminals, disfigured persons, persons of mixed blood, those with psychological maladies, and other similar groups, were all placed before the anthropologist's camera and measuring devices and under the anatomist's scalpel. To this, we can add the native and Aboriginal peoples of colonized territories. These people had been rejected, uprooted, and vomited out. I prefer to call them "the abject," following Julia Kristeva. However, these people were not simply excluded or thrown aside. These people were absolutely necessary for the "viewers" of society to establish their own homogeneity, and in fact their existence was an existence vomited out from the viewers themselves. However, in the same way that the repressed returns, so too do these abject appear before the viewer. How so?

As is commonly known, modern naturalist and realist art fully bloomed in the fertile soils of the imaginative power of modern natural science, especially anthropology. The theory of evolution forms the backdrop for this development. Humanity's new self-understanding—which is to say, anthropology's rise to prominence as a branch of study—would have been impossible without the theory of evolution.[13] In this world, the author served as the "anatomist of the soul and body" and "vividly described the animalistic nature, the physical strength, and the violent tendencies" of the "human-beast"—in short, he became a student of anthropology.[14]

The human-beast, to rephrase in Kristeva's terms, is an abject; someone who exists as an "in-between," someone with traits that are "ambiguous," and someone who represents a "composite" of various qualities.[15] Dirty, disgusting, creepy, and ghastly, the abject is neither a subject nor an "object" that, by standing opposite from me, ultimately guides me toward a world of homogeneity and meaning. As dirty and revolting as fecal matter, urine, pus, blood, or vomit, the abject forms the "border" of my existence. My body, as a living entity, can survive only up to the point at which such toxic substances are released. Only corpses exist on the other side of that border. I live only to the point that I release such filth; thereafter, in the moment at which nothing else remains, my body will have crossed that border. Therefore, "refuse and corpses show me what I permanently thrust aside in order to live."[16] Corpses are truly the outer limits of the abject.

As mentioned previously, the abject are not objects that lead me toward some sense of homogeneity. Rather, they "disturb identity, system, order."[17] Just as corpses reveal the limits of existence, the abject mark the furthest boundaries of the system. People with ambiguously defined identities must be put forward as beings that manifest the limits of identity. This is the case with criminals who, as their tricks become increasingly vulgar and cruel, assume the qualities of the human-beast and reveal the last and furthest frontier that the system must defend. As long as they exist, law and order will not only ceaselessly devolve into disorder, but the system's weakness will also ever be exposed. For order to exist, then, these nasty by-products must be continuously discharged.

Given the threat posed by the abject, it was imperative that they be located, defined, and ejected—those who stood on the border as the in-betweens, those who presented composites of characteristics from the inside and the outside, and those who shook the foundations of the imperial system and order and its sense of homogeneity. As a result, the indigenous inhabitants of colonies consistently found themselves branded as criminals (or at least, latent criminals) and subsequently were surveyed, observed, quarantined, and ultimately pushed past the boundaries of society and treated as if they were refuse. The fate of empires hangs on how these individuals are categorized and treated. The colonists focus their gaze relentlessly onto the colonized. The net of this gaze, stitched together from countless categorizations and borders, is constantly thrown over the bodies of the colonized. There is nowhere to flee. Even if one becomes a corpse, the gaze of the colonist still looks on. This is to say nothing of the experiences of the living. What is one to do? Yŏm Sangsŏp's *On the Eve of the Uprising* presents one example of a topography or natural history that carefully records the conditions of those caught under the net of the gaze.

On the Eve of the Uprising—from Abject Bodies to Abject Bodies

The question of where to find the origin of the gaze that structures this particular work continues to present difficulties. Some read it as the introspective gaze of a colonial intellectual who, upon his homecoming, is awakened to the bitterly painful state of the nation. Others point out that the "naturalist" gaze itself—as the protagonist observes his "kind"—is an effect of the internalization of the distorted views of the colonizer and reveals the class limitations of the author. However, I do not think these two viewpoints necessarily conflict. At least as far as the gaze is concerned, the narrator cannot be classified as either colonized or colonizer but as both. Literally, he is an in-between, a gray figure with a murky identity. This, of course, has no bearing on the oft-mentioned objectivity of the gaze that emerges in discussions of Yŏm's fiction. Rather, he radically persists in his own subjectivity as a "gray person"; in his own subjectivity as an abject, ever in danger of being expelled beyond the border. Let us examine how *On the Eve of the Uprising* unfolds in accordance with this subjective gaze. The following passage merits particular attention:

> As I was traveling from Tokyo to Shimonoseki, I was neither attempting to behave like a Japanese person, nor, for that matter, was there any need to behave like a Korean—as such, I simply was at ease, going about my business.[18]

Of course, the protagonist Yi Inhwa could let go and go about his business without having to act like either a Japanese person or a Korean because his face is indistinguishable from that of a Japanese person. While "traveling from Tokyo to Shimonoseki"—that is to say, while he was in "Japan proper"—not only was he free from the gaze of others, but he also became a subject gazing at and observing others. In the first scene of the novel, after he receives a telegram from his hometown and prepares to return, he sits on the Tokyo city tram staring at the surrounding passengers, who have "contorted faces with skin shriveled up from hard work, starvation, and the cold." He even provides a lengthy exposition of the "practice of surveying those around them," which is a habit that "all humans have." (22)[19]

However, his ability to unilaterally scrutinize others extends only so far. The moment he leaves Japan proper—that is, the moment he enters the waiting room for the connecting boat in Shimonoseki—he is caught in the gaze of a detective who "spontaneously became aware of his presence." (34) However, Yi Inhwa had no way of knowing that the gaze of this particular imperial policeman—a gaze focused intently on his outward appearance, which was supposedly indistinguishable from that of a Japanese—was no ordinary gaze but rather a systematized gaze attuned to racial differences, developed out of the lengthy and intense examination of the bodies of colonized natives. The imperial police had already, for instance, developed secret guidelines, such as the following, to better manage abject persons with ambiguous external features:

1. Their height is no different from people of Japan. Because of their straight postures, there are few with bent or curvy backs.
2. Their faces are no different from those of the Japanese, their hair is smooth and lacks density, there is little hair on their faces, so-called "flat faces" are numerous, and their beards generally appear thin.
3. Tooth decay is infrequent because, from early childhood, they use salt when brushing.[20]

In 1913 the Department of Security of the Home Ministry, in order to better regulate Koreans (who were often "difficult to distinguish from people of Japan proper"), released a secret document containing forty-six different guidelines to help determine whether or not someone was Korean. We need not dwell on the question of whether the guidelines worked effectively; rather, we must focus on the fact that this document worked in concert with an anthropological gaze to systematically dig into, cut apart, measure, and classify the bodies of colonial subjects. And as long as this was the case, it would seem that Yi Inhwa's assertion that he need not "attempt to behave like a Korean or a Japanese person" amounted to nothing more than a misapprehension. Indeed, in all of his subsequent journeys he finds himself consistently under the vigilant gaze of the police.

Of course, forces other than the police subject Yi Inhwa to their gaze. From the moment he leaves Japan and sets foot on Korean ground, he discovers that both Japanese and Korean people cast suspicious stares his way. However, Yi too constantly scrutinizes and classifies others. In this sense, *On the Eve of the Uprising* seems to use the protagonist Yi Inhwa's paranoid sensitivities to these intersecting gazes to drive the narrative. Here, I want to focus on how that sensitivity develops into racial and phrenological descriptions of others.

In a famous scene in the bathing area on the passenger boat, our protagonist sits beside Japanese passengers and describes their appearances as they converse. He observes the shifting of "large innocent eyes back and forth" in a "dark, rugged face" and "large and copper-colored bodies" that call to mind "peasants fresh from the countryside." Similarly, he classifies people with "predatory eyes" who have a "condescending, imposing manner of speaking, coupled with thin lips" like "a pawnbroker's middleman or something along those lines." (35)[21] Having been subjected to the gaze of the Japanese detective shortly beforehand, Yi Inhwa experiences an "undisguised burst of superiority, mingled with inferiority" (47) as he vengefully classifies Japanese people according to their appearances and the occupations he associates with them. His subsequent travels also clearly demonstrate how these feelings of superiority and inferiority are cast in accordance with a phrenological gaze.

Finishing his bath and entering the changing room, Yi Inhwa's identity as a Korean is revealed by a Korean detective who states that "in my estimation, though he does speak Japanese fluently, I needn't inquire into his way of speaking—it is clear that he is a Korean." Yi subsequently becomes "the recipient of hateful stares from many people" and feels his "energy diminish and his shoulders hunch." (41-42) In sum, as soon as he leaves the Japanese mainland, where he has "no need to act either as a Japanese person or a Korean person," he begins to react with great sensitivity to gazes that distinguish between Koreans and Japanese. Arriving at Pusan, the gateway to the colony, he once again encounters the "eyes of an assistant policeman and an assistant gendarme, neither of whom carried their own revolvers." He stands "hoping and praying that they would take me for Japanese." (50)

Naturally, his wishes do not come to fruition. It is not in Tokyo but rather in his own hometown that he is exposed as a "person of Chosŏn." "Cold sweat trickled down [his] back," and he "was at a loss for words, overcome by anxiety and fear." (51)[22] It is only on the train that his hopes materialize ever so briefly. Inside the train, he carefully observes the other passengers in his vicinity and describes their behavior. The scene in which he engages a merchant peddling Korean-style hats is of particular interest here. Yi, who had attracted the suspicion of "inspectors and relief officers every time he arrived in the train station," focuses on the "protruding cheekbones and thick lips that extended outward from the dark face" of this "rural villager of approximately 30 years, who wore a protective covering on his hat and tied a towel to his umbrella." The man carefully inspects Yi's face as well, out of a "concern whether he was Japanese or not." (76) Ultimately, it is not the imperial power that mistakes Yi for a Japanese but a colonial abject who is positioned outside imperial law.

This very hat merchant is an archetypal abject who threatens the system and throws the established order into confusion. In response to Yi's questioning about why he does not cut his hair, the man answers:

> If you want to cut your hair, you must first know how to speak Japanese and have some knowledge of current affairs. If a person has short hair but can't speak Japanese, he's likely to be harassed even worse by officials and policeman. But if his hair is worn up in a traditional topknot, they let minor offenses pass, because he's just a yobo. So doesn't it make more sense not to get a haircut? (77)[23]

In 1902, Mochiji Rokusaburō, who oversaw policy toward indigenous peoples in the Civil Affairs Bureau of the governor-general of Taiwan, stated that "under the laws of the Japanese Empire, there is no relationship between the empire and native persons." They existed entirely outside the law. Mochiji also stated: "While in sociological terms, the raw savages [*seiban*] who have not surrendered are human beings, they are analogous to animals from the perspective of international law."[24] In other words, the hat merchant that Yi Inhwa meets on the train is the *seiban* of Chosŏn. He is not a *seiban* who "wore a hat," "walked with a Western cane," "cut his hair," "learned the language of Japan," and "surrendered" but rather is an "undomesticated" *seiban* who continues to wear Korean-style hats and *manggŏn* and never cuts his hair—he is, in fact, a *yobo.* The laws of the empire do not apply to him. He has been pushed outside the confines of the law and rendered the equivalent of an animal.

Yi Inhwa witnesses these base and haggard human-beasts on the train ride to Seoul. When the train briefly stops at Taejŏn station, Yi sees four or five criminals, bound and tied, under police guard. Though we have no way of knowing what crimes these people have committed, when we consider Yi Inhwa's tone when observing them it becomes clear that these are not criminals of conscience or political offenders. "A young married woman, whose general appearance was rather unseemly, what with her hair let out and her jacket stained with blood," "stared blankly at Yi Inhwa and nodded her head," as if to say that "she was not ashamed." Yi says that after seeing these people, "his heart fluttered and his legs shook, as this entire spectacle seemed a recreation of something taken from a book." (83) As we can see, for him fear and hatred overwhelm feelings of compassion and pity. When Yi looks upon these rope-bound abject bodies and says he feels as if the scene was like something in a book, he is expressing his sense of shock after witnessing concrete manifestations of the border between the legal and the illegal, as well as forms beyond that border, which the imperial order constantly reinforced and inculcated in the colonized people (and therefore made extremely familiar to them) through various methods, including books. Returning once more to Kristeva, revolutions, liberation movements, or crimes that carry some degree of solemnity, like suicide terrorism, are not reflections of the abject. Cunning, merciless, and shameful crimes are the true abject, for these show the fragility of the law.[25] The abject do not, then, emerge as the objects of indoctrination or correction but rather as entities to be thrown outside society's boundaries; entities who, though captured by the law, are to be thoroughly excluded; entities who, in the eyes of the law, are the equivalent of animals. It is from this that Yi Inhwa's fears originate.

Yi Inhwa's pessimism and despair reach a climax here. Amid a swarm of abjects, Yi spits out that famous exclamation: "This is a grave! A grave full of maggots!" (83) This exclamation, a condensation of the gruesome reality of colonial life, points toward the ends of the abject, namely corpses and the filth streaming forth from them. Nevertheless, he seeks out both the conditions that give rise to the abject and also a new world where such conditions no longer obtain from the perspective of the theory of evolution. In this sense, his despair never reaches the level of a total denial of the system but targets the interior of the system, which can be maintained only by constantly reproducing and expelling abject bodies:

> Everyone is a maggot. You and I are maggots. Even inside the grave, the evolutionary process continues, not ceasing for even a minute! There will be natural selection and the struggle for survival . . . Each of these maggots will soon disintegrate into elements, turn into earth . . . Be ruined, utterly! If we could only be over and done with, maybe something better might grow.(83)[26]

In the last line of the novel, Yi—who has finished his work in Seoul and is preparing to return to Tokyo—says of himself: "I am barely escaping from this grave." (107) Though we cannot know what happens to Yi Inhwa after his return to Tokyo, based on the discussions we have had to this point we cannot help but question whether he is able to be at ease without having to worry about whether he should behave like a Japanese person or a Korean person.

Regarding the many Yi Inhwas of the world, in 1940 Yi Kwangsu wrote the following:

> Now, thinking back on things, I am certain that the faces of peninsular Koreans have changed over the past thirty years. But it is not only their faces that have changed. The way they dress, the way they walk, their manners, and their thoughts all have changed. Taken together, these things have resulted in their faces changing. It is especially so with young people. Women are even more difficult to recognize.[27]

In thrusting the figure of the colonized whose faces have changed before the colonizer who demands "assimilation," Yi Kwangsu shows us the strategy of "mimicry," what Homi Bhabha describes as "one of the most elusive and effective strategies," which allows the colonized to look "almost the same, but not quite" to "at once resemble and menace."[28] Be that as it may, we must attend to the fact that the gaze that observes the changed faces of "peninsular Koreans" looks out through the ethnological frame of empire. Rather than subverting the police's keys to identifying Koreans, his assertion, or perhaps hope, that "one cannot distinguish the faces of Koreans and Japanese" in actuality mimics them with great accuracy, though in the opposite direction. Moreover, this approach serves to position all those other Yi Inhwas who left the grave-like confines of a colony that overflowed with abject bodies squarely within the ethnological and phrenological imperial frame. Regardless of whether one's face or outfit changed, as long as one remained within this racial framework one could never escape this net of classifications and boundaries nor could one's fate as an abject be changed.

This indeed came to pass. Twenty years after Yi Inhwa returned to Tokyo—the same period in which Yi Kwangsu wrote the above words—his exclamation became reality. The implementation of the Korean Volunteer Soldier System in 1938 and the Conscription System in 1944 pushed countless Yi Inhwas into graves full of maggots. Caught in the finely knit web of countless classifications and boundaries that constituted the racial distribution of the empire, these other Yi Inhwas were disposed of as corpses, the utmost limit of the abject, and thereby sustained the system. And, as is well known, the cost of this was a promise about the lives of those within the boundaries, within the system. The abject bodies of the colony "could live only in death."[29]

The Response of the Abject

As mentioned above, as faithful companions of modern biopolitics, modern naturalist and realist art were born with the discovery of abject bodies. Rey Chow, in an attempt to problematize primitivism through an analysis of contemporary Chinese cinema, finds in Western "high modernist" art—represented by painters such as Picasso, Gauguin, Matisse, and Modigliani and authors such as James

Joyce, D. H. Lawrence, and Henry Miller—a process in which "Western signification systems become modernized and high-tech'd by primitivizing others" through the "continual primitivization of non-Western lands and peoples."[30] Chow also points out that none other than anthropology was implicated in these "artistic aspirations." Furthermore, she not only stresses the West's exploitation of non-Western peoples but focuses on the "primitivization of the other" that emerged in representations of female sexuality and the fact that such representations are found not only in the West but also in the writings of authors from the Third World:

> In the "third world," there is a similar movement to primitivize: the primitive materials that are seized upon here are the socially oppressed classes—women, in particular—who then become the predominant components of a new literature. It would not be far-fetched to say that modern Chinese literature turns "modern" precisely by seizing upon the primitive that is the subaltern, the woman, and the child. We would therefore need, once again, to reverse the conventional way literary history is written: not that modern Chinese intellectuals become "enlightened" and choose to revolutionize their writing by turning their attention to the oppressed classes; rather, like elite, cultured intellectuals everywhere in the world, they find in the underprivileged a source of fascination that helps to renew, rejuvenate, and "modernize" their own cultural production in terms both of subject matter and form.[31]

The foregoing passage argues that a new modern literature appeared through the discovery of a source of fascination with and the primitivization of "the underprivileged" or, in the terminology of this article, abject bodies, by Western and Third World authors alike. This can be applied to modern Korean literature as well. In fact, the modern literature of colonial Korea overflows with representations of the abject body. Equipped with the imperial anthropological gaze, elite colonial male authors figured all manner of abject bodies—persons of lower social classes, criminals (especially female criminals), deformed persons, the insane, and so on. What has continuously emerged in postcolonial Korean literary history, in its linking of the figuration of such bodies with nationalist discourse, is precisely "the conventional way literary history is written."

Yi Hyeryŏng, in an article that carefully analyzes how elite males monopolized the figuration of female sexuality in colonial fiction, thoroughly overturns the "conventional way literary history is written." Like Chow, Yi points to the tendency of modern Korean novels to "portray a primitive world, where instinct dominates and the cunning of reason holds no currency, through the lives of those in the lower strata of society."[32] Moreover, Yi brings to light how the transformation of these abject bodies into a spectacle occurred primarily through male authors' representation of female sexuality. Analyzing the appearance of the lower-class femme fatale in works such as Na Tohyang's "Mulberry" and "Waterwheel," Kim Tongin's "Potato," Hyŏn Chingŏn's "Fire" and "Chastity and the Price of Medicine"; the presence of the New Woman in Yŏm Sangsŏp's *Love and Crime* and *Two Minds;* and the appearance of the lower-class prostitute in works such as Kim Yujŏng's "Wanderer among the Hills," "The Kettle," "Wife," and "A Sudden Shower," Yi points out how repeated depictions of the bodies of abject women in Korean fiction from the 1920s and the 1930s are "always presented as entities inextricably bound up with nature and instinct" and how the sexuality of these women is in fact a "mere projection of the repressed desires of male elites."[33]

The important point here is that masculinity's monopoly, through the representation of female sexuality or the bodies of the lower class, comes into contact with the ethnological gaze of imperialism. Yi explains the process by which the abject become naturalized by noting that male elites, who created the lower-class femme fatale in the first place, never appear in the novel itself. The male elites, by standing outside the work and so concealing their gazes, "carry out the function of invisible steel bars, bars that allow the semblance of a state of nature at a zoo." That is, they function much like the anthropologist's camera or the anatomist's scalpel. This unseen gaze functions as "the perspective of civilization" through which abject bodies accordingly find themselves "fixed as entities more natural than nature."[34] Needless to say, this whole process serves as a method of colonial rule—on the one hand, by primitivizing and naturalizing the inhabitants of a colony it alienates and suppresses impulses lodged within itself, and on the other, it imitates an imperialist racism that affirms the position of the "civilized" by fixing its gaze upon "savages" caught in a state of nature. Accordingly, "if we recall that the abject became incarnate in women and the cast-offs of society, then we must expose the complicity not only of the colonial rulers, but also of the colonized male elite."[35]

I completely agree with the foregoing analyses provided by Rey Chow and Yi Hyeryŏng. At the same time, I want to propose one further question: Are abject bodies entities that are always only made visible? If not, how might these bodies, ever on the opposite side of the camera lens or maintaining silence under the scalpel of the anatomist, respond to the gaze of the observer? That is, how might they reverse the camera lenses and scalpels that observe, measure, cut open, and dissect? How can they expose the gaze of their observers? Furthermore, how can they disturb a system that reinforces the borderline of its own internal identity by constantly pushing the abject outside that boundary? How can the gaze upon abject bodies be scattered?

My goal here is not to discover an opportunity for positive, active subject formation in the appearance of abject bodies and thereby to group them under some alternate category of self-identity. There is nothing the abject bodies can do when placed before the gaze of authority. However, as we see in Torii Ryūzō's photograph from Manchuria, the abject pictured therein reveals, in a completely unexpected and unintended manner, the existence of the unseen gaze that frames this racial exhibition. It momentarily evokes for the spectator the "invisible steel bars" of the zoo. If the violent gaze targeting the abject ever were to display a crack, even if only microscopically, it likely begins with this moment of realization (fig. 5.1).

Figure 5.1. In this photograph taken by Torii Ryūzō, an elderly person shields his face as he clasps his hands together. According to an explanation provided by the Tokyo University Museum, "At the time, one of the most difficult aspects of anthropological surveys was the fact that people would often run away out of fear of having their picture taken. This elderly person, as well, likely raised his hand due to fear of being photographed." The subconscious reaction of the abject before the camera lens reveals the existence of the people on the opposite side of the lens and thereby momentarily unsettles the boundary between the viewer and the viewed. We must turn our attention to the moment when violence begins—which is to say, the moment when these disturbances begin. In my view, this image seems to symbolize this moment. Source: Tokyo University Museum Database.

I want to focus on this moment. The abject, which elicit nausea and disgust, are things that I have pushed and spat out, that I have eliminated from myself in order to establish my own identity. Nevertheless—or rather, precisely for this reason—they stand constantly between two borders, and I am constantly exposed to the risk of contamination. Though pushed outside the border through stigmatization and classification, their very existence has the capacity to mark that boundary, a capacity without which the system would be absolutely unable to subsist. Yet at the same time they are contagions—germ carriers that can or will perforate that system (or that system's self-identity). In short, they are subsumed in their exclusion and excluded in their subsumption. By being excluded, they uphold the system, but the very moment (point) they begin to both threaten the system and uphold it is the moment (point) when an equivalence between exclusion and inclusion emerges—the moment (point) the abject is born. Moreover, this moment (point) heralds the birth of the apprehension and fear shared by the system and the abject. Ultimately, the abject both stands beyond the boundary line and marks that boundary, existing within the moment of apprehension and fear. Without it, there would be no boundary. Because of its existence, the system is stabilized, but at the same time it is also always exposed to instability.

The response of the abject also emerges at this moment (point). Small gestures that may be seen or may go unseen, covert glances, an undomesticated roughness, an interior craftiness that others cannot discern, a silence and expressionlessness that incites unease, strange signs of disquiet—these sorts of things represent what the abject, trapped by invisible steel bars, can do or show. However, that sort of ambiguity and lack of transparency can perplex and disquiet onlookers. Yi Yŏngjae, in an analysis of *The Volunteer* (1941), a propaganda film shot during the Pacific War, discusses how the "scowling expressionlessness" of colonized peoples confuses and perplexes the colonizers.[36] According to Yi, the "uniform expressionlessness seen in the scowling faces of the actors straddled the line between laughing and crying" and in its indecipherability presented Japanese movie critics with difficulty. In my view, this expressionlessness, which dominates the whole of the symbolic space of the colony, presents one mode of response from abject bodies.

Figure 5.2. The black hole of expressionless that completely devours the gaze of the viewer. Anxiety is induced when the gaze of the colonizer is distorted in reflection when coming up against the (image of) the bodies of "human-beasts." Source: Tokyo University Museum Database.

This sort of reaction completely swallows the gaze of the viewer, much in the same way that a black hole devours light. Before that black hole of expressionlessness, the gaze of the viewer is thrown into confusion while the appearance of the photographed subject is scattered. For example, what of the following case?

> On the exterior, these people may seem indifferent—yet, whence their menacing stares, deeply suspicious glances, lips struggling to conceal mocking smiles, sluggish deportment, traces of dark shadows of doubt, and distrust of the Karak people? This is hardly a sign of powerlessness, but rather a method of resistance—and one need not be a statesman of Silla to know this.[37]

This passage from Ch'oe Chaesŏ's *Marriage of the Peoples* (1945)—a piece of national-policy fiction (*kukch'aek sosŏl*) written in Japanese that obliquely advocates for the ideal of the Greater East Asian Co-Prosperity Sphere through its representation of Silla's unification of the Three Kingdoms—depicts the disturbance of the colonizer's gaze upon the colonized, as seen earlier. When confronted with the "menacing stares, deeply suspicious glances, lips struggling to conceal mocking smiles, sluggish deportment" and the undomesticated bodies of the human-beasts, the gaze of the colonizer becomes both scattered and confused.

Pegasus—"Blurry Figures, Malicious Laughter"

A pioneering description of this scattered gaze may be found in Kim Saryang's *Pegasus*. Before touching on the novel's content, I want to call attention to the fact that the social status and developmental history of both the author and the novel reflect those of the archetypal abject. Kim Saryang's name repeatedly appears in debates over the identity of Korean literature, much like Chang Hyŏkchu, the first Korean author to debut in Japanese writing. During the colonial period, Chang Hyŏkchu, Kim Saryang, and both authors' Japanese-language novels were considered ambiguous entities existing in an ambiguous space between Korean and Japanese literature and therefore, were ostracized.[38] In these novels, imperial authors not only gained a taste of the odd exoticism generated by a distant colonial Aboriginality but also expressed their sense of superiority (with a mix of scorn and praise)[39] over the colonial natives' fumbling attempts to mimic the imperial language. In effect, this shows how Kim's and Chang's novels were seen as heterogeneous, positioned on the fringes of Japanese literature. At the same time, their novels were pushed outside the bounds of Korean literature.[40] Moreover, in postcolonial South and North Korea, they have either been forgotten or branded sell-outs, criminals, traitors, or collaborationists. These two were abjects who stood on the borders of existence and threw identities into confusion and who assumed the function (or, who had to assume the function) of strengthening internal homogeneity by being pushed outside predominant social boundaries.

Let us consider one further example. In 1987, North Korea's Munye Publishing Company assembled the works of Kim Saryang as part of an effort to reframe him as a patriotic revolutionary author. In the introduction to the collection, a North Korean critic provides the following commentary on *Into the Light,* one of Kim Saryang's representative works: "Although one cannot deny that the [book] presents the plight of the Korean people," the shortcoming of the novel actually consists in its treatment of "the problems of children of mixed blood."

> This particular work's limitations are seen in the fact that the mixed-blooded adolescent Haruo is established as the central matter of concern. It is not possible to develop a portrait of the destiny of the ill-fated Korean nation through such a problem set. Why? The fate of the Korean nation is a matter pertaining to Koreans, who have endured great oppression and exploitation at the hands of Imperial Japan—not to a mixed-blood child like Haruo.[41]

In the context of a discourse that attempts to rehabilitate Kim Saryang as a revolutionary patriot, there is no place for a child of mixed blood. A child of mixed blood presents an archetypal abject that muddies the purity of blood and the identity of the nation. Therefore, in treating the issue of the "fate of the Korean nation" through the lens of a child of mixed blood, Kim Saryang himself assumes the position of an abject.

In this regard, the name of the protagonist in *Pegasus,* Genryu (K. Hyŏllyong), merits particular attention. As opposed to the names of the Japanese and the Koreans who appear in this book—those names with "clear identities" such as Tanaka, Omura, Yi Myŏngsik, and Mun So'ok—the name "Genryu" is extremely ambiguous and confusing. One finds it difficult to determine whether the person is a Korean or a Japanese person by his name alone. Genryu could be either; however, whatever the answer, the name still carries an odd feeling. The very name Hyŏllyong—which feels as though it lacks a clear definition, in that it could be one thing or the other, or perhaps neither—exemplifies aspects of abject existence, of an entity with a "mixed-blood" background.

The novel begins with a description of the novelist Hyŏllyong walking dizzily toward "the street most bustling with Japanese people in all of the capital city" after spending the night in the red-light district.[42] Words like "tick," "bedbug," "young rat," "trash," and "stray dog" describe this intellectual male writer (who carries a sexually transmitted disease and walks pigeon-toed through the streets). All such words are used repeatedly when calling attention to this character with a sinister personality disorder. When one considers the prevalent use of women and the lower class in colonial novels to describe abject bodies, the debased representation of this elite intellectual male seems without precedent.

Therefore, Hyŏllyong seems rather different from all of the abject seen to this point. He is not a native who devours the gaze of the rulers with a cold and stark expressionlessness. He bears no resemblance to downtrodden lower-class folk who "manifest themselves not through language, but through their bodies." Rather, he bears greater resemblance to a Frankenstein-made monster who, in his ability to speak the language of the rulers, becomes difficult to treat.[43] This "monster" that "cuts his hair, speaks Japanese, and has knowledge of current affairs," which the hat merchant spoke of in *On the Eve of the Uprising*, has no concern for the gazes cast upon him and first speaks of himself as a heap of garbage or a bedbug. However, the hateful and scornful looks cast on his strange behavior are often scattered or refracted in unexpected directions.

The reason why Korean literati "hate and exclude him as if he were some horrible thing like a bedbug" has not only to do with the fact that he exhibits major personality flaws, such as lying, boasting, and other strange behaviors, but even more with the fact that he continuously speaks without care or caution, saying things like: "Writing in the Korean language disgusts me. The Korean language should go eat shit. It is simply a talisman of destruction." (253) For this reason, "Korean literati banded together and forced him outside the cultured world." (238) Once he is pushed outside this boundary, those on the inside find "solidarity." The interior is, of course, "Korean culture." The critic Yi Myŏngsik, in a gathering dedicated to criticizing the "Hyŏllyong faction," fulminates against Hyŏllyong as he strongly decries the deplorable state of literary production in the Korean language.[44] Hyŏllyong sneers at Yi Myŏngsik, who in response grabs a plate and throws it at him. Even though Hyŏllyong is hit on the head and falls backward, he continues giggling, and Yi Myŏngsik is subsequently imprisoned for assault.

Nonetheless, we must ask: Who was chastising whom? Who cast whom out? Are Yi Myŏngsik and Hyŏllyong truly different types of figures? Can we not read Yi Myŏngsik as some sort of superego while reading Hyŏllyong as some sort of id? Unlike Hyŏllyong, who is consistently described with generous amounts of sarcasm, humor, and irony, Yi Myŏngsik is described with a rigid, formulaic, and argumentative style of writing. After Yi briefly appears in and disappears from the novel, Hyŏllyong's self-despairing wildness, much like a horse without its reins, fills the absence Yi has left. We can read this abject figure much like an id that has escaped the control of the superego. However, if so, whose "id" is this?

This abject, who "has been abandoned by the Koreans" and would "have no choice but to die in the streets" (259) if also abandoned by the Japanese, alternately behaves in a clingy manner, begs, displays anger, jeers, threatens, flees, or squirms when confronting his observers. As a result of this struggling, the gaze upon the subject wavers and generates unintended reflections. Consider the following example. Hyŏllyong becomes the object of hatred from Yi Myŏngsik and his colleagues, who strongly support the notion that "Korean literature has a distinct identity." However, when one realizes Kim Saryang's personal history of activity in the world of Tokyo letters and considers that many of the statements made by Yi Myŏngsik in the novel directly reference statements appearing in other Kim Saryang works, it becomes increasingly difficult to determine the meaning of the dispute between Hyŏllyong and Yi Myŏngsik. In this regard, how might one best classify the "Korean literati," who branded Hyŏllyong a "tick on Korean culture" and decided to exclude him from their world? These literati, ever involved in a flattery competition to "present themselves as the representatives of Korean literature on the occasion of a visit from some reasonably well-known figure from the Japanese art scene," are no different from Hyŏllyong, who spends his day gasping and panting, wandering in search of authors from the Japanese mainland. They are simply lodged in a competition over patriotic fervor. In the end, as the scornful gazes cast on Hyŏllyong grow ever stronger, the Korean literati ultimately come to cast similar gazes on themselves.

Hyŏllyong's relationships with Japanese intellectuals present one further case worthy of examination. Due to a series of incidents, Hyŏllyong finds himself trembling with fear as Omura, "the head man of a project to publish a magazine on current affairs that aims to strengthen the patriotic solidarity of the Korean people," demands that he temporarily enter a temple and improve his behavior. Hyŏllyong, who thinks that he will "certainly die in the streets if Omura abandons him," spends the entire day in Chongno and Honmachi searching out Tanaka, a Japanese author from Japan, who he believes will help rescue him. While observing the harried wanderings of this pitiable abject, we find that he eventually meets the powerful people from Japan whom he so desperately sought. It goes without saying that these Japanese people view Hyŏllyong as if he were an insect. At the same time, one sees their ignorance, arrogance, phoniness, and vanity in their treatment of Hyŏllyong. For example, Professor Tsunoi, who held a chair at a "State Professional School," claimed that "to be a Korean youth is to belong to a clan [*choksok*] that, without exception, has a cowardly mettle, a highly skewed temper, a shameless disposition, and a strong proclivity for factionalism." (270) Yet according to the speaker, he "is just one of many scholars who came to Chosŏn for the purpose of earning money" and therefore "can be considered a Japanese Hyŏllyong." (268) Then there is Tanaka, who landed in Chosŏn "following an excursion in Manchuria, where he concluded that he might be able to re-brand himself and start a new line of work in Korea." (269) After listening to Hyŏllyong's lengthy exposition concerning "how he, when encountering Japanese, out of a sense of mean-spiritedness, could not suffer the meeting without shooting off a long string of Korean-style insults," (270) Tanaka finds himself very moved. He then experiences a profound internal happiness as he says to himself: "It is indeed true that one can only write imperial literature if one is completely confined to Japan. But here, one sees the sufferings of continental people . . . So it is decided. Japan must be made to know the self-reflections of Korean intellectuals . . . Those who say that the Chinese cannot be known are incomparably foolish. I came to know Koreans in just two days—at such a pace, the Chinese can then be known in four." (271) Finally, we find that Omura, after instructing Hyŏllyong that he should "carefully study the signs of the times," is truly the type of person who "struts about excitedly, moved by the eloquence of his own speech." (273)

These are important moments, when the hateful and scornful gazes cast upon the abject Hyŏllyong suddenly reflect back onto the appearances of the gazers, causing them to realize that they are little different from the people they observe. The author captures this with great descriptive precision. Consequently, many figures emerge as targets of derision and exclusion. In addition to Hyŏllyong, we can include the literati, as well Korean culture and Korean cultural identity, all of which cast gazes onto Hyŏllyong. We can also include patriotism, imperial literature, and the Japan and Korea as One policy, not to mention the Japanese literati and the Japanese themselves. The following scene depicts the suddenly flustered appearance of Tanaka—who had previously observed Hyŏllyong with the demeanor of one "conducting a survey of the Korean people"—and the origins of his reaction:

> Hyŏllyong, wondering if the time was right, ran to the side of Tanaka, panting.
>
> "Mr. Tanaka."
>
> Hyŏllyong spoke in a grave tone with Tanaka, his voice caught in his throat.
>
> "Please ask a favor of Mr. Omura for me. Please convince him not to send me to the temple. Please!"
>
> Listening to his voice tremble with such passionate sadness, Tanaka found himself caught off guard, staring Hyŏllyong straight in the face. Suddenly, Hyŏllyong's figure, which was so hardened that it gave one goose bumps, became scattered, and he began to laugh wryly. (275–276)

This colonist, who had "surveyed and observed the Korean people," feels both confusion and surprise the moment he is confronted with the sudden disarray and malicious laughter of the object of his observations. The monster who can speak the language of the colonial rulers is no longer a noble savage but a source of gloom, discomfort, and embarrassment. Caught in the act of looking, the observer's gaze becomes jarred, and the form of his object becomes distorted when the monster (who is "fixed as an entity more natural than nature") begins to laugh and look back at him. Tanaka may even finally recognize the presence of the "unseen steel bars" between himself and his target. In other words, he likely feels confused after realizing that a long-suppressed part of himself has appeared on the other side of those unseen steel bars.

Whatever becomes of this abject and his "malicious laughter"? After all his efforts yield no results, he begins to shout, "I must die! Wedge me between a car and a train and kill me as with a bomb!"—and, just as in the first scene of the novel, he is left wandering the alleys of the red-light district of Shinmachi. He feels suffocated and surrounded by the people proceeding to Shinto worship, who are comprised of "an endless line of gaiter-wearing middle school students and professional students, followed by teachers wearing khaki-colored clothing, not to mention people from newspapers or magazine offices, or even literati with acquaintances." Hyŏllyong wanders through the labyrinthine alleyways as he hallucinates tens of thousands of people shouting "Senjin! Senjin!" at him, forcing him to shout in response, "I am not a Senjin! I am not a Senjin!"

> "Please rescue me, a man of Japan—rescue me!"
>
> He cried out as he panted for breath. Then, he ran to a different house and knocked on the door.

> "Please open up! Please allow me, a Japanese man, to come inside!"
>
> Again he began to run. He knocked on the door.
>
> "I am not a Senjin! I am Kennogami Ryūnosuke, Ryūnosuke! Please allow me inside!" (281)

Having been thrown outside the boundaries, this abject man boldly invokes a sacred symbol of self-identity (Ryūnosuke) from the world within those boundaries and demands to be let inside. He knows that Pegasus can only be born if Medusa is killed. Therefore, he passionately wails that the "Senjin" has died and that he can become a "Japanese man." As we saw with many of the other colonial abjects above, he too can "live only in death."

Conclusion

Where does violence begin? Violence is a basic condition of all living things. If life is a product of violence, we must focus our attention not on eliminating it but on the conditions under which it materializes, on "those moments where actors experience a looming presentiment of violence."[45] When we speculate on the sort of violence that emerges and is actualized in everyday life—rather than the violence of states of exception and emergency—we begin to understand how the violence of colonialism continues well after colonialism's political end and how resistance to colonialist violence easily transforms into the same sort of violence.

If we capture the very first moment that violence materializes, we can also discern the moment when resistance to violence begins (or perhaps, must begin). In the first moment of contact with the other, signs of violence begin to flicker. We must direct our attention, then, not to the scenes of massacre or slaughter—the result of the colossal bursting forth of these signs of violence—but rather to the place where these signs originate. Only by standing in that place can we stop "speaking on behalf of the dead" and start "letting the dead speak for themselves."[46] How is the speech of the dead to be understood?

Can we even begin to understand the meanings conveyed by the menacing stares, deeply suspicious glances, lips struggling to conceal mocking smiles, and sluggish deportment[47] of these human-beasts? Can we read in that expressionlessness—the black hole that devours the gaze of the master—the potential to produce small fissures in a system of violence? Can we detect traces of microscopic contagions spread by those "monsters," ventriloquists who "speak two languages with one mouth?"[48] To put it differently, the purpose here is not to focus on a "field of active potential, as with acts of revolutionary overthrow or disobedience" but rather on the political significance of minor or even unintended "transgressions."[49] If the modern nation-state's systems of oversight and discipline newly mold the bodies and senses of its citizens, the possibility of "violations" of discipline remains "ever-present in their lives and self-formation."[50] If we turn our eyes, then, toward these minor transgressions as a "sort of critical point" that "perforates the unjust monopoly system of the state"—and upon the slight fever or perhaps a certain "sorrow" arising from the anxiety the transgressor feels at that moment—we can perhaps find some point at which the system of violence is thrown into disorder. In other words, "in order to observe these critical points—indistinct and difficult to properly grasp—we must carefully examine the significance of these tepid or sporadic transgressions, and perhaps that fever spread through the body of a transgressor of humble appearance."[51] To reflect on violence, to search for the point at which these cracks emerge, is to turn our ears to things that are difficult to hear and our eyes to things that are difficult to see. In this regard, we may simply be anthropologists of another sort.

Notes

This chapter was translated from the Korean by Matthew Lauer.

1. The measurements of the bodies of Koreans completed in 1887 by Koike Masanao (a Japanese army surgeon stationed in Pusan who examined the bodies of seventy-five Koreans between the ages of twenty and fifty) is thought to be the first example of such research. However, the records of this research are not extant. See Kohama Mototsugu, "Chōsenjin no seitei keisoku" (Bodily measurements of Koreans), in *Lectures on Anthropology and Archaeology*, vol. 4 (Tokyo: Yuzankaku: 1938). The following year, in 1888, Koganei Yoshikiyo presented results from his measurements of the skulls of four Koreans. See Yutaka Imamura, "Chōsenjin no taishitsu jinruigaku ni kansuru bunken mokuroku" (Catalog of documents pertaining to the physical anthropology of Koreans), in *Lectures on Anthropology and Archaeology*, vol. 7 (Tokyo: Yuzankaku: 1938). When one considers that the first Japanese anthropological society was formed in 1884 and that the first anthropological journal (*Journal of the Tokyo Anthropological Association*) was printed in 1886, one realizes that research into the physical anthropology of Koreans began at a rather early point in time. For recent research into Kubo Takeshi, see Hoeŭn Kim, "Anatomically Speaking: The Kubo Incident and the Paradox of Race in Colonial Korea," in *Race and Racism in Modern East Asia* (Leiden, Netherlands: Brill, 2013).

2. Ibid., 85.

3. Michel Foucault, *Society Must Be Defended*, trans. David Macey (New York: Picador, 2003).

4. For a thorough explanation of the development of prewar Japanese anthropology, see Sakano Tōru, *Teikoku nihon to jinruigakusha, 1884–1952 nen* (Anthropologists and imperial Japan, 1884–1952) (Tōkyō: Keisō Shobō, 2005); and "Kiyono Kenji no nihon jinshuron" (Kiyono Kenji's theory of Japanese race), *History of Science—Philosophy of Science* 11 (Tokyo: Tokyo University Press, 1993). In addition, for in-depth analysis of the relationship between the history of anthropology and colonialism, see Tomiyama Ichirō, "The Birth of the Citizen and 'The Japanese Race,'" in *Thought* 845; Takezawa Yasuko, *Jinshu gainen no fuhensei o tou* (An inquiry into the universality of the concept of race) (Kyoto: Jimbun Shoin: 2005); Yamamuro Shin'ichi, *Shisō kadai toshite no ajia* (Asia as a conceptual problem) (Tōkyō: Iwanami Shoten, 2001); Tessa Morris-Suzuki, "Ethnic Engineering, Scientific Racism and Public Opinions Surveys in Mid-century Japan," *positions* 8 (2000): 499–529.

5. The methodological inversion of an ethnology that first establishes the conceptual categories of "Koreans" and "Japanese" and then defines them as "races" with basic biological traits on the grounds of body measurements derived from those initial categories calls the scientific value of this scholarship into question. The 272 research articles written on the physical

anthropology of Koreans since 1938 plainly display the futility of such an approach. See Imamura Yutaka, "Chōsenjin no taishitsu jinruigaku ni kansuru bunken mokuroku."

6. Arase Susumu, "Chōsenjin no taishitsu jinruigaku teki kenkyū" (Research into the physical anthropology of the people of Chōsen), in *Journal of the Chōsen Medical Association* 24, no. 1 (1934): 60.

7. Ueda Tsunekichi, "Chōsenjin to nihonjin to no taishitsu hikaku" (A comparison of the bodies of Koreans and Japanese), in *Nihon minzoku* (The Japanese race) (Tokyo: Iwanami Shoten: 1935).

8. For a treatment of Torii Ryūzō's "source material survey" and the body measurements of Koreans taken by Japanese anthropologists, see Sŏgyŏng Ch'oe, "Ilche ŭi 'Chosŏn in sinch'e e taehan singminji chŏk sisŏn" (The Japanese Empire's colonial gaze onto the bodies of the 'People of Chosŏn') (Chuncheon, South Korea: Institute of Japanese Studies, Hallym University, 2004). As part of this research, Torii collected around thirty-eight thousand photos of the customs and bodies of Koreans. These photos are now stored in the National Museum of Korea.

9. Sakano, *Teikoku nihon to jinruigakusha.*

10. Tomiyama, *Birth of the Citizen,* 43.

11. Sakano, *Teikoku nihon to jinruigakusha,* 37.

12. Hang Kim, "The Sovereignty of Citizens and Partisan Publicness—A Reinterpretation of *Before the March First Movement*" (K. Inmin chugwŏn kwa p'arŭt'ijan konggongsŏng—*'Mansejŏn' chaedokhae*), The Shape of Thought, the Alleyway Entrance Author: In Search of the New Literature of Yŏm Sangsŏp (K. *Sasang ŭi hyŏnsang, pyŏngmun ŭi chakka: Saeroun yŏm sangsŏp ŭi munhak ŭl ch'ajasŏ*) (academic conference, Academy of East Asian Studies, Sŏnggyun'gwan University, January 17, 2013–January 18, 2013).

13. However, here we must draw a strong distinction between Darwin's theory of evolution and Spencer's theory of social evolution (social Darwinism). Darwin denied any and all attempts to find a force of "internal necessity" in the timeline of evolution. Conversely, social Darwinism grafted the concept of "time as a phase in the march toward civilization" or "time as initiating and 'completing' the process of evolution" onto the theory of evolution. In this way, social Darwinism transformed Darwin's theory into a tool and thereby discovered a scientific framework that placed the development of society and the ideology of progress within time. It goes without saying that anthropology, as a discipline, was established with the help of this framework. For a more thorough explanation of this point, see Johannes Fabian, *Time and the Other: How Anthropology Makes Its Objects* (New York: Columbia University Press, 1983).

14. Chongyŏn Hwang, "Naturalism and Beyond," in Shape of Thought, the Alleyway Entrance Author.

15. Julia Kristeva, *Powers of Horror: An Essay on Abjection,* trans. Leon Roudiez (NewYork: Columbia University Press, 1984), 4.

16. Ibid., 3.

17. Ibid., 4.

18. Yŏm Sangsŏp, *On the Eve of the Uprising,* in Yŏm sangsŏp chŏnjip (The complete works of Yŏm Sangsŏp), vol. 1 (Seoul: Minŭmsa: 1987), 47. Quotations are taken from this original text and from this point on will be cited in-text with page numbers in parentheses. The English translations here are generally based on the version found in Sunyoung Park's "On the Eve of the Uprising," in *On the Eve of the Uprising and Other Studies from Colonial Korea* (Ithaca, NY: Cornell East Asia Series, 2010), 5–114. I have made changes where appropriate, including the addition of passages from the original omitted in the translation. When I have relied on Park's translation I cite the page number in endnotes.

19. Park, "Eve of the Uprising," 16.

20. Kyŏngsik Pak, ed., *Zainichi Chōsenjin kankei shiryō shūsei* (Collected documents concerning Koreans residing in Japan), vol. 1 (Tokyo: San-ichi Shobō 1975), 28.

21. Park, "Eve of the Uprising," 30.

22. Ibid., 47–48.

23. Ibid., 78–79.

24. Robert Tierney, *Tropics of Savagery* (Berkeley: University of California Press, 2010), 45–46.

25. Kristeva, *Powers of Horror,* 4.

26. Park, "Eve of the Uprising," 85–86.

27. Yi Kwangsu, "Kao ga kawaru" (Faces have changed), in *Spring and Autumn Arts,* 1940, 11; Yi Kyŏnghun, *The Complete Pro-Japanese Works of Ch'unwŏn Yi Kwangsu* (K. *Ch'unwŏn Yi Kwangsu ch'inilmunhak chŏnjip*), vol. 21 (Seoul: P'yŏngminsa, 1995), 140–141.

28. Homi Bhabha, *The Location of Culture,* trans. Na Pyŏngch'ŏl (Seoul: Somyŏng, 2002). Translation taken from *The Location of Culture* (New York: Routledge, 2004), 122–123.

29. Hang Kim, *The Threshold of Imperial Japan* (J. *Teikoku nihon no iki*) (Tokyo: Iwanami, 2010).

30. Rey Chow, *Primitive Passions: Visuality, Sexuality, Ethnography, and Contemporary Chinese Cinema* (New York: Columbia University Press, 1995), 20.

31. Ibid., 21.

32. Hyeryŏng Yi, "Tongmulwŏn ŭi mihak" (The aesthetics of the zoo), in *Han'guk sosŏl kwa kolsanghak chŏk t'aja tŭl* (Korean fiction and the phrenological other) (Seoul: Somyŏng, 2007), 38.

33. Ibid., 31.

34. Ibid., 38.

35. Ibid., 41.

36. Yŏngjae Yi, "Cheguk ilbon ŭi chosŏn yŏnghwa" (Korean films under imperial Japan), in *Hyŏnsil munhwa* (Realist culture) (Seoul: Yŏngu, 2008), 61.

37. Chaesŏ Ch'oe, *Minjok ŭi kyŏrhon* (The marriage of the peoples), in *Ch'oe chaesŏ ilbonŏ sosŏl chip* (The collected Japanese-language fiction of Ch'oe Chaesŏ), trans. Yi Hyejin (Seoul: Somyŏng, 2012), 235.

38. For an analysis of how Chang Hyŏkchu and Kim Saryang have been represented in the history of modern Korean literature, see Chul Kim, "Tu gae ŭi kŏul—minjok tamnon ŭi chahwasang kŭrigi" (Two mirrors: Drawing a self-portrait of nationalist discourse), in *Singminji rŭl angosŏ* (Embracing colonialism) (Seoul: Yŏngnak, 2009). Kwŏn Nayŏng has also used the concept of the abject to analyze the "disquiet" experienced by imperial critics because of Kim Saryang's use of two languages. According to Kwŏn, the imperial critics who nominated Kim Saryang for the Akutagawa Prize attempted to expand the formal boundaries of Japanese literature by assimilating colonial literature, even though they sensed the possibility that colonial literature could contaminate the "purity" of Japanese literature. My own analysis in this article is highly indebted to Kwŏn's analysis of this "two-faced gesture, that both includes and excludes colonial authors" and the sense of disquiet that it generated. See Nayŏng Kwŏn, "Cheguk, minjok, kŭrigo sosuja chakka" (Empire, nation, and minority authors), in *Han'guk munhak yŏn'gu* (Korean literature) 37 (2009).

39. Frantz Fanon has analyzed the scorn shown to a black man who asks for a banana in broken French and the hypocritical racist praise that "turns a black man who quotes Montesquieu into an exceptional case." See Fanon, *Black Skin, White Masks,* trans. Sŏkho Yi (Seoul: In'gan sarang, 1998).

40. In a special report from August 1936 in the magazine *Samch'ŏlli,* in which Korean literature is defined as "writing in the Korean language, by Koreans, for Koreans," it is concluded

that "the work that Chang Hyŏkchu presented in Tokyo literary circles is not Korean literature." For a more detailed explanation, see Chul Kim, "Tu gae ŭi kŏul."

41. Hyŏngjun Chang, "Chakka kim saryang kwa kŭ ŭi munhak" (The author Kim Saryang and his work), in *Kim saryang chakp'um chip* (The collected works of Kim Saryang) (P'yŏngyang: Munye, 1987), 10. This particular review's commentary that "[the book] cannot appropriately treat the fate of the Korean nation" is in fact a retort to the review of Sato Haruo made for the Akutagawa Prize, which claimed that the book "fully treated the pitiable fate of the Korean nation." According to Kwŏn Nayŏng, Sato Haruo's review clearly displays both the arrogance of the imperial literati—who continuously demanded that colonial authors write "work that represents the colony and presents a foreign flavor"—and also something of the colonial consciousness. See Kwŏn, "Cheguk, minjok." However, when the North Korean critic responded to Sato Haruo by saying that "the fate of the nation cannot be depicted through a 'child of mixed blood,'" he also fully adopted the racism of the old empire.

42. Saryang Kim, *Tenma* (Pegasus), in *Kim Saryang zenshū* (The collected works of Kim Saryang), vol. 1 (Tokyo: Kawade Shobō Shinsa, 1973). For an English translation of this novel, see Christina Yi, *Tenma*, in *Rat Fire: Korean Stories from the Japanese Empire* (Ithaca, NY: Cornell East Asia Series, 2013). The pages numbers used for quotations from this book are from the version in the Korean translation and from this point on are cited in-text in parentheses.

43. Yi, "Tongmulwŏn ŭi mihak," 18.

44. On this occasion, Yi Myŏngsik said, "For the benefit of the work of people who either do not enjoy writing in Japanese or simply cannot, we must organize a translation service with the support and funding of Japanese who sympathize with this situation. The notion that one must either write in Japanese, or not at all, dumbfounds me." These words appear to reflect other statements by Kim Saryang in September 1940 in *Chōsen Bunka Tsushin* (Korean culture news).

45. Tomiyama Ichirō, *Bōryoku no yokan* (Premonitions of violence), trans. Sŏgwŏn Song (Seoul: Greenbee, 2009).

46. See Tomiyama Ichirō, *Memories of the Battlefield* (J. *Senjō no kioku*, K. *Chŏnjang ŭi kiŏk*), trans. Im Sŏngmo (Seoul: Isan, 2002).

47. See note 41.

48. Chul Kim, *Pokhwasulsa tŭl* (The ventriloquists) (Seoul: Moonji, 2008).

49. Yerim Kim, "Kukka wa simin ŭi pam—kyŏngch'al kukka ŭi yagyŏng, simin ŭi yŏhaeng" (Night of citizens and the state—the night watch of the police state, and the nighttime travels of citizens), in *Hyŏndae munhak ŭi yŏn'gu* (Contemporary literature), (*Han'guk munhak yŏn'gu hakhoe* [The association for research on Korean literature]) 49 (2013): 398.

50. Ibid., 380.

51. Ibid., 409.

Faces that Change

Physiognomy, Portraiture, and Photography in Colonial Korea

From the Portrait of the Ideological Criminal

After the March 1st Movement in 1919, extensive reports providing images of the faces of "ideological criminals" (*sasangbŏm*) became increasingly prevalent within popular journalism in colonial Korea. The need for a system of identification had become all the more pressing, to enable surveillance and control of the people involved in the huge independence movement. It is said that the 1919 movement was a watershed of Japanese imperialism, which forced the colonial officials to replace the policies of "military rule" with a new guiding policy of "cultural politics." But the new governance necessitated more effective and elaborate techniques of surveillance. The police archive was established in the late 1910s in this context—for the systematic identification and classification of anticolonialists under the inspecting gaze of the Government-General of Chosŏn. Forensic photography was in use even before the official announcement of the Ordinance for the Probation of Ideological Criminals (Chosŏn Sasangbŏm Poho Kwanch'al Ryŏng) in 1936, and its primary purpose was to help with the identification and capture of potential criminals, as well as regulating their probation afterward.[1]

From the 1920s on, the portraits of ideological criminals began to circulate in the public sphere through various media. The collected mug shots of the 146 Kando criminals appeared in the *Chosŏn Daily News,* and the faces of these fugitives, otherwise destined to remain invisible and imperceptible to the end, were for the first time exposed to the public (fig. 6.1).[2] With the circulation of their portraits, the faces of the underground resistance became the objects of mass gaze.[3] Stories about them circulated in the public arena via gossip and rumor. Once their faces were exposed, the struggle between anonymity and celebrity began. The face of Yi Chae-yu, one of the leaders of the Chosŏn Communist Party, was highlighted in the daily newspapers, together with detailed information on his disguises, legendary camouflage techniques, numerous hideouts, and elusive getaways (fig. 6.2).[4] For these ideological criminals, being an unidentifiable presence and hiding beneath an assumed identity was a tool of resistance. They countered the physiognomic system of the police archive with

朝鮮日報

間島事件被告面影

Figure 6.1. The profile photographs of the defendants of the Kando accident. *Chosŏn ilbo*, September 25, 1933.

a strategy of deception, using masks and make-up, code-switching, and physical disfiguration. In other words, the Socialists resisted the power of the imperial authority by remaining faceless and nameless.

My analysis, however, stops here, for I cannot explain how Yi's portrait was circulated or its precise relationship to the contested identities of the underground Socialists. The reasons for this lack of historical data are many: colonization, continuing wars and mobilizations, national separation, massive movements of people, immigration to North Korea, and huge massacres under the military regimes. As a result, only a scant amount of evidence remains as to the early practice of portraiture and studio photography in Korea. While it would be untrue to claim that no material has been collected, only a few scattered visual resources exist, and no photography magazine or bulletin was issued before 1948. The shortage of archival materials makes it difficult to completely de-

(二) 昭和十三年二月十八日 (金曜日)

神出鬼沒는李載裕等
幹部七名公判廻附
昨日、朝共再建事件豫審終
十三名은來月中

Figure 6.2. "Seven Communists including Yi Chae-yu Are Brought to Trial," *Tong'a ilbo,* February 18, 1938.

scribe the actual conventions of portraiture, the agencies behind its production, and the audiences that consumed it. Therefore, I have followed another path in examining the contexts of early photographic portraiture by taking popular literature as the main object of my study. These mundane archival sources, such as daily newspapers and popular magazines, guide me in unexpected directions to consider the nonvisual materials and discourses of photography. The portraits of the underground Socialists were enveloped in a cloud of constant gossip, hearsay, and visual metaphor, all of which depended upon photography to make claims of identity and identification.

Reading through a wide and expansive range of popular archives, my inquiry begins with the "face," one of the terms used and circulated most in association with photographic portraiture from the 1920s through the 1940s. In particular, the growing number of photographic studios, whose main business was to produce portraiture highly desired by urbanites, forged the linkage between the face and photography. But the bond was established at a more conceptual level. The increasingly popular practice of portraiture introduced a new visual paradigm that crystallized a different mode of looking, speaking, and representing the faces of self and others based on physiognomy (*insang* or *kwansang*). As the study of character through one's facial traits, physiognomy inaugurated an idea and manner of seeing that stressed the boundaries of different races, genders, and classes in late nineteenth-century Europe. It provided a way of perceiving oneself and others through a particular set of visual judgments, modes of interaction, and techniques of representation. By approaching physiognomy from the vantage point of colonial Korea, I address the limits and possibilities of shaping subjectivity under the colonial regime; examine why the face, among other possible factors, was the primary stake in the process of representing and performing identity; and consider how photography ultimately promised and compromised at once the modernist assumption, built on racial ideas and distinctions, of the face as a veridical screen reflecting human interiority. Indeed, such a physiognomic way of seeing the human face is still with us today, especially prevalent in the media technologies and medical industries in Korea. It facilitated diverse developments from the boom of plastic surgery to elaborate security systems based on facial recognition. In this contemporary context, how do we reorient the essentialist way of looking at the face as it has been historically constructed? Is it possible to think of the face beyond the physiognomic concepts of frame and power?

This chapter provides an entry point to ask these broader questions about the face by focusing on the historical moments when the first questions of perception began to be posed within particular photographic systems and representations. The first part of this chapter offers a brief history of photography as a technology of imperial differentiation, elaborated and exercised by Japanese scholars and civil authorities. The second part sheds light on the new mode of physiognomic gaze and how its affective orientations solicited different identity politics and power struggles. The final section concludes with the promise of photographic portraiture as a means toward the constitution of a better self. The racist colonial debasement of the Korean subject produced the desire for a set of technologies that might aid in the recovery and rehabilitation of the nation's unhealthy face. Photography offered such a technology.

The Negative Portrait

As the nineteenth century progressed, physiognomy emerged as a field of knowledge that encompassed a broad range of studies on the representation of different facial types. It was a widespread practice in urban locations, licensing the public to make social judgments about others based on the sense of sight.[5] The expansion of urban space proceeded in tandem with the development of physiognomic skills, which enabled urban dwellers to acquire a certain level of visual literacy to read the complex layers of the city. By judging other people's faces through their own eyes, physiognomy offered "pocket knowledge" to the middle-class men who would identify and discriminate among the increasing number of immigrants moving into the cities.[6]

Physiognomy was also a key technique within nineteenth-century racial sciences, which claimed a tight connection between particular races, their inner characters, and facial features. Underlying this practice of assessment was the presumption that the face is a transparent screen onto which the inner mind of a human being is projected. The face's perceived truth-telling functionality was exploited via elaborate systems of media and optic technologies, such as profile photography and anthropometry.

Under this rapidly changing urban environment, the classification of people grew across the wide social spectrum in 1920s Korea. Keijō (K. Kyŏngsŏng) went through a huge expansion after an urban development project created an urgent need for quickly evaluating people in the city.[7] Although systematic records of criminals were established in the late 1910s, the potential for using photographs in criminal investigation emerged in 1909, spurred by the assassination of the colonial governor Itō Hirobumi by the anticolonialist An Chung-gŭn in Harbin. The increasing number of terrorist and guerrilla attacks on imperial authorities provoked the state's urgent interest in what Allan Sekula called "a new juridical photographic realism" to aid in the effective regulation of the "dangerous classes."[8] The police archive was established at this moment and expanded during the 1930s as an oppressive system of state surveillance was activated, marking Socialists, anticolonialists, and anarchists collectively as "ideological criminals."[9]

When it comes to understanding the role photography played in the demarcation of social ethnic others, it is helpful to address the bioethnographical studies on the "Japanese race" (Nihon Jinshūron) conducted by Japanese scholars from the late nineteenth century on. At the center of their physiognomic and phrenologist project was the Tokyo Anthropological Society (Tōkyō Jinruigaku Gakki 東京人類学学会), organized around the Department of Anthropology at the Imperial University of Tokyo. From Torii Ryūzō to Tsuboi Shōgorō, a group of archaeologists and anthropologists struggled to collect, record, categorize, and visualize the facial types of different ethnic groups to define the specific features of the "Japanese race." They conducted their studies on races and species in various ways, including colonial expeditions and racial exhibitions. Both Torii and Tsuboi, among others, actively embraced photographic portraiture as a main methodology in theorizing the physical characters of social deviants, criminals, and colonial ethnic groups. While Torii employed Alphonse Bertillon's mug-shot-profile photography to define and classify the facial types of the ethnic groups under the Japanese protocol, Tsuboi was more interested in Francis Galton's composite portrait to define the generic images of criminals

Figure 6.3. Torii Ryūzō, anthropometric photographs of Korean people, ca. 1913. National Museum of Korea.

(figs. 6.3 and 6.4).[10] Their uses of the camera raise a puzzling question about the extent to which these scholars made serious use of photography, and its evidential status, to formulate knowledge for imperial control.[11] Despite the ambiguity of their initial intentions, crucial to their experiments is the way photography came to mark, theorize, and classify social ethnic others—a system of control concurrent with the rapid expansion of Japanese imperialism in the first half of the twentieth century.[12]

The two methodological poles that Torii and Tsuboi established continued to be elaborated in Japanese academia up until the wartime period.[13] In the early 1940s, the anatomist Yamazaki Kiyoshi invented an "anthropology of faces" that shows the physical characters of the different ethnic groups of the Pan-Asian co-prosperity, expanding Bertillon's anthropometric method to its utmost level.[14] On the other hand, the anthropologist Nishimura Shinji followed Galton's method of composite portraiture through the channel of Tsuboi.[15] Nishimura presented the standard facial type of the Japanese race through superimposed portraits of the different ethnic groups under the Japanese multiethnic empire (fig. 6.5). Despite different approaches, these viewpoints and visual practices all shared the belief that the surface of the body, especially the face and head, bore the outward signs of inner character.[16]

What made such physiognomic data *coherent* is the system of the archive. The archive gives conceptual unity to these images of bodies. In other words, only when operating within the rule of the archive and its institutional spaces did the images come into existence as intellectual facts about colonial faces. The physiognomic data served as an immediate means of surveillance for the police, especially during states of emergency such as war, natural disasters, or political incidents. One of the most compelling examples is the huge archive of Korean residents in Japan, which during the notorious 1923 massacre of Korean residents in Tokyo identified certain physical characteristics of Korean people by their verbal accents and specific physiognomies, like the "flat face (*nopperi kao*), the trace of topknot on the forehead, and protruding cheekbones."[17]

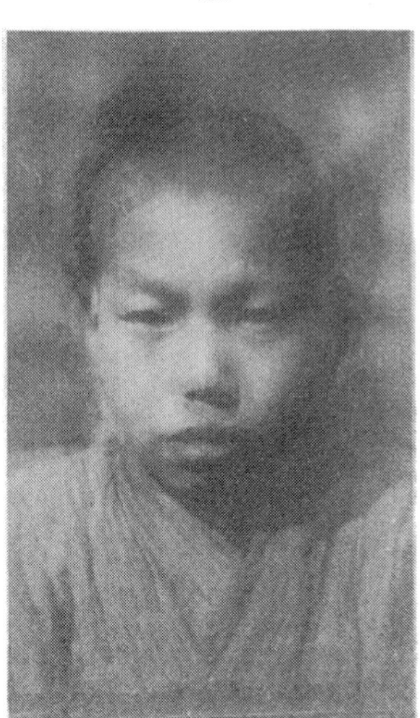

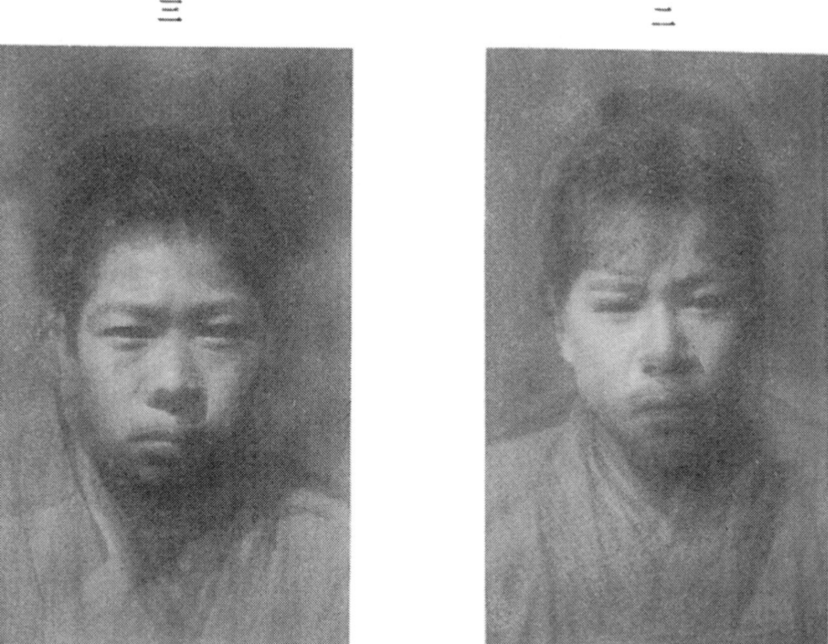

Figure 6.4. Tsuboi Shōgorō, composite portrait of juvenile criminals. *Tōyō gakugei zasshi*, vol. 2, no. 157 (October 1894).

Figure 6.5. Nishimura Shinji, "The Japanese Folk: From an Ethnological Point of View," *NIPPON*, no. 27 (1941).

As Paul Barclay points out in his study of Taiwanese postcards, the technique of "negative portrait" was most fully developed in the colony of Taiwan, in close connection with medical pathology. At the heart of this project was the relationship between imperial anthropologists and colonial informants. Their collaboration contributed not only toward law enforcement but also to the proliferation of a postcard industry that provided titillating, savage imagery of the colony for viewers back at home in Japan.[18] This was also the case in colonial Korea. Racial physiognomy was embedded in the curriculum of medical pathology at Keijō Medical College, where a group of experts in anatomy and physical anthropology, such as Kubo Takeshi, Koganei Yoshiko, Kiyono Kenji, and Hasebe Kotondo trained both Japanese and Korean students. In particular, Kubo asserted that Korean facial expressions and muscle movements revealed the signs of racial inferiority, which were in turn associated with the historical backwardness of Korea.[19]

Michel Foucault has argued for the positive aspects of social power when operating in the context of new regulatory knowledge about the body. The sciences of the body made individual subjects visible and legible by positing those subjects onto the nexus of power knowledge. These sciences worked for individuation by conferring on people the status of the subject while at the same time configuring them as objects of knowledge. Hence, it was not coincidence that the legal system of the registration of colonial migrants was established *after* the 1923 earthquake and massacre in the Japanese metropole. The identification card of each immigrant was posthaste created, managed, and archived in the department of police affairs and the local Concordia Association (Kyōwakai 協和会). As a positive deployment of power onto the body, this new system required detailed descriptions of the physical characters of individual immigrants. The basic template of the written record is fairly similar to that of the imperial conscription initiated under the Conscription Law of 1873.[20] Both created a "verbal portrait" to illustrate the physical characters of immigrants or soldiers, including their full names, addresses, physical and biological data, family makeup, friends' names, talents, careers, and more.[21] The identification card differs in that it contains a photographic record of the individual body—namely, a mug shot of a colonial immigrant that forms a frontispiece to the card (fig. 6.6).

According to John Tagg, this specific type of portraiture was invented in late nineteenth-century Europe in response to the urgent need for a disciplinary mechanism in which the bodies of social deviants could be discerned and identified in relation to other bodies.[22] Tagg's point is apposite to the mug shots of the colonial immigrants under the Japanese imperial regime. What we have in these identification cards is more than a picture of a Korean man living in Japan. It is a portrait of the "product of the disciplinary method: the body made object, enclosed in a cellular structure of space, separated and individuated, and subjected and made subject."[23] Unlike a mug shot taken in a prison or a hospital, the portrait of a Korean man is juxtaposed together with the score of the national anthem, "Kimigayo," which is printed on the final page of the card. If the mug shot codifies the body in the service of modern disciplinary techniques, the national anthem builds on a structure of feeling that enables the regionally specific recodification of the individual within an expanding imperial body living through "thousands of years of happy reign" and ruling on until "what are pebbles now/by ages united to mighty rocks shall grow."[24] This marks a curious and precarious convergence of disciplinary technique and affective mechanism. What emerged in this collision was an individual body to be reconfigured into a timeless incorporeal body existing solely for the empire.

The ominous archive of *futei senjin* ("malcontent" or "unruly" Koreans) grew in many different forms beyond the imperial metropole, especially after the introduction of mug shot photography within the police archives of the colonies.[25] The photographic archives of racial others generated and maintained an essentialist's logic of the face as a reflection of an individual's interior character. At the same time, it brought about a new technique of looking at and reading faces. The operation of the police archive, most of all, required a horizontal conception of inquiry and knowledge about faces, presupposed and practiced in the very heart of common people's lives. The emerging techniques of observation needed to be extended beyond the walls of the police precinct, since physiognomic knowledge never worked on its own unless people participated as faithful and vigilant witnesses. People were watching—and being watched—in

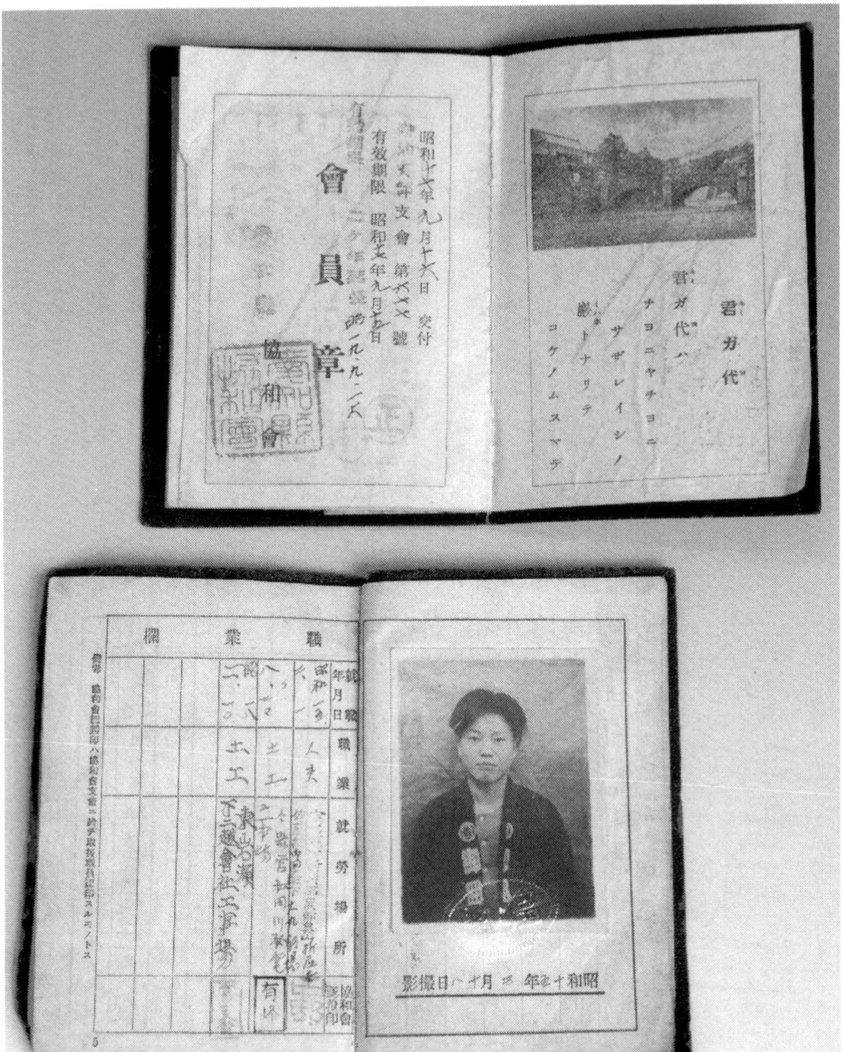

Figure 6.6. The registration cards of Korean residents in Japan, ca. 1922. History Museum of J-Koreans (Tokyo) (在日韓人歴史資料館).

this climate; at this basic level of looking, they were equal.[26] An important skill for obtaining equality was to capture, quickly and accurately, the fleeting impressions of others' faces based on one's own sense of vision. Concurrently, people should be able to distinguish themselves from the faces of others. Such comparative physiognomic analysis offered protection from being attacked and, ideally, from being suspected. Popular physiognomy emerged as a form of witnessing and surveillance for those who ventured into the light of legality; at the same time, it established the ability as well as the right to look, especially under the imperial censorship imposed on popular print culture.

Physiognomy and Communal Looking

The idea of communal witnessing proliferated throughout the 1930s in Korean mass print culture, especially in the popular contemporary magazines focusing on gossip, rumor, scandal, and everyday knowledge. Rhetoric and representation were to be found in many forms, including writings about people (*inmulji* 人物誌), commentaries on one's face (*insang'gi* 人相記), and worldly physiognomy (*kwansang ch'ŏsesul* 觀相處世術).[27] The article titled "How Should You Look at Men?" in *Samchŏnri* (April 1936) was targeted at a female audience, offering various ways to observe men in social situations. Another article, "Who Is Saving Money?," analyzed the physiognomy of rich men and introduced several promising occupations for the twentieth century. The former piece emphasized the importance of urban knowledge and a quick grasp of others' faces in the city, whereas the latter relied on the skills of facial reading developed in classical Chinese physiognomy.[28] Due to its wide conceptual spectrum of basic knowledge and an emphasis on pragmatism in application, physiognomy continued to survive throughout the times of turbulence (*nanse* 亂世).[29] The term *insang* or *kwansang* that refers to physiognomy permeated both intellectual and popular discourses, even after the harsh censorship imposed in the 1940s.

Popular magazines and newspapers forged a link between the surface signs of the body and interior depth, in which faces were naturally connected to gendered and racialized interior essences. And yet, this "surface politics of the body" was not simply given but achieved through practices of looking.[30] To recognize, identify, and classify another's face, one should learn the new social uses of eyes—such as the frontal stare, quick screening, instant observation, stealing a glance, and peeping. One should learn how to deal with contexts of communal watching and witnessing, which shaped an important part of the visual experiences of the urban public sphere. Popular physiognomy stepped in here, providing guidance toward becoming an expert at seeing and being seen and becoming better able to participate in this game.[31]

The act of communal looking had been a rather restricted convention throughout the long history of the Chosŏn dynasty. Its negative connotations still existed in the early twentieth century, since looking itself was entrenched in ideas of class and gender. Common people and females were restricted from looking at the face of a privileged male elite, since it hugely challenged or even blasphemed social norms and authority. In contrast, for lower-class people, being looked at or inspected by male authority evoked a sense of fear because it was often accompanied by physical punishment. Due to the rigid rules that governed the gaze, even painters had to draw portraits without making any eye contact with their models.[32] The portrait of Yun Chŭng (尹拯, 1629–1714), one of the most representative Confucian scholars in the late Chosŏn period, was secretly created by an artist who had to camouflage himself as a literati in order to observe and sketch Yun's appearance at a ceremonial party of literati scholars.[33] This episode reveals not only the Confucian devaluation of picture and image making but also the taboo against using one's eyes for social contact in the eighteenth century, at a time when the literati self-portrait was socially acknowledged as a form of moral cultivation. The avoidance of communal looking may also explain why female portraits are so rare in the artistic tradition of Korea.[34]

Marking a distinctive break from the traditional way of viewing, popular physiognomy embraced an egalitarian idea of looking. It leveled the hierarchical zone between watching and being watched. One radical shift is apparent in the way that faces of male intellectuals were illustrated as an object of physiognomic gaze in the contemporary popular literature. *Byŏlgŏngon* (別乾坤), a magazine renowned for its strong coverage of popular trends and taste, published a serialized article titled "The Commentaries on the Physiognomy of Famous Intellectuals." This article discusses the different physiognomies of nine leading intellectuals while juxtaposing nine illustrations corresponding to each man. Cho Myŏng-hŭi, a famous leftist novelist, is characterized as "the one who has deep eyes, sharp thought, and burning passions; he seems to have an unyieldingly grand voice that speaks a thousand words eloquently, yet actually stumbles over his own words. And it is this contradiction that shows the comic aspect of the poet!"[35] The small caption beside the illustration even exaggerates his feeble physiognomic character, stating that "Cho Myŏng-hŭi should pinch his own cheek to speak out" (fig. 6.7). As illustrated here, popular literature frequently played with the discrepancies between the interior mind and the exterior features of contemporary male elites. The facial character of male intellectuals became an object of assessment, losing any attachment to Confucian ideals of keeping the physiognomic unity between the inner depths and surface signs.

The physiognomic satire about male elites presents a radical break from prior conventions of portraiture. In effect, the ancient idea of portraiture as a means of "conveying the spirit" (*chŏnsin* 傳身) continued to exist in the Chosŏn period, during which the diverse practices of literati portraiture were executed—from the political manifestation of sovereign loyalty to portrait making for self-cultivation by literati scholars.[36] Even after the deployment of the camera, the traditional idea of portraiture survived. For example, the 1910 photographic portrait of Kim Yun-sik, a famous literati scholar and government official of the Great Han Empire (1897–1910), straightforwardly conveys male elite virtue and authority within the neo-Confucian tradition of portraiture, albeit using the new media of photography. The model is located at the center, striking a steep and authoritative pose and evoking the idea of *jŏnsin* through a full framing of the body. Very minute details of eyes and hairs are depicted while a particular set of props that connoted the elegant taste of a literati elite, such as the Confucian classics and a small fan, are displayed (fig. 6.8).[37]

Figure 6.7. "The Commentaries on the Physiognomy of Famous Intellectuals," *Pyŏlgŏngon* (別乾坤), February 1927.

By contrast, popular physiognomy occasioned a tricky combination of entertainment and documentary impulse, especially when its target was the face of male elites. Painters and illustrators were "forced to go outside to capture the facial characters of famous intellectuals on the street based on their fleeting impressions."[38] As an outcome of their street observations and sketches, the faces of national ideologues like Yi Kwang-su came to be represented and publicized by means of caricature. Once framed by the physiognomic gaze, the faces of these male elites were transformed into hyperbolic images that affected a humorous and sarcastic comment on celebrity. Cynicism penetrated the stories

Figure 6.8. Portrait of Kim Yun-sik, 1910. Source: Ch'oe In-jin, *Han'guk sajin sa, 1631–1945* (Seoul: Nunbit, 1999).

that accompanied these caricatures, regardless of the different classes and the political stances of the people being watched within the physiognomic matrix. Popular physiognomy married politics with entertainment, and in so doing, knowledge about the intellectuals was constructed and, in turn, deconstructed.

This physiognomic satire shows a certain sense of democracy that took place through the process of communal looking. To some extent, physiognomy guaranteed a verification of one's equality in demonstrating both the ability and the right to look. Walter Benjamin proclaimed that the "ability to read facial types" became of vital importance, as one had to get used to looking and being looked at.[39] He especially found in August Sander's photographs a social function of portraiture that could destabilize the honorable bourgeois portrait through its direct and anatomical gaze out onto the faces of different classes. Such a physiognomic distance, Benjamin believed, would enable the deconstruction of the mythic aura of bourgeois culture and ultimately constitute a counter-hegemonic action against the dominant order of society.

Benjamin's view of physiognomy provides the context for examining the everyday experiences of communal looking and facial recognition through the wide distribution of portraits of celebrities in early twentieth-century Korea. Popular magazines strategically displayed photographic portraits on the covers, combined with quizzes inside asking about the identification of a given celebrity, especially when in guise with masks or wearing makeup for film productions. The editor sent rice to the selected readers who provided correct answers to the physiognomic quizzes, and a list of those winners was distributed throughout the city and countryside.[40] The media events contributed to the creation of a large body of active physiognomic readers who possessed a certain level of visual literacy, cultural competency, and an ability to make decisions about their own and others' faces. They could discuss other's faces and turn this into a source of information; more important, they observed and were aware of being observed, and this observational exchange entailed specific physiognomic actions. To a certain extent, this physiognomic looking led to a critical moment of interface when a sharable code, affection, and expectation could be recognized and distributed in the colonial public sphere. Underlying this new practice of looking was a knowledge equally distributed, built on a broad configuration of fact and fiction, which functioned as "a magic lantern illuminating all kinds of stories" (*pyŏl a pyŏl kŏt*) about people and society.[41]

And yet, it should be noted that the loose, open, and egalitarian colors of physiognomy were part and parcel of imperial censorship, which allowed fairly limited room for discussions about the present and the future of the society. What Benjamin envisioned through the politics of the physiognomic gaze was entrenched in the actual politics of imperialism that controlled and determined the very channels of interface. Physiognomy demonstrates the liminality between what Jacques Rancière termed the police and the politics. Following Rancière's definition, the police signifies more than the political institution in this context. The term points to the systems that legitimize the "distribution of the sensible." In legitimating actors within a distributed order, the power of the police operates by dividing the visible and the nonvisible, the sayable and the unsayable, and the representable and the unrepresentable. Politics emerges at this point as a practice that "undoes the perceptible divisions of the police order." It implements and demonstrates "the sheer contingency of that order."[42]

In examining the tension between Rancière's idea of the police and the politics, I want to introduce specific materials of the underground Socialists that circulated around 1932 and 1933. Titled *Recommendations for Contact with the*

Masses, this work was published by and shared among the members of the Kyŏngsŏng Reading Society, a resistance group of Communist students, anarchists, and factory workers. The guidelines suggest several techniques for disguising yourself, such as: "Hide your face within the collars of a coat or scarf; avoid eye contact with others on the trolley; at the same time, try to remember the physiognomy of the people around you; always bring a bourgeois-like book or magazine with you; prepare hats and glasses; and do not leave your handwriting anywhere."[43] Many of the Socialists were experts at hiding and masking their faces, and their legendary actions often disrupted the security systems of the imperial police in Kyŏngsŏng. For instance, the police once arrested the legendary Socialist Yi Chae-yu based on his portrait as filed in the police cabinet, only to quickly set him free because they did not recognize him. This episode shows how physiognomy worked in-between the police and the politics, identification and disidentification, and imperial politics and the everyday practices of communal looking. On the other hand, the failure of the police archive illuminates the constructed and contingent nature of physiognomy as a mechanism of signification. Rather than affirming the self-presence of the subject, physiognomic looking introduced *affective orientations* and solicited an open-ended field of expression that constituted different identity politics and power struggles. It invited a "structure of feeling" that initiated a new form of cultural politics for "inducing, amplifying, and transmitting capacities to affect and be affected."[44] But how could this structure of feeling be conceptualized as a new modality of physiognomy? With its intensity, contingency, and indeterminacy, would it be possible to imagine other outcomes, other political possibilities, than racialized and gendered interiorities circumscribing the face? It is within these inquiries on the affect of faces that I turn to the concrete materials of photographic portraiture that promised, solicited, and delivered a certain set of intensities, which in turn constituted a new form of sociability encircling the colonial public sphere.

Portrait Photography and the Racialization of Face

In the early 1930s, physiognomy encountered the new techniques of portrait making. Studies of the face and facial expressions became popular among contemporary commercial and amateur photographers. The Association of Portrait Photography (Insang Sajin Yŏnguhoe) was organized in 1932, proclaiming its goal as "studies on the new techniques of lighting and print in order to create a new form of portraiture distinctive from the previous studio-photo style portrait."[45] The members of this association seemed to pursue so-called art photography (*yesul sajin* 藝術寫眞) separate from commercial photography. Many leading photographers were members of this association, including Hyŏn Il-yŏng, Sŏ Sun-sam, Kim Kwang-bae, Pak P'il-ho, Sin Ch'il-hyŏn, and Sin Nakkyun. They held their first exhibition on the second floor of the Ozawa photography store in the Namch'on area where the Japanese town was located. According to the memoirs of Kim Tong-ho, who published the first photographic magazine in Korea in 1948, *Photography Culture* (*Sajin munwha*), these members used to employ female dancers and modern girls as models for their photographic studies. The members took pictures together, discussed their results, and exhibited their photographs in their own studios. Members of the group produced high-quality portraits. Any sitter was honored to stand in front of their cameras, and thus people used to pay more to obtain a portrait from the members of this association.[46] Female photographers began their own studios in the 1920s and began producing and circulating portraits, and they often lied about their qualifications to their clients in order to "sooth the anxiety of a female audience who was not inclined to bear any confrontation with a male photographer."[47]

It is likely that the visual paradigm of popular physiognomy came to be refracted onto a collective anxiety of looking at and obtaining a portrait of a desired face. Even "negative portraits" from prisons began to be reproduced and circulated through various channels starting in the mid-1920s. This began with Song Hak-sŏn, who attempted to assassinate Satō Kojirō, a Japanese resident in Korea, in 1926. The police examination proved that Song misidentified Satō as Saitō Makoto, then governor-general of colonial Korea, based on an image of Saitō's portrait he had studied for the assassination.[48] In court, Song was asked if he had seen a portrait of An Chung-gŭn, the aforementioned national hero who had attempted to assassinate the previous governor Ito Hirobumi a decade earlier. Song said that he had secretly bought An's portrait from a Japanese photographer in the Namch'on area. Looking at An's portrait was a daily ritual for Song, which ultimately guided him to take the same path as his predecessor. The portrait of An had been initially produced as a mug shot of the criminal. A few portraits of An, presumably taken in prison, appeared in the daily newspapers and popular magazines, but its reproduction and circulation were strictly banned by the colonial government due to its affective power.[49] However, An's portraits were suddenly commercialized in the form of postcards inside and outside the colony. Many Japanese photographers produced a package containing An's portrait along with his biography and background stories of the assassination to cater to the demands of the colonial people (fig. 6.9).[50] The photographic portrait of An rapidly spread as far as Harbin, Paris, Hawai'i, and San Francisco, beyond the reach of the colonial government. It was then imported back to Korea through the global photographic circuit and continued to be reproduced in the black markets of the colonies. The distribution of An's portrait shaped a "community of affect" running across different colonies, a community in which Song was one of the most devoted members.[51] Japanese printmakers participated in this community by facilitating its material-affective process; yet within this community the Japanese imperial government controlled all distribution.

As both a representational form and a material object, An's portrait created a set of relationships—relations between different individual subjects in the colonies and the empire, their relations to the state power activated in different countries, and a form of relations not entirely determined by the power of the imperial state. The portrait of An might form what Ariella Azoulay termed a

Figure 6.9. "An Chung-gŭn Arrested by Japanese Residents—General of Korea," *Manchu il'il sinbo,* April 15, 1910, *left;* and *Kyŏngsŏng ilbo,* November 10, 1909, *right.*

"civil contract of photography," one that conceptualizes the relations between "diverse actions that contain the production, distribution, exchange, and consumption of the photographic image."[52] Photography opens up a new space of "civil relations" that includes both addressers and addressees of a photographic meaning/action—regardless of their status of citizenship—and often transcends the boundary of the modern form of sovereignty and its territorial articulation. This "citizenry of photography" crosses over the templates of state power, just as An's portrait responded to the anxieties of stateless people, modulating the tensions and affections raised at the boundaries between the legal and the illegal, the visible and the invisible, and the sayable and the unsayable.

Within the complex political relations of civic space, and as a way of responding to it, the popular literature of the 1930s began to discuss the generic face of Korean people in gendered and racialized terms. The idea of "proper physiognomy" was initially elaborated in the search for a generic type of Korean female beauty that might encapsulate the essential beauty of the nation under the colonial regime. Informed by the cultural nationalism movement, a group of male artists set out to define the facial characteristics of Korean women and incorporated the results into their artwork. The article titled "Painters' Evaluation of Beautiful Women," published in *Samchŏnri* in 1936, presents a long round-table discussion among leading painters, illustrators, and filmmakers, such as An Sŏk-yŏng, No Su-hyŏn, and Yi Sang-bŏm, who talked about the ideal facial type of the Korean woman (*mi'in* 美人). In their debates, No argued that "the faces of Korean girls are characterized as less rosy and less glossy than that of Japanese girls; but I would say the bodyline of the Korean girl is superior, and they show off really beautiful leg lines." While agreeing with No, An made an additional comment that "beautiful legs are the pride of this country indeed. Perhaps the best in the world!"[53]

Although the painters discussed the facial characteristics of Korean women, they did not present a single profile image of a face to accompany their studies. A couple of photographic portraits were shown, yet they were arbitrarily juxtaposed without providing a specific reference to the generic type of Korean female beauty. It is even more striking that the distinctive features of beauty in Korean women were often described in very indirect and elusive terms—the silhouette of a woman's attire, her shy gaze, the pose of her hands—and not articulated through the face. Another article titled "The Beauty of the Korean Woman Seen through the Painter" actually presented a few illustrations indicating the prototype of the beautiful woman, and yet none showed a frontal view. The women's backs were to the viewer (fig. 6.10). The painters conceptualized the beauty of the Korean woman not through the face but through the "tightly braided black hair, neatly folded lines on her traditional garment, a silhouette that secretly reveals a well-proportioned body line, etc."[54] The back profile view of the standing lady consistently appeared in both fine art and the mass media as one of the most popular generic images of Korea.

The absence of facial iconography could be understood in terms of what the painters conceived as beauty, existing only in one's inner mind and thus transcending physicality. The painters, however, agreed that their conception of the character of the Korean female visage might render it unfit for use as a visual icon, especially due to the stereotype of Korean faces as pale and dry. They assumed that such facial traits of Korean women were due to inadequate hygiene and unbalanced nutrition resulting from the poor condition of the country. Note that an ironic twist happens here as the face begins to be articulated as an acquired and nurtured quality of appearance rather than a purely inherent surface matter. Moreover, the face could be continually renewed and reformulated throughout different times and spaces and even evolve into a better face that reflects a better mind, depending on the achievement of civilization. The painters thought that Korean women would ultimately be "able to compete with Western women, should they get proper nutrition and treatment."[55] The contemporary newspapers shared this idea of the potential transformability of the face, especially because it dealt with the female face as the measurement of modernity.

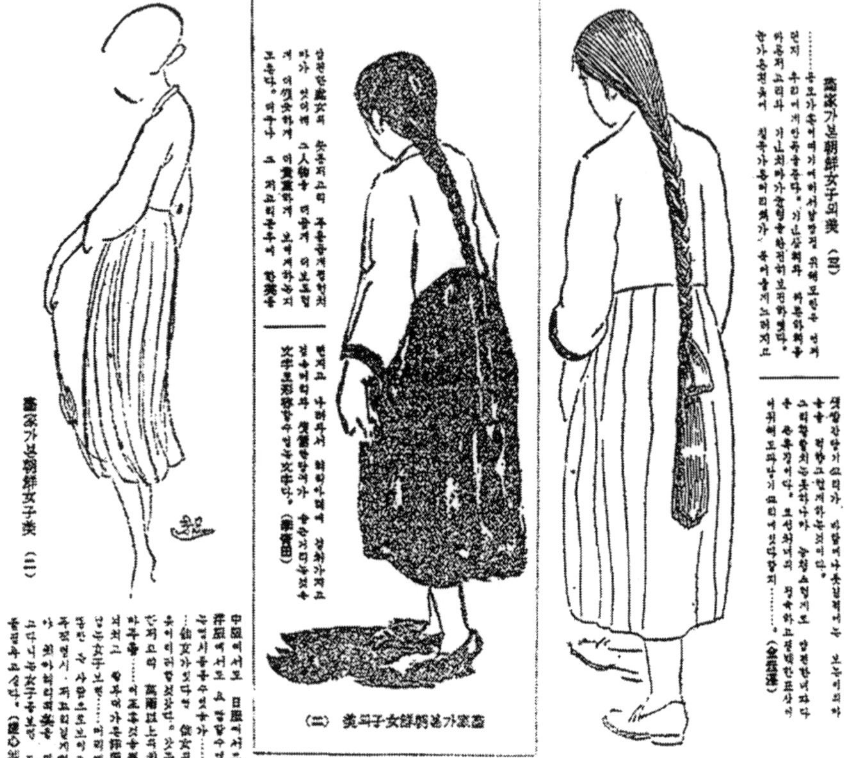

Figure 6.10. "The Beauty of the Korean Woman Seen through Painters," *Pyŏlgŏngon* (別乾坤), May 1928.

For example, "the Korean lady could almost succeed in passing into the circle of civilized women through a simple set of bodily performances and representations, like doing facial massage, showing elegant movements of the hands, making Western-style vibrant eyes with fake eyelids, and keeping a *lively-looking portrait.*"[56]

The anxiety with maintaining a natural, healthy face caused an obsession with the technologies of recovery and the rehabilitation of the vernacular colonial body. It is in this context that studio photography stepped into the contested arena of beauty by promising the appearance of a better face in a better portrait, which was believed to redeem the racialized subject. Some photo studios boasted of their incredible powers in rendering one's dry and pale face into a rosy and glossy one while preventing an overly whitened and thus artificial-looking face. Right after the Second Sino-Japanese War of 1937, a small advertisement for a photo studio appeared in *Samchŏnri,* one of the most popular, longest-surviving magazines throughout the colonial period. The studio was in the Kwanghwamun area, the urban center where the entrance to the formal Yi dynasty palace complex as well as the headquarters of the Government-General of Chosŏn were located. This studio showed off its specific techniques of lighting and retouching that could provide people with a pleasing portrait of a "naturally white face."[57] The underlying ideas produced results similar to today's techniques of digital photography, such as the blurring and sharpening effects of Photoshop, rendering one's face into a willfully constructed image. What is different here is the particular definition of the face desired most—that is, looking "naturally white." This is a nuanced expression implying that one's face should be *properly* white rather than just white or overly white. In particular, this specific degree of whiteness was encouraged in contrast to depictions of the Japanese female face, which was viewed as "unnaturally pale" and thus artificial.[58] To stay natural, paradoxically, one had to evade nature by getting the photographic operations and manipulations that the studio photographers commercialized.

In a similar context, Sunlight Healing House advertised its secret healing technique that used sunlight for people suffering from diseased and scarred bodies wounded or disfigured as a consequence of being jailed.[59] They believed that bathing in sunlight could cure everything from hair loss to nervousness. Although a limited number of written records remain, these examples illustrate how the face was centrally grounded in a widespread perception of the recovery of physical and national health. The sunlight therapies and the photographic surgery were concerned with perceptions of the face as an object of rehabilitation, which ultimately promised a curative racial reconstruction and healing of the nation's unhealthy population.

These therapeutic techniques and medical metaphors seemingly appeared for just a brief time. Such advertisements disappeared after the 1940s, once the total war regime began. But there is an interesting revisiting of this rehabilitation of the face during the height of the war period, when pure spirituality replaced the physical mark of race. Yi Kwang-su argued in his writing in 1941 that the face is something changeable and transformable, should one's convictions to the empire be strong enough. That is, the deeper one's belief and love for the emperor, the brighter and happier one's face would be. This is what he conceived of as the face of the imperial race (*yamato minzoku*). The logical ground of physiognomy was reversed in Yi's writing, since it was one's mind that could determine, promise, and even redeem the face of the racialized subject. Yi ultimately believed that Koreans might appear indistinguishable from Japanese in terms of physiognomy should they be able to reach a higher status of imperial assimilation and thus acquire a higher degree of imperial subjectivity.[60] Paradoxically, Yi's physiognomic idea undoes the modernist assumption of the face as a clear marker of the interiority of the gendered and racialized subject. As a matter of belief, physiognomy in Yi's writing turned toward moral, affective, and spiritual ends rather than remaining a visible and quantifiable marker of identification. The surface politics of the body turned back to an almost Hegelian concept of the subject whose selfhood is only fulfilled by its form of negation.

But as Kim Chul indicated in his chapter on the ethnological gaze within the Japanese Empire, the modernist assumption of the face often failed outright, and the reverse, altered form that Yi Kwang-su wrote of in 1941 never came to pass.[61]

Racial physiognomy was unable to distinguish between the imperial and the colonial body, and it could never promise a rosy future of rehabilitation of the colonial body, particularly in the context of the Japanese Empire, where defined racial affinity was an integral condition of imperial formation. In contrast, racial physiognomy enabled the colonized to pass, emulate, and often compete through the facial code of the imperial while also causing the imperial to be mistaken for the colonial. Given this complex traverse of identity, can we usefully recast the physiognomic framework as a new way of understanding the face? How might it be possible to use it as a heuristic device with which to conceive the human visage? I want to end with a small story that may help us address these problems of the racialization of the face and its association with power.

Hosoi Hajime, a private mentor of Saitō Makoto, the governor-general of Chosŏn from 1919 to 1927, avidly argued that the policy of imperial assimilation was a "utopian daydream" impossible to reach because of the very racial differences between Japanese and Koreans.[62] In fact, he had originally been a fervent assimilator but changed his position after narrowly escaping being killed by Japanese rioters at the 1923 massacre in Tokyo. At that moment, Hosoi was suspected of being Korean due to his facial characters—the flat face and protruding cheekbones—and so to assert his ethnicity, he had to show his photographic portrait as a means of evidence. This anecdote might suggest the dilemmas of the physiognomic frame of race under the Japanese Empire, especially due to its close cultural and racial affinity to the colony. But it concurrently tells us how, and in what contexts, the photographic portrait promises, or fails in its promise, to offer final proof of the racialized face. The marker is definitely drawn but in an arbitrary way. Our problem is thus to locate the contingent nature of this power and historicize it.

Notes

1. In colonial Korea, forensic photography went through several stages of development: (1) both profile photography and finger prints were used from the late 1920s, although their techniques were still at the preliminary stage; (2) triggered by the March 1st Independence Movement, forensic photography rapidly developed, and its changing phases were highlighted in newspapers during the late 1920s and 1930s; (3) a total of 354,736 forensic photographs were archived and utilized for the identification of criminals from 1920 to 1935; (4) the colonial government introduced brand new techniques in 1934, such as special chemical rooms, new fingerprinting machines, and special microscopes and mercury lighting systems; (5) a new surveillance system was invented for Korean residents in Manchuria, which took the form of an ID card with the holder's mug shot.

2. *Chosŏn ilbo*, September 25, 1933, 4.

3. Tom Gunning discusses how the circulatory possibilities of photography play a regulatory role and therefore, how photography became the ideal tool of the process of detection. See "Tracing the Individual Body: Photography, Detectives, and Early Cinema," in *Cinema and the Invention of Modern Life*, ed. Leo Charney and Vanessa R. Schwartz (Berkeley: University of California Press, 1995), 18–34.

4. *Tong'a ilbo,* February 18, 1938. About more detailed stories of Yi Chae-yu, see Kim Kyŏng-il, *Yi Chae-yu, na ŭi sidae, na ŭi hyŏkmyŏng* (Yi Chae-yu, my era, my revolution) (Seoul: P'urŭn Yŏksa, 2007).

5. For the reformulation of physiognomy as popular urban knowledge, see Sharrona Pearl, *About Faces: Physiognomy in Nineteenth-Century Britain* (Cambridge, MA: Harvard University Press, 2010), 26–56.

6. Pearl used the term "pocket physiognomy" to explain how physiognomy was popular and accessible in late nineteenth-century Britain as a subjective science for everyone with practical applications in daily life. See ibid., 6.

7. For the various data regarding the urban development of Keijō, see Son Chŏng-mok, *Ilche kang'jŏmki tosi kyehoek yŏngu* (Studies on the urban planning of the Japanese occupation period) (Seoul: Iljisa, 1990) and *Ilche kang'jŏmki tosi sahoesang yŏngu* (Facets of urban society during the Japanese occupational period) (Seoul: Iljisa, 1996).

8. Allan Sekula, "The Body and the Archive," *October* 39 (Winter 1986): 5. In this article, Sekula explores the emergence of the interrelation between photography, scientific discourse, and police archives in late nineteenth-century Europe. Christian Phéline also argues that photography became encoded in the nineteenth century as a ritual of power in which the body of the deviant was subjected to a gaze and a recording apparatus possessed by authority. See Phéline, *L'Image accusatrice* (Paris: Cahiers de la Photographies, 1985), 8–15.

9. The Ordinance of the Probation of Ideological Criminals (Chosŏn Sasangbŏm Poho Kwanch'al Ryŏng, 朝鮮思想犯保護觀察令) was passed in 1936 and continued in force until the end of the Pacific War. Although this ordinance promoted the conversion of Socialists rather than imposing a punishment on them, it is regarded as one of the most violent laws enabling police to keep suspects and ordinary people under constant surveillance. About the system of surveillance, see Chi Sŭng-jun, "1930 nyŏndae ilche ŭi 'sasangbŏm' taech'ek kwa sahoeju'ŭijadŭl ŭi chŏnhyang nonri" (The Japanese policy of the ideological criminals and the logic of Socialists' conversion during the 1930s), *Chungang sahak* 10–11 (1998): 267–292.

10. Alphonse Bertillon was the Paris police official who invented the first effective modern system of criminal identification that combines anthropometric photography and a file cabinet system. Francis Galton, a British eugenicist as well as a cousin to Charles Darwin, invented a method of composite portraiture in search of a biologically determined criminal type.

11. For example, Tsuboi once applied Francis Galton's composite photography for defining the ideal type of beautiful Japanese woman, with the support of the Mitsukoshi department store. He created the generic image of the beautiful women by overlayering the different portraits of seven different women from the Shinbashi area. For the composite portrait he made, see "Risōteki Nihon bijin" (The ideal Japanese beauty), *Mitsukoshi Times* 8, no. 4 (1910).

12. Japanese intellectual history often overlooks how early Meiji intellectual works came to be politicized in relation to Japanese imperialism while overweighting their struggles and even playing with Western intellectual thoughts. For example, Yamaguchi Masao considers Tsuboi Shōgorō's various experiments as evidence of his naïveté and playfulness originating from Edo popular culture in the previous period. See Yamaguchi Masao, *Haisha no seishinshi* (Tokyo: Iwanami shoten, 2005). But Sakano Tōru argues that this interpretive tendency always assumes the universality of Western knowledge, leading to a denigration of Japanese intellectual activities, including Tsuboi's composite portraits, not only as crude and immature but also as naïve, innocent, and apolitical. See Sakano Tōru, *Teikoku Nihon to jinruigakusha 1884–1952* (Tokyo: Keisō shobō, 2005), 45–52.

13. For Torii and Tsuboi's studies and experimentations on "Japanese race" and its relation to the formation of the national empire, see Tomiyama Ichirō, "Kokumin no tanjō to 'Nihon jinshū,'" *Shisō* 845 (November 1994): 37–56.

14. Yamazaki Kiyoshi, *Kao no jinruigaku* (Tokyo: Tenyū shobō, 1944), 1–34.

15. Nishimura Shinji, "The Japanese Folk: From an Ethnographical Point of View," *Nippon* 27 (1941): 39–45.

16. Tsuboi especially discussed the physiognomy of juvenile criminals and their inner characters on the basis of their composite portraits. See Tsuboi Shōgorō, "'Kasane shashin' o riyōshita kansōhō" (Physiognomy that uses "composite photography"), *Tōyō gakugei zasshi* 2, no. 157 (October 1894): 542–552. Likewise, Torii analyzed the physical traits of Taiwanese indigenous peoples based on the photographic data he had taken during his several expeditions in Taiwan from 1895 through 1899. See Torii Ryūzō, *Jinruigaku shashinshū—Taiwan kōtōsho no bu* (Tokyo: Tokyo teikoku daigaku rika daigaku, 1899).

17. The document of the police affairs department of the Government-General indicates the facial, bodily, and linguistic characteristics of Korean people. See Chōsen sōtokufu keihokyoku, "Chōsenjin shikibetsu shiryō ni kansuru ken" (The references for the identification of Koreans), October 28, 1913, in "Zainichi Chōsenjin shuzai no naimushō nado tsūchō," *Zainichi Chōsenjin kankei shiryō shūsei,* vol. 1, ed. Pak Kyŏng-sik (Tokyo: San'ichi shobō, 1975–1976), 28–29.

18. See Paul Barclay's chapter in this volume.

19. For more details of Kubo's racial theory and Korean students' response, see Hoieun Kim, "Anatomically Speaking: The Kubo Incident and the Paradox of Race in Colonial Korea," in *Race and Racism in Modern East Asia: Western and Eastern Constructions,* ed. Rotem Kowner and Walter Demel (Leiden, Netherlands: Brill, 2013), 411–430.

20. For the medical record made under the Conscription Law, see Takashi Fujitani, "Technologies of Power in Modern Japan: the Military, the 'Local,' the Body," *Shisō* 845 (November 1994): 163–176. The present citation refers to p. 167.

21. The registration card of Korean residents in Japan (在日朝鮮人登録証) was made and institutionalized by the Department of Police Affairs (警保局), in collaboration with the Concordia Association (協和会). For more details regarding the registration card, see Higuchi Yūichi, ed., *Kyōwakai kankei shirōshū: Senjika ni okeru zainichi Chōsenjin tōsei to kōminka seisaku no jittai shiryō* (Tokyo: Ryokuin shobō, 1991), 395–490.

22. John Tagg, *Burden of Representation: Essays on Photographies and Histories* (Minneapolis: University of Minnesota Press, 1988), 66–102.

23. Ibid., 76.

24. The entire passage of "Kimigayo," translated by Basil Hall Chamberlain, is: Thousands of years of happy reign be thine; Rule on, my lord, until what are pebbles now; By ages united to mighty rocks shall grow; whose venerable sides the moss doth line.

25. *Futei senjin* was a term created around the 1923 Great Earthquake of Kantō. It referred to the Korean residents in Japan, who were marked as disturbing elements that threatened social stability.

26. Pearl's study highlights this correlative and communal nature of physiognomy, which, she argues, provided a new mode of "shared subjectivity" to the Victorians. See Pearl, *About Faces,* 5.

27. I refer to popular magazines including *Samchŏnri* (三千里), *Pyŏlgŏngon* (別乾坤), and *Sinyŏsŏng* (新女性), along with daily newspapers such as *Chosŏn ilbo* (朝鮮日報) and *Tong'a ilbo* (東亜日報).

28. See "Ŏttŏn saram i tonmoŭgo sana?" (Who is saving money?), *Samchŏnri,* February 1936, 456–460; and "Namsŏng ŭl ŏttŏke ponayo?" (How should you look at men?), *Samchŏnri,* April 1936, 156–158.

29. This kind of expression frequently appeared in the physiognomic articles written in the total war period. See "Kwansang yŏngu" (Physiognomic studies), *Samchŏnri,* March 1940, 252–

254; and "Pugwi chi sang yŏngu" (Physiognomic studies on good-looking faces), *Samchŏnri,* April 1940, 522–529.

30. I borrowed the notion of the "surface politics of the body" from Judith Butler. As she puts it, "interiority is an effect and function of a decidedly public and social discourse, the public regulation of fantasy through the surface politics of the body." See Butler, *Gender Trouble: Feminism and the Subversion of Identity* (New York: Routledge, 1990), 136.

31. Most of the articles on physiognomy and first impression discussed the etiquette of looking and being looked back at: "Manna pogi chŏn kwa manna pogi hu" (Before and after meeting), *Pyŏlgŏngon,* January 1927, 40–43; "Munsa ŭi chŏtinsang" (The first impressions of celebrities), *Samchŏnri,* January 1936, 36–44; "Ŏttŏn saram i tonmoŭgo sana?," *Samchŏnri,* 456–460; and "Namsŏng ŭl ŏttŏke ponayo?," *Samchŏnri,* 156–158.

32. For the convention of portraiture making in Edo Japan, see Timon Screech, *Obtaining Images: Art, Production and Display in Edo Japan* (London: Reaktion Books, 2012), 165–204.

33. Yun denied his disciples' request to make a portrait due to his conviction to the Confucian ideal that considered images fictitious and secondary to the essential world. The disciples of Yun then intentionally organized the portrait project to portray him in an ideal light as the leader of their Confucian school. When Yun attended a Confucian ceremony at the private academy, the painter came dressed like students and joined the crowd to observe his face. They peeked through windows to get a look at him. About the process of making Yun's portrait, see Moon Dong Soo, *The Secret of Joseon Portraits* (Seoul: National Museum of Korea, 2012), 210.

34. For the tradition of female portraiture in Korea, see Cho Sŏn-mi, *Han'guk ŭi chosanghwa* (Portraiture of Korea) (Seoul: Tolbege, 2009), 44–48, 533–549. The rarity of female portraiture might be similar in the cultural context of Japan, although there were traditional woodblock prints picturing beautiful women, popular among urban commoners during the eighteenth and nineteenth centuries. However, Hamanaka Shinji points out that the so-called painting of beautiful women (*bijinga*) emerged as a pictorial genre in the early twentieth century, along with the development of the Nihonga tradition (Japanese-style painting) and the industry of picture postcards. See Hamanaka Shinji, "Nihon bijinga no tanjō, soshite yūkei," in *Bijinga no tanjō,* ed. Yamatane Bijutsukan (Tokyo: Yamatane Museum, 1997).

35. "The Commentaries on the Physiognomy of Famous Intellectuals," *Pyŏlgŏngon,* February 1927, 100.

36. For the literati portraiture and neo-Confucian ritual culture in the Chosŏn dynasty, see Kang Kwan-sik, "Literati Portraiture of the Joseon Dynasty," *Journal of Korean Art and Archeology* 5 (2011): 25–57.

37. For the relations between traditional portraiture and photographic portraiture at the turn of the century in Korea, see Pak Chŏng-a, "Han'guk kŭndae chosanghwa yŏngu—Chosang sajin kwa ŭi kwan'gye rŭl chungsim'ŭro" (The study on modern Korean portraiture: With emphasis on the relation to photography portraiture), *Misulsa yŏngu* 17 (2003): 201–232.

38. "Nosang ŭi in" (People on the street), *Pyŏlgŏngon,* January 1927, 25.

39. Walter Benjamin, *One Way Street and Other Writings* (London: New Left Books, 1979), 252.

40. The list of the winners was posted on the inside back cover of *Pyŏlgŏngon,* August 1928.

41. "Pando ŭi inmulji" (The people of the peninsula), *Samchŏnri,* May 1934, 86–89.

42. Jacques Rancière, *Disagreement: Politics and Philosophy* (Minneapolis: University of Minnesota Press, 1999), 28–30.

43. For the secret guidelines of the society and the police's struggles to arrest Yi, see Kim Kyŏng-il, *Yi Chae-yu, na ŭi sidae, na ŭi hyŏkmyŏng,* 124–126, 177–186, 247–249.

44. Ben Anderson, "Modulating the Excess of Affect: Morale in a State of Total War," in *The Affect Theory Reader*, ed. Melissa Gregg and Gregory J. Seigworth (Durham, NC: Duke University Press, 2010), 161.

45. Yi Kyŏng-min, "Pak P'il-ho rŭl malhada—sajin chedo ŭi hyŏngsŏng kwa chŏngch'ak" (Pak Pil-ho and the formation and establishment of the photographic institutions), in *The Commemorative Conference of the 100th-Year Anniversary of the Birth of Hyŏn Il-yŏng, Sŏ Sunsam, and Pak P'il-ho* (Seoul: Han'guk sajinsa yŏnguso, 2003), 31.

46. Yi Dong-ho, "Wishing for New Photography," *Photography Culture* (*Sajin munhwa*) 12 (June 1950): 44.

47. Yi Kyŏng-min, *Kyŏngsŏng, sajin e pakida—sajin ŭro ilnŭn Han'guk gŭndae munhwasa* (Kyŏngsŏng pictured: Reading the cultural history of modern Korea through photographs) (Seoul, Sanch'ekja, 2008), 123–131; and Ch'oe In-jin, *Han'guk sasjinsa, 1631–1945* (History of Korean photography, 1631–1945) (Seoul: Nunbit, 1999), 198–202.

48. The details of his story appeared in the article "The Crime Due to the Misrecognition of the Governor-General," *Tong'a ilbo*, May 2, 1926, 3.

49. For example, there is a record that the two people who reproduced An's portrait—depicting him tied up with handcuffs and shackles—were jailed and punished in 1926. See *Chosŏn ilbo*, January 17, 1926, 2.

50. According to Yun Pyŏng-sŏk's research, there is a record written in 1925 in the archive of the Ministry of Japanese Foreign Affairs regarding the circulation of An's photographs and postcards. See Yun, "The Photographs of An Chung-gŭn," *Hanguk tongnip undongsa yŏngu* 37 (December 2010): 339. Also, see Yi Kyŏng-min, *Kyŏngsŏng, sajin e pakida*, 138–145.

51. The records in the Ministry of Japanese Foreign Affairs indicate that An's portrait was in demand in China because Chinese people regarded his assassination as a heroic expression of anticolonialism. See ibid., 401.

52. Ariella Azoulay, *The Civil Contract of Photography* (New York: Zone Books, 2008), 86.

53. "Hwabaek ŭi mi'in pyŏng" (Painters' evaluation of beautiful women), *Samchŏnri*, August 1936, 116–122.

54. "Hwagaga pon Chosŏn yŏja ŭi mi" (The beauty of the Korean woman seen through the painter), *Pyŏlgŏngon*, May 1928, 117, 191, 219. Also, it should be noted that at the peak of imperial subjectification, the cultural specificities of Korea were celebrated rather than excluded as unique and essential artifacts to be preserved for the crucial assets of Asianness. In particular, female robes and clothing were highly valued as marks of Koreanness and coloniality.

55. "Hwabaek ŭi mi'in pyŏng," 116–122.

56. *Chosŏn ilbo*, April 14, 1939, 4.

57. The advertisement of Yŏng kwang sajinkwan, *Samchŏnri*, November 1938, 317.

58. *Chosŏn ilbo*, April 14, 1939, 4; and *Tong'a ilbo*, September 16, 1934, 3.

59. "T'aeyang kwangsŏn chiryowŏn" (Sunlight healing house), *Samchŏnri*, September 1932, 58–60.

60. Yi Kwang-su [Kayama Mitsurō], "Kao ga kawaru" (Faces that change), *Bungei shunjū*, November 1940, 19–21.

61. See Chul Kim's chapter in this volume.

62. Hosoi Hajime, "Dai Nihonshūgi no kakuritsu to chōsen tōchi hōshin no henkei" (The establishment of "great Japaneseness" and the changing policies toward Chōsen), September 17, 1923, in *Saitō Makoto bunsho: Chōsen sōtoku jidai kankei shiryō* (Seoul: Koryŏ sŏrim 1990), 44–49.

Speaking Japanese

Language and the Expectation of Empire

> Taiwan's Taroko, what is its specialty?
> Gold sand, gourds, Taroko paper, paulownia sandals of plums and silk floss
> A Taroko maiden's "Hello."
>
> —"Taroko Melody" (Taroko fushi), ca. 1930s

The policy of forced Japanese-language education in colonial Taiwan and Korea has been widely portrayed as the exemplar of Japan's attempt to assimilate colonial populations to Japanese norms. Yet early Japanese travelers came to Taiwan with two contradictory expectations about the role of Japanese in the empire: one, that a shared language would eventually make a cohesive nation out of the colonial and metropolitan populations; and two, that Aborigines in Taiwan's so-called Savage Territory (*banchi*) would not speak Japanese and therefore would remain outside the nation. Encounters with Japanese-speaking Aborigines challenged these expectations, however, and led to the production of a form of linguistic inequality between colonizer and colonized based not on skill but on race. Represented in the language of sentiment, linguistic expectations in colonial Taiwan illuminate a broader racialization of difference within the Japanese Empire in the 1930s.[1]

Expectations

By the 1930s, Japanese travelers to Taiwan's Taroko Gorge had come to expect a "hello" from the region's Aboriginal women. The greeting would be polite, nonthreatening, and above all, in Japanese (*konnichiwa*). Such an encounter might have connoted a significant success for Japanese colonial policy. Japan acquired Taiwan in 1895, and after considerable debate, established a Government-General to rule the island outside the jurisdiction of Japan's constitution. Evading the designation of Taiwan as a colony (*shokuminchi*), the government argued that the people of Taiwan would need to be gradually assimilated to Japanese norms before it would fully incorporate the island into the nation. Taiwan's indigenous population was excluded even further from the nation. Overwhelmed by the prospect of establishing Japanese control over the indigenous populations in

Taiwan's mountainous central region, the Government-General revived the Qing practice of confining a great majority of Aborigines within this region and declaring the area "ungovernable." Making use of technology that had been unavailable to the Chinese, the Government-General of Taiwan wrapped the border of the Savage Territory with electrified fences and guard posts. Japanese who wished to visit the interior were required to apply for a permit and told that they entered the Savage Territory at their own peril.[2]

Three decades later, Japanese-speaking Aborigines were so common as to become material for a popular song. Yet Taroko Gorge, on the periphery of the Savage Territory, was not, with all the fanfare of modern nationalism, incorporated fully into the Japanese nation. Nor were Aborigines, forced to undergo Japanese language and cultural education from a young age, embraced as subjects of the Japanese emperor equal to those from the metropole. Rather, despite the rhetoric of gradual assimilation, Aborigines—and residents of Taiwan in general—became the subjects of regular evaluations of their fitness for incorporation into the nation, the first and foremost of which was the evaluation of their ability and willingness to speak Japanese.

The idea that language and nation are coterminus, that nation comes from language, and that nations are definable through language is a form of language ideology rather than historical truth.[3] Indeed, it would be hard to find an existing nation that meets the standards of cultural histories of nationalism. Language is notoriously variable, with even the most codified of tongues open to internal debate over the "correct" way to conjugate a verb, how to gender speech, and which registers are appropriate for different classes of people. For this reason, Michael Silverstein has argued that language is a metalinguistic category, a subjective matter of where boundaries between languages, dialects, and creoles should be rather than an objective description of what they truly are.[4] Indeed, despite the confidence with which they drew the linkage between language and nation, more often than not nineteenth- and twentieth-century linguistic nationalists found themselves confronting language as a problem to be solved rather than a reality to be embraced.[5]

Within this highly politicized realm of speech, language expectations played an outsized role in producing and reproducing a flexible hierarchy of inclusion and exclusion in the Japanese Empire. Language expectations became powerful precisely at the fuzzy border between inside and outside, where the question of whether a person spoke Japanese fluently *enough* or spoke *pure* Japanese could mean the difference between violent death at the hands of a rampaging mob or safe passage (as in the aftermath of the Great Tokyo Earthquake of 1923) or, in a more mundane but no less important example, between access to higher education or the denial of upward mobility (in the case of colonial subjects in Taiwan).

This chapter focuses on language expectations in colonial Taiwan, where the record of Japanese travelers' linguistic encounters with three distinct ethnic groups throws the history of language expectations into stark relief. Japanese accounts of colonial Taiwan divided the island into Japanese (*naichijin*), Chinese (*hontōjin* or Taiwanjin), and Aborigines, who were almost indiscriminately referred to as savages (*banjin*). Colonial educators developed distinct educational tracks for each group, and Japanese travelers arrived with distinct expectations for how members of each group would and should speak Japanese. In particular, Japanese travelers commented on the Japanese-language speech of Aborigines. This chapter explores language expectations as a way of thinking more broadly about the history of race, language, and nation in the Japanese Empire.

As sentiments, language expectations emerged out of the particular context of Japanese imperialism and linguistic nationalism. At the same time, expectations produced new contexts for imperial encounters by pushing travelers and governments to reevaluate the end goals of imperialism and the character of the Japanese nation. Early travel writers exclaimed at the ability of Aborigines to speak Japanese, exposing their own expectation that Aborigines would be incapable of speaking Japanese (or at the minimum not very good at it) despite the intense focus of the Government-General of Taiwan on language education. Later travel writers, particularly those writing in the 1930s, continued to express surprise at the Japanese-language speech of Aborigines. Yet these travel writers also spent considerable time evaluating the appropriateness of Aboriginal speech. The primacy of the question of whether or not Aborigines spoke Japanese in an *appropriately Aboriginal way* belied the new expectation that the Japanese-language speech bridged two immutably different and unequal social groups within the empire. These language evaluations excluded Japanese-speaking Aborigines as "not-quite Japanese." They also, however, reified a new sense of ethnic Japaneseness within a multilingual empire, that is, the inherent ability to evaluate "pure" Japanese.

Traveling Expectations

In 1924 and 1925, Ōyama Takeshi and Hamada Tsunenosuke traveled to Taiwan. Ōyama was an official in the Bureau of Colonization (Takushokukyoku). Hamada was the chief of the bureau, touring the colonies to get a firsthand account of their conditions. They traveled around the entire Japanese Empire, from Karafuto; to Korea and Manchuria; and finally, to Taiwan. In 1928, Ōyama published a report on the journey, in which he wrote enthusiastically about how his encounters with colonial territories and peoples challenged his original expectations. The book's title, *Waga shokuminchi* (Our colonies) summed up his bold attempt to capture what he termed "the reality" of colonial conditions through firsthand observation.[6]

Ōyama and Hamada were only two of thousands of metropolitan Japanese who traveled to the colonies on what were known as investigative (*shisatsu*) travel missions between 1905 and 1945. The first investigative travel mission took place at the dawn of Japan's informal colonization of Manchuria. In 1905 an international cadre of diplomats, journalists, and other notables, sponsored by the Japanese government, boarded the *Manchuria Maru* in Yokosuka and arrived in Inchŏn a few days later. They traveled through Korea to Manchuria, filing reports in newspapers around the country. Their accounts provided metropolitan residents with their first look at peacetime Manchuria.[7] The following year, the Ministry of the Army, the Ministry of Education, and the South Manchuria Railway Company sponsored the first imperial school field trip (*shūgaku ryokō*) to Manchuria and Korea. The practice of sending students to Korea, Manchuria, and Taiwan to investigate various aspects of colonial conditions continued throughout the imperial period. In addition to student groups, educational associations, local chambers of commerce, intellectuals and artists, and government officials boarded steamers in Yokohama, Kobe, Shimonoseki, and Moji to see the empire firsthand. While Korea and Manchuria were the most popular destinations, a surprising number of school groups, public intellectuals, and officials traveled to Taiwan as well to report on the progress of colonialism there. To encourage this sort of travel, local officials published guidebooks and pamphlets, many of which insisted that cholera, which had famously killed Prince Kitashirakawa of the Konoe Division in 1896; malaria; and head-hunting barbarians were under control. For their part, travelers remained unconvinced.

Despite the ongoing efforts of local tourism boosters in Taiwan and Korea to persuade travelers that the colonies were quite modern, one of the most common tropes of colonial travel writing was the expression of surprise at the modernity of colonial infrastructure. Travelers were shocked to find that it equaled or at times even surpassed that of the metropole. Itagaki Hōki, who traveled with his wife to Taiwan in 1931, reported their surprise when they disembarked the train at Taihoku (Ch. Taipei) Station only to find themselves in the middle of a modern boulevard. "This is so civilized," Itagaki said. "But I thought we were going to Taiwan!" his wife replied.[8] Travelers to Korea recorded similar shock at the "Japanification" (*naichika*) of Pusan, the gateway to Korea. "It's not just *like* Japan," wrote Arakawa Seijrō in 1918, "it *is* Japan."[9]

Travelers expected to find that the colonies reflected the system of political exclusion built around their supposed "backwardness." In the case of Taiwan, the act to be justified was not imperialism per se but rather the exclusion of Taiwan from the jurisdiction of the constitution. Following the acquisition of Taiwan in 1895, the Meiji government balked at formalizing Taiwan as a colony, which suggested that Japan was simply reenacting the inequities of European imperialism in Asia.[10] The government placed Taiwan under the authority of a military government, declaring it outside the boundaries of the constitution yet not quite a colony. Instead, it would be governed by a governor-general, who had the power to issue ordinances "with the force of law"—a power that in the metropole was reserved for the emperor.[11] The effect of removing Taiwan, and later Korea, from the Japanese legal and political system excluded residents of these territories from participation in parliamentary elections and permitted the use of corporal punishments, such as flogging, that were outlawed elsewhere. The justification for this exclusion was that residents of Taiwan, unfamiliar with modern ways, were not prepared to participate fully in a modern nation. The Government-General of Taiwan thus declared its commitment to gradual assimilation (*dōka*) while maintaining harsh terms of colonial rule.[12]

When travelers found modern infrastructure instead of undeveloped backwaters, they struggled to rearticulate the relationship of the colonies to the metropole. Events on the ground exacerbated their confusion. Colonial uprisings intensified the question of whether Japanification and acculturation policies would actually result in a "Japanese" colonial population. In Korea, the March 1, 1919, independence uprising brought the feasibility of Japanification to the forefront of popular debate. The colonial police responded violently and aggressively to the nonviolent movement, raising questions about the future of "military rule" in colonial Korea in both the international and the domestic press. In response, the prime minister, Hara Kei, vowed to integrate the metropolitan and the colonial legal and political systems under a new policy of "extending Japan" (*naichi enchō*). Yet many Japanese commentators saw the uprising as evidence of the inevitable failure of Japanification. While it was one thing to alter the infrastructure to match the metropole, it was quite another to alter the mindset of the people. In Taiwan, protests took a different but equally contentious tack: in 1921, the League for the Establishment of a Taiwanese Parliament (Taiwan Gikai) began to advocate for the establishment of a legislative body "popularly elected by *all* residents of the island irrespective of race."[13] Arguing that Taiwan was a unique place whose special features required local rather than imperial government, the movement thrived for nearly fifteen years with broad support from local intellectuals and the middle class.

By the early 1920s, the certainty with which colonial officials embarked on projects of assimilation in the early days of colonialism had faded, replaced by a palpable insecurity about the future of the empire. Ōyama and Hamada experienced as much when they visited schools in Keijō (K. Seoul). There, they were treated to stories of Korean students asking their Japanese teachers, in Japanese, "When will you let Korea be independent?"[14] On the one hand, Ōyama acknowledged, the student asked the question in Japanese, thus demonstrating the success of Japanese-language education, a cornerstone of colonial policy throughout the empire. On the other hand, the content of the question was troubling. Would Japanification and assimilation create Japanese subjects, or was it time to reconsider what a Japanese subject was?

Language Expectations in Colonial Taiwan

The Japanese Empire has long been treated as an "anomaly" among empires for its geographic contiguity and presumed cultural or ethnic cohesion.[15] Yet like the empires of France and Britain, the imperial Japanese government and the colonial governments-general engaged in their own work of cultural homogenization, first under the banner of assimilation, which aimed to bring colonials "up" to the modern level of Japanese, and later, imperialization, which sought to legitimate Japan's supremacy in Asia by demanding that colonial populations both perform a distinct ethnic cultural heritage and demonstrate that they had internalized their loyalty to the Japanese emperor. Japanese-language education was a core principle in the assimilation phase of Japanese imperialism, and Japanese-language *evaluation* was a key feature of the imperialization phase. In both cases, language expectations disguised the political relationship between colonizer and colonized as a matter of linguistic competence and inherent sensibility.

The centerpiece of colonial education in Taiwan was Japanese-language training. As the Government-General of Taiwan framed it, the basis for assimilation would be language. Officially referred to as "national language" (*kokugo*) rather than "Japanese" (Nihongo or *naichigo*), early linguistic nationalism linked Japanese-language use to membership in the national polity as well as to the spiritual or affective body of the nation. For this reason, the Government-General of Taiwan as well as of Korea relied on Japanese-language training as the foundation of their programs of assimilation.

By 1906, the Government-General of Taiwan had established two distinct schooling systems for Chinese and Aboriginal residents of colonial Taiwan. Taiwanese Chinese who could afford to send their children to school sent them to one of 180 common schools (*kōgakkō*), which provided six years of elementary education and were the first step in matriculating into the teacher-training college and the medical college. Later, these schools would become the gateway to a wide variety of secondary options and central to social mobility in the colony.[16] For Aboriginal residents of the colony, the Government-General established "centers for educating for savage children" (*bando kyōikujo*) in Aboriginal provinces. In 1910 there were two dozen education centers, with around two hundred students enrolled. By 1920 there were over one hundred education centers, with over two thousand children enrolled.[17] The education center curriculum differed markedly from that of the common schools. Under the broad rubric of "acculturation" (*kyōka*), the education centers emphasized basic tasks. In particular, the centers taught Japanese-language communication, as officials considered this skill to be necessary for assimilating Aborigines to Japanese cultural norms and incorporating Aborigines as laborers into the colonial economy.[18] As one colonial official explained in the pages of *Riban no tomo* (The savage manager's friend), "Reading before writing, and speaking before reading."[19]

If he followed colonial policy at all, which as an official in the Bureau of Colonization Ōyama certainly did, Ōyama should thus have had every reason to expect that at least some Aborigines would speak Japanese. Yet Ōyama was taken aback by the ability of Aborigines to speak perfect, polite Japanese. In his travelogue, Ōyama reported arriving at a station in southern Taiwan to find dozens of Aborigines, whom he called *seiban* (raw savages), standing outside the police building.[20] He noted the other-worldliness of their appearance: colorful long clothes on the women, strange jewelry, and arms that were covered from wrist to shoulder in "savage tattoos." To his surprise, "everyone understood Japanese." "Isn't your belt tight?" he asked. "No, it's not a problem," a smiling man answered. Ōyama noted their barefootedness. "Aren't your feet hot?" he inquired. "No, they are not hot," another answered. Ōyama thought of the men running through the jungle barefoot and asked, "Well, don't you ever get cut and injured by thorns?" "Not very often," the man replied. "And anyway, if we do get injured we get better within three days." This, Ōyama thought, was probably a thinly disguised sneer at the weakness of the Japanese.[21]

Ōyama was not alone in his surprise. Ishikawa Toraji, who traveled to Taiwan in 1918, reported speaking with several people. But the only people whose speech he commented on were the Aborigines he met in the Savage Territory. "I grabbed my sketchbook and walked here and there," he wrote in his contribution to the volume, *Shin Nihon kenbutsu* (Sightseeing new Japan). "Along the way, every male savage I met gripped his sword and greeted me with "Hello" (*konnichiwa*)." The encounter was worthy of note, he wrote, because "this state of affairs was somehow uncanny."[22] The appearance of Japanese-speaking Aborigines and, moreover, *polite* Japanese-speaking Aborigines struck Ishikawa as strange and unsettling.

Travelers' fascination with the fluency of the Aborigines was in marked contrast to their disappointment with everyone else. Similar to the distinction between official expectations for Japanese, Taiwanese, and Aboriginal language learners, conversations with Aborigines operated within a different set of expectations than those applied to the island's Chinese population. Itagaki Hōki, who published his *Taiwan kenbutsu Man-Sen manpo* (Sightseeing in Taiwan, meandering in Manchuria and Korea) in 1931, had nothing but disdain for the Taiwanese he encountered because they could not speak Japanese. Itagaki had expected to find Japanese the lingua franca of colonial Taiwan. Instead, he found endless frustration with non-Japanese-speaking locals. Wandering into a small market, Itagaki's wife, Rikiko, asked a fishmonger, "What kind of fish is this?" The reply came as a nonsequitur, "Three hundred seventy-five grams for twenty *sen*—cheap, cheap."[23] Itagaki summarized the encounter: "Even if you ask a *wanjin* [Taiwanese], Japanese doesn't work."[24] His emphasis on the "even" in that statement suggested that he expected that *at least* the Taiwanese would be able to speak Japanese. A visit to another market in Takao resulted in a similar identification of the linguistic failings of the Taiwanese, in this case women: "Again we went to the market. There were a lot of Taiwanese women (*wanpu*), who sold [their goods] in broken Japanese."[25]

Itagaki was not alone in his frustration with the uneven spread of Japanese-language use in Taiwan. Writing in the journal *Kokugo kyōiku* (National language education) in 1925, a teacher at the Nisshin Common School in Taihoku expressed his dismay at the rapidly diminishing abilities of native-born Japanese speakers to speak proper Japanese. He explained that two problems faced Japanese-language educators in Taiwan. One was the difficulty inherent in the Japanese language itself for those who had never been exposed to it. In this category he included the use of honorifics, the question of when to drop the subject, and the use of postfixed particles. More serious than the difficulty of the Japanese language itself, however, was the lack of a proper Japanese-language environment in which to be immersed. Taiwanese students were not the only ones using Taiwanese as their everyday language. The Japanese around them were using "Made in Taiwan Japanese" (*wansei kokugo*). After relating a conversation he overheard at the vegetable market, in which the speaker repeatedly conjugated verbs and adjectives incorrectly, the teacher pleaded, "Are there women in Japan *anywhere* who would use words like this?"[26]

In this context of disparate expectations, travelers treated Aboriginal Japanese-language speech as a positive sign of assimilation. Whereas reports of dialogues with Chinese Taiwanese and Japanese emphasized the corrupted nature of their Japanese-language speech, Ōyama's and Ishikawa's reports presented Aboriginal speech as fluent Japanese. In contrast to Ōyama's report on Korean students and the independence problem, the Aborigines in these travelogues spoke in polite forms, never straying from the boundaries of acceptable conversation (leaving Ōyama to wonder whether or not he had been insulted rather than bristling from an explicit jab). Despite the apparent differences in customs to which Ōyama and Ishikawa referred, the deferential attitude with which Aborigines greeted and responded to Japanese travelers suggested that the gap between Japan and the Aboriginal territory was shrinking. Indeed, Ishikawa commented that although it was a strange experience, being greeted by Aborigines in the Savage Territory in Japanese "could not but make one feel pleased."[27]

The Racialization of Expectations

A number of scholars have noted a change in Japanese representations of Aborigines in the early 1930s from "savagery to civility," in the words of Leo Ching.[28] The shift to representations of Aborigines as civil participants in the imperial regime paralleled larger changes in imperial ideology, which T. Fujitani has characterized as a shift from the "vulgar" racism of the early years of empire to the "polite" racism of the late 1930s. In contrast to the assimilation rhetoric of the early years of colonialism, polite racism constituted certain populations as "somehow different" yet able to be incorporated into the imperial national body.[29] This new racialization was circulated through an explosion of appreciation for and consumption of local and colonial culture in the metropole and among travelers to the colonies.[30] Korean folk songs swept the charts in the metropole. Travelers to Taiwan flocked to performances of "savage dances." Travelers embraced the ethnic difference, or what they called the "local color" (*rōkaru karā*) of the colonies.

Within this imagination of a multiethnic nation, colonial populations were marked as not only "somehow different" but timelessly so. Reports of encounters with Japanese-speaking Aborigines suggest that travelers also reimagined their own place within the nation. The ability to hear and evaluate the purity of Japanese-language speech belonged to the "pure Japanese" people, distinct from their fellow countrymen (*dōhō*) in the colonies. It demarcated a sharp boundary of ethnoracial difference within the imperial nation.

By the mid 1930s, travelers had come to expect that Aborigines would speak *kokugo* (national language) to the point that travelers recorded encounters with Aborigines as Japanese-language examinations. The idea that Japanese travelers were the ultimate arbiters of the appropriateness, purity, and meaning of colonial Japanese speech united these representations of Aboriginal speech. Japanese speech, as Osa Shizue has argued, was split into a sensibility and a skill that ethnic Japanese innately possessed, the performance of which was mandated for colonial populations throughout the empire.[31] Nakanishi Inosuke, a left-wing writer who traveled to Taiwan specifically to critique the dominant representation of the island and its inhabitants, exposed this relationship of evaluator-evaluated when he challenged the trope of the polite Aborigine in his *Taiwan kenbunki* (Record of things seen and heard in Taiwan). Guided by one Mr. O, Nakanishi visited an Aboriginal house in a small village. As they waited for their servings of *yahō*, a staple vegetable dish, an Aboriginal chief (*tōmoku*) berated Nakanishi's guide: "Although you insisted that we throw a big reception for him because it's still uncommon for a Japanese (*naichijin*) to come from Tokyo to stay the night in an Aboriginal village, you brought him to *this* kind of house. My house is built in Japanese style (*naichi shiki*), with *tatami* mats no less. Why didn't you bring him there?"[32] The speech struck Nakanishi as mysterious. Not only did the chief speak Japanese, "he spoke not in the Japanese of an islander or a Korean, or even in the Japanese of a Chinese. This was the Japanese of a pure Japanese (*jun Nihonjin no Nihongo*)."[33]

Nakanishi broke the chief, Buruna, out of the standard frame of polite call-and-response. The chief had traveled to Japan as part of a Japan tour group (*naichi kankō dan*) in 1907. The Government-General sponsored these trips in the hopes that a firsthand encounter with the industrial and military power of metropolitan Japan would convince the Aboriginal elders that resisting the colonial government was futile. The itineraries included visits to ammunition and weapons factories, newspaper printing presses, and the brick hearts of Japan's major cities.[34] Yet for Buruna, these institutions were secondary to his experiences of life in the metropole. Nakanishi reported Buruna's view of the imperial center: "There are a lot of people in the *naichi*. So many it's like they're ants wriggling around. Why do they live like that?"[35] In allowing Buruna to comment on life in the metropole, Nakanishi reversed the ethnographic gaze of Japanese imperial travel literature and illuminated the standard boundaries of representations of Aboriginal speech.

What Nakanishi could not overcome, however, were his expectations about his own role in the multilingual Japanese Empire. Nakanishi positioned himself as the arbiter of linguistic purity, praising Buruna for speaking a Japanese so delocalized that ironically, it would have been difficult to find outside the highly regimented and highly unequal interactions of colonizer and colonized. Lacking sound recordings of conversations, readers had no way of evaluating the truth of reports such as, "He spoke the Japanese of a pure Japanese," as Nakanishi described Buruna's speech. Rather, these evaluations of Aboriginal fluency, of purity and of Japaneseness, relied on the reader's expectation that the author possessed the ability to differentiate between pure and impure Japanese. More important, these narratives assumed that both reader and author shared a definition of what pure Japanese was.

In the 1930s, encounters with Aboriginal individuals appeared in travel narratives as evaluations. These encounters constituted the Japanese-Aboriginal relationship as one of coercive expectation: Japanese expected Aborigines to prove their linguistic competence at each encounter, which simultaneously reaffirmed their own competence as evaluators. Shinoda Jissaku, who traveled to Taiwan in 1935 as part of the entourage of Korea's Prince Yi, found little to appreciate when he encountered an Aborigine at Sun-Moon Lake who did not, or would not, speak to him in Japanese. "I asked him, 'Do you understand *kokugo?*' and the response was, 'Mo-ura,' which I took to mean, 'Nope' (*wakaranu*—N.B.: this phrasing would have been quite rude)."[36] Taking it as his responsibility to investigate the spread of *kokugo* in Taiwan, Shinoda did not initiate conversation for the purpose of listening to what Aborigines had to say. Rather, he simply assessed whether or not they could understand what he was saying *to* them. Shinoda later attended a national language speech contest in Takao where, to his delight, the majority of speakers used *kokugo* flawlessly. He reproduced parts of the speeches in his narrative yet reserved his commentary for the question of whether the *kokugo* was good, fluent, perfect, or accentless.[37]

When Aborigines did speak *kokugo,* travelers had expectations about the kind of topics with which an Aborigine should be concerned. Matsuda Kiichi, an Osaka middle school student who traveled to Okinawa and Taiwan in 1937, recorded his surprise that Aborigines were not only concerned about money but were savvy about earning it. Arriving at Taroko, by this point famed for the polite "hellos" of its "Taroko maidens," Matsuda encountered two Aboriginal men near the train station. They offered to take a picture with him for ten *sen* each. At first, he reported being excited by what he saw as the significance of their demand: "That savages (*banjin*) have come to appreciate money so much made me happy. With no tattoos, and a yukata tied with a red *obi,* they are not a bit different from Japanese (*naichijin*)!" The Aborigines' embrace of money struck Matsuda as un-Aboriginal. Upon reflection, this was a positive sign that the gap between Japanese and Aborigines was diminishing.[38] Yet Matsuda quickly reset his expectations about what made a person "Japanese": "But, the threateningness of their eyes and their black faces are parts that can't be denied."[39] In other words, at the moment that his Aboriginal interlocutors engaged him in terms defined and advocated by the colonial authorities for inclusion in the Japanese nation, Matsuda changed the terms. Their black faces were now a barrier that no linguistic or cultural adaptation could overcome.

It now seems time to come back to the question raised above, of whether how to be a Japanese subject changed in the 1920s and the 1930s. Early linguistic nationalists, such as Ueda Kazutoshi, argued that language was the lifeblood of the nation. Ueda, the leader of the campaign for a standardized national language in Japan (*kokugo undō*), famously articulated this claim in 1894 when he argued that "the Japanese language is the spiritual blood of the Japanese people."[40] During this era of monolinguistic nationalism, speech diversity, as Hiraku Shimoda has argued, "was not a problem of function . . . rather, it was a problem of political psychology."[41] As Ueda saw it, the problem was not that people could not understand each other but rather that they would not *feel* like a unified nation if they did not speak the same language. "Dialectism" threatened the unity of the nation because "even though we are all Japanese, it is like meeting foreigners."[42] During this time, the Governments-General of Taiwan and Korea inaugurated intense Japanese-language education campaigns that intended to transform colonial subjects into Japanese through linguistic conversion. In the metropole, the education system waged a similar (if less violent) campaign against dialect. Students who slipped into their own local dialect in school were publicly chastised by having to wear dialect tags (*hōgen fuda*) on their uniforms.[43]

By the 1930s, however, rural revitalization programs in the metropole and pressure from settler and colonial groups in the colonies sparked a serious discussion of the political and social value of provincial vernaculars, replacing the binary logic of monolinguistic and assimilation-based nationalism of the early twentieth century with the integrative logic of cultural pluralism. Faced with rising movements for independence and self-rule in Korea and Taiwan, Hoshina Kōichi, a student of Ueda Kazutoshi and a frequent contributor to *Kokugo kyōiku,* argued that the stability of the empire depended on the recognition of "ethnic" languages as acceptable in private contexts and the concomitant declaration of Japanese as the "official" language of government. To continue to deny a place for local language would only encourage colonial independence activists to make language the object of their struggle.[44] In the metropole, the search for a timeless Japanese identity that could survive the destructive, assimilating forces of capitalism led scholars to regional dialects, which came to be seen as markers of cultural authenticity.[45] Even Ueda reconsidered his policy on dialect, writing in the first issue of the journal *Hōgen* (Dialects) that "dialect is a speech that is perfectly appropriate for the people of that region. There is no reason whatsoever to feel that speaking in dialect is shameful or strange."[46]

Conceiving of Japanese-language speech as a political rather than a natural expression of spirit had significant consequences for the conception and the significance of difference within the imperial community. While dialects had been an object of linguistic curiosity since at least the 1870s, the spread of Japanese in the form of *kokugo* throughout the empire delinked Japanese speaking from Japanese identity. At Osa Shizue argues, it was at this juncture that Japanese ethnology turned to dialect as the authentic expression of a primordial Japanese identity as *kokugo* transformed standard Japanese into the pragmatic universal language of the imperial state.[47]

Such changes in the intellectual realm were visible in colonial tourist publications, which quite suddenly began to encourage Japanese travelers to explore Korea and Taiwan through local languages. The Government-General of Korea's 1934 *Chōsen ryokō annai ki* (Notes on travel in Korea) encouraged travelers to learn a few phrases in order to interact more smoothly with local Koreans. The phrase guide described Korean as a local alternative to a national language: "While nowadays *kokugo* has spread to the degree that there is no place where one cannot communicate through it, for the person who wants to understand Chōsen and the people of Chōsen, it is necessary to understand Korean. Even if you only memorize two or three words, you can create an extremely friendly environment."[48] This contrasted markedly with the 1926 guidebook published by the Korea-Manchuria Information Bureau, which boasted that "as the mother tongue (*bokokugo*) has spread throughout the land, Japanese travelers should not worry about being unable to communicate."[49] The Keijō Tourism Association (Keijō Kankō Kyōkai) offered even more specific preparations for Japanese travelers, including the following phrases: I love you; you are a beautiful woman; let's go together by car; please sing one more time; that was really delightful.[50]

In Taiwan, the Government-General and the Taiwan branch of the Japan Tourist Bureau represented the authenticity of Aboriginal culture through language. *Takasagozoku no hanashi* (A conversation about Taiwan's Aborigines), a 1941 booklet published by the Taiwan branch of the East Asia Travel Company (Tōa Ryokō Sha), contained dozens of pages of local songs, each written out phonetically in "the savage tongue" (*bango*) and then translated into Japanese so the reader could "pass the time with the feeling of travel."[51] In the metropole, Yanagita Kunio's folk ethnography popularized dialect as the expression of an authentic and timeless Japanese identity. Dialect was not only definable by its distance from national language speech. It was, Yanagita argued, also definable by the sensation it evoked in Japanese.[52] Dialect was the feeling of home.

As both culture and skill, *kokugo* was a double-edged sword. In colonial Taiwan, the Government-General engaged in its own policy of replacing vulgar racism with what we might call polite "linguicism," or a set of ideologies and practices used to produce and legitimate social inequality on the basis of language.[53] In the early 1920s, the Government-General integrated Taiwanese and Japanese school systems. In 1922, Governor-General Den Makoto declared that all Japanese-speaking children could attend the formerly Japanese-only primary schools, which led to the prestigious higher schools, regardless of race. Non-Japanese-speaking children would attend common schools, which offered an elementary-level education and a limited upward trajectory.[54] The Government-General framed integration as an explicit move away from race. The Integration Rescript, as the declaration was known, did not "recognize racial (*shuzoku*) appellations like 'Japanese' and 'Taiwanese' at all," the chief of the education bureau wrote. "Its distinctions are based on the use of the Japanese language."[55]

The integration of the colonial school system did not result in an influx of Taiwanese and Aboriginal students in the prestigious hallways of postprimary education, however. Rather, the racial and ethnic distinctions that the colonial government had used to bar Chinese and Aboriginal students from matriculating into Japanese-only primary and secondary schools were quickly replaced by a new barrier: the assertion that an individual did not speak Japanese fluently *enough* to matriculate into the more prestigious primary school system. The distinction was used to prevent large numbers of Taiwanese students from matriculating into middle and higher schools, which were the gateway to a university education.[56] Aboriginal students, who as a matter of policy received very little training in writing and reading in the "education centers for savage children," were placed at an even greater disadvantage.[57] The Government-General reported in 1936 that *kokugo* use had spread to an average of 43 percent of all Aborigines, with a higher average percentage for men than women. Of this group, 6 percent, or nearly six thousand people, were reported to have achieved an advanced level of *kokugo* fluency, and 23 percent were reported to have advanced or intermediate fluency.[58] Yet despite these gains, only a handful of students were able to matriculate into the higher levels of schooling, such as a higher elementary school, a normal school, or a vocational school. Kitamura Kae reports that of some nearly seven thousand Aboriginal students enrolled in school in 1930, only sixteen were enrolled in a common or higher elementary school, three in agricultural school, and four in middle school. The rest were in education centers, from which only approximately half the students graduated on any given year.[59]

Implicit in the linguicism of the colonial education system was the idea that the culture of Japanese, envisioned as the ability to evaluate fluency and perfection, was open to a select few. In an environment where access to the central institution of social mobility was barred to those who did not speak Japanese fluently *enough,* the question of who could evaluate fluency and who had to prove their fluency marked a boundary between Japanese and not Japanese. These boundaries were relational—Japanese from dialect-rich rural areas such as Tōhoku had to work harder to perfect their national language than students in Tokyo, whose dialect formed the basis of the national language. As Miyako Inoue has shown, women struggled to speak in the forms classified as "women's language" even though in practice very few women actually spoke in such an upper-class, Tokyo-inflected way. In the context of colonial encounters, however, the inner conflicts of Japanese-ness disappeared. Reports of Aboriginal speech—and indeed of Taiwanese speech and "Made in Taiwan" Japanese—effaced these distinctions by pitting an imagined community of native linguistic evaluators from the metropole against the aberrations and abominations of the unenlightened in the colonies. Although Chinese Taiwanese and Koreans could "look just like a metropolitan Japanese" (*naichijiin to sokkuri*), their fluent, non-dialect-inflected national language marked them as colonial.[60] And Aborigines, as Matsuda declared, had "black faces . . . that just can't be denied." Imperial linguicism flagged Aborigines for special scrutiny as it absolved Japanese of the self-same requirement.

Silence, Violence, and the Opaque Mind

The colonial government presented Japanese-language speech as the basis for inclusion into the nation and access to the empire's institutions of social mobility. Yet for Aborigines in colonial Taiwan and other colonial subjects, this was an impossible task. By the 1930s, success had itself become a marker of difference. Perfect, accentless Japanese speech marked the colonial subject as colonial, as engaged in a process of translating his or her authentic linguistic self into a performance of obedience through national-language speech. Indeed, for all of our historical studies of the colonial uses of Japanese language, perhaps the most poignant example of the racialized gap that imperial linguicism opened between Aborigines and Japanese was not speech but silence.

In the early years of colonialism, travelers portrayed Japanese-language greetings as a signal of safety. Ishikawa, for example, noted that the Aboriginal men who greeted him did so while gripping their "savage swords." Yet after being greeted with a polite "hello," he relaxed and marveled at the bright future of colonialism and assimilation. Twenty years later, however, speech could not erase the fear of violence. Matsuda Kiichi, who traveled in 1937, argued that one could not squash the fear (or expectation) of violence at the hand of Aboriginal men. "While it's to be expected that savage women and children will be polite," Matsuda wrote after an encounter with a mother and child, "when you meet a savage man in his prime you wonder, will he just not greet me or will he also pierce my body [with his sword]?"[61] Silence engendered a panic in Itagaki Hōki's account. Writing in 1931, he used the silence of the Aborigines to signify danger. Stopped in the car on their way to the town of Keishū (Ch. Xizhou), Itagaki asked the driver why they had halted:

> When I asked the [Taiwanese] malaria assistant (*mararia joshu*), he avoided an explanation with frighteningly simple Japanese:
>
> "Connection. Connection."
>
> The sun was blazing down and it was very hot, so we settled into the middle of the car. As soon as we did so, a person peered into the car. We looked up: it was a savage. And not just one, but three or four, each doing his own painstaking investigation. I felt chills on my neck, as if our necks were being evaluated for head-hunting just as the books on head-hunting said.
>
> "Connection. Connection."
>
> What was the malaria assistant thinking?[62]

In the end, Itagaki discovered that the assistant had stopped the car in order to transfer Itagaki and his wife to a different one, hence the "connection, connection" (*renraku, renraku*) line. But not before a second group of Aborigines arrived and examined the car's inhabitants, leading Itagaki to wonder, "How long will we be pilloried by the savages?"[63]

Japanese travelers and the Government-General framed the representation of the most famous Aboriginal uprising in terms of silence. On October 27, 1930, a group of Taiyal tribe members killed 134 Japanese officials and residents in the village of Musha. Prior to the uprising, Musha had been known as a model "tamed" village. As one Government-General of Taiwan publication put it in 1925, Musha offered an experience of the "magnificent beauty" of the savage world, "bathed in the atmosphere of the savage highlands."[64] After the incident, however, tourist literature portrayed the Japanese-language voices of the village's past inhabitants as ghostly sounds whose comprehensibility was shattered by the unexpected violence. The 1935 *Taiwan tetsudō ryokō annai* (Guide to railway travel in Taiwan) described the village before the incident as occupying an important position in Taiwan's savage management system, economy, and transportation network—a place where Japanese, islanders, and Aborigines lived together and where the Aboriginal children "happily puppeted (*ayatsuri*) *kokugo* and sang 'Kimi ga yo' [the imperial anthem]."[65] Although Musha had been a place of Japanese-language conversation and interaction, in the end the guidebook argued that speech was not enough to prove the loyalty of the Aboriginal community.

The trope of silence framed Musha as an example of the inability of language to transcend the gap between Aboriginal and Japanese minds. Aboriginal minds were, in this representation, opaque—national language was a bridge between two peoples, but its use could not reassure Japanese colonial authorities of Aboriginal intentions. Savage Manager (*ribanka*) Suzuki Tadashi explained the difference in 1932 when he wrote that the purpose of *kokugo* education was to create a shared language that made clear the "shared consciousness" (*dōrui ishiki*) of Japanese and Aborigines and fostered "close friendship" between the two peoples.[66] Linguistic anthropologists have argued that the idea that other minds are "opaque" is a form of language ideology prevalent in local, non-Western communities. Indeed, the "opacity of other minds" is often treated as a cultural clash between a Western language ideology in which speech is presumed to be a transparent reflection of intention and particular or local language ideologies that assume the impossibility of knowing the mind of another, regardless of what he or she says. The difference is one between two distinct "theories of mind," one Western and psychological, one local and culturally determined.[67] The treatment of Aboriginal speech in the Japanese Empire suggests, however, not a preexisting, culturally determined binary of opacity and transparency but that modern imperial cultures style their speech transparently, *in opposition to* indigenous opacity.[68] The consequences of such presumed opacity, as the overwhelming, violent response to the Musha uprising indicates, are severe because the trope of opacity delegitimizes communication and dialogue in favor of unilateral action.

After the "Musha Incident" (Musha Jiken), Musha became a site of uncanny silence in fact as well as in representation. The actual village was destroyed; its remaining Aboriginal residents moved to a neighboring village. The guidebook assured travelers that the colonial government had exacted swift and overwhelming retribution to reassert Japanese authority. Following the uprising on the morning of October 27, the colonial government killed over one hundred Taiyal and removed nearly three hundred "submissive" (*kijun*) Aborigines to a neighboring village.[69] Even for Nakanishi Inosuke, the village became a place of silence. He cut off sound by placing a transparent barrier between himself and the Aborigines in a conversation with his travel companion:

> Musha! . . . "I'd like to see it one time. Are there still savages from that time alive?"
>
> "I think so. Over that mountain . . . in a place called Kawanakashima . . ."

> When the car passed by Horikai (Ch. Puli) the figures of savages were visible through the car window.[70]

Conclusion

The future of empire studies, as Antoinette Burton argues, resides in the use of "mobile subjects" who can disable "the persistent fiction that home and empire were separate spheres."[71] The coercive, unstable expectations that I have identified here constitute what we might call an affect of empire, one that was not limited to the formal boundaries of the Japanese Empire or even of empire itself. Indeed, we have seen the linguistic politics of expectation and evaluation replayed in other empires and within self-styled multicultural nations.[72] These affects of empire further illuminate the shifting measures of inclusion and exclusion in modern nations. As Ann Stoler argues, probing these "troubled, ill-defined boundaries" is key to bringing the question of "What is empire?" back to the forefront of public debate and to overcoming the increasingly unpalatable distinction between "good nation, bad empire" that elides the shifting politics of inclusion and exclusion in both nation and empire.[73]

Japanese-language speech was a social barrier whose measures shifted as colonized groups achieved fluency. The metapragmatic politics of Japanese-language use, and their reification on increasingly racialized lines, mirrors what we have seen in the United States, France, and other postcolonial, multicultural societies: the expectation that certain populations should have to prove their linguistic "fitness" for membership in the nation by using specific registers that signify obedience. David Theo Goldberg, a scholar of race in the United States, has called this the "integration" model of multiculturalism. While allowing expressions of minority culture at the periphery and in private, integrative multiculturalism demands adherence to what are called a "neutral set of common values" in the public sphere. Upon closer inspection, these "common" values show themselves to be the values of the dominant group.[74] This hegemony is reinforced by the constant evaluation of other expressions as "not-quite," as in the declaration of local Japanese as "Made in Taiwan Japanese" or, more poignantly, in the constant and coercive evaluation of Aboriginal speech and its eventual rejection as a meaningful act of communication.

If we take seriously the claims of Benedict Anderson and other cultural historians of nationalism who argue that the spread of a vernacular language within a given territory gave birth to the modern nation, we should also take seriously the same claim that colonial governments and administrations have made—that Japanese-language training would make the speaker Japanese. To fail to do so—to naturalize dialect eradication in the national context while problematizing national language in the imperial context—would be to conceal the lie at the heart of "national language" itself: only certain populations within the nation are required to prove their linguistic bona fides as part of their claim to inclusion. The history of Japanese-language speech in the imperial context illuminates the fluidity with which language assumed a double character in the 1930s: as a signifier of ethnic belonging and as a signifier of voluntary political commitment, obedience, or loyalty. Linguistic Japaneseness was both a territorial identity and an affective one that when linked to the coercive institutions of colonial rule conferred upon its owner the power to demand performances of others while excusing Japanese bodies from the same in colonial encounters.

Notes

Epigraph. Quoted in Nakanishi Inosuke, *Taiwan kenbunki* (Tokyo, Jissensha: 1937), 583.

1. Todd Henry has coined this mode of racism "affective racism" for its use of "cultural sensibilities" rather than scientific biology to determine racial difference. Henry, "Assimilation's Racializing Sensibilities: Colonized Koreans as *Yobos* and the '*Yobo*-ization' of Expatriate Japanese," *positions* 21, no. 1 (2013): 11–49, 14.

2. Takekoshi Yosaburō, *Japanese Rule in Formosa,* trans. George Braithwaite (New York: Longmans, Green, 1907), 211; Robert Tierney, *Tropics of Savagery: The Culture of Japanese Empire in Comparative Frame* (Berkeley: University of California Press, 2010), 40; Matsuda Kyōko, "Shokuminchi shihaika no Taiwan genjūmin o meguru 'bunrui' no shikō to tōchi jissen," *Rekishigaku kenkyū* 846 (2008): 97–107, 104–105. See also Government of Formosa, *Report on the Control of Aborigines in Formosa,* 1911, Tokyo, 10–19.

3. Michael Silverstein, "Whorfianism and the Linguistic Imagination of Nationality," in *Regimes of Language,* ed. Paul Kroskrity (Santa Fe: School of American Research Press, 2000), 85–138.

4. Michael Silverstein, "Encountering Language and Languages of Encounter in North American Ethnohistory," *Journal of Linguistic Anthropology* 6, no. 2 (1996): 126–144.

5. Hiraku Shimoda, "Tongues-Tied: The Making of a 'National Language' and the Discovery of Dialects in Meiji Japan," *American Historical Review* 115, no. 3 (June 2010): 714–731.

6. Hamada Tsunenosuke, *Waga shokuminchi* (Tokyo: Toyama-bō, 1928), 2.

7. Kō En, "Kankō no seijigaku: Senzen sengo ni okeru 'Manshū' e no kankō" (PhD diss., University of Tokyo, 2004), 29–32.

8. Itagaki Hōki, *Taiwan kenbutsu Man-Sen manpo* (Tokyo: Itagaki Rikiko, 1931), 13.

9. Arakawa Seijirō, ed., *Sen-Man jitsugyō shisatsu danshi,* 1918, Tokyo, 22.

10. In fact, the first official use of "outer territory" (*gaichi*) was in 1929 with the establishment of the Ministry of Colonial Affairs (Takumushō). But the concept was embedded in the articulation of Japan "proper" as "inner territory" (*naichi*), such as in the Naichi Hōsei Enchōshugi (Extension of the Japanese Legal System) policy of the late 1910s. The colonies were in fact not referred to in any systematic terms because the Meiji government wished to avoid the terminology of "colony" and "colonialism." In this sense, Taiwan and Korea occupied an ambiguous place within the Japanese nation. Nakamura Akira, "Shokuminchi hō," in *Kindai Nihonhō hattatsu shi,* vol. 5, ed. Ukai Nobushige (Tokyo: Keisō shobō, 1958).

11. Harry J. Lamley, "Taiwan under Japanese Rule, 1895–1945: The Vicissitudes of Colonialism," in *Taiwan: A New History,* ed. Murray A. Rubinstein (Armonk, NY: M. E. Sharpe, 2007), 204.

12. Daniel Botsman, *Power and Punishment in the Making of Modern Japan* (Princeton, NJ: Princeton University Press, 2007), 201–220.

13. Edward I-te Chen, "Formosan Political Movements under Japanese Colonial Rule, 1914–1937," *Journal of Asian Studies* 31, no. 3 (1972): 477–497, 484 (emphasis in original).

14. Hamada, *Waga shokuminchi,* 315. As reported, the question is in grammatical Japanese. However, it is not clear from the text if the impolite form of the question is because it is being reported second-hand or because this is how the student asked the question. Unlike Ōyama's

encounters with Taiwanese Aborigines, he does not comment directly on the Japanese-language use of the Korean students nor does he include their comments within quotation marks.

15. See, for example, Mark R. Peattie, "Japanese Attitudes toward Colonialism, 1895–1937," in *The Japanese Colonial Empire, 1895–1937*, ed. Ramon H. Myers and Mark R. Peattie (Princeton, NJ: Princeton University Press, 1984), 6; Ann Laura Stoler and Frederick Cooper, "Between Metropole and Colony: Rethinking a Research Agenda," in *Tensions of Empire: Colonial Cultures in a Bourgeois World*, ed. Ann Laura Stoler and Frederick Cooper (Berkeley: University of California Press, 1997), 23.

16. Ming-Cheng M. Lo, *Doctors within Borders: Profession, Ethnicity, and Modernity in Colonial Taiwan* (Berkeley: University of California Press, 2002).

17. E. Patricia Tsurumi, *Japanese Colonial Education in Taiwan, 1895–1945* (Cambridge, MA: Harvard University Press, 1978), 233. Tsurumi notes that by 1920 there were also a handful of Aboriginal common schools (*banjin kōgakkō*), but the number of these institutions declined dramatically after the Government-General integrated the school system in 1922.

18. Matsuda Yoshirō, *Taiwan genjūmin to Nihongo kyōiku: Nihon tōchi jidai Taiwan genjūmin kyōikushi kenkyū* (Kyoto, Japan: Kyōto shobō, 2004), 54.

19. Suzuki Tadashi, "Bandō kyōiku no ni dai ganmoku," *Riban no tomo* 1, no. 1 (January 1932): 7. Education centers, especially the centers at Kappanzan and Urai, were also popular stops for travelers who wished to investigate the progress of assimilation in colonial Taiwan. See Paul Barclay's study of representations of Aborigines from Kappanzan in colonial picture postcards, "Peddling Postcards and Selling Empire: Image-Making in Taiwan under Japanese Colonial Rule," *Japanese Studies* 30, no. 1 (2010): 81–110.

20. The Japanese colonial government adopted the terms of the former Qing government to describe Taiwan's Aboriginal population. Aborigines were divided into two categories: "raw" (*seiban*) and "cooked" (*jukuban*), the latter of which was used to describe Aborigines who had been acculturated to Chinese norms. Tierney, *Tropics of Savagery*, 7–8.

21. Hamada, *Waga shokuminchi*, 594.

22. Ishikawa Toraji, "Taiwan ryokō," in *Shin Nihon kenbutsu*, ed. Kanao Shujirō (Tokyo: Kanao Bun'endō, 1918), 70.

23. The actual phrase is *hyakume nijūsen*. Hyakume is a measure of weight by length for stick-shaped items, such that one item is 375 grams.

24. Itagaki, *Taiwan kenbutsu Sen-Man manpo*, 158.

25. Ibid., 161.

26. Kawamigome Tarō, "Taiwan no kōgakkō ni okeru kokugo kyōiku no nanten," *Kokugo kyōiku* 10, no. 12 (December 1925): 84–87, quote from page 86.

27. Ishikawa, "Taiwan ryokō," 70.

28. Leo Ching, "Savage Construction and Civility Making: The Musha Incident and Aboriginal Representations in Colonial Taiwan," *positions* 8, no. 3 (2000): 795–818. See also Tierney, *Tropics of Savagery*, 38–77.

29. T. Fujitani, *Race for Empire: Koreans as Japanese and Japanese as Americans during World War II* (Berkeley: University of California Press, 2011), 25.

30. E. Taylor Atkins, *Primitive Selves: Koreana in the Japanese Colonial Gaze, 1910–1945* (Berkeley: University of California Press, 2010); Kimberly Brandt, *Kingdom of Beauty: Mingei and the Politics of Folk Art in Imperial Japan* (Durham, NC: Duke University Press, 2007); Noriko Aso, *Public Properties: Museums in Imperial Japan* (Durham, NC: Duke University Press, 2014).

31. Osa Shizue, *Kindai Nihon to kokugo nashonarizumu* (Tokyo: Yoshikawa kōbunkan, 1998), 5.

32. Nakanishi, *Taiwan kenbunki,* 202.

33. Ibid., 203.

34. The Government-General of Taiwan began sponsoring tours of Japan for Aborigines in 1897. For a concise history of *naichi kankō,* see Suzuki Sakutarō, *Taiwan no banzoku kenkyū* (Taipei: Taiwan shiseki kankōkai, 1932), 374–402. Similar programs of co-optation were deployed in other Japanese colonies as well. See Senjū Hajime, "Nihon tōchika Nan'yō guntō ni okeru naichi kankōdan no seiritsu," *Rekishi hyōron,* no. 661 (2005): 52–68.

35. Nakanishi, *Taiwan kenbunki,* 203.

36. Shinoda Jissaku, *Taiwan o miru* (Tokyo: Rakuryō shoten, 1935), 69. Shinoda, who thought he heard some strange (*kii*) phonetic overlaps with Korean, then took the unusual approach of re-asking the question in Korean. "I went down the line, asking 'Do you understand?' in Korean, but still nobody understood. Then, since there were a lot of Korean laborers in the area, I asked the women in Korean if they understood, but still nobody understood."

37. Ibid., 149–159.

38. Matsuda Kiichi, *Taiwan Okinawa no tabi* (Osaka: Yanagihara shoten, 1937), 117.

39. Ibid. In the 1920s and the 1930s, the colonial government had expanded assimilation to include a policy of educating Aboriginal communities on "economics," in the form of wage labor and forced group savings plans, in an effort to transform them into willing participants in the colonial labor regime. The Japan Tourist Bureau's 1935 guidebook for Taiwan, which was produced in the Railway Bureau of the Government-General, advertised the success of this particular aspect of assimilation specifically, stating that "they [the Takasago-zoku, or Taiwan tribes] have abandoned their primitive lifestyle, and their pathway to engaging in an economic lifestyle (*keizaiteki seikatsu*) is remarkable." As of 1934, nineteen thousand Aboriginal laborers had placed (most likely not voluntarily) nearly 350,000 yen in savings. Japan tsūrisuto byūrō Taiwan shibu, *Taiwan tetsudō ryokō annai* (Taipei, Taiwan: Japan tsūrisuto byūrō, 1935), 35.

40. Ueda Kazutoshi, "Kokugo to kokka to," *Meiji bungaku zenshū,* vol. 44 (Tokyo: Chikuma shobō, 1968), 110, quoted in Miyako Inoue, *Vicarious Language: Gender and Linguistic Modernity in Japan* (Berkeley: University of California Press), 87.

41. Shimoda, "Tongues-Tied," 729.

42. Ueda Kazutoshi, "Shōgaku no kyōka ni kokugo no ikka o moukuru no gi," *Dai Nippon kyōikukai zasshi,* 2nd ed. Tokyo, 1884): 138, quoted in Shimoda, "Tongues-Tied," 722.

43. Florian Coulmas, "Language Policy in Modern Japanese Education," in *Language Policies in Education: Critical Issues,* ed. James W. Tollefson (Mahwah, NJ: Lawrence Erlbaum, 2002), 213.

44. Yeounsuk Lee, *The Ideology of Kokugo: Nationalizing Language in Modern Japan,* trans. Maki Hirano Hubbard (Honolulu: University of Hawai'i Press, 2010), 184–185.

45. Marilyn Ivy, *Discourses of the Vanishing: Modernity, Phantasm, Japan* (Chicago: University of Chicago Press, 1995).

46. Ueda Kazutoshi, preface to *Hōgen* 1, no. 1 (1931), quoted in Shimoda, "Tongues-Tied," 730.

47. Osa, *Kindai Nihon to kokugo nashonarizumu,* 147–183.

48. Chōsen sōtokufu, ed., *Chōsen ryokō annai ki* (Seoul: Chōsen sōtokufu, 1934), 109.

49. Mantetsu Sen-Man annaijo, ed., *Chōsen Manshū ryokō annai: Tsuketari Shina ryokō annai* (Tokyo: Mantetsu Sen-Man annaijo, 1926), 78.

50. Mōri Motoyoshi, ed., *Keijō jōsho* (Seoul: Keijō kankō kyōkai, 1934), 26–27.

51. Ueda Hachirō, ed., *Takasagozoku no hanashi* (Taipei: Tōa ryokō sha Taiwan shibu, 1941).

52. Ivy, *Discourses of the Vanishing,* 66–97.

53. Robert Phillipson, *Linguistic Imperialism* (New York: Oxford University Press, 1992), 47.

54. Tsurumi, *Japanese Colonial Education,* 99.

55. Yoshino Hideo, *Taiwan kyōiku shi* (Taipei: Taiwan nichi nichi shimbunsha, 1927), 467–468, for the original Japanese. The translation is from Tsurumi, *Japanese Colonial Education,* 99.

56. Tsurumi, *Japanese Colonial Education,* 97. The claims were mostly spurious. As Tsurumi notes, a secret 1923 study by the Government-General of Taiwan showed that Taiwanese students were performing at or above the level of their Japanese (Naichijin) counterparts in all subjects.

57. A 1936 report by the Police Bureau of the Government-General noted that students in "education centers for savage children" spent the largest blocks of time on *kokugo* education and "practical" education (*jikka*), which included instruction in farming and husbandry. While the report indicated that *kokugo* time was spent on "speaking, reading, composition, handwriting," Matsuda points out that in fact the majority of this time was devoted to education in speaking. The reading section, which after 1916 used the *Banjin dokuhon* (Primer for savages), taught students to read in katakana, the script of simple government directives, and placed relatively little emphasis on the ability to read hiragana or Chinese characters, both of which would be necessary for advancement within the normal education system. See Taiwan sōtokufu keimukyoku, *Takasagozoku no kyōiku* (Taipei: Taiwan sōtokufu, 1936), 100–101; Matsuda, *Taiwan genjūmin to Nihongo kyōiku,* 52–53.

58. Taiwan sōtokufu keimukyoku, *Takasagozoku no kyōiku,* 61. The population of Aborigines in the Savage Territory in 1935 was reported to be around ninety thousand.

59. Kitamura Kae, *Nihon shokuminchika no Taiwan genjūmin kyōiku shi* (Sapporo: Hokkaidō daigaku shuppankai, 2008), 243–253. The Government-General documented the reasons why students left school before completing the course. The most common was that school was a burden on the family. Movement, sickness, and death were also common reasons. See the table on p. 246. Of the students who did successfully matriculate to higher schools, Kitamura could confirm the progress of only eleven. These students became nurses, public doctors, police officers, and farmers. Many were only able to continue to higher levels of education because they received scholarships or other support from the local colonial police, often in exchange for their fathers' support or compliance.

60. Matsuda, *Taiwan Okinawa no tabi,* 39.

61. Ibid., 120.

62. Itagaki, *Taiwan kenbutsu Sen-Man manpo,* 154.

63. Ibid., 155.

64. Taiwan sōtokufu, ed., *Saikin no Taiwan* (Taipei: Taiwan sōtokufu, 1925), 30, quoted in Kate McDonald, "The Boundaries of the Interesting" (PhD diss., University of California, San Diego, 2011), 202.

65. Japan tsūrisuto byūrō Taiwan shibu, ed., *Taiwan tetsudō ryokō annai* (Taipei: Japan tsūrisuto byūrō Taiwan shibu, 1935), 142.

66. Suzuki, "Bandō kyōiku no ni dai ganmoku," 6–7.

67. For the cultural clash model of transparent/opaque language ideology, see Joel Robbins and Alan Rumsey, "Cultural and Linguistic Anthropology and the Opacity of Other Minds," *Anthropological Quarterly* 82, no. 2 (2008): 407–420.

68. Michelle Z. Rosaldo famously argued that speech act theory is itself a local language ideology in her seminal article, "The Things We Do with Words: Ilongot Speech Acts and Speech Act Theory in Philosophy," *Language in Society* 11, no. 2 (1982): 203–237. On speech act theory, she writes, "Our theoretical attempts to understand how language works are like the far less explicated linguistic thoughts of people elsewhere in the world, in that both inevitably tend to reflect locally prevalent views about the given natures of those human persons by whom language is used" (ibid., 203).

69. Itagaki, *Taiwan kenbutsu Sen-Man manpo,* 143.

70. Nakanishi, *Taiwan kenbunki,* 272.

71. Antoinette Burton, "Who Needs the Nation? Interrogating 'British' History," in *Empire in Question: Reading, Writing, and Teaching British Imperialism* (Durham, NC: Duke University Press, 2011), 41–55, 44. Originally published in *Journal of Historical Sociology* 10, no. 3 (1997): 227–248.

72. See Terrence G. Wiley, "Continuity and Change in the Function of Language Ideologies in the United States," in *Ideology, Politics, and Language Policies: Focus on English,* ed. Thomas Ricento (Philadelphia: John Benjamins, 2000), 67–85.

73. Arguing that imperial forms with "distinctly rendered boundaries . . . represent only one end of the spectrum," Ann Stoler has suggested that historians of colonialism and empire analyze those imperial forms that operate precisely at the "troubled, ill-defined" boundaries of citizenship, territory, and legal rights. See Stoler, "Degrees of Imperial Sovereignty," *Public Culture* 18, no. 1 (2006): 125–146, 128, 136–137.

74. David Theo Goldberg, "Introduction: Multicultural Conditions," in *Multiculturalism: A Critical Reader,* ed. David Theo Goldberg (London: Blackwell, 1994), 1–41.

Race behind the Walls

Contact and Containment in Japanese Images of Urban Manchuria

Manchukuo (1932–1945) was a land of paradox. Founded by the Japanese Kwantung Army, the territory was a militarily strategic bulwark between the Japanese homeland and the Soviet Union and provided a base for the Japanese invasion of the Asian continent.[1] At the same time, Manchukuo also became a site for the projection of a myriad of visionary Japanese ideals—a utopian social experiment where Chinese, Japanese, Manchurians, Mongolians, and Koreans might live in peace and harmony. Japanese military advisors, government officials, and corporate advisors saw it as a "blank page" (*hakushi*) and ideal spatial "laboratory" where cutting-edge urbanization initiatives could take form.[2] Here was both a regimented, militarized space yet also a place for indulgent play—a luxury destination for cosmopolitan travelers, offering the finest accommodations, exotic scenery, cultural enrichment, and a host of leisure activities from sunbathing to skiing.[3] Pastoral and industrial, peaceful and dangerous, a multicultural paradise and the site of unspeakable violence on Chinese inhabitants, Manchukuo was in short both a progressive nation-building experiment grounded in the new discourse of decolonization and a state subject to coercive colonial rule.[4]

At the core of these multifarious descriptions of Manchukuo lies the insurmountable tension between the claim of the state's sovereignty and its occupation by the Japanese army. These narratives have been in constant competition with each other from the Manchukuo period through the present. For example, historians Prasenjit Duara and Yamamuro Shin'ichi each have examined different facets of the complicated writing of Manchukuo. Duara exposed the complex mechanisms at work in constructing claims of sovereignty and cultural authenticity necessitated by the growing ideology of anticolonialism and anti-imperialism during the interwar period.[5] Yamamuro's provocative study examined the darker side of Japanese idealism on the continent, proposing that Manchukuo was not just a puppet state of the Japanese Empire but—given the horrors suffered by "roughly one million victims"—"an Auschwitz state or a concentration-camp state."[6] What, then, was Manchukuo? How can one reconcile these multiple meanings?

An analysis of images featured in Japanese media during the 1930s reveals how these diverse, sometimes conflicting ideas were not mutually exclusive. In fact, though the goals of different Japanese offices like the Kwantung Army and the South Manchuria Railway Company (Minami Manshū Testsudo Kabushikigaisha, hereafter referred to as Mantetsu) were divergent, their respective visualizations of Manchukuo demonstrate how discourses of independence and military occupation intermingled in a larger web of signification that had accrued meaning over several decades. Indeed, symbolic coding of Manchukuo in Japanese media preceded the nation's founding in 1932. Since the Russo-Japanese War (1904–1905), Manchuria had figured large in the Japanese collective imagination as the land of the "red setting sun," the melancholic site where tens of thousands of soldiers had lost their lives in pitched battle, a vast frontier of exotic peoples, and a dangerous space of warlord factionalism. Images produced during the 1930s could not ignore these entrenched meanings; rather, they built on them and capitalized on the profound emotions they aimed to elicit.

The most notable examples of such multilayered imagery are photographs of the old walled cities of Manchuria, regularly featured in Mantetsu's illustrated materials promoting tourism on the continent. These photographs exemplify the complicated visual coding of space and continental culture in the context of Japanese militarism and the sovereignty of Manchukuo. Mantetsu's public relations magazine, *Manshū graph* (Pictorial Manchuria), presented the walled cities, such as the old provincial capital of Mukden, as ideal tourist destinations, describing them as "squalid" (*waizatsu*), "noisy" (*kensō*), and distinctively "Manchurian" sites at which to take in the exotic culture of the local inhabitants.[7] Moreover, images of the old cities testified to the continuity of indigenous culture despite the unofficial occupation of the region by the Japanese. As such, images of the bustling streets and smiling inhabitants of these cities underscored the utopian, multiethnic ideal that acted as the conceptual foundation for Manchukuo. Whether articulating cultural commodities or sites of cultural autonomy, the walls marked spaces of difference.

This chapter examines photographs of the walled-city portion of Mukden (also known as Fengtian) in Mantetsu's media to expose how these spatial narratives of difference constructed complex social and political relationships on the continent.[8] Drawing primarily on photographic essays published in *Manshū graph* in the mid-1930s, I first discuss how representations of the old walled cities separated out the indigenous population and culture, framing them as exotic commodities for Japanese tourist consumption. As these photographs imaged what spaces different ethnic groups occupied, I argue that they functioned in concert with formative imperial slogans espousing "racial harmony" (*minzoku kyōwa*) and the "harmony of the five races" (*gozoku kyōwa*) on the continent.[9] As such, they must be understood as constituent parts of the overlapping Japanese discourses of belonging and superiority in Manchukuo. To further draw out the significance of the differential categories of inclusion at work in these images, the final section considers the discursive relationship between Japanese military occupation, Manchuria's ongoing "bandit problem," and the popular cultural attraction in the walled city known as the "thieves' market." Here, it becomes apparent that the wall functioned not only as a tourist spectacle but also as a fortification, a means to control and contain potentially dangerous bodies residing within the old city. Through a discussion of representations of the old walled cities in Manchuria, I aim to reveal the complex entanglement of race, space, cultural authenticity, and military occupation in Manchukuo and how Mantetsu harnessed affects of difference—curiosity, desire, aspiration, anxiety, and revulsion—in illustrated materials that promoted not only travel and tourism but also the achievements of empire during the 1930s.

Selling Mantetsu and Continental Progress

In the 1930s, Mantetsu's influence in Manchuria was second only to the Kwantung Army. As Japan's largest corporation, Mantetsu had had a hand in many facets of Manchukuo's economy and infrastructure since it was established in 1906. The company described the vast scope of its activities in a 1935 report:

> In addition to its extensive railway undertakings which constitute its main business, the Company continues to operate accessory enterprises, coal mines, railway workshops, harbors and wharves, warehouses, and hotels; it administers the Railway Zone; it conducts schools, libraries, hospitals, and various hygienic institutions; it controls a number of joint-stock companies, electric and gas works, shipping and dockyard companies, and several industrial concerns and factories; and it carries on a chemical research laboratory, a geological research institute, an economic research committee, and several agricultural experimental stations and farms.[10]

As this list of activities demonstrates, Mantetsu's interests were heavily tied to the economic, industrial, and commercial development of Northeast Asia. In fact, the company claimed that it was "more than a mere railway company"—it was "the carrier of the light of civilization into Manchuria."[11]

Mantetsu's enthusiastic self-aggrandizement of its achievements in Manchuria is evident in the wealth of illustrated promotional materials it published, from postcards and tourist pamphlets to magazines and photographic annuals. In 1933, a year after the Kwantung Army proclaimed the formation of the new, supposedly sovereign state of Manchukuo, Mantetsu launched its flagship public-relations magazine, *Manshū graph,* as a means to advertise the company's continental activities as well as Manchukuo's distinctive culture and customs.[12] Mantetsu distributed the magazine through the Korea-Manchuria Information Offices (Sen-Man annaijo) on the continent and in major Japanese cities, including Tokyo, Osaka, and Nagoya. Published primarily in Japanese with occasional English text, the magazine attracted potential tourists and emigrants among a predominantly urban Japanese readership.[13]

Manshū graph was a critical tool in the production of knowledge about Manchukuo and actively contributed to the visual tropes used to define the new state, from nostalgic frontier vistas to bustling urban street scenes illuminated by neon signs. The magazine's editor and renowned art photographer, Fuchikami Hakuyō

(1889–1960), utilized the latest in design and photography trends such as New Objectivity and Soviet-inspired Constructivism to enervate the featured landscapes and people.[14] Dramatic perspectives, montage, and diagonal layouts presented the new nation as a dynamic, exciting space where tradition met transformation. This expressive component demonstrates how *Manshū graph,* though intended as a means to introduce Japanese readers to Manchukuo, was not a news magazine per se. Rather, it was a vehicle of persuasion. As an extension of Mantetsu's advertising and public-relations protocols, it carefully avoided negative or gloomy images of the new state.[15]

A testament to the modernization occurring on the continent, images of urban Manchuria were among the most common in *Manshū graph.* Photographs of the newly built spaces of the South Manchuria Railway Zones (SMR Zones) in cities like Mukden and the new Manchukuo capital of Xinjing advertised the ingenuity of Japanese urban planning to both domestic and international audiences. The new continental city spaces featured the latest in modern amenities, including lush parks, luxurious Mantetsu-owned Yamato Hotels, and department stores. *Manshū graph* also drew attention to monumental civic spaces, inviting the virtual tourist to stroll down grand axial boulevards and visit architectural achievements such as Xinjing's State Council Building, which featured a stripped-down neoclassicism reminiscent of the National Diet Building that was completed in Tokyo in 1936.

Early in the summer of 1935, Mantetsu dedicated an entire issue of *Manshū graph* to the city of Mukden. Briefly referencing the infamous 1931 Mukden Incident that triggered Japanese military expansion in the region, the issue sought to recode the city as a peaceful space of flourishing commerce and industry and rapid new development that was seeing the transformation of the surrounding suburbs.[16] Given Mantetsu's central involvement in these urban and industrial transformations in Mukden, it is not surprising that the magazine dedicated several layouts to the new commercial, administrative, and leisure spaces of the city. The expansive SMR Zone of Mukden, like those in other major Manchurian cities, was nothing short of a monumental achievement.

A major element in rebranding Mukden was selling the city as a must-see destination on the Manchuria Tour. To this end, Mantetsu drew on evocative images of historic Mukden. The city had functioned as the capital of the Manchu people prior to 1644 when the Manchu-led Qing dynasty displaced the Ming dynasty in Beijing. While the city no longer functioned as the center of imperial Manchurian rule, the city became an important provincial capital. Underscoring the rich history of the city, Japanese media referred to Mukden as the cradle of the Qing dynasty and as an important historical site, featuring two imperial mausoleums and the old Manchu imperial palace, all of which dated from the first half of the seventeenth century.

Photographs of these landmarks acted as tantalizing monuments in the company's destination-marketing campaign. In the pages of *Manshū graph,* Mukden was represented as a distinctive, fantastic site that could satisfy the tourist's wish to experience foreign lands. Capitalizing on—or producing—a desire among his readership to see the different cultures of the continent, Fuchikami used a dramatic photograph of the West Pagoda of Yanshou Temple, located just over a mile outside the city, for the cover of the Mukden issue (fig. 8.1). The subject of many postcards and pamphlets advertising the city, the unique dome and spire of the West Pagoda had long been associated with Mukden's rich history. Fuchikami canted the pagoda on a diagonal axis, energizing an otherwise static monument and heightening the anticipatory excitement of Mukden's historic, cultural spaces featured on Mantetsu's Manchuria Tour. These photographs had a secondary effect as well. They suggested that Mantetsu was instrumental in the appreciation and preservation of important cultural sites in Manchuria. By bringing the viewer in close to the crumbling brick edifice of the pagoda and focusing on the texture of the failing masonry, Fuchikami both aestheticized the landmark and suggested that such fragile historical sites were under the protective care of Mantetsu. According to *Manshū graph,* then, Mantetsu was critical in modernizing and developing Manchukuo as well as acting as attentive steward of the new nation's cultural past.

The old walled city of Mukden occupied a curious place in this spatial modern/historical binary (fig. 8.2). Like the SMR Zones, it was a bustling commercial and residential district, a living space filled with people and activities; at the same time, as the site of the old Qing palace, it was also an important historical site. Interestingly, while a caption accompanying the photographic layout dedicated to the old city mentions the palace, the photographs do not focus on it. Instead, the dominant visual motifs used to define the old city are the people and the monumental city wall. Indeed, the caption underscores what features Mantetsu thought important to highlight in the old city:

> Two walls, inner and outer, enclose the native town of Mukden. Square in shape and with two entrance gates in each side of the square, the inner wall, 10 metres in height and 6 metres in thickness, is constructed of brick. This wall embraces the most thriving business quarter with the ancient palace of the Ching monarchs in the centre. It is here within this wall that the local colour of Manchuria can best be seen in all its various exotic forms.[17]

The focus on the wall is not entirely surprising. At more than thirty feet tall, the Mukden wall was a visual spectacle, and the photograph certainly draws attention to its tremendous physicality. This is perhaps why Mantetsu republished this same image in its annual *Manshū gaikan* (Overview of Manchuria) in 1935, 1936, and 1937. The massive wall fills the right side of the composition, towering high above the street. As the photographer shot the image from atop the wall, the people seem tiny in comparison. The structure is overwhelming, squeezing the small figures on the street to the left and almost out of frame. These continental walls were quite unlike anything the Japanese would see at home, where cities were not fortified with such structures. Consequently, walls from all over Manchuria frequently appeared in Mantetsu's promotional media. From the colossal ornamental gate at Liaoyang to the more picturesque city wall at Chinchou, these were objects of fascination.

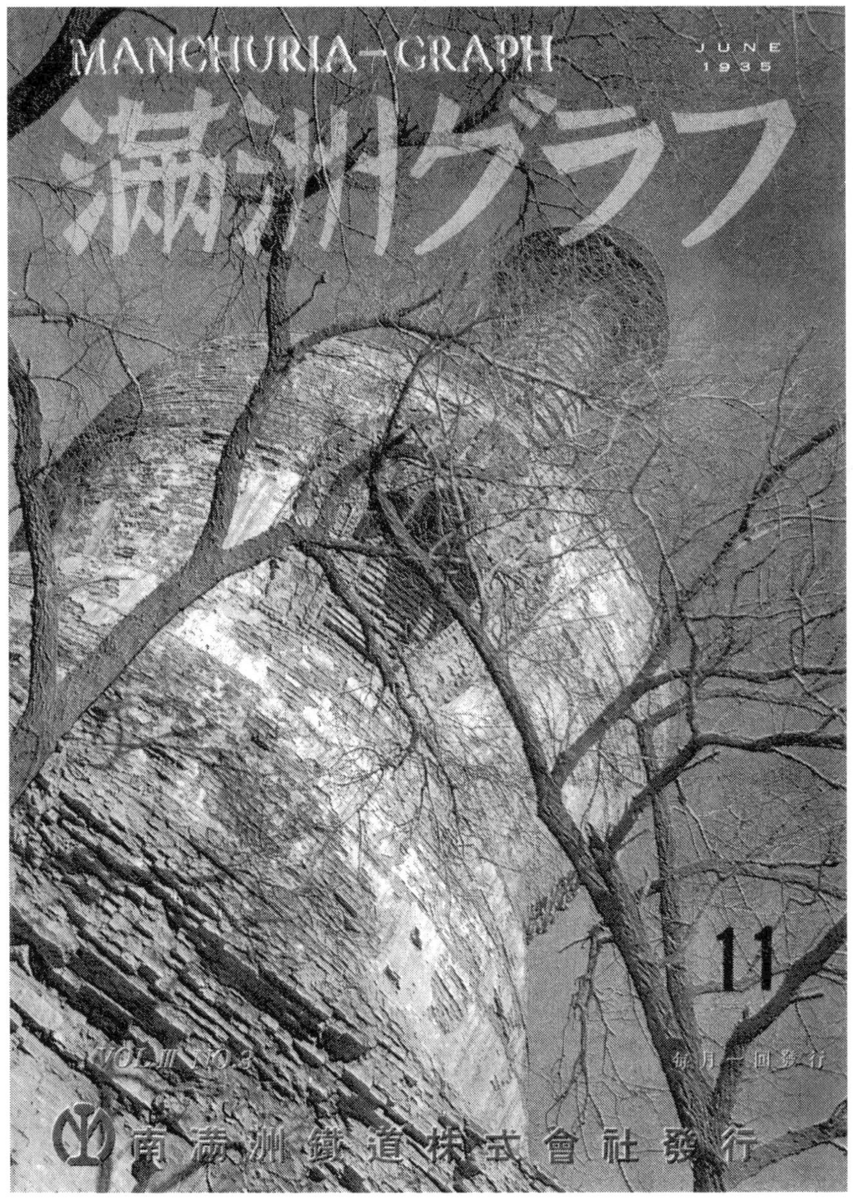

Figure 8.1. Cover (featuring the West Pagoda of Yanshou Temple), *Manshū graph* 3, no. 3 (June 1935). Yumani shobō reprint, University of Minnesota Library.

Figure 8.2. "The Walled City of Mukden," *Manshū graph* 3, no. 3 (June 1935). Yumani shobō reprint, University of Minnesota Library.

Yet while its size and unfamiliarity made the wall worthy of attention, it also performed a special function: according to the caption, it encapsulated the "local color" of the city. Here, the wall created a distinctly separate space for the apprehension of an exoticized form of Sino-Manchurian culture.[18] As the Mukden issue of *Manshū graph* makes clear, the SMR Zone and the old walled city were spaces of difference. The magazine states that each section of the city "possess[es] peculiarities of its own."[19] Highlighting these differences in the pages of the magazine was a productive way to market Mukden as a unique and desirable destination, a common strategy in tourism marketing campaigns that offer would-be visitors unique historical, cultural sites as well as the comforts of modern amenities. *Manshū graph* repeatedly portrayed the SMR Zone of Mukden (and other major Manchurian cities) as a place of luxury, comfort, and modernity. This neighborhood was the picture of urban, bourgeois modernity. In contrast, the walled city offered an exoticized spectacle of supposed cultural authenticity. Literature presented the old city as smelly and squalid, with a "chaotic market and picturesque slums."[20]

Manshū graph posited the old walled cities not just as spaces of visual and spatial alterity; the magazine makes clear that these were spaces of ethnic and racial difference as well. The Japanese-language caption notes that Japanese inhabitants made up more than 70 percent of the population in the modern SMR Zone, and, while this suggests that a minority of other racial and ethnic demographics would also have resided in this space, images of these ethnic others are notably absent from photographs dedicated to the SMR Zone. Both text and image marked it out as a space for Japanese consumption and inhabitation. Further adding to this schism is the textual framing of the old walled city—the Japanese caption states that, of Mukden's total population of 480,000 people, 80 percent were Manchurian and lived within the walls of the old city.[21]

These photographs and captions of these varied spaces had multivalent meanings. Young states that the "dichotomy of the old and new" provided a compelling "'before and after' advertisement of Manchurian development."[22] Indeed, the differences between the old city and the new urbanization projects were powerful tools in rationalizing the enormous outlay of Japanese resources on the continent. However, I argue that these spaces of difference were also important tools for the visualization of transforming social identification in Manchukuo. As Jeremy Foster has argued, "The discursive representation of imaginary spaces (or 'places') in some sense creates the community which belongs to them,"[23] and *Manshū graph* provided just such a discursive means through which Japanese readers could imagine the spaces they could inhabit on the continent.

Further, *Manshū graph* makes clear to its Japanese readers that there were specific spaces in Manchuria for different people and that while Japanese could enjoy the SMR Zones, they were also free to visit and consume other spaces, including the old walled city. The magazine did not afford all of Manchukuo's diverse populations this kind of free virtual movement. Indeed, in the pages of *Manshū graph,* Japanese readers possessed greater access and mobility. This underscores the unequal ordering of the space for respective populations on the continent. Mukden—like other growing Manchurian metropolises featuring coexistent SMR Zones and old walled sites—was, in media if not entirely in practice, a segregated city.

Given the colonial and racial violence segregation implies, the textual and visual coding of Mukden as a segregated city seems at odds with authorities' claims of Manchukuo's inclusionary, multicultural ethos. How did such images operate vis-á-vis competing discourses of sovereignty and occupation? What purpose did such claims serve? Certainly, the politics of belonging and authority on the continent complicated this narrative of the segregated city. On July 1, 1936, the Japan-Manchukuo Extraterritoriality Treaty went into effect, thereby transferring administrative rights in the SMR Zone to the Manchukuo government.[24] However, as Japanese military officials supervised even top government positions, Japanese authority remained in those zones, though dictated by the military rather than Mantetsu. Despite these significant shifts in the political landscape in the mid-1930s, Mantetsu's images of place, race, and culture featured in the 1935 Mukden issue of *Manshū graph* exemplify how Mantetsu's media negotiated themes of cultural containment, harmonious racial sovereignty, and, more problematically, the military occupation of the continent. To better understand the way these photographs operated in a larger political and social schema, it is important to address how they fit in to the discursive ordering of bodies in the 1930s, namely, through Manchukuo's formative national slogans of "racial harmony" and the "harmony of the five races."

"Racial Harmony," Belonging, and Dominance

While the concept of the segregated city initially seems at odds with the formative Manchukuo slogans of "racial harmony" (*minzoku kyōwa*) and the "harmony of the five races" (*gozoku kyōwa*), in fact they have much in common, acting in concert with each other to form a larger racial and spatial paradigm of Japanese belonging on the continent. Promoted by the Japanese Manchurian Youth League (Manshū Seinen Renmei) in the late 1920s, the idea of "racial harmony" was a founding principle for the Japanese occupation of Manchuria.[25] The concept was borrowed from the discourse of Chinese Nationalism, specifically Sun Yat-sen's call in 1912 for a "civic nationalism" that was predicated on the unification of China's five major ethnic groups: Han Chinese, Manchus, Mongols, Tibetans, and Muslims.[26] It was also a response to the growing Nationalist and anti-Japanese sentiment among Chinese in the first years of the 1930s. According to Yamamuro, in June 1931, the Manchurian Youth League called for "harmony among the various peoples presently resident in Manchuria-Mongolia," thereby calling for the *right to live* in the region and equal treatment of the small ethnic group of Japanese living on the continent.[27] This was, then, a defensive slogan and an early means of inscribing a sense of Japanese belonging in Manchuria.

In 1931, the Manchurian Youth League also began cooperating with the Kwantung Army to combat the economic and political control of Chinese warlords, the greatest threat to Japanese authority and power in the region.[28] The Kwantung Army soon recognized the potential political and social benefits of promoting "racial harmony" in Manchuria and so created new propaganda campaigns to promote the concept in both Japan and on the mainland. Ishiwara Kanji (1889–1949), a high-ranking officer in the Kwantung Army and one of the primary architects of the Manchurian Incident, invented the slogan *Gozoku kyōwa ōdō rakudo* (Paradise ruled by kingly virtue, where five races harmonize).[29] Here, the politics of belonging become more apparent: the five races constituting this new paradise were Chinese, Manchurian, Mongolian, Korean, and Japanese, the latter two replacing the Tibetans and the Muslims of Sun Yat-sen's earlier Nationalist paradigm.

Visualizations of these formative defensive slogans were crucial to the process of persuading multiple demographics—Chinese, Korean, and Japanese alike—that the various racial and ethnic groups residing in Manchuria and Mongolia should be recognized and afforded rights to inhabitation. In part, this was because images promoting *minzoku kyōwa* and *gozoku kyōwa* used representative individuals of each race or ethnicity to embody these concepts, decontextualizing their symbolic bodies from the political and social weight attached to their population sizes in the region. This is clearly evident in two *gozoku kyōwa* examples: the 1933 poster "The Mutual Prosper-

Figure 8.3. "Gozoku kyōei," (The mutual prosperity of the five races), Manchukuo Ministry of Police, 1933. Yusei Nostalgia Museum (Yusei deai no kan).

ity of the Five Races" (*gozoku kyōei*) (fig. 8.3), issued by the Manchukuo Ministry of Police, and an undated poster that proclaimed, "Let the five peoples living under the five radiant colors of the Manchurian flag live in togetherness and glory" (fig. 8.4).[30] The *gozoku kyōei* poster depicts five women, dressed in different ethnic costumes. They walk toward a raised open-air

Figure 8.4. "Let the five peoples living under the five radiant colors of the Manchurian flag live in togetherness and glory." Concordia Association (n.d.). Yusei Nostalgia Museum (Yusei deai no kan).

pavilion erected on a foundation inscribed with "The Imperial Nation of Manchuria" (Manshū Teikoku) and bearing a sign that reads *ōdō rakudo* (paradise of the kingly way). Each woman bears a Chinese character designating her race: Chinese, Manchurian, Japanese, Korean, and Mongolian, *left to right*, respectively. They hold aloft the flags of Manchukuo and Japan, signifying the nations through which this racial harmonization and enlightened rule has been realized.

The second poster, published by the Japanese Concordia Association (Manshūkoku Kyōwakai) for a Korean audience, similarly uses representative bodies for each of the five ethnic groups, united under a large flag of Manchukuo. However, this poster differs slightly in that the figure of the Japanese man—shown standing, *second from the left*, between two men wearing variations of the Chinese *changshan*—wears Western attire, set apart by his trousers, trench coat, and fedora.[31] This sartorial statement suggests that the symbolic figure of Japan embodied the Western modernization that would transform Manchukuo and marks him as the rightful inhabitant of the urban spaces being built in the new nation. Importantly, by abstracting the concept through the individual embodiment of ethnic difference in these posters, the vast discrepancy in population sizes disappears.[32] Aggrandizing the Japanese body through the repetition of the Japanese flag and the association with modernization, these images suggest more than the right to be in Manchuria and the equal agency of these constituent groups. These images speak to a racial hierarchy as well.

These subtle hierarchies are also evident in Mantetsu's media. In January 1940, *Manshū graph* featured a two-page montage titled "Manchoukuo, the Land of Racial Harmony" (Minzoku kyōwa no koku) (fig. 8.5) with the figures of five smiling women—(*from right to left*) Japanese, Chinese-Manchurian, White Russian, Mongolian, and Korean—in different ethnic dress. What stands out

Figure 8.5. "Minzoku kyōwa no koku" (Manchoukuo, the land of racial harmony), *Manshū graph* 8, no. 1 (January 1940). Yumani shobō reprint, University of Minnesota Library.

immediately is the collapsing of the Chinese and Manchurian races (labeled in the caption as "Kan-Manzoku") into one body and the subsequent inclusion of the White Russian. This speaks to the greater flexibility and license that editors took in defining race through the more general "racial harmony" slogan *minzoku kyōwa.*[33] Despite this difference from the earlier *gozoku kyōwa* promotional posters, this layout also presents a visual hierarchy. The Japanese woman, *furthest right,* commands the most prominent position. She stands almost a head taller than the Chinese-Manchurian woman next to her. In fact, as the eye moves across the two-page layout, each subsequent figure grows increasingly smaller, culminating in the figure of a Korean woman who appears half the size of her Japanese counterpart. The healthy roundness of the Japanese woman's face and her fine kimono indicate that she is a woman of a middle or upper economic class. While the kimono marks her as the bearer of Japanese tradition and culture, the permanent wave of her hair demonstrates that she is also Westernized, a symbol of a modern Asian woman. Her affluence and modernity contrast with the rather abject, impoverished figure of the Mongolian woman, *second from the left.*

In addition to displaying subtly coded socioeconomic hierarchies, these three images exemplify how the visual language of multiculturalism and racial diversification relied on maintaining the image of cultural difference. Indeed, the visualization of the slogan relied on markers of cultural difference, such as costuming, to demonstrate the difference between population groups. This cultural differentiation had a spatial component as well. The visualization of this harmonious coexistence existed in a symbolic, illustrated space or one sutured together through montage. Notably absent in "racial harmony" representations are photographs capturing the smiling bodies of the diverse races of Manchukuo in a singular physical space. *Gozoku kyōwa* and *minzoku kyōwa* promotional images do not utilize photographs of models smiling while interlocking arms in identifiable Manchurian landscapes such as the broad avenues of Mukden or Xinjing. These bodies do not inhabit the same space. Rather, they were drawn, composed, and pasted into a multiethnic community. They touched only in fiction. Harmony, then, became associated with distance.

Images of Manchurian segregated cities featured in *Manshū graph* can be appreciated as spatial-pictorial translations of these sociopolitical relationships. Each ethnic group could enjoy its respective space in Manchukuo, even in the densely populated spaces of the city. Implicated in this spatial and social ordering was the tension between the idealism of multicultural sovereignty and the regimes of colonial dominance. This became particularly delicate terrain to negotiate as the interwar period saw increasing calls on the world stage for decolonization. In theory, a city split between modern and traditional spaces for immigrant (occupying) and indigenous populations, respectively, satisfied the call for national self-determination without compromising the goals of the colonial regime that occupied the territory. Gwendolyn Wright has argued that European colonial powers used urban design in the early twentieth century as a means of making colonialism more palatable to critics in the West and "tolerable to the colonized peoples."[34] In order to reconcile competing international and indigenous interests with imperial plans, urban engineers simultaneously created modern spaces—with new administrative buildings, large boulevards, water and electrical infrastructure, gardens, and transit systems—while trying to preserve traditional culture.

This "dual city" produced political and economic effects. In the French protectorate of Morocco, for instance, resident-general Hubert Lyautey (1854–1934) allowed for historic districts within Casablanca that maintained ancient artifacts, mosques, street fronts, and other kinds of Moroccan cultural forms. These historic sites were separated from the new, French-built urban spaces by no-build zones or "sanitary corridors" such as a green belt, a ravine, or some other "natural inclusion."[35] This spatial segregation played multiple roles. It supposedly gave indigenous people a feeling of cultural autonomy, limited the contact between colonizer and colonized, and provided the French with the opportunity to market the "quaint charm" of traditional spaces as a tourist commodity.[36] This negotiation of autonomy and commodification certainly parallels Mantetsu's destination marketing in *Manshū graph.*

These dual/segregated spaces also facilitated the reconciliation of the conflicting European feelings of desire and revulsion—affects of difference—that emerged as Europeans engaged with foreign cultures. Jean-Louis Cohen and Monique Ebb write how, in 1907, French reporter Georges Bourdon lamented Casablanca's "squalid carapace," warning "tourists who 'have a love of beauty and suave fragrances' against the town's 'repugnant filth' and 'seedy quarters.'"[37] British reporter Reginald Rankin described the city in much different terms, likening it to a townscape in the background of one of Masaccio's paintings, enlivened with a celebratory crowd wearing vividly colored *djellabas* (robes).[38] Another British traveler, S. L. Bensusan, apparently wrote "in disgust" about the *medina*'s "muddy lanes whose rickety paving stones barely cover up the drains" yet remarked that the local market (*jutiya*) "offered as oriental an image as any Westerner might wish to see."[39]

The affective language of these travelers speaks to the tension between curiosity, disgust, desire, and anxiety in the experience of the historic sections of Morocco. It is remarkably similar to the kind of language Mantetsu used to describe the old walled city in 1935: "noisy," "squalid," and authentically "Manchurian." These statements express the Othering of the historic district, marking it out as something distinctive from the hygienic, ordered spaces of the new developments. On one hand, the coding of these spaces was a necessary component in selling culture for tourist consumption—as Chris Ryan has argued, exoticization "depends on cultural difference and *spatial distance.*"[40] The wall and the sanitary corridor, then, were necessary in the physical articulation of cultural autonomy and marketable difference.

Difference, however, was predicated on a deprecatory language that underscored the unequal social and political relations at work in these spaces and their representations. Herein lay the tensions between desire and anxiety, occupation and sovereignty. *Manshū graph*'s textual and visual treatments of the old city suggest both the promotion of an exotic cultural experience and an underlying anxiety regarding a fetid and disorderly environment. This speaks to the larger conflict between contact and distance or inclusion and exclusion seen in broader colonial discourse and the perception that the body of the Other was somehow diseased or unhygienic.[41] These were bodies that required control and containment.

This tension underscores the paradox of the wall. On one hand, the wall might be understood as a physical symbol of the cultural autonomy of Chinese and Manchurian residents and, taken more broadly, the authentic sovereignty of Manchukuo. On the other hand and as Wendy Brown writes, the symbolism of walls should be appreciated from an alternative perspective wherein the weakening of state sovereignty fuels the "frenzy" for wall building.

> Rather than resurgent expressions of nation-state sovereignty, the new walls are icons of its erosion. While they may appear as hyperbolic tokens of such sovereignty, like all hyperbole, they reveal a tremulousness, vulnerability, dubiousness, or instability at the core of what they aim to express—qualities that are themselves antithetical to sovereignty and thus elements of its undoing.[42]

While Brown focuses on the relationship between the current proliferation of newly constructed walls and diminishing national identification, her statement provides productive insight into the ambiguous function of the historical Manchurian walls. The recurrent referencing of the continental walls in Mantetsu media connotes not spaces of stable autonomy but rather spaces of instability and flux. The repeated iteration of the wall became a necessary means to visualize control over spaces of sociopolitical insecurity.

In the representation of the walled cities, then, one sees the convergence of the language of belonging and the language of domination. Japanese publications like *Manshū graph* provided Japanese readers with a sense of place and continental identity. Yet the insecurity of the Japanese position on the continent necessitated the visualization of a defensive, dominant position in the cities—and, read more broadly, the state of Manchukuo—as a bulwark against any threats to this position: a vulnerability to heterogeneity from both within and without that compelled the need to build "higher walls around the boundaries and borders of the national collectivity and to mobilize people towards exclusionary politics."[43] But what danger lay behind the walls of the old city? What was the potential threat? To articulate this last layer of signification in the walls, it is useful to look at one of the principal advertised spaces for the appreciation of "local color" in the old walled city—the thieves' market—and its relationship to discourses of banditry, danger, and militarism on the continent.

Containing the Thief, Containing the Threat

In 1919, Mantetsu advertised Mukden's spectacular wall and the old city in the *Minami Manshū testudō ryokō annai* (South Manchuria Railway Company travel guide). The guide touched on several unique characteristics of the walled city, marking it out as a space of physical and cultural alterity. Using a language similar to that seen in *Manshū graph* more than fifteen years later, the travel guide states that, in addition to housing the old Qing palace and government offices, the "disorderly" (*fukisoku*) neighborhood inside the wall is home to "humble people" (*senmin*) and small businesses that occupy the "narrow, dirty backstreets" (*rōkō*).[44] The guide then makes a surprising observation, stating that "on top of the inner wall is a battle turret; if ever there is a brief incident, the width of the wall is great enough to accommodate tens of thousands of soldiers and to lay down an abundant barrage of fire from field artillery."[45] The rhetoric of "tens of thousands of soldiers" may have been a means to express the physical scale of the inner wall. It may also have been a nod to the city's militaristic past as the site of a bloody battle between 200,000 Japanese soldiers and more than 275,000 Russian infantrymen during the Russo-Japanese War (1904–1905).[46] Or, it may have been an acknowledgement of the political and military unrest in Northeast Asia. Certainly, this text reveals the contemporary entanglement of militarism and tourism in Mantetsu's promotion of the continental tour and recognizes that the old city is a site of difference *and* potential danger. It also shows how the wall, a monumental tourist spectacle, functions as a vehicle for containment and, if need be, forceful subordination.

Years later, the theme of potentially dangerous bodies in Manchuria would appear in Mantetsu promotional literature, this time in the pages of *Manshū graph*. There were subtle changes, however, as the company commodified and packaged potentially menacing figures into a cultural commodity: the thieves' (*kosodoro*) market. Operating in much the same way as Oriental bazaars featured at French fairs, these Manchurian street markets held inside the city walls were often advertised as one of the primary attractions for tourists interested in witnessing an authentic form of Manchurian culture. In May 1936, the magazine dedicated a two-page layout to these markets (fig. 8.6). A caption accompanying the photographs states that "in practically every Manchurian walled city, there is at least one open market. Popularly, these markets are known as 'markets for petty thefts' and the wide range of articles displayed there tends to make one believe that nothing in this world is fit to be discarded."[47]

This layout, featured in an issue dedicated to the lives of Chinese coolie laborers in the port city of Dalian, associates the "local color" of the walled city with a transient social class and low-quality goods. The feature takes the reader on a virtual tour of the market. A large photograph spanning the two pages provides a panoramic view of this distinctive commercial venue. Utilizing the elevated perspective seen in the photograph of the Mukden wall in 1935, the photograph captures the event from high above the unfolding action. The photograph is intercut with a montage of close-up shots of smiling market vendors and various trinkets, including shoes, secondhand cookware and utensils, and heaps of clothes. Each operates in sharp contrast to the well-dressed, commercial affluence advertised in the SMR Zones.

The subjects of these photographs do not appear as immediate threats, but by framing the markets through the trope of the "thief," the magazine

Figure 8.6. "Open-Air Markets," *Manshū graph* 4, no. 5 (May 1936). Yumani shobō reprint, University of Minnesota Library.

transforms the people into transgressive bodies. They become *potential* threats. Moreover, they invite comparison to the bandit (*hizoku* or more commonly, *bazoku*), a figure inextricably bound up with Japanese images of Manchuria's vast frontier since Japan won concessions in Northeast China from Russia in 1905. Most often envisioned as armed brigands who survived through kidnapping and robbery, these notorious bandits figured heavily in stories about China in the Japanese and foreign press.[48] As Yaqin Li notes, media from the 1920s associated banditry with "disorder" in China and sociopolitical problems in Manchuria; consequently, foreign interventions such as the Japanese military's own "bandit suppression" undertaken since the Manchurian Incident were conducted in the spirit of "maintaining peace and order."[49] Japanese print media such as *Manshū graph* built on this association between the "bandit problem" and political and military instability in China, often describing the culture within the walled city as disorderly. Dangerous bodies resided in these culturally authentic and chaotic spaces. These bodies necessitated regimes of control, and foreign powers—including the Japanese—used the bandits as an excuse for military intercession and occupation.

Despite an ongoing campaign of bandit suppression in the new state of Manchukuo by the Japanese Kwantung Army, the bandits continued to be a problem. In part this was due to the flexibility of the term, referring to various armed forces marauding in the Manchurian hinterland and seeking out economic opportunities through theft and kidnapping. But the term also worked as a means to rebrand military and political insurgency: bandits could simply mean those who "resist[ed] Japan and the Manzhouguo regime."[50] Used in this way, the Japanese army did not have to acknowledge armed, ideological resistance to Japanese occupation in the new state. Violence could be attributed to economic stakes rather than military action. Through these multiple iterations, the bandit then became a faceless repository of violence and danger, inextricably bound to the experience of the Manchurian frontier. Moreover, bandit suppression was a means to reconcile the optimistic ethos of "racial harmony" and the virtuous "paradise ruled by the kingly way" with the transformation of the fledgling nation into a "garrison state."[51] As Yamamuro has argued, opponents of this state and its moral foundation "had to be liquidated," and consequently, "everyone had perforce to keep an eye on everyone else."[52]

Yamamuro's statement highlights the importance of the gaze in the negotiation of space and race in Manchukuo. Certainly, the walls and their representations must be understood as critical components of the discourse of Japanese domination on the continent. A primary means of visualizing Japanese authority over the walled city was in the use of the elevated perspective, utilized most notably in the 1935 Mukden issue and also in Mantetsu's *Manshū gaikan 2598* (Overview of Manchuria, 1938) (fig. 8.7). As mentioned previously, taking a photograph from atop the wall was useful for expressing the massive scale of the wall and capturing an expansive view of the scene below. It was a sight to see and a site from which one *could* see. The position of the photographer and, by extension, the Japanese reader produced what Tony Bennett has described as a kind of

Figure 8.7. "Rekishi no miyako" (The historical city), *Manshū gaikan 2598* (An overview of Manchuria, 1938). Waseda University Central Library collection.

"specular dominance" that rendered people and things knowable.[53] In this way, the photographs taken from on top of the great Manchurian walls demonstrated an exhibitionary impetus. They revealed and mapped the "humble people" and the "thieves" of the old walled city. Moreover, the "commanding view" of these photographs, to borrow from David Spurr, affords the photographer and reader a sense of mastery over the "unknown" and what is perceived as "the strange and bizarre."[54]

The elevated perspective produced a spectacle as well as a system of surveillance. The wall, wrapping around the old city, functioned as a kind of reverse panopticon. Spurr remarks that this elevated perspective facilitated the "superior and invulnerable position of the observer," thereby "affirming the political order that makes that position possible."[55] Linking the physical occupation of the wall to its symbolic function in Japanese media, photographs transferred this authority, situating the reader in the position of the "prison warden."

While Spurr may speak to the figurative authority this field of vision entails, it is far more literal in the case of the Manchurian walls. Following the Mukden Incident in 1931, the Japanese Kwantung Army took up a strategic position on the Mukden wall as a means to suppress anti-Japanese forces. Photographs of soldiers on the wall proliferated as a result (fig. 8.8). The soldiers featured on the cover of *Manshū jihen gahō* (Manchuria incident pictorial) from October 18, 1931, look out from the wall, away from the city, suggesting that the threat lay beyond its borders. On the other hand, photographs, such as the one (fig. 8.9) published in *Asahi graph* on September 30, 1931, and republished in Mantetsu's 1934 *Manshū gaikan* in a photo essay dedicated to remembering the Mukden Incident, demonstrate how the soldiers' guns and disciplinary gaze easily turned upon the inhabitants inside the city as well.[56] The wall made possible the surveillance and military subjugation of the dangerous bodies below. As such, the palimpsest of militarism overlays these seemingly innocuous Mantetsu images of spaces of cultural difference.

Further, the composition of Mantetsu's wall photographs affected another symbolic form of domination on the Sino-Manchurian inhabitants of the old cities. Many photographs of Mukden's wall featured in *Manshū graph* and *Manshū gaikan* between 1934 and 1939 depict the wall and people or vehicles on the street below. However, the framing of the photograph does not reveal the flow of bodies through gates and beyond the structure. This is certainly evident in the aforementioned June 1935 photograph and 1938 photograph from Mantetsu's annual. Both images show movement within the old city but do not visualize points of entry or exit into this neighborhood. These are images of containment. In Mantetsu's media, these potentially dangerous bodies could not move freely. These visual representations underscore a unidirectional cultural contact. The Japanese reader or traveler may move freely about these spaces, look from empowered positions, and consume Sino-Manchurian culture.

While the thief or the bandit provided a lexical repository for images of the threatening Other, the visual narrative of containment and mobility of Sino-Manchurian inhabitants in the old city may also be read in the context of Japanese concerns regarding the movement of Chinese coolies into Man-

Figure 8.8. Japanese soldiers on top of the wall at Mukden. *Manshū jihen gahō* (Manchuria incident pictorial), October 18, 1931. Image originally appeared in *Certain Victory: Images of World War II in the Japanese Media*, (ME Sharpe, 2008, p. 73). Reprinted by permission of the David C. Earhart Collection of Japanese Primary Sources from the Asia Pacific War, 1931–1948.

chukuo. In 1936, Mantetsu expressed its apprehension regarding mass migrations from China, which had numbered in the millions since the late 1920s, and the subversive politics such people may bring. Speaking to the necessity for "effective control of labor and immigration" from China, the company averred that

Figure 8.9. Japanese soldiers stationed on top of the Mukden wall. *Asahi graph*, September 30, 1931.

> politically speaking, pending the promulgation of the naturalization law, it became necessary to draw a clear distinction between the citizens of Manchoukuo and the citizens of China in order to solidify the foundations of the new State. Moreover, plain-clothed Chinese soldiers, the trained anti-Manchoukuo propagandists, and even communists were discovered flowing into Manchuria in great numbers under the guise of Shantung coolies.[57]

While immigration control was integral to maintaining the distinct cultural and ethnic boundaries that defined citizens of one nation or another, this claim also crucially points to the association of the coolie with possible political and military subversion, the same dangerous figures whom Japanese offices subsumed under the "bandit" designation. Given this association, it is not surprising that, while Mantetsu often featured layouts on the outdoor street markets of the old city in *Manshū graph*, it emphasized the trope of the thief in its coolie issue. It also provides a compelling reason why images of the Mukden walls emphasized containment of the dangerous, ethnic Others of the old city.

Interestingly, Mantetsu used the thieves' market not just as a means to posit Chinese and Manchurian residents as potentially threatening bodies. Rather, *Manshū graph* transforms the transgressive body of the thief—a less menacing variation of the bandit—into a controlled commodity, a marker of "local color" and "exotic" culture. In other words, Mantetsu repackaged the threat, taking the very real danger of the bandit and coding it as a product for consumption.

Yet, the thief was not entirely stripped of his or her dangerous potential, and the threat was itself an element in coding the market as a cultural spectacle of difference and the racial Others of the old city as potential risks. This underscored the unspoken need for urban segregation and continued military occupation. Harmony in the new multiethnic state necessitated firm control. The image of this control reassured would-be visitors that they would be safe during their continental tour. According to *Manshū graph,* Japanese staying in the posh new hotels in the SMR Zone could visit the supposedly dangerous old walled city and thereby experience a cultural adventure, the exotic spectacle of indigenous life. Yet, as the wall contained the bodies of the Sino-Manchurian ethnic Other and, by extension, the threat of the "thieves," Japanese visitors could maintain the fiction of safety once they left the historical city.

Conclusion

In 1939, part of the monumental Mukden wall collapsed, causing a number of casualties. Consequently, city authorities began discussing a five-year plan to demolish it and its gates.[58] *Manshū graph* addressed the dismantling of the wall in its November 1941 issue, noting that demolition of the famous structure finally commenced in June of that year. Given Mantetsu's recurrent treatment of the wall in its promotional literature, it is fitting that *Manshū graph* imaged its destruction (fig. 8.10). What was once a formidable, towering structure was now an expanse of stone rubble. The caption accompanying the layout speaks to the earnest deep emotions (*kangai*) elicited by the process, highlighting the affective meaning of the wall. Interestingly, the text overtly references the wall's relationship to Manchuria's military past, perhaps an indication of the Kwantung Army's increasing control over media messages and a nod to Japan's "blood debt"

Figure 8.10. "Kie iku Hōtenjō," *Manshū graph* 9, no. 11 (November 1941). Yumani shobō reprint; University of Minnesota Library.

on the continent. It stated, "As for the government, it is more and more resolved to preserve eternally the fortified city's Great South gate, through which Ōyama [Iwao], Commander-in-Chief of the Japanese armies in Manchuria, had boldly entered during the Russo-Japanese War. As for the other gates, they will be demolished completely."[59] In this layout depicting the wall's destruction, the meaning of the structure and its mediation of sociopolitical relationships changed. The wall was no longer a fortification that contained bodies and subjected them to the dominant gaze of the Japanese photographer or soldier. At the end of 1941, as the Kwantung Army entered the fifth year of the second Sino-Japanese War (1937–1945), the wall came down almost completely and exposed potentially dangerous bodies. This was both a physical and an important symbolic flattening of Mukden's famous fortification. Now, there was nowhere to hide.

Of course, Mukden's wall was not the sole focus of Mantetsu's media in the 1930s. As a massive structure, it was merely one of the most photographed and most visible. An examination of these photographs provides a richer understanding of a complex discursive relationship between race and space in Japanese media during this transformative decade in Manchuria. These photographs were more than the product of Mantetsu's advertising and public-relations efforts; they were lodged in a complicated web of signification informed by Mantetsu's activities as well as those of other offices like the Kwantung Army and the Manchuria Youth League.

Consequently, these images must be appreciated for the multiple meanings they accrued as they coexisted with idealistic slogans espousing racial harmony, stories of military unrest, and news of ongoing bandit suppression on the continent. While some of these narratives might seem incompatible, Mantetsu's promotional media such as *Manshū graph* demonstrate how the company was able to negotiate tensions in representation to sell its achievements in Manchukuo and the Manchuria Tour. Drawing on the cultural spectacle of the walled city, the magazine emphasized the exoticism of Sino-Manchurian culture, making the indigenous population visible and spatially accessible. At the same time, Mantetsu's photographs of the walled cities suggested that these were controlled spaces. In this way, these historic urban sites bore the palimpsest of military domination that, in turn, tempered stories of the dangerous bodies that continued to plague the frontier. In locating the racial Others securely behind walls, Japanese media like *Manshū graph* provided Japanese urban readers with a comforting fiction of the multiethnic utopia of Manchukuo.

Notes

1. Common ways to romanize the name of the nation-state "満州国" (Manshūkoku) are Manchukuo, Manchoukuo, (which is the romanization that often appeared in Japanese-published media from 1932 to 1945) and, using the pinyin system of romanization, Manzhouguo. As Yamamuro Shin'ichi notes, postwar Chinese histories written on both the mainland and in Taiwan refer to the nation-state as *wei Manzhouguo* (illegitimate Manzhouguo) or simply *wei Man* in order to emphasize how Japanese occupation created a puppet state. Yamamuro Shin'ichi, *Manchuria under Japanese Dominion*, trans. Joshua A. Fogel (Philadelphia: University of Pennsylvania Press, 2006), 3.

2. David Tucker, "City Planning without Cities: Order and Chaos in Utopian Manchukuo," in *Crossed Histories: Manchuria in the Age of Empire,* ed. Mariko Asano Tamanoi (Honolulu: University of Hawai'i Press, 2005), 54.

3. Louise Young, *Japan's Total Empire: Manchuria and the Culture of Wartime Imperialism* (Berkeley: University of California Press, 1998), 259–268.

4. Yamamuro, *Manchuria under Japanese Dominion,* 3.

5. Prasenjit Duara, *Sovereignty and Authenticity: Manchukuo and the East Asian Modern* (Lanham, MD: Rowman and Littlefield, 2004), 1.

6. Yamamuro, *Manchuria under Japanese Dominion,* 4.

7. *Manshū graph* 3, no. 3 (June 1935): n.p.

8. Mukden (Fengtian) today is known as Shenyang. While many historians refer to the historical city as Fengtian, I use Mukden in this paper, as it better articulates the city's embattled past, most notably the Mukden Incident (also known as the Manchuria Incident) in September 1931.

9. Louise Young translates *gozoku kyōwa* as "harmony of the five races." Young, *Japan's Total Empire,* 276. Other scholars such as Angela Yiu translate the slogan as "harmony of the five ethnic groups." Angela Yiu, "From Utopia to Empire: Atarashikimura and *A Personal View of the Greater East Asia War,*" *Utopian Studies* 19, no. 2 (2008): 213–232. One translation is not necessarily more accurate than the other. As Mariko Asano Tamanoi has observed, scholars of nationalism and imperialism face a difficult task in translating *minzoku.* It usually translates as "ethnicity," whereas *jinshu* and *shuzoku* translate as "race." However, Tamanoi rightly points out the absence of a clear distinction between the culturally defined ethnicity and biologically determined "race." Therefore, it is common to see *mizoku* translated as "people," "ethnicity," "race," or even "nation." In this section, I too use "race" and "ethnicity" interchangeably because the difference between the two in the context of the Japanese Empire are decidedly blurry. See Mariko Asano Tamanoi, *Memory Maps: The State and Manchuria in Postwar Japan* (Honolulu: University of Hawai'i Press, 2009), 166.

10. South Manchuria Railway Company, *Fifth Report on Progress in Manchuria* (Dalian, China: South Manchuria Railway, 1935), 68.

11. Ibid.

12. Mantetsu's public relations department published the *Manshū graph* bimonthly from September 1933 to August 1935 and monthly thereafter until January 1944.

13. English captions were more common during the 1930s than in the early 1940s. Even when included, there were disparities in meaning between the Japanese and the English text.

14. Fuchikami Hakuyō was a renowned art photographer recruited by Mantetsu in the late 1920s to spearhead publication projects in its public relations department. He worked for Mantetsu from 1928 to 1941, when he returned to Japan. For a more in-depth analysis of the artistic vision Fuchikami brought to the company, see Kari Shepherdson-Scott, "Fuchikami Hakuyō's *Evening Sun*: Manchuria, Memory, and the Aesthetic Abstraction of War," in *Art and War in Japan and Its Empire, 1931–1960,* ed. Ming Tiampo, Louisa McDonald, and Asato Ikeda (Leiden, Netherlands: Brill, 2012), 275–291; Kari Shepherdson-Scott, "Utopia/Dystopia: Japan's Image of the Manchurian Ideal" (PhD diss., Duke University, 2012), 118–171, 292–318; and Annika A. Culver, *Glorify the Empire: Japanese Avant-Garde Propaganda in Manchukuo* (Vancouver: University of British Columbia Press, 2013).

15. The magazine exemplifies the blurring between news, Mantetsu's advertising, and the still nascent field of public relations. Isomura Yukio, "Jōhō/ Kōhō katsudō," in *Mantetsu chōsabu: Kankeisha no shōgen,* ed. Imura Tetsuo (Tokyo: Ajia keizai kenkyūjo, 1996), 408.

16. The Mukden Incident or Manchurian Incident refers to the explosion of a section of Mantetsu's rail line just outside Mukden on September 18, 1931. The event was staged by the

Japanese military and made to look as though Chinese insurgents were responsible. The Japanese army then used the Mukden Incident as the pretext for invading Manchuria, supposedly to secure Japanese economic interests in the region. This issue of *Manshū graph* references the Mukden Incident, stating, "Even up till the outbreak of the 'Incident' this city of a thousand tales remained the stronghold of the notorious warlord, Chang Hsueh-liang, but with the auspicious establishment of Manchoukuo, Mukden relinquished to Hsinking its title of the 'Capital City.' Today it is purely an industrial and commercial city as well as the center of both education and transportation." See *Manshū graph* 3, no. 3 (June 1935): n.p.

17. Ibid.

18. While the English caption uses the phrase "local color," the Japanese caption refers to the old walled city as a place with an "exotic atmosphere" (*ikoku jōcho*).

19. Ibid.

20. Young, *Japan's Total Empire,* 268.

21. *Manshū graph* 3, no. 3 (June 1935): n.p. The English captions do not mention these population dispersals. Only the Japanese captions discuss what populations reside in these spaces.

22. Young, *Japan's Total Empire,* 268.

23. Jeremy Foster, "Capturing and Losing the 'Lie of the Land': Railway Photography and Colonial Nationalism in Early Twentieth-Century South Africa," in *Picturing Place: Photography and the Geographical Imagination,* trans. Joan M. Schwartz and James R. Ryan (London: I. B. Tauris, 2003), 143.

24. The negotiation of Japanese voluntary relinquishment of extraterritorial rights was underway in 1935 but not signed until June 10, 1936. A key point in the negotiations was the adoption of measures by the Manchukuo government perfecting "various means to facilitate the residence, travel, and business activities of Japanese subjects" and (more generally) assuring "the prevailing degree of protection enjoyed by the Japanese subjects under the Japanese administration." See South Manchuria Railway Company, *Sixth Report on Progress in Manchuria to 1939* (Dalian, China: South Manchuria Railway, 1939), 26–27, 40.

25. The Manchurian Youth League formed in 1928 and used *minzoku kyōwa* as a means to solicit support for Japanese living in Manchuria. Kevin McDowell, "Colonizing Manchuria: Racial Harmony and Agricultural Emigration in the Japanese Empire" (master's thesis, University of British Columbia, 1992), 11.

26. Mariko Asano Tamanoi, "Introduction," in *Crossed Histories: Manchuria in the Age of Empire,* ed. Mariko Asano Tamanoi (Honolulu: University of Hawai'i Press, 2005), 11.

27. This small group of Japanese, many of whom were running small and mid-sized businesses on the continent, comprised less than 1 percent of the roughly thirty million inhabitants of the region. Yamamuro, *Manchuria and Japanese Dominion,* 62.

28. Ibid., 14.

29. Tomoko Hamada, "Constructing a National Memory: A Comparative Analysis of Middle-School History Textbooks from Japan and the PRC," *American Asian Review* 21, no. 4 (Winter 2003): 124.

30. Translation by Dafna Zur.

31. The men flanking the Japanese man likely represent Chinese and Manchurian ethnic groups. The men who are furthest to the right wear Korean and Mongolian clothing.

32. At the end of 1932, Japanese numbered 135,597, constituting roughly 4.5 percent of Manchukuo's population of 29,968,835. *Japan-Manchoukuo Year Book 1936* (Tokyo: Japan-Manchoukuo Year Book, 1936), 45, 655.

33. Such slippages, omissions, and inclusions in racial categories articulate how the Japanese media delicately negotiated representations of the diverse populations in the region. For ex-

ample, even when acknowledged, the Russian population was repeatedly marked as an outsider population on the decline, often referred to in *Manshū graph* as émigrés (*emigurantotachi*). Understanding how to reference the many different ethnic groups and races in Manchoukuo was also problematic because of a fundamental difficulty in differentiating one race from another. Mariko Asano Tamanoi argues that these blurred definitions were entangled in the space between "idioms of dominance" and idioms of "ambivalence and confusion." In other words, the fluidity of these taxonomies was the result of disinformation and the strategic need for colonial legitimation. Mariko Asano Tamnoi, "Knowledge, Power, and racial Classification: The 'Japanese' in 'Manchuria,'" *Journal of Asian Studies* 59, no. 2 (May 2000): 251.

34. Gwendolyn Wright, "Tradition in the Service of Modernity: Architecture and Urbanism in French Colonial Policy, 1900–1930," in *Tensions of Empire: Colonial Culture in a Bourgeois World,* ed. Frederick Cooper and Ann Laura Stoler (Berkeley: University of California Press, 1997), 322.

35. Wright, "Tradition in the Service of Modernity," 327–332. See also Paul Rabinow, *French Modern: Norms and Forms of the Social Environment* (Cambridge, MA: MIT Press, 1989), 286.

36. Ibid., 325.

37. Jean-Louis Cohen and Monique Ebb, *Casablanca: Colonial Myths and Architectural Ventures* (New York: Monacelli Press, 2002), 30.

38. Ibid.

39. Ibid.

40. Chris Ryan, "Tourism and Cultural Proximity: Examples from New Zealand," *Annals of Tourism Research* 29, no. 4 (2002): 957 (my emphasis).

41. Ming-Cheng M. Lo also discusses this from an interesting perspective in *Doctors within Borders: Profession, Ethnicity, and Modernity in Colonial Taiwan* (Berkeley: University of California Press, 2002). Lo addresses how Taiwanese doctors, who were both mentored and oppressed by Japanese doctors, were called on to protect the health of the nation by severing racial and ethnic ties to China. China, writes Lo, "was both the site of the enemy and the source of disease, against which Taiwan needed to defend itself" (ibid., 115). Fear of miscegenation and the subsequent blurring of racial and ethnic divisions that informed colonial taxonomies also played a role in the perceived threat of physical colonial encounters. Ann Stoler discusses the sexual contact between colonizer and colonized and how it led to cultural and social anxieties in the metropole. See Ann Stoler, "Sexual Affronts and Racial Frontiers: European Identities and the Cultural Politics of Exclusion in Colonial Southeast Asia," in Cooper and Stoler, *Tensions of Empire,* 198–237.

42. Wendy Brown, *Walled States, Waning Sovereignty* (Cambridge, MA: MIT Press, 2010), 24.

43. Nira Yuval-Davis, Floya Anthias, and Eleonore Kofman, "Secure Borders and Safe Haven and the Gendered Politics of Belonging: Beyond Social Cohesion," *Ethnic and Racial Studies* 28, no. 3 (May 2005): 528.

44. *Minami Manshū testudō ryokō annai* (Dalian, China: Minami Manshū Kabushikaisha, 1919), 75.

45. Ibid.

46. Dennis Warner and Peggy Warner, *The Tide at Sunrise: A History of the Russo-Japanese War, 1904–1905* (New York: Charterhouse, 1974), x.

47. *Manshū graph* 4, no. 5 (May 1936): n.p.

48. Yaqin Li, "'Bandit Suppression' in Manchukuo (1932–45)" (PhD diss., Princeton University, 2012), 4.

49. Ibid., 4–5.

50. Yamamuro, *Manchuria and Japanese Dominion,* 208.

51. Ibid., 209.

52. Ibid.

53. Tony Bennett, *The Birth of the Museum: History, Theory, Politics* (New York: Routledge, 1995), 66.

54. David Spurr, *The Rhetoric of Empire: Colonial Discourse in Journalism, Travel Writing, and Imperial Administration* (Durham, NC: Duke University Press, 2004), 15.

55. Ibid., 16.

56. This photograph was taken on September 19, 1931, the day after the Mukden Incident, but featured in the *Asahi graph* in the September 30, 1931, issue.

57. South Manchuria Railway Company, *Fifth Report on Progress in Manchuria,* 121–122.

58. Fujikawa Yūji, ed., *Saraba Hōten: Shashinshū* (Tokyo: Kokushokankōkai, 1995), 65.

59. *Manshū graph* 9, no. 11 (November 1941), n.p.

Imagining an Affective Community in Asia
Japan's Wartime Broadcasting and Voices of Inclusion

Imperial Formation, Radio, and Affect

While Benedict Anderson focused on print media in explaining the role of modern mass communication technology in the formation of the "imagined community" of nationhood, other scholars of media have pointed out that radio during the first half of the twentieth century played a similar role in an even more powerful and far-reaching manner.[1] Electronic technology enabled radio to be the first medium that literally realized the synchronicity of parallel action by dispersed bodies of media audiences, which Anderson noted as crucial to national identity formation. As an auditory medium, radio extended the awareness of parallel action to nonelite populations, spreading imagined nationhood to "the largest grouping of people ever known."[2] Many studies have drawn attention to the affect-producing effects of broadcasted voices with regard to radio's role in mediating the imagination of the nation as a community. Although the effects of such mediation were never predetermined, with its profound bodily and emotional impact the medium tended to facilitate a strong sense of affinity among listeners and contributed to the formation of the self-conscious but empathetic, community-minded self.[3]

Yet what has often been forgotten in historical studies of radio and national formation is that the most advanced radio nations in the first half of the twentieth century were imperialist powers, and these empires in one way or another came under growing pressure to reconfigure their nationhood in relation to various regional and ethnic others. With a few noteworthy exceptions, the relationship between the medium and "imperial formation" has been a relatively understudied topic.[4] Regardless of what caused this lacuna—the categorical distinction between research on domestic and overseas operations; a postwar historiography that focused exclusively on domestic affairs and made it difficult to go beyond the framework of national history; or postwar disdain for wartime broadcasting as an agency of propaganda and mass deception—bringing empire into perspective compels us to reframe the question of radio and the imagined community of nationhood.[5] How did radio, both its technology and cultural practices, work—or fail—to evoke a sense of community when the demand for imperial expansion inevitably posed a challenge to an exclusively imagined nationhood?

I will attempt to answer this question by exploring the radio broadcasting of the Japanese Empire at its zenith of expansion, namely during the last phase of the Asia-Pacific War. During this era the growing demands of the war effort forced the empire to make inclusionary gestures to its colonial subjects and the various ethnic groups in newly occupied territories under the banner of the Greater East Asia Co-Prosperity Sphere.[6] The Japanese imperial state, colonial governments, and occupation forces utilized all means of communication and cultural institutions to win over diverse populations under their purview. As the chief of the Second Section of the Japan Broadcasting Corporation (NHK)'s International Department put it, radio's unique capacity to overcome spatial and temporal barriers—which no other medium available at the time possessed—made it an "absolutely crucial . . . propaganda machine" for the empire.[7]

Radio broadcasting in Japan started in 1925, and as the empire continued its territorial expansion, its broadcasting network expanded accordingly. Regular broadcasting service in Japan's colonies began during the interwar period, in 1927 in Korea and in 1928 in Taiwan. Japan's overseas broadcasting, later known as Radio Tokyo, began its service for the West Coast of North America and Hawai'i in 1935. With the escalation of the war with China and the Allied powers, Japanese broadcasting expanded its target audience to include various peoples under the rapidly expanding empire. By 1944 Radio Tokyo was broadcasting its programs to sixteen regions (including China, India, Thailand/Indochina/Burma, and the Philippine/Dutch Indies in Asia) in twenty-five different languages.

Yet at the same time, overemphasizing the functionality of broadcasting prevents us from considering the concrete ways in which radio engaged with dispersed listening subjects to develop a sense of community and affective bonds between them.[8] As I shall show in the following pages, contemporaneous Japanese broadcasters, like their counterparts in other advanced radio-listening nations, were deeply aware that broadcasting technology alone did not automatically turn listeners into a group. They realized that, in addition to the awareness of simultaneous colisteners, emotional ties were necessary to sustain a strong sense of community. Wartime Japanese broadcasters thus developed various strategies to boost the audience's sense of connectedness with the speaker and imagined colisteners.[9] By analyzing these strategies and listeners' reactions, I wish to draw attention to the broadcasting-mediated social and cultural practices of emotions and feelings situated in the context of Japan's propagation of the Greater East Asia Co-Prosperity Sphere.

Specifically, my study maps out how these radio practices attempted to construct and sustain an affective community in Asia by using radio listening and audience participation as a generative mechanism of imperial identification. Although these practices were designed to educate the multiethnic listeners into a normative way of feeling amid the processes of imperial formation, we should not discount the subversive possibilities of the audiences' decoding and local radio practices aimed to counteract the effects of Japanese broadcasting or even to oppose the empire. While space does not allow me to discuss such possibilities extensively, a few exemplary cases presented in the closing section will help us critically assess the actual effect of the Japanese broadcasters' attempts to generate imperial identification.

In examining the interplay between radio broadcasting and Japan's imperial formation, I consider both domestic and overseas operations "in a single analytic field."[10] The elevation of the war and the concomitantly growing imperial aspiration for the political, economic, and cultural integration of the Asia-Pacific region increasingly blurred the boundaries between domestic and overseas broadcasting. Asia's diverse populations heard many programs at the same time as the Japanese through the NHK's relay networks and shortwave broadcasting. Likewise, it became a matter of everyday experience for domestic audiences to listen to material transmitted from overseas stations and the speeches and performances of various Asians. In other words, the empire's broadcasting became a reciprocal activity between the metropole and its colonies and occupied territories in Asia and the Pacific. Thus, it is imperative to consider the empire's domestic and overseas broadcasting together.

Synchronizing the Expanding Empire

Japanese imperial aspirations to build a "New Order" in Asia and the start of the war in the Pacific strongly conditioned both Japanese domestic and overseas broadcasting. The Cabinet Information Bureau (*Naikaku Jōhōbu*) issued a series of guidelines for opinion formation and directed all forms of media to support the war effort.[11] In terms of the nature of the intended messages, which were tailored to the Cabinet Information Bureau's guidelines, radio broadcasting might not necessarily be distinguishable from other media. Yet perhaps no other medium could make the copresence of diverse places and peoples under the rapidly expanding empire "feel" as real as radio did; the advancement of relay broadcasting technology enabled radio to conjure a sense of connectedness with the remote colonies and the newly occupied territories.

The broadcasting system linking Tokyo and radio stations in Japan's formal colonies, Manchuria, and the occupied territories in China—informally called relay broadcasting to outer lands (*gaichi renraku hōsō*)—had developed following the emperor's enthronement ceremony in November 1928. In its early years, the empire's network functioned primarily as the extended service of domestic radio to Japanese settler communities. Yet the network did not remain a unidirectional means of communication from the metropole to the colonies and the areas under Japanese influence. The broadcasting system incorporated programs originating from the colonies to the metropole to "enhance a deeper understanding" in the Japanese population of the diverse places and peoples under the empire.[12]

For instance, in the case of Taiwan, Japan's first formal colony, Taiwan-originated programs were aired to all parts of Japan almost once a month following the first such broadcast on September 9, 1934. The programs included "Taiwanese music, full of exotic atmosphere of the southern land," children's plays, lectures on the current state of the nation's development, human stories of Aboriginal youths' Japanese-language training, and so on. By 1940, these programs were broadcast up to eighteen times per month, and in 1942 the NHK launched a new monthly program called *Letters from Taiwan* (*Taiwan dayori*).[13]

The NHK formally named the broadcasting system East Asia Relay Broadcasting (Tōa Chūkei Hōsō) and improved infrastructure facilities. The time of broadcasting increased from eight to thirteen hours a day from January 1941 and continued to grow. In early 1943, the NHK and broadcasting companies in the "outer lands" cooperated to conduct a basic survey of various matters of radio listening in order to improve East Asia Relay Broadcasting, thereby contributing to the synchronicity between the mainland and its imperial holdings.[14]

By the time of the outbreak of the war in the Pacific, advanced shortwave technology enabled the NHK to make transmissions directly (sometimes via the retransmission facilities in occupied Singapore) to the home receivers of diverse populations in Asia and the Pacific region. The goal of Japan's overseas broadcasting gradually shifted toward the dispersal of imperial propaganda that corresponded with the escalation of the war in Asia.[15] Shortwave broadcasting allowed listeners to virtually experience the expansion of the empire in real time. Short pieces of audio taken from real-life scenes relayed to listeners at home the events taking place on the war front and in the empire's occupied territories. They also "heard" the fall of Hong Kong through a relay from the spot. On December 25, 1941, the day after the broadcast, the *Asahi Newspaper* described "the explosive roar of tanks, the resounding boots of marching soldiers" and "the thunder of artillery" that made listeners feel "as if they were witnessing" the event.[16] According to an estimate by the NHK's recording staff, regular relay broadcasts of live recordings from its colonies and occupied territories for listeners in the metropole numbered more than twenty per month as of November 1942. If we take irregular relay broadcasts into account, the number was significantly higher.[17]

Relay technology enabled an even more dramatic representation of the synchronized experience of expanding empire in the form of multilateral broadcasts. The NHK's journal *Broadcasting Research* (*Hōsō kenkyū*) provides a glimpse of one such broadcast titled "The Roundtable of the (Greater East Asia) Co-Prosperity Sphere Networked by Electronic Waves" (*Denpa ni musubu kyōeiken zadankai*). The fifty-minute evening program, which aired on October 13, 1942, attempted to link the metropole and three separate locations in newly occupied territories in Southeast Asia: Singapore, Batavia (Jakarta), and Manila. Receiving shortwaves from Southeast Asia, Tokyo rebroadcast these to each site. The speakers were the vice-director of the Singapore Museum and advisers to the military governments in Batavia and Manila. They discussed "rich local themes" (*genchi no hōfu na wadai*) for the empire's listeners.[18]

Of course, it would be misleading to assume that the simultaneous copresence of diverse places and peoples under the purview of the empire itself automatically generated a sense of community. Contemporary Japanese broadcasters raised doubts about such technological determinism, well aware that the listeners' mental and emotional engagement with radio was a far more complex process. In contemplating ways to build a national forum through radio, Furu Takeo, an NHK producer and media scholar, noted, "It is said that listeners form a sense of solidarity around the single voice [of the speaker] just because radio voices reach to every corner [of the world] simultaneously. Yet in my opinion this view attends only to the functionality of radio, ignoring the position of listening subjects (*kiku shutai*)."[19] Broadcasters were deeply concerned about the ways in which they could take the awareness of simultaneous colisteners a step further to generate a "sense of belonging" (*kyōzoku no ishiki*) and an "emotional bond" (*jōshoteki ketsugō*) among the dispersed bodies of listeners. They studied and introduced research on the psychology of radio listeners, including the classic work by the American scholars Hadley Cantril and Gordon W. Allport, to map out strategies to boost the sense of connectedness between radio speakers and listeners and among listeners. In the following section, I will discuss some remarkable strategies that Japan's wartime radio adopted to generate a sense of belonging and emotional ties among the colisteners of the various ethnic groups in Asia.

Passionate Announcements, Affective Community

Finding a way to strike a chord with listeners was one of the enduring concerns of Japanese announcers. Further, as wartime radio was expected to serve as a vehicle for spiritual mobilization, broadcasters faced demands to project a voice around which the empire's diverse listeners could build a strong sense of unity and commitment to the war effort. To this end, Japan's wartime broadcasting actively worked to develop intimate and chatty forms of radio talk in an attempt to reconstruct the sociability and interaction of oral settings.

In a roundtable discussion on radio announcements organized by the NHK and held in October 1942, social critics, radio performers, and NHK announcers discussed concrete strategies to intensify the affective ties between the radio speaker and listeners as a crucial basis for generating empathy for the war effort. By showing their personalities (*kosei*) and expressing their subjective view (*shukan*), for instance, announcers could help give listeners a basis on which to personally connect with or develop affection for the speaker. Another strategy to enhance sociability between announcers and listeners was to make announcements "as if talking to listeners." In so doing, announcers were instructed to imagine their listeners not as a mass of anonymous people but as a small group of several people in a private setting. Small-group listening was the most common mode in real life. Targeting the small group would allow announcers to develop a friendly and intimate mode of address.[20]

The implementation of these strategies in response to wartime demands resulted in a notable transition in the normative mode of radio announcement and its aesthetics, a shift from a detached tone (*tantanchō*) to a passionate (*jōnetsuchō*) or emotional (*jōshochō*) tone. Between the outbreak of the Pacific War and mid-1943, the NHK's *Broadcasting Research* journal carried a series of roundtable discussions and feature articles that reflected the shift. As NHK announcer Kawana Shōichi explained in his review of Japanese broadcasting for the first year after Pearl Harbor, the outbreak of the war in the Pacific was a key factor behind the shift that made the detached tone—once considered ideal for radio announcements, particularly news announcements—obsolete. According to Kawana, the stunning military success of the Japanese Empire during the early phase of the Pacific War made it inappropriate for announcers to deliver war news in a detached, objective manner.[21]

The significance of the passionate tone did not decrease even after the war moved "from the stage of dazzling military achievements to that of rather unglamorous construction [of the Greater East Asia Co-Prosperity Sphere]." Rather, NHK broadcasters emphasized the importance of the emotional tone more than ever as they were called upon "to cheer up one million compatriots and encourage them to go in the directions instructed by the nation" in the face of the protracted war. Such emotional appeal, they expected, could attract disinterested people to their broadcasts and leave an impression on their minds. Kawana Shōichi wrote:

> If we [announcers] understand the content, we can make accurate announcements for programs like *Primer for National Subjects* (*Kokumin dokuhon*), saying that "the national subject must do such and such because the current situation is such and such." These accurate (*seikakuna*) announcements may win listeners' approval. Yet such approval is merely based on intelligence, which will burst like a bubble once the listener moves away from the radio set. . . . According to [Henri] Bergson, "It is the emotion which drives the intelligence forward in spite of obstacles." Does not here lie the base for compelling even passersby to listen attentively [to radio]? . . . What strikes the chord [with listeners] is neither intelligent understanding nor a call to jump on the bandwagon; its base exists beyond the awareness of the situation. The foundation for a new announcement should be what propels the awareness, which is emotion. . . . The compelling announcement must take a form that penetrates into the sub-consciousness of listeners. What moves listeners is emotional appeal. The announcement that forces intelligent awareness is mere coercion.[22]

How, then, should the announcer arouse empathy for the empire's cause among listeners? Kawana argued that in order to move listeners' emotions the announcer himself or herself should be moved by the significance of the matter he or she was to announce. The foundation for the passionate tone should be "the sensation the announcer has of being hit directly in the gut (*chokugeki na kandō*)." When expressing such a sensation, the announcer should exert his or her personality so that listeners could find his or her address lively and compelling. Yet that personality was to reflect less an autonomous individuality than a singular perspective thoroughly permeated by the communicative needs of the empire and originating from the proper "view of current affairs, the nation, and the world that have penetrated into the body (*niku*) of the announcer." Put differently, Japanese announcers identified their role as emotionally drawing listeners into normative ways of feeling defined by the wartime state and the governing elite.

Broadcasters such as Kawana assumed a priori that Japanese citizens and colonial subjects had already formed a strong empathy for the war effort. As such, the announcers' job was to express their shared feeling as representatives of the preexisting affective community. In this line of thinking, the announcer's expression of his or her subjective feeling was to represent some sort of broader collective feeling shared by the entire nation. Kawana observed that even though the highly emotional announcements on the start of the Pacific War violated the existing norms for the techniques of radio addresses they did not encounter resistance from listeners. This was because "the touched feeling of the announcer was not a peculiar feeling of a private individual but a shared feeling of one million [national subjects]." In other words, it was a "natural manifestation of the national feeling that the Japanese in general shared."[23]

Yet to other keen-minded contemporaries such as Furu Takeo, the affective community was not a fait accompli but rather a condition to be created out of the dispersed individuals that made up the listening population in order to "shift the core of the listener's ego from an individual to a national domain." To create an interactive affective connection among listeners with the radio speaker at the center (what Cantril termed the "circular relationship"), radio should enhance mutual contact among multiple listeners. Yet because listeners did not have direct contact with each other, the circular relationship among them remained an imagined one. The broadcasting-mediated pseudocircular relationship "lacked a sense of reality" and therefore tended to dissipate easily.

On the premise that an individual is always a social being, Furu sought a solution to this absence of real social contact from theories of community, holding that if affinities (*ruijisei* or *dōrui ishiki*) and common interests facilitated the formation of *Gemeinshaft* (community), broadcasting might capitalize on these already existing affinities and common interests to strengthen the circular relationship among radio listeners.[24] Japanese broadcasting adopted several strategies designed to evoke affinities and common interests among its diverse listeners, and I turn to these concrete practices in the following section.

Exploiting Intimate Affection, Connecting Warfront and Home Front

Perhaps no other group could have attracted greater sympathy from general listeners than the soldiers fighting for the empire at the risk of their lives. Japanese broadcasting took advantage of this widespread sympathy for the soldiers, inviting them to speak or perform on radio. *On-Site Recording* (*Genchi rokuon*) occasionally broadcast soldiers' voices. The broadcast on April 19, 1942, for instance, featured a soldiers' roundtable (*heishi zadankai*), which one listener, in his letter to the program, described as "truly interesting" and during which he "felt as if he were watching the cool and collected soldiers." He suggested that the broadcast had "far greater effect on listeners on the home front than one hundred exhortations."[25]

Several feature programs went further, exploiting the affection between the soldiers and their families in order to raise the sense that the battlefront and the home front were a community sharing the joys and burdens brought on by the war. *Connecting Battlefront and Home Front* (*Zensen jūgō o musubu*), a program arranged to exchange messages between soldiers at war and their families and friends at home, made its debut on August 25, 1942. Utilizing the empire's extensive broadcasting networks, radio stations in Manchuria, northern China, central China, Southeast Asia, and some Pacific islands dispatched recording staff to Japanese troops stationed in those areas and recorded the voices of sixteen soldiers in the format of "letters to home." The NHK's domestic personnel then visited each soldier's hometown, let his family and friends listen to his message, and recorded their replies. Each soldier's voice was paired with that of his family and broadcast across the empire.[26] As a preview article in the *Asahi Newspaper* commented, the show was designed to produce "wild excitement on both warfront and home front, as it would air soldiers' and their families' voices back-to-back from the same microphone, transcending the distance between Japan and [Greater] East Asia."[27]

The October 1942 issue of *The Broadcast* (*Hōsō*), the NHK's magazine for listeners, carried the scripts of the messages from soldiers and their families. These scripts reveal patterns designed to steer listeners toward normative ways of feeling under the "spiritual mobilization" of wartime empire. The letters carried inquiries about the safety and health of each soldier and his family members, along with updated news and brief reports about how they were supporting the war effort on the warfront and the home front. The soldiers expressed their determination to serve the empire while showing their concern for their families. The families tried to relieve the soldiers' anxiety and remind them that people on the home front were also faithfully supporting their efforts. The messages of the soldiers' families ended with requests for the soldiers to focus on their duties and to take care of themselves. One letter from an army corporal in a detached unit stationed in central China to his father at home read:

> As July starts in central China, summer is really here. I hope you and all other family members have been well. How is grandmother doing? In the picture you sent me before you looked much older, so I hope you can take it easy. I am working cheerfully every day. In face of the great operation that attacked Chiang Kai-shek (Jiang Jieshi)'s troops . . . our airmen hit every shot with full fighting spirit and excellent techniques. Yet considering that it is up to us, chair-borne soldiers enabling aircraft to run at full capacity through close inspection and care, I feel great responsibility and also feel honored. I am healthy, with my body completely tanned. I wish you all the best for your good health. Good-bye.

His father in Ōoka Village of Suntō County at Shizuoka Prefecture responded by writing:

> Dear Haruo,
>
> Your grandmother and the whole family, neighbors, and relatives assembled upon hearing the news that we could listen to your letter on the radio, to which we are listening right now. Don't worry about your family. We want you to commit yourself to your job without worries. National subjects on the home front unite to serve sincerely in their own fields. A moment of inattention may cause an air crash. Even when tightening a screw or affixing a piece of wire, we want you to keep in mind that the fate of the airplane relies on [the assembly of] its individual pieces and devote yourself to your job. Haruo, please persevere in your military duty while taking better care of your body, as it was offered to the emperor. Good-bye.[28]

The ways that soldiers and their families talked to each other indicate that these participants consciously conformed to the norms of behavior expected of loyal imperial subjects at war. Even when talking to their own family members, they were not free from normative modes of expression and feeling strongly conditioned by the spiritual mobilization for the empire's war effort. During the recording and listening, for instance, participants had to pose for photographs, to be publicized through NHK publications. Those photos captured the soldiers speaking on the microphone to their family members, usually a young wife and her little children. While themselves subject to interpretation, the visual images often seemed to belie the determination expressed in the audio messages, implying the pressure under which the soldiers and their families spoke for the empire. While some soldiers did not hide their excitement and the smiles on their faces appeared genuine, overall the speakers appeared to restrain their emotions. The soldiers' wives in particular tended to maintain a nearly expressionless face.[29]

No matter how scripted, however, we cannot simply dismiss the emotional impact of this sort of project on the sense of connection among listeners. The wife of a hospitalized soldier described the thrill of listening to her husband's voice as being "like a dream."[30] The younger brother of a conscripted soldier explained the possible emotional impact of those programs on the warfront in general, saying that "as far as they were the voices of adorable Japanese children, even the voices of complete strangers would evoke wistful affection for the soldiers' own children they had left at home."[31]

The listeners' column of *The Broadcast* indicated that the program achieved its aim of evoking a strong affective response and empathy among general listeners. It was not unusual for listeners to find themselves in tears. A resident of Kawaguchi City wrote:

> I was truly touched by *Connecting Battlefront and Home Front,* aired on August 27. It made me ever more greatly appreciate broadcasting. The success of this broadcast was so touching that as a listener I could not help but to take up my pen [to write a letter to NHK]. I was unconsciously moved to tears by

> the affection between siblings and spouses, the fierce determination for the Greater East Asian War that firmly linked warfront and home front, and the scenes of exchanging messages as if they were seeing each other.[32]

Another listener's letter from Niigata Prefecture described *Connecting Battlefront and Home Front* as "a timely project" that left him "grateful and touched." He was deeply moved by, more than anything, the "completely genuine voices of old parents, wives, and children replying to the cheerful voices of brave soldiers on the warfront."[33]

The NHK later modified the show's format into a recreational program for soldiers titled *Evening Show for the Battlefront* (*Zensen ni okuru yū*). For the first broadcast, on January 7, 1943, soldiers' families were invited to Hibiya Public Hall as an audience, and popular entertainers were recruited to perform Japanese traditional comic monologues (*rakugo*), popular songs, and so on, as requested by soldiers at the front. Soldiers took their turn through another program called *From Battlefront to Home Front* (*Zensen kara jūgo e*), delivering choruses, harmonica performances, and poetry readings to domestic listeners.[34] Like their predecessor, these programs drew positive reactions from listeners. According to the NHK's analysis of listeners' letters, *Evening Show for the Battlefront* continued to rank as one of the most favored programs throughout the spring of 1943.[35] A listener, in his letter, assessed the broadcast as a success while confessing that a little girl's solo performance caused him to dissolve in tears. "Soldiers must have burst into tears of joy," he wrote. "We on the home front also spent an enjoyable, spiritually rich evening."[36]

Voices of Inclusion: Audience Participation and Multiethnic Colisteners

The aforementioned programs aimed to connect the warfront and the home front and attempted to provoke empathy primarily among the Japanese. Yet the empire's proclaimed goal of creating a Greater East Asia Co-Prosperity Sphere pushed the NHK to expand the affective community beyond the exclusively imagined ethnic nation. An important strategy the NHK utilized to facilitate affective community across Asia was to invite diverse populations to participate along with Japanese citizens in round-the-empire programs, linking audiences by allowing them to speak and perform on radio. Empire-wide participatory events would serve two ends. First, they were meant to strengthen a sense of connectedness, if not affective ties, among performers and listeners. Hearing the actual voices of diverse peoples of Asia would make the existence of multiple colisteners feel more real. The experience of speaking to each other and performing together—in a sense, actively participating in empire—would contribute to intimacy and affinities among members of ethnically diverse audiences. The large-scale radio events, aired simultaneously to the entire region under the empire's purview, would purportedly make it much easier to imagine the whole region as a continuous space and the inhabitants of that space as a community. Second, these participatory practices would announce the inclusionary gesture of the empire, consciously orchestrated under the slogan of "building the Greater East Asia Co-Prosperity Sphere."

Wartime radio networked the voices of Japanese citizens and the diaspora, international students and intellectuals residing in the metropole, and locally mobilized Asian peoples. For example, on December 31, 1941, the NHK aired an assembly of boys and girls from Asian countries titled *Greater East Asian Little National Subjects' Meeting* (*Daitōa shokokumin no tsudoi*). In June 1943, to "deepen the understanding about current circumstances in the Southern Regions (*Nanpō*) and strengthen the bond among children" in different locations, the program *Little National Subjects' Hour* (*Shōkokumin no jikan*) relayed the stories and singing performances of Japanese children abroad as well as Japanese and local songs performed by native children in the "Southern Regions."[37]

The NHK organized even more ambitious, widely publicized, empire-wide participatory radio events. One of these, the *Greater Asian Children's Singing Contest* (*Daitōa jidō shōka taikai*), was held in 1941. The NHK had run the national chorus contest for schoolchildren, the *School Children's Singing Contest* (*Jidō shōka konkūru*), since 1932. The contest called for voluntary participation. The applicants went through a preliminary round at the prefectural level, then on to local contests at seven central stations, and finally on to a national contest. Such procedures displayed participants in the final event as local representatives, implying synchrony and an equal footing across national spaces, seen as a crucial basis for community making. In tandem with the empire's aspiration to build a New Order in Asia, the national contest developed into an imperial event with an extended range of participation.[38]

In 1942, the NHK took advantage of broadcasting technology's capacity to actualize synchrony and elevated the singing contest to a new type of imperial event. The *Convention for the Little National Subjects All over the Country to Sing Together* (*Zenkoku shōkokumin minna utae taikai*) attempted to have "little national subjects (*shōkokumin*) from all over the country sing the same song at once" by networking the central venue and each local meeting place with group listening facilities.[39] In the following year, the NHK attempted to expand the same practice to the entire Japanese Empire with the modified title *Convention for Greater East Asia's Little National Subjects to Sing Together* (*Daitōa shōkokumin minna utae taikai*). This festival invited both Japanese schoolchildren and other Asians from "all over the Greater East Asia Co-Prosperity Sphere" who resided in Tokyo to sing in a chorus at the central venue, Hibiya Public Hall. The NHK planned to mobilize group-listening facilities on the Japanese mainland and in each country within the Greater East Asia Co-Prosperity Sphere so the concert could be heard at exactly the same time, and children in various local meeting places could join the chorus. This ambitious project to allow all Japanese and other Asian children of school age to simultaneously sing in chorus was inconceivable and impracticable without the broadcasting networks of the Japanese Empire. It was "what broadcasting made possible in the first place (*hōsō ni oite hajimete kanō na koto*)," as the broadcasters proudly remarked.[40]

Though the NHK boastfully announced that listeners "greatly welcomed" these events, due to a lack of reliable sources the actual attitudes of the diverse participants remain unclear, and we cannot discount the possibility of exaggeration in such an assessment.[41] Yet it is not unreasonable to argue that these participatory radio events created shared simultaneity of experience among multiethnic participants and listeners. As Naoki Sakai has suggested, singing in chorus often functions as a powerful mechanism for generating a sense of community based upon strong sympathy.[42] The aforementioned imperial radio events were programmed to channel the emotional effect of singing together into the imagination of the empire as a community.

It is also true that regardless of their inner conviction, participants not only chorused nationalist and imperialist songs but also performed a series of rituals designed to forge imperial identification and loyalty to the emperor. For example, the 1943 program for the *Convention for Greater East Asia's Little National Subjects to Sing Together* included pledging allegiance to the nation, vowing to the emperor, singing the national anthem, praying for the war dead, and shouting "Long live the emperor" as well as chorusing imperialist songs.[43] Following Leo Ching, we may see this series of corporeal activities not as the externalization of inner faith but as the crucial mechanism that constituted people as imperial subjects. In this light, cross-empire and multiethnic audience participation in imperial radio events can be considered as just such a performative ritual, "a generative foundation" of imperial identification and an affective community.[44]

Concluding Thoughts

Analyzing several remarkable strategies utilized to boost the sense of connection and affective ties among ethnically diverse listeners, I have attempted here to examine the role of radio broadcasting in Japan's imperial formation during the last phase of the Asia-Pacific War. In doing so, I have tried to show the ways in which broadcasting technology and practices of radio listening and participation became a mechanism for forging imperial identification when imperial expansion necessitated the reconfiguration of an exclusively imagined nationhood. The improvement of the empire's broadcasting network and the advancement in relay technology made diverse populations under the Japanese Empire aware of their simultaneous colisteners. In order to channel such awareness into affective ties, Japanese wartime broadcasters adopted an intimate style of radio address and a passionate tone of announcement. Some radio programs aimed to utilize affective ties already existing among listeners, such as affection for one's own family, to foster empathy in the national audience. Other round-the-empire programs and large-scale imperial radio events invited both ordinary Japanese citizens and other Asian peoples in as speakers and performers to facilitate a sense of participation in the empire and foster emotional bonds among participants and listeners.

As recent studies based on oral interviews, diaries, and memoirs have shown, imperial subjects had diverse reactions to the experience of war and to wartime media messages.[45] We cannot expect that radio broadcasts had a homogeneous effect on different listeners. At the same time, some Japanese listeners testified that wartime radio broadcasting let them imagine the multiethnic people of Asia as a community bound together by a common cause and that such imagination emotionally moved them, intensifying the effects of normative modes of feeling under wartime imperial discourse. Listening to stories of Southeast Asian children's Japanese-language training and their performances in Japanese, for instance, an Osaka resident stated in her letter to the NHK that "the fact that we can communicate with children in the Southern Regions in the Japanese language made me feel as if I were watching the dawning of the *hakko ichiu* (all eight corners of the world under one roof) ideal and I shed tears of gratitude for the heavenly blessings of the emperor."[46]

The remaining question is whether Japan's wartime radio had a similar mental and emotional impact on other Asian peoples who came under the empire's rule in the latter phases of the war. Japanese broadcasting made inclusionary gestures, such as audience participation, to non-Japanese populations, and Japan's overseas broadcasting addressed diverse Asian populations. Between November 1, 1942, and October 1943, East Asia Relay Broadcasting aired *Invitation to Greater East Asia* (*Daitōa ni yobu*). Transmitted from Tokyo to various locations in "Greater East Asia," this program aimed to boost affinity across national and ethnic populations in Asia through lectures and news reports. The announcer interpellated listeners in an intimate mode of address, with "Dear All in Asia" (*Tōa no minasama*). The tactics of directly addressing Asian listeners were employed in other programs as well. For example, Japanese programs for soldiers and civilians in Asia attempted to capture the listeners' attention by intimately addressing their program to "Dear All" (*shokun*) multiple times in each broadcast.[47]

Calling on Asian peoples to be "unified with (*kiitsu*) the Japanese," the empire's broadcasting emphasized what Furu considered the major bases for emotional bonds. First, Japanese broadcasting stressed affinities in history, culture, religion, and so on, between the Japanese and other ethnic groups. At the same time, following the Cabinet Information Bureau's *Guidelines for Overseas Broadcasting* issued on December 8, 1941, the NHK tailored the contents "in consideration of the differences in the history and the national character between Japan (*kōkoku*) and other foreign countries" when explaining the necessity of building the Greater East Asia Co-Prosperity Sphere. This was a common rhetoric of the empire's differential inclusion.[48]

Second, Japanese radio tried to persuade diverse listener groups to realize their common interests in the "liberation of Asia" from Euro-American colonialism. The NHK employed "Asia for Asia" (*Ajia no tame no Ajia*) as the slogan for overseas broadcasting. Accordingly, it allowed the prominent Indian nationalist movement leader Rash Behari Bose (1886–1945) to transmit a series of nationalist speeches from Tokyo to the Indians under British rule using Japanese overseas broadcasting facilities. Bose called on unified efforts to achieve Indian independence while expressing his sympathy toward Japan's proclaimed goal of liberating Asia.[49] The NHK even aired a song dedicated to Bose's Indian National Army titled "Independent March" through its imperial networks.[50]

The case of the Dutch East Indies suggests the inclusionary gestures of Japanese radio broadcasting met some success in drawing sympathy from intellectuals. Around the time of the attack on Java, the Japanese military aired "Indonesia Raya" frequently in an attempt to request the native populations to cooperate with the Japanese forces. "Indonesia Raya," a nationalist song banned by the Dutch at the time, was selected as the national anthem when Indonesia proclaimed its independence in 1945. The empire's gesture drew nationalist intellectuals into Japanese broadcasting as they enthusiastically listened to Japanese shortwave radio and even voluntarily assisted Japanese broadcasters, hoping to help their nation achieve independence from the Dutch.[51]

However, the empire prematurely revealed its motivations underlying the slogans of Asian coprosperity. The independence of the Dutch East Indies was postponed in the name of the cultural underdevelopment of the people, and "Indonesia Raya" was banned by military proclamation only twelve days after the fall of Java to Japanese forces. The swift shift greatly disappointed and disillusioned the nationalist movement leaders and intellectuals in the Dutch East Indies who had enthusiastically listened to Japanese radio and showed some sympathy with the Japanese Empire's slogan of "liberating Asia."[52]

Japanese radio in the Philippines, on the other hand, exemplified the failure of aggressive and hastily launched radio propaganda campaigns. In a meeting at Broadcasting Headquarters (*Hōsō Shireibu*) on May 19, 1942, Komori Shichirō, the head of NHK at the time, expected that "it would be impossible to transplant the Japanese spirit (*Yamato damashii*) [into Asian peoples in newly occupied territories] in a hurried manner."[53] Japanese scholar Terami Motoe documents such failure, noting continued counterpropaganda by U.S. Army Forces Far East against Japanese broadcasting and the lukewarm attitudes of Filipino politicians and cultural figures mobilized by the Japanese military to speak on the radio. Listeners distrusted Japanese radio news, pejoratively describing the acronym of the Japanese Domei News Agency (*Dōmei Tsūshin*) as that of the "Distributor of the Most Erroneous Information" behind the Japanese soldiers' backs.[54]

The limited material capacity of the empire constituted an important reason for such failure. The low distribution rate of radio sets and the lack of broadcasting infrastructure in Southeast Asia and some Pacific islands left a significant number of people unaffected by attempts to imaginatively constitute the Japanese Empire as a community.[55] The NHK constantly struggled to secure the finances and personnel necessary to improve the situation in remote occupied territories. The records of the Propaganda Unit (*Sendenhan*) of the Japanese occupied forces stationed in the Philippines also show the limited influence of Japanese broadcasting. The mission of this agency was to pacify and educate the native populations in the empire's occupied territories through all sorts of media. However, this agency's cultural activities for facilitating propaganda and cultural integration were limited to the urban spaces of a few major cities. In other parts of the country, the occupation forces' major activity remained confined to the mere maintenance of order.[56]

My approach here has been to expand our analysis beyond a domestic history of the functionality of media technology to consider concrete strategies and practices of wartime radio and listener responses alike, allowing us to see, from different perspectives, the complicated and contested processes of imperial formation. While the "absolute presence" of radio allowed a sense of simultaneity and a potential for community building, commentators were also aware that an imperial sense of belonging was a constructed one, requiring the co-option and participation of the listening population. I have thus traced self-conscious attempts to build such an affective community across ethnically and linguistically diverse populations under Japanese empire. Despite the clear potential of radio broadcasting as a powerful means of forging an affective community in Asia for the Japanese Empire, however, newly devised techniques of broadcasting alone could not realize the great expectations of broadcasters and policymakers, whose inclusionary gestures remained a strategy of differential inclusion for an overexpanded empire.

Notes

1. Benedict Anderson, *Imagined Communities: Reflections on the Origin and Spread of Nationalism,* rev. and extended 2nd ed. (London: Verso, 1991). On radio and national community, see Susan J. Douglas, *Listening In: Radio and the American Imagination, from Amos 'n' Andy and Edward R. Murrow to Wolfman Jack and Howard Stern* (New York: Times Books, 1999); Michele Hilmes, "Radio and the Imagined Community," in *Sound Studies Reader,* ed. Jonathan Sterne (New York: Routledge, 2012), 351–362, especially, 351–352; Jason Loviglio, *Radio's Intimate Public: Network Broadcasting and Mass-Mediated Democracy* (Minneapolis: University of Minnesota Press, 2005); Joy Elizabeth Hayes, *Radio Nation: Communication, Popular Culture, and Nationalism in Mexico, 1920–1950* (Tucson: University of Arizona Press, 2000).

2. Hadley Cantril, *The Invasion from Mars: A Study in the Psychology of Panic* (1940; repr. Princeton, NJ: Princeton University Press, 1982), xii.

3. See Walter Ong, *Orality and Literacy: The Technologizing of the Word* (1982; repr. London: Routledge, 2002), 133–135; Steven Connor, "Sound and the Self," in *Hearing History: A Reader,* ed. Mark M. Smith (Athens: University of Georgia Press, 2004); Paddy Scannell, *Radio, Television and Modern Life: A Phenomenological Approach* (Oxford: Blackwell, 1996); Hadley Cantril and Gordon W. Allport, *The Psychology of Radio* (New York: Harper and Brothers, 1935); and Hayes, *Radio Nation,* 22–23. Susan Douglas demonstrates that radio cultivated both a sense of nationhood and a validation of subcultures, which can be resistant to claims of nationhood, often simultaneously. Douglas, *Listening In,* 22–39.

4. On the concept of imperial formation, see Ann Laura Stoler, "Imperial Debris: Reflections on Ruins and Ruination," *Cultural Anthropology* 23, no. 2 (May 2008): 193. For recent studies that address the links between radio broadcasting and imperial formation, see Simon J. Potter, *Broadcasting Empire: The BBC and the British World, 1922–1970* (Oxford: Oxford University Press, 2012); Marie Gillespie Alasdair Pinkerton, Gerd Baumann, and Sharika Thiranagama, "*South Asian Diasporas and the BBC World Service: Contacts, Conflicts, and Contestations,*" special issue, *South Asian Diaspora* 2, no. 1 (2010); Thomas Hajkowski, "The BBC, the Empire, and the Second World War, 1939–1945," *Historical Journal of Film, Radio*

and Television 22, no. 2 (2002): 135–155. In Japan, most studies on radio during the 1930s and the 1940s have focused on its relationship with war rather than empire. For a notable exception, see part 2 of Kishi Toshihiko, Kawashima Shin, and Son Ansuk, eds., *Sensō, rajio, kioku* rev. and extended ed. (Tokyo: Bensei Shuppan), 2015.

5. Potter, *Broadcasting Empire,* 6; some keen scholars of wartime media suggest that both pejorative connotations associated with propaganda and prejudices against broadcasting as a mere tool of unilateral, top-down transmissions were the effects of the particular postwar perspectives on the war era. See Mark Wollaeger, *Modernism, Media, and Propaganda: British Narrative from 1900 to 1945* (Princeton, NJ: Princeton University Press, 2006), 1–37; and John Durham Peters, "The Uncanniness of Mass Communication in Interwar Social Thought," *Journal of Communication* 46, no. 3 (Summer 1996): 108–110.

6. See Eiji Oguma, *A Genealogy of "Japanese" Self-Images* (Melbourne: Trans Pacific Press, 2002); and Takashi Fujitani, *Race for Empire: Koreans as Japanese and Japanese as Americans during World War II* (Berkeley: University of California Press, 2011).

7. Sawada Shinnojō, *Sugata naki tatakai: Sekai no tanpa hōsō* (Tokyo: Kibundō Shobō, 1944), 15–17.

8. Furu Takeo, "Rajio ni yoru kokuminteki ba no keisei ni tsuite," *Hōsō kenkyū* 3, no. 6 (June 1943): 53, 55.

9. Although the portrayal of World War II as a psychological war is a cliché, and radio served as a primary medium for psychological warfare in the Asia-Pacific region, scholars of Japanese history and media have not necessarily taken the psychological effects of Japanese wartime radio broadcasts seriously. This tendency, again, has much to do with the dominant postwar understanding of Japan's wartime broadcasting simply as an apparatus of mass deception. For a series of strategies that interwar Euro-American broadcasters invented to avoid alienating effects and to boost the affections of listeners through personalized addresses, studio audiences, sound effects, and so on, see Peters, "Uncanniness of Mass Communication," 108–123.

10. Ann Laura Stoler and Frederick Cooper, "Between Metropole and Colony: Rethinking a Research Agenda," in *Tensions of Empire: Colonial Cultures in a Bourgeois World,* ed. Frederick Cooper and Ann Laura Stoler (Berkeley: University of California Press, 1997), 15.

11. Nai Kaku Jōhōkyoku, "Nichi-Ei-Bei sensō ni taisuru jōhō senden hōsaku taikō (December 8, 1941)" and "Daitōa sensō ni taisuru jōhō senden hōsaku taikō (December 15, 1941)," reprinted in *Taiheiyō Sensō hōsō senden shiryō*, vol. 1, ed. Kitayama Setsurō (Tokyo: Ryokuin Shobō, 1997), 283–299.

12. For a brief summary of the development of the empire's networks linking Taiwan, Korea, Manchuria, and other occupied territories and East Asian relay broadcasting, see *The History of Broadcasting in Japan* ed. NHK Hōsō Bunka Kenkyūjo (Tokyo: Nihon Hōsō Kyōkai, 1967), 102–104, 110–116; Ji Hee Jung, "Nanhang hanŭn cheguk ŭi chŏnp'a net'ŭwŏk'ŭ: Cheguk Ilbon ŭi Tongasia pangsongmang chaego," *Tongasia munhwa yŏn'gu* 57 (May 2014): 277–306.

13. Hōsō Bunka Kenkyūjo 20-seiki Hōsōshi henshūshitsu, *Hōsōshi shiryōshū Taiwan Hōsō Kyōkai* (Tokyo: Nihon Hōsō Kyōkai Hōsō Bunka Kenkyūjo, 1998), 30; Denpa Kanri Iinkai, *Nihon musenshi,* vol. 12 (Tokyo: Denpa Kanri Iinkai, 1946), 102–103.

14. Nihon Hōsō Kyōkai, *Nihon hōsōshi,* vol. 1 (Tokyo: Nihon Hōsō Shuppan Kyōkai, 1965), 580–586; Tōa Hōsō Kyōgikai Jimushō, "Tōa Hōsō: Tōa Hōsō no kihon chōsa," *Hōsō kenkyū* 3, no. 2 (February 1943): 117–118.

15. For the general account of Japan's overseas broadcasting, see Jane Robbins, *Tokyo Calling: Japanese Overseas Broadcasting, 1937–1945* (Florence, Italy: European Press Academic, 2001).

16. "Denpa ni todomeku bakugeki: Honkon kōrayku no jikkyō hōsō," *Tokyo Asahi shinbun,* December 25, 1941, morning edition.

17. "Jikkyō rokuon: Gaichi yori no hōsō," *Hōsō kenkyū* 2, no. 11 (November 1942): 80.

18. "Denpa ni musubu kyōeiken zadankai," *Hōsō kenkyū* 2, no. 11 (November 1942): 71.

19. Furu, "Rajio ni yoru kokuminteki ba no keisei ni tsuite," 53.

20. Wada Shinken, "Anaunsu zadankai," *Hoso Kenkyū* 2, no. 10 (October 1942): 14–16, 25.

21. Kawana Shōichi, "Anaunsu: Nyūsu anaunsu o chūshin to shite," *Hoso kenkyū* 2, no. 12 (December 1942): 50.

22. Kawana Shōichi, "Anaunsu no miryoku," *Hōsō kenkyū* 3, no. 6 (June 1943): 63–64.

23. Kawana, "Anaunsu: Nyūsu anaunsu o chūshin to shite," 50–51.

24. Furu, "Rajio ni yoru kokuminteki ba no keisei ni tsuite," 53–57.

25. "Chōshūsha no koe," *Hōsō* 2, no. 6 (June 1942): 134.

26. I thank Takeyama Akiko for bringing the program and listeners' letters to my attention. Takeyama Akiko, *Sensō to hōsō: Shiryō ga kataru senjika jōhō sōsa to puropaganda* (Tokyo: Shakai Shisōsha, 1994), 86–87, 97–100. I also thank her for sharing *The Broadcast* magazine from her own collection.

27. "Zensen to jūgo: Natsukashii 'koe' de musubu getsumatsu kara ureshii hōsō," *Tokyo Asahi shinbun,* August 20, 1942.

28. "Zensen to jūgo o denpa ni musubu," *Hōsō* 2, no. 10 (October 1942): 85.

29. See the unpaginated picture section attached to chapter 4 of Nihon Hōsō Kyōkai, *Nihon hōsōshi.* The section carries a photograph of the soldiers recording their messages to their families and three images of their families listening to the soldiers' voices and recording their messages back to the warfront. Two photographs of soldiers' families are reproductions of the images featured in the unpaginated photograph section of *Hōsō kenkyū* 2, no. 9 (September 1942), front matter.

30. "Zensen to jūgo o denpa ni musubu," 88.

31. "Chōshūsha no koe," *Hōsō* 3, no. 3 (March 1943): 104.

32. "Chōshūsha no koe," *Hōsō* 2, no. 10 (October 1942): 134.

33. "Chōshūsha no koe," *Hōsō* 2, no. 11 (November 1942): 134.

34. Nihon Hōsō Kyōkai, *Nihon hōsōshi,* 544, 551.

35. See Matsuzawa [first name unspecified], "Hankyō," *Hōsō kenkyū* 3, no. 2 (February 1943): 43; "Hankyō," *Hōsō kenkyū* 3, no. 3 (March 1943): 12; and "Hankyō," *Hōsō kenkyū* 3, no. 5 (May 1943): 83.

36. "Chōshūsha no koe," *Hōsō* 3, no. 3 (March 1943): 104.

37. Nihon Hōsō Kyōkai, *Nihon hōsōshi,* 538–539.

38. NHK Shichōsha Honbu Jigyōbu Bangumi Seisakukyoku Gakkō Kyōikubu, *NHK zenkoku gakkō ongaku konkūru 50-nen no ashi ato* (Tokyo: NHK Shichōsha Honbu Jigyōbu Bangumi Seisakukyoku Gakkō Kyōikubu, 1983), 9–12.

39. For the *Minna utae taikai,* see also Nihon Hōsō Kyōkai, *Nihon hōsōshi,* 538.

40. "Dai 2-kai Daitōa shōkokumin 'minna utae' taikai," *Hōsō* 3, no. 10 (October 1943): 26–28.

41. "Dai 3-kai kinrōsha ongaku taikai," *Hōsō* 3, no. 9 (September 1943): 40.

42. On the community of sympathy, see Sakai Naoki, *Nihon eiga Beikoku: Kyōkan no kyōdōtai to kokumin shugi* (Tokyo: Seidosha, 2007): 67–176.

43. Ibid., 27–28.

44. Leo Ching, *Becoming Japanese: Colonial Taiwan and the Politics of Identity Formation* (Berkeley: University of California Press, 2001), 89–90.

45. For example, Haruko Taya Cook and Theodore F. Cook, eds., *Japan at War: An Oral History* (New York: New Press, 1992); Samuel Hideo Yamashita, ed., *Leaves from an Autumn of Emergencies: Selections from the Wartime Diaries of Ordinary Japanese* (Honolulu: University of Hawai'i Press, 2005); NHK Sensō Shōgen Purojekuto, ed., *Shōgen kiroku heishitachi no sensō,* vols. 1–7 (Tokyo: NHK Shuppan, 2009–2012); and Hildi Kang, ed., *Under the Black Umbrella: Voices from Colonial Korea, 1910–1945* (Ithaca, NY: Cornell University Press, 2001).

46. "Chōshūsha no koe," *Hōsō* 3, no. 1 (January 1943): 134–135.

47. Jōhōkyoku Dai 2-bu Hōsōka, "Taiteki denpasen dai 1-gō (January 1943)," reprinted in *Taiheiyō hōsō senden shiryō,* vol. 4, ed. Kitayama Setsurō (Tokyo: Ryokuin Shobō, 1997), 9–19.

48. Naikaku Jōhōkyoku, "Nichi-Ei-Bei sensō ni taisuru jōhō senden hōsaku taikō," 289. For the scripts of the domestically broadcast programs on Southeast Asia based on the rhetoric of differential inclusion of Asian others, see Sawada Ken, *Nanyō minzokushi* (Tokyo: Nihon Hōsō Kyōkai Shuppan, 1942). On the concept of imperial racism as a strategy of differential inclusion, see Michael Hardt and Antonio Negri, *Empire* (Cambridge, MA: Harvard University Press, 2000), 191–195.

49. On Bose's activities in Tokyo, including his broadcasting to India through Japanese overseas broadcasting facilities and Pan-Asianism, see Nakajima Takeshi, *Nakamuraya no Bōsu: Indo dokuritsu undō to kindai Nihon no Ajia shugi* (Tokyo: Hakusuisha, 2005).

50. "Indo Kokumingun ni kyōshinkyoku o okuru," *Hōsō kenkyū* 3, no. 12 (December 1943): 58–59.

51. Sawada Shinnojō, "Taitōa sensō to kaigai hōsō," *Hōsō kenkyū* 2, no. 1 (January 1942): 24–25; Kitayama Setsurō, *Rajio Tokyo II: "Daitōa" e no michi* (Tokyo: Tabata Shoten, 1988), 62–63.

52. Miyoshi Shunkichirō, "Jawa gunsei kaikoroku 6," *Kokusai mondai* 67 (October 1965): 198–199. Miyoshi served with the Japanese occupation forces during the military operation in Java.

53. "Nanbō hōsō no naiyō kentō," Nihon Hōsō Kyōkai, *Nihon hōsōshi,* 509–510.

54. Terami Motoe, "Nichijōji no naka no tatakai: Firipin ni okeru bunka sensen," in *Tōnan Ajiashi no naka no Nihon senryō,* new ed., ed. Kurasawa Aiko (Tokyo: Waseda Daigaku Shuppanbu, 2001), 258–268.

55. On the NHK's observation of a range of difficulties related to the lack of infrastructure and broadcasting facilities and the low level of education in general, see "Tōnan Ajia no rajio chōshusha," *Hōsō kenkyū* 1, no. 3 (March 1941): 20.

56. See Watari Shūdan Hōdōbu, ed., *Hitomi Sendentai senden kōsaku no kiroku* (Tokyo: Ryūkei Shosha, 1996).

Racialized Sounds and Cinematic Affect

My Nightingale, the Russian Diaspora, and Musical Film in Manchukuo

This chapter examines cinematic representations of the Russian diaspora and the placement of sound, singing, and music with respect to movement and affect in the film *My Nightingale* (*Watashi no uguisu,* 1943), shot in Manchukuo (1932–1945) and directed by Shimazu Yasujirō (1897–1945).[1] "Affect" here refers primarily to cinematic affect, which means bringing "the body back into the understanding of emotion."[2] Defined as an ability to affect and be affected, affect is a "prepersonal intensity corresponding to the passage from one experiential state of the body to another and implying an augmentation or diminution in that body's capacity to act."[3] In conjunction with this concept, I specifically focus on the use of close-up shots in the film that highlight the character's face, defined as "affection images" by Deleuze, and explore the significance of these images and their affectivity.[4] A propaganda musical, *My Nightingale* recounts the hospitality and generosity of Sumida, a Japanese merchant, toward White Russian exiles from the Russian Imperial Theater who settle in the city of Harbin, and the story of his daughter, Maria/Mariko, who matures musically under the care of Dmitrii, her adoptive Russian father. The hospitality of the Japanese exemplifies the feeling of pity that comprises their affective commitment to the exiles—the film calls particular attention to the multivalent yet historically specific racial positioning of stateless Russians and their cultural legacies in 1940s Manchuria.

My central concern is to explore how the production of culture by a stateless people, even if mediated by Japanese imperial power, can be associated with and simultaneously dissociated from the projects of nation and empire building. In particular, I examine mechanisms of boundary making at the intersection of race and culture in terms of sound, vocality, and cinema technology on the levels of surface and deep structures—representational techniques that stage the inclusion or exclusion of stateless Russians. With a focus on sonic, sensory, and vocal aspects as productive of cinematic affect, the chapter further addresses how the film produces sensory resonance using audiovisual images and affection images, going beyond the ideological and pedagogical apparatus of film production and thereby extending outside the controlling contours of state power.

I first analyze the ways in which architectural images are represented in intimate connection with sound and music in constructing the racialization of space, a visual inscription of the cultural legacies of diasporic Russians in Manchukuo. The chapter then moves on to explore the historical background of the film's production and the significance of the creation of the film's theme song, "My Nightingale," in the history of Japanese musical film. The third section discusses how the film's audiovisual images—particularly scenes featuring the micromovement of objects, the sound of objects, and human singing—create their own temporality and dimensionality for the spectator; I show how the film provokes visceral responses and affective engagement as part of the spectators' viewing processes. The final section focuses on how vocality and scenes with discord between the source of sound, speech acts, subtitles, and affection images are rendered and presented as pure potential and indeterminacy in simultaneous tension with both actualizing, identifying forces and transitive, mobile forces.

Stateless White Russians were racially and culturally positioned within multiethnic Manchukuo, producing various kinds of cultural capital in relation to nation and empire building. An analysis of sound and audiovisual images in *My Nightingale* will illuminate the significant meaning and values of the Japanese musical film in cinematic and colonial historiography, a rich research area that has been little explored in modern Chinese and Japanese studies. The employment of music and sound in images acts as a mechanism for boundary making, and *My Nightingale* captures and represents mobile moments with sound and music to create a hermeneutic space without a definite, stable center. This space locates the meanings of the Russian diaspora and the legacies of colonial cultures within Manchukuo and the Japanese Empire. In short, representations of White Russians and their diasporic culture in the film were utilized to embody the West and modernity, as well as to highlight Japan's leading role in the preservation of "high culture" and its hegemonic power in rescuing stateless White Russians from Communist rule and forced social dislocation. At the same time, because audiovisual images, singing, and affection images are not presented as definite cultural sources for identification upon which nation, empire building, and identity formation are to be founded, they reveal the multifaceted, complex, and ambiguous nature of colonial cultural production.

Constructing Harbin as a "Western" Cultural City: Movement, Spatiality, and the Russian Diaspora

My Nightingale opens with an encounter between Razmovski, a White Russian count, and Sumida, a Japanese manager of the Matsuoka Company's branch office, traveling by steamboat down the Sungari (Songhua) River toward Harbin. In a flashback within this scene, the film also shows Sumida's hospitality toward White Russian musicians employed in the Russian Imperial Theater. Sumida invites Razmovski, along with other Russian vocalists and musicians, to dinner in his company's parlor, welcoming them with a generous feast. Because of domestic geopolitical instability during the Chinese warlord regime, Sumida, his wife, and his daughter Mariko, together with Razmovski and his friend Dimitrii—a vocalist who performed at the Russian Imperial Theater before the 1917 Russian Revolution—travel by wagon to seek refuge. After they all become separated, Sumida travels to Shanghai, Tianjin, and Beijing searching for his daughter on the basis of information from Razmovski, but he has no success.

Three years later, Sumida drops by Razmovski's barber shop in Harbin to tell him that he will return to Japan and then go to Southeast Asia. After another fifteen years have passed, Razmovski spots a newspaper advertisement for a performance by Dmitrii and mentions it to Mr. Tatsumi, Sumida's friend. It turns out that after Sumida was separated from his family his wife was killed, and Dmitrii adopted Mariko, whom he calls Maria, and is now teaching her how to sing. Tatsumi meets Dmitrii in a theater and tells him that Sumida is in Southeast Asia.

In the meantime, Dmitrii's performance at a theater is disrupted by Bolshevik sympathizers in the audience who respond to his song with aggressive boos and hisses. As a result of this sudden fiasco, Dmitrii loses his job, and Maria quits her studies to sell flowers in the square of the Cathedral of St. Nicholas. When a Chinese policeman orders her to stop, Ueno, a young Japanese painter, tries to defend her and purchases all her flowers for his house. The movie cuts to a scene in which Maria practices singing with Dmitrii, after which she has a chance to sing "My Nightingale" at a charity concert benefiting Russian émigrés and is warmly applauded by the audience. Ueno also attends the concert, but Dmitrii is displeased to see him speaking to Maria. Right before the outbreak of the Manchurian Incident, Dmitrii and Maria try to move to Shanghai in the forlorn hope that people in that city will acknowledge and cherish his art as much as those in Harbin do, but the trains stop running due to the war between Japan and China.

Their lives threatened, Dmitrii asks Maria to wear Chinese clothes and takes her to a harbor where the Japanese are hiding themselves, but he himself goes to a Russian refuge. Finally, the Japanese defeat the Chinese warlord regime and establish the puppet state of Manchukuo. Afterward, Sumida comes back from Southeast Asia and asks Dmitrii, whose poor health has prevented him from performing, to participate in an opera performance. At the earnest behest of Sumida, Dmitrii takes the stage to sing "Song of the Golden Calf" from Gounod's *Faust,* but during the performance he suffers a heart attack. As Dmitri is dying, he pleads for Maria to return to Japan, the country of her biological father, along with Sumida. At the end of the film, Maria sings "My Nightingale" in front of Dmitrii's gravestone, and Ueno stands beside her at a slight distance.

Harbin, a narrative pivot of the film where White Russians make their livelihood through musical performance, is represented in *My Nightingale* as a modern "Western" city, marked with churches, theaters, classical music, and Western fashions—an audiovisual spectacle for the viewer. At the same time, it is a gendered and nationalized space: Sumida travels to Shanghai, Tianjin, and Beijing to look for his daughter after becoming separated from her and his Russian friends, an act that not only indicates the male capacity to move but also symbolically embodies important cultural and spatial features of those Chinese cities that filmmakers strove to construct and promote to use as backdrops in contrast to modern, civilized, Westernized Harbin. Sumida's movement is accompanied by music and noises, in diegetic or nondiegetic form, that convey geographical, cultural, and political meanings attached to particular city spaces. Importantly, Harbin stands out as a culturally advanced, vibrant hub where Russian characters express an unwavering passion for art and musical talent—part of the flourishing of Western culture in a city filled with cultural resources. It is particularly in relation to churches and theaters that the film represents the spatial and temporal characteristics of Harbin in its association of architecture and music.

Above all, Harbin is represented in *My Nightingale* as a religious city replete with Orthodox churches, which are symbolically tied to the Russians' construction of the city.[5] Designed and established by railway engineers, Harbin grew rapidly, fueled by an influx of Russians who began building the Chinese Eastern Railway (CER) in 1898. Russians administered Harbin until the 1917 revolution, after which China governed it until the establishment of Manchukuo in 1932. Harbin was known as the "Paris or Moscow of the East," and its architecture had a European look. The film highlights the Russian community and its religious and cultural features, although Harbin consisted of Chinese, Japanese, European-Russian and other ethnic communities divided into several districts.[6] In the film, the churches are initially presented in a city overview. As the narrative develops, more concrete images appear, including the Cathedral of St. Nicholas, St. Iverskaia Church, and Pokrovskaia Church.

Chiming bells and a female choir singing a low-pitched, somber melody accompany images of the Cathedral of St. Nicholas and St. Iverskaia Church (the same music is playing at a hospital where Sumida has his injured leg treated after he is separated from Maria and his Russian friends during their escape). The bells are diegetic music—ambient or territory sounds, to use Chion's terms—but the choirs are nondiegetic, hinting that Sumida's mood and recollection of separation from Maria are tinged with apprehension, inner dolefulness, and concern over his illness.[7] The combination of the images of the two churches with territory sounds and music also contributes to the representation of Harbin as almost the filmic apotheosis of Russian Orthodoxy and high culture, forged and accented by Western classical music. Moreover, the music creates a pious atmosphere within the narrative space of the film, a more authentic mise-en-scène that foregrounds the important symbolic and historical meanings of such religious spaces for Russian émigrés in Manchuria at that time, as detailed below.

The Cathedral of St. Nicholas, erected in 1899, and its square are an important narrative space; it is here that Maria sells flowers after Dmitrii loses his job. Pokrovskaia Church is shown in an establishing shot, indicating the passage of the three years during which Sumida travels to Shanghai, Tianjin, and Beijing looking for Maria. In the final scene, Maria sings "My Nightingale" in front of Dmitrii's gravestone at Uspenskoe Cemetery, and crosses dominate the shot. Harbin was divided into four districts, and the Cathedral of St. Nicholas stood in the district the Russians called Novy Gorod (New Town), and the Chinese called Nangang (South Hill); it was the administrative center of the new city, where the CER offices, the station, and foreign consulates were located. The dominant population groups were Russo-European, and most Chinese inhabited the district known as the Daowai (literally "outside the tracks," also known as Fujiadian), though the number of Chinese living in other districts later increased. The Cathedral of St. Nicholas was a symbol of the city, and its cultural, religious, and administrative centrality was expressed in its location at the top of the hill, with other buildings placed around it.[8] The centrality and the symbolic value of the Cathedral of St. Nicholas are also reflected and affirmed in the film. As a unique cultural monument of Harbin, the cathedral sets an overall visual tone for the narrative, conveying a religiously charged atmosphere underscored by music and serving as a pivotal spatial point in storyline development.

Like the Cathedral of St. Nicholas, the two other churches also have important historical and symbolic meanings for Russian émigrés to Manchuria. St. Iverskaia, a military-centered church, was built in 1907 on the orders of a Russian general to commemorate Russian soldiers who died in the Russo-Japanese War (1904–1905). Pokrovskaia Church, marked by its cupola, had a cemetery for Russians.[9] Koshizawa Akira notes that the first staff members of the CER were buried at the cemetery and that there was a wayside shrine for soldiers who died in the Boxer Rebellion (1900).[10] These churches were erected to honor and sanctify the Russian people who sacrificed their lives in the city's founding. Thus, the images of the churches symbolically embody the centrality of the city and are inserted with fastidious care to commemorate the foundation of the Russian community and its legacy in Harbin.

Sumida's travels to Shanghai, Tianjin, and Beijing illustrate how the filmmakers strove to construct the cultural preeminence of Harbin by presenting simplified yet typical images of the three cities. Shanghai is represented by the Union Assurance Company building.[11] Sumida looks at an advertisement showing a couple dancing at a bar, and a theater is also seen, accentuating a popular aspect of Shanghai culture. Beijing is represented by the Zhengyangmen Gate, also known as the Qianmen (Front Gate), and by Pailou, the ceremonial arch. Depictions of traditional architecture are accompanied by music that evokes Beijing opera. Stores selling antiques symbolize Tianjin, along with street noises, sounds common in Shanghai as well with its raucous urban soundscape. Both Shanghai and Beijing stand for the hurly-burly of the city, packed with a hodgepodge of trolleys, bicycles, and rickshaws rushing through Chinese crowds dressed in Chinese clothing, though Beijing looks less bustling. Further, only in Harbin are automobiles displayed as a major means of transportation; the pedestrians on Kitayskaya Street (currently called Zhongyang Dajie, or Central Street) are mostly Russians who stroll gracefully in Western outfits with hats, scarves, and bags, racially charged signs of their urbane sophistication in manners and sartorial practice.

In tandem with the transient glimpses of select images of the three cities used to establish Harbin's cultural superiority, theaters where musical performances take place show the contrast between Tianjin and Harbin. Dmitrii sings the Russian folk song "Sten'ka Raizn" in the Tianjin Theater. This theater has a traditional indoor design with an end stage, an orchestra pit, and an auditorium. Harbin's modern, outdoor amphitheater—an annex of the CER's club—provides the setting for Maria's musical debut, where she performs "My Nightingale." In Judith Strong's view, a traditional indoor theater with its proscenium arch limits audiences to a passive relationship with the performance.[12] The amphitheater of Harbin, however, has a bandshell that bears a strong resemblance to that of the Hollywood Bowl, a representative modern amphitheater.[13] The Harbin amphitheater does not have a separate orchestra pit, and thus the audience is positioned closer to the performers onstage. This design allows the audience to observe performers' expressions, gestures, and nuances more clearly, increasing theatrical intimacy and immediacy.[14] The unique architectural structure of the amphitheater is a visual manifestation of the Western nature of Harbin, its modernity, and its proliferation of cultural activities that encourage closer interactions with audiences to render performances as authentic as possible.

Sumida's travels to Shanghai, Tianjin, and Beijing are identified and structured by music and noises that highlight the unique nature of the physical and cultural landscapes of each city, bearing symbolic connotations of their respective heritages. Their architecture represents the crystallization of cultural and religious heritages from the past. In this respect, music and sound function as a signifier of spatiality that is mostly racially charged and overlaid with cultural codes. Moreover, Sumida's physical movement (re)frames the space by dint of acoustic effects of sound and music that further the narrative flow and its development, hierarchically displaying the cinematic symbolism of the culturally and religiously privileged space of Harbin with Western classical music, modern architecture, and symbols of Russian Orthodoxy.

The Status of Man'ei and Japanese Musical Film in Wartime: Musical Scores and Cultural Hegemony

My Nightingale was produced by Man'ei (Ch. Manying), the Manchurian Motion Picture Association (MMPA, established in 1937), in collaboration with the Toho Film Company.[15] According to Yamaguchi Yoshiko (the actress starring as Maria/Mariko, also known as Ri Kōran or Li Xianglan), this film was considered the first full-fledged musical in the history of Japanese film and was further remarkable because it was abundantly infused with an exuberance of Western music adopted from enemy countries.[16] However, Yamaguchi's claims pose key questions about the status of Man'ei and Japanese musical film at the time of *My Nightingale*'s production. In the 1930s and the 1940s, music was already considered a powerful medium whose universal appeal linked the Japanese to non-Japanese-speaking colonial subjects, and filmmakers were regularly urged to use this effective medium to convey their message to the colonized. Moreover, Japanese moviegoers had come to expect both visual and audio satisfaction, so Japanese filmmakers had begun to insert popular Japanese songs (*sonyu-uta*) into their films to improve profitability and audience satisfaction.[17] At that time, Japanese filmmakers did not typically produce musical scores composed solely for specific films.

Sasagawa Keiko points out that Japanese critics and musicians suggested the American film *One Hundred Men and a Girl* (directed by Henri Koster, 1937)—a comedy about an orchestra and a big hit at the time in Japan—as a model for Japanese musical film production. They perceived it as an epoch-making, modern musical film. The employment of European classical music, namely Wagner, was regarded as an artistic novelty, particularly given the overall cultural milieu of the United States, where jazz music was popular; Japanese musical films, on the other hand, used premodern music, and their songs were usually produced in partnership with record companies. The Japanese critics' enthusiasm for *One Hundred Men and a Girl* was due in part to its use of classical music, which allowed them to place Europe over the United States in a politicized schema conceptualizing the two as competing and diametrically opposite ideologies. The critics affirmed and objectified the cultural value of the film, praising it as a canonical work that Japanese filmmakers should emulate due to its international characteristics, which equated European modernity with civilization through European classical music.[18] The Japanese critics' recommendations were accepted and later reified by Man'ei's filmmakers. As Monma Takashi points out, Man'ei planned to film a story concerning an orchestra of White Russians and set in Harbin, one of the major music cities in East Asia in the 1940s; a plan to produce a remake of *One Hundred Men and a Girl* was also mentioned in a newspaper.[19]

However, this plan was directly at odds with the principal doctrine of Amakasu Masahiko (1891–1945), who became head of the MMPA in 1939, to develop Man'ei as a means to enlighten the Chinese masses, since *My Nightingale* was neither legible nor accessible to Chinese audiences, who did not know the Russian language, could not read Japanese subtitles, and presumably lacked the cultural sensitivity to appreciate Western classical music. Amakasu reorganized the structure of the MMPA by employing more Chinese film directors and technicians, rendering it more inclusive in racial composition.[20] He was deeply aware of the paramount significance of reaching the Chinese masses through film production and transforming them into objects to be inculcated; he thus insisted in 1943 that "Man'ei's works should be first targeted at the Chinese masses, who are the majority in the state—it is important to embrace them. As we teach children about things, we must maintain an explanatory attitude toward them."[21]

The cultural and political imperative to include the Chinese in storylines and in film production was announced before *My Nightingale* was shot; it is highly likely that these guidelines influenced the overall direction of filmmaking in Manchukuo. At the same time, Amakasu's goal of producing films specifically targeting Chinese audiences seems to have been entirely squelched, as Shimazu assigned the Chinese characters in *My Nightingale* only marginal roles, such as policemen, servants, or fugitives in a crowd scene, a visible sign of their complete exclusion from the content and the language of the film. Yet Amakasu was pursuing a far more ambitious goal for Man'ei's development. Michael Baskett notes that Amakasu challenged the authority of the Japanese film industry and aspired to build a self-sufficient film studio for Man'ei, independent of Japan proper (*naichi*).[22] Shimazu also adhered to this formidable, contentious blueprint, mentioning to Ikeda Toku, the assistant director, "I cannot say this openly, but Japan will definitely be defeated in the war. So we should leave evidence that Japan was making an excellent artistic film that was not outstripped by famous European or American films, as well as war films, for a time when the American army occupies Japan."[23]

Amakasu's ultimate goals for Man'ei reveal the self-contradictory nature of his management and vision: an unbridgeable rupture between the reality on the ground and the cultural hegemony he hoped to achieve, vying with Japan in the long run and even going against the national policy of the "harmony of the five races." Furthermore, the production of an outstanding artistic film was only possible through the complete silence of the Chinese, the majority in the state, thereby creating more linguistic and cultural barriers for them—a trenchant revelation of the inherently unenforceable and unattainable nature of the state policy. Seen in this light, Amakasu seems to have fallen into the same trap as those critics in Japan who pursued European classical music as a mere cultural source for Japanese musical film production.

My Nightingale, however, stands out as an innovative departure from the tradition of Japanese musical film in that its music director, Hattori Ryōichi (1907–1993), composed its theme song, "My Nightingale," solely for the film, rather than inserting existing popular songs in partnership with record companies. This composition signaled the emergence of full-scale film scores. Although Hattori also composed the theme song for the film *China Nights,* "Suzhou Serenade" (Soshū yume), its title differs from that of the film title.

The production of score music heralded Manchukuo's cultural breakthrough and signaled its cultural advancement over Japan. Moreover, the filmmakers and the music director worked closely with the Harbin Opera, rather than with record companies, to select music by and for themselves.[24] A wide range of classical music was thus carefully chosen to thematize the narrative or even to go beyond storylines to impart diverse layers of meaning. The film includes a broad gamut of Russian classical music, such as the "Trépak" dance from Tchaikovsky's *The Nutcracker* and songs from his *The Queen of Spades,* performed in the film by Dimitrii, as well as folk music, such as "Sten'ka Razin," and folk-influenced popular music, such as Vasily Andreyev's "In the Moonlight," played on the domra and the balalaika, together with Gounod's *Faust.*

Given the wide variety of musical genres employed in the film, the Manchurian concept of being European was thus made to seem more extensive and musically diverse than that of the Japanese in that it was not merely limited to Western Europe but extended the boundary of what counted as "European" or "Western"—as was the case in *One Hundred Men and a Girl,* which utilized Wagner's music. The producer and the director's avid efforts to represent an artistically and culturally advanced Manchukuo were thus reflected not only in the use of eye-catching architectural images of Harbin but also through the selection and performance of music understood as culturally representative and arranged in a hierarchy of value in line with the expansive hegemonic imperatives of the Manchurian film industry.

Audiovisual Sounds as Effects and the Malleability of Cinematic Time and Space

My Nightingale illustrates the power of cinema to not only reify but also destabilize categories of perception and identity in the production of audiovisual images and cinematic affect. The opening credits and the sequence of Sumida's steamboat travel with Dimitrii's friend Razumovskii to Harbin, presented in a flashback at the beginning of the film, show how visual images are juxtaposed with rhythmic effects, sounds of objects, and the human singing voice to yield wide ranges of visual and sonic effects.[25] These effects are intimately linked to the audience's perception of time and space in the movement of images. In the workings of image and sound, they create expressive and informative "added value," serving to enrich existing images with sound and rendering them more impressive.[26]

Both the cast information and the first establishing shot show micromovements of nature on the sunlit sea, ultimately affecting the viewer's reception of them. Quivering leaves, like fluttering shadows on a white background, are superimposed on the cast information. They linger, producing a visual microrhythm—a temporality of movement created on the image's surface through the representation of smoke, rain, snowflakes, or waves on the surface of water.[27] Along with the men's choir in the introduction, the audience's attention is naturally directed to this visual microrhythm that generates an effect similar to vibrating sonic undulations. The opening establishing shot is another example of a visual microrhythm that affects spectators at a tactile level—an affective cinematic experience with the tactility of the visual image wherein their bodies respond to it as if the image were vibrating on their skin. This opening shot displays a steamboat sailing on the Sungari River in an extreme long shot, an overview of the film's locale in Harbin. The ship makes headway, its steam engine emitting sounds. A gentle breeze ruffles the river; its tranquil surface glitters with myriad cross-shaped waves. This visual microrhythm gives viewers a sense of horizontal movement and generates dimensionality.[28]

In addition to the visual microrhythm, the film also shows how the combination of a human singing voice and the sound of an object form a temporality of movement and dimensionality in images in both sonic and visual forms. As Razumovskii starts to sing, his low-toned voice delicately overlaps with the steamboat engine, producing a regular beating rhythm, a combination of kinetic and sonic movements. As he continues, the engine sound decreases gradually, so that the singing voice is well articulated and audible. Moreover, the engine's consistent sound adds a regular, rhythmic beat to his plaintive voice, which alternates a low-tuned pitch with a deep yet subtle timbre, thereby accentuating both the regularity and the changes of rhythms and tones in a moving object and a human voice.

In watching the three images described above, viewers are more likely to sense interlocking points of audio-visuality layered within the images, where they apprehend visual images in an auditory mode or vice versa. The images in turn evoke a sense of cinematic space and cinematic affect. A world of concurrent audiovisual sensory stimulation, particularly those sonic qualities embedded within visuality, is opened to viewers, who can engage in the audio-visuality of images and appreciate the intricate interface between the aural and the visual. The viewers' horizon of reception is thus expanded to include multiple modalities of reception within and beyond images seen and sounds heard with delicately overlapping audiovisual sensory inputs.

Just as audiovisual images carry a temporality of movement and dimensionality, sound and noise impart spatiotemporality and dimensionality to images in such a way that the timing and spacing of images look like they are managed by sound. To take one example, the film's depiction of Sumida and his Russian friends' escape brims with sound and noise from humans and the movement of objects, serving as sonic spectacles in tight parallel with the visual spectacles the urban images from the four different locales create. Chion observes the significant use of punch sounds as accented synch points in martial arts and fighting films, noting that they can keep audio and visual continuity tight and create "temporal elasticity," bringing in a vertical dimension just as a chord does in music.[29] The escape sequence in *My Nightingale* contains different pitch levels and scales ranging in volume from low to high: horses galloping, bells ringing, shells falling, birds singing, and guns firing. These sounds are heard consecutively and simultaneously at certain intervals and in a specific order. The galloping movement accelerates with the sound of shells, adding temporal elasticity to the fast flow of the narrative, and creates an effect of time contracting on an audiovisual level.

The sound of artillery shells is first heard from outside the parlor twice before the characters escape a battle. On the first occasion, Sumida explains the noise to his Russian friends, saying, "It's a battle between warlords." Shells are next heard exploding when Sumida's Chinese male servant reports the current geopolitical emergency: "Chou's army seems to be surrounding the city at a distance." The third and final volley of shells occurs in the sequence of horse riding on the broad plain, where it maximizes the exigency of escaping from the war, a life-or-death situation, and is coupled with the acceleration of the wagons. Compared to the high and quickly passing sounds of gunshots coming from nearby, the exploding shells seem to be falling far away to maximally dilate the audience's perception of space or, in Chion's term, they became a "vast extension" in which the audience can expect to hear a variety of sounds emanating from on and off the screen.[30] In short, the sounds of the gunshots and shells belong to different temporal and spatial dimensions even though they bring forth the characters' actions and generate a movement of objects in fast-forward mode: the former contracts time, and the latter creates an extended image of a cinematic space that communicates the characters' perspective of the vastness of the plain via the periodic movement of sound.

Singing beyond Signification: Vocality and Affection Images

While sound adds spatiotemporal elasticity, scenes featuring incongruity between image and sound sources show how a new cinematic space can be opened to viewers for creative imagination, offering them affective engagement with the image. The film includes a scene in which Maria is cared for by a Russian au pair whose voice is inaudible but provided by Japanese subtitles. When Dmitrii travels to Tianjin by train for his musical performance, a Russian woman holds Maria, standing in for Maria's birth mother. While patting Maria's body, the au pair waves her arms as she looks at Maria's face, and the Japanese subtitle "*Yoshiyoshi* Mariko," meaning "Hush, hush, Maria," is shown. However, the Russian woman does not quite move her lips, though there seems to be a slight lip movement too quick to catch. Viewers cannot even hear her voice in Russian.

Maria also cries in this scene, and the au pair tries to calm her down. Maria's crying, however, is inaudible because of the sound of the train. This imperceptible crying seems to stem from a technical glitch that fails to match the characters' speaking and crying with the Japanese subtitles. Technically, this scene shows the audience the source of the sound is onscreen, a synchronous sound. However, it is presented as an asynchronous sound, coming from offscreen, like a dubbing or lip synchronization but without any actual sound and source that should be heard. From the standpoint of the development of cinema technology, the failure to provide the baby's crying and to match the woman's voice with the Japanese subtitles shows the film's lack of "fidelity of sound," producing a gap between the image and viewers' expectations.[31]

This disparity yields an audiovisual and imaginary space for spectators to listen to an onscreen voice, seeping in from some outer source or into their minds through the image of the shot. Noting the significance of this mismatch from the viewpoint of characters and spectators, Chion calls it "a voice in exile," awaiting a body.[32] He picks two scenes from *Psycho*: one presenting other characters' voices apparently inside the head of nervous, guilty Marion as she is driving away with the stolen cash; the other at the end of the film presenting the voice of Norman Bates's mother, Norma, inside his head. Chion explains how voices are bifurcated and directed for the character and spectators. "The internal voices that fascinate Marion resonate in her head," he writes, "whereas the embracing voice that speaks over the image of Norman resonates in us. It's a voice in exile."[33] This is

> an effect of corporeal implication, or involvement of the spectator's body, when the voice makes us feel in our body the vibration of the body of the other, of the character who serves as a vehicle for the identification. The extreme case of corporeal implication occurs when there is no dialogue or words, but only closely present breathing, groans or sighs.[34]

A prevocal expression, a voice that does not yet articulate words, only sounds, is another example of a corporeal implication.[35] Chion's discussion of corporeal implication is strictly confined to how spectators can feel the vibration of the character through their own bodies owing to the presence of the character as a definite source for identification. The scene of mismatch between the dialogue and the subtitles in the image is an example of corporeal implication, but it also illuminates how sound (even if not heard, or not heard as a source of actual sound) and image resist a direct relationship, failing to serve as a source of identification solely predicated on the characters. They are presented as beyond the domain of the characters' influence for identification, particularly in reception on account of multiple modalities of viewing processes and the unsettled, elusive nature within images and their unlocatability.

More specifically, the presentation of the Russian woman's lips, with or without their slight motion, and the subtitles lead the audience to transform the latter into the character's words as if she had spoken them, effectively turning the subtitles into an internal, diegetic sound. In other words, the subtitles function as a subjective internal voice, as if she were uttering words in her mind.[36] Ironically, in terms of cinema sound technique, the technical flaw of the arrangement of sound effects or the underdevelopment of synchronization technique during production makes possible more complex sonic dimensions and effects on the spectators than were usually available in the film industry at the time. The Russian woman's unuttered voice is in "exile" and can be imagined in her mind or in the minds of audience members who read her dialogue onscreen. In this case, the image and the subtitles presented to spectators delay direct identification of the two, turning the source of voice/sound, the external diegetic sound, into an internal, nondiegetic sound imagined and heard only in the character's and the viewers' minds.

Thus, the boundary between distinct sounds, external and internal, can be blurred and traversed in the spectators' viewing. The possible interplay of the two sound sources at the levels of acting and reception renders the world of diegesis an imaginary and sensory space filled by the viewers' working minds and their sensibility, depending on the extent to which the layout of sound sources enables them to watch the scene from diverse directions. Viewers can imagine the baby crying, singing, babbling, breathing, or all four, or they may imagine other possible sounds without dialogue as well as a mixture of the woman's lulling words and the baby's preverbal expressions. The image produces a more complicated cinematic space: not a space to identify the source of the sounds, but a space for the audience to creatively imagine and capture the indefinite source unrestricted to the visual image presented to them.

The film also presents Dmitrii and Ueno singing without lyrics. This entails different ways of using the voice through speaking and singing, an illuminating example of how vocalization and vocality are crucially connected to language and its materiality, as discussed by Dunn.[37] When Maria visits Ueno's painting studio to give him the flowers that he purchased from her on the street, he imitates a vocalist's singing exercise as a way of expressing interest in her. He stands up, opens his arms, and sings with "Ah" sounds and a full range of pitches, a maximization of his voice. By contrast, Dmitrii sings to his piano accompaniment as he plays for Maria so that she can practice singing at home. At the level of diegesis, this mise-en-scène outwardly reveals his role as Maria's musical instructor and his professionalism. Dmitrii's singing to his piano accompaniment (i.e., *solfège*) presents a fuller and richer contour of a melodic line covering a full chromatic scale of pitches rising to a crescendo and falling. His sonorous singing voice and the dramatic changes in the melodic line's contour are matched with a fairly fast and lively tempo. The quick transition of his pitches from ascending to descending, a sign of the breadth of his tessitura, is highlighted by the piano's fast beat. The rise and fall of the pitches accented by the piano in the process of vocalization suggest how the voice is pronounced, projected, and intensified by the various movements of the singer's body, and draw our attention to the implication of the singing voice in vocal performance for the interpretation of music, particularly concerning the semantic aspect of meaning (i.e., signification).

Dunn notes that unlike speech, the process of vocalization in singing involves more body movements, such as a wider mouth, deeper breath, and the use of deeper diaphragm muscles. Since vocalization carries more intense body work, this heightened materiality of language yields indeterminacy of meaning. Roland Barthes' essay "The Grain of the Voice" probes the dialectic relationship between signification and materiality in language and singing. He uses the term "grain" to refer to the voice produced in vocal music and to situate the singing voice and its meaning in conjunction with language, a system of signs composed of *signifiant* (signifier) and *signifié* (signified). "When the latter [the voice] is in a dual posture, a dual production—of language and of music," then "the 'grain' is the body in the voice as it sings."[38] Barthes notes that the grain forms

> a signifying play having nothing to do with communication, representation (of feelings), expression; it is that apex (or that depth) of production where the melody really works at the language—not at what it says, but the voluptuousness of its sounds-signifiers, of its letters—where melody explores how the language works and identifies with that work.[39]

The materiality of the singing body carries "the voluptuousness of its sounds-signifiers," or *significance,* which leaves the singing voice unbound by semantic restraints. The listener also relates to the vocalist's body through identification with the music.[40] In this respect, the film does little to illustrate simple gender and race relations, such as the White Russian father teaching Western classical music to an adopted Asian daughter or the father's engagement in culture and the mother's engagement in preverbal education. Instead, it essentially touches upon the interlocking yet liberating sites where signification becomes obscure and is subverted by *significance.* Moreover, singing without lyrics also involves a greater degree of corporeality, the intensive affect, thus spectators also have affective cinematic engagement and resonance with the movements of the singing bodies; the changes in tones; and the vibrations in human, instrumental, and technical sounds. Therefore, the singing scenes exemplify the bodily excess of singing or the excess of affect, whose force is free of semantic restraints and references, thereby embodying the "not yet"-ness of a body and a world—a body simultaneously engaged with affectual doings and undoings.[41]

Along with the unfettered potential of male vocality unbound by signification, the camera work closely interweaves the mobile images of the singing body and face in the form of the "affection image." Maria's singing scenes, set on stages or in private rooms, are presented in medium or close-up shots, especially when she moves into a crescendo at the climax of the songs and the absence of instrumental accompaniment creates a purely vocal space for the character and the audience. Maria's face is highlighted even when she stands with other vocalists on stage or watches the opera performance as an audience member with other characters offstage. The technique of the close-up shot is further used to underpin Maria's Japanese identity as the dying Dmitrii urges her to return to Japan, her biological father's home country. The camera captures her face in an extreme close-up, and the image of Maria on the verge of tears parallels the caption *Nihon e* (to Japan), rendered in Japanese characters.

Ott notes that "affects involve a corporeal continuum, which ranges, on one end, from the experiencing body (i.e., immediate sensations of movement, color, and sound, for instance) to, on the other end, our body of experience (i.e., our body's memory of previous sensations)," arguing that in fact, affect is political, since there is a gap between the existing body of experience and the experiencing body in the theater, which would lead viewers to experience either affective repulsion or embrace the given images.[42] The image of Maria's face with the text "to Japan" visibly identifies Maria with Japan, an affective association that draws on spectators' memories of the phrase and implies the restoration of her Japanese origin. It echoes and corroborates the state's filmic propaganda for the racial superiority of the Japanese and Japan's primordial centrality in identity formation and the triggering of political affect among diverse viewers in multiracial Manchukuo.

In another scene in Ueno's painting studio, however, Maria's face is shown in an extreme close-up when Ueno asks about her father's occupation and biological paternity. Her lightly smiling face fills the screen completely. When Ueno tries to ascertain whether Dmitrii is her biological father, her perplexed face is again shown in a close-up. On the level of diegesis, these distinctively contrasting images manifest a dramatic shift in her emotional countenance from elation to bewilderment, arising from her current admiration of Dmitrii's masterful musicality and her utter unawareness of the facts of her birth. The close-up is the best example of the affection image, and this framework provides a new perspective for interpreting the film, deviating from its outright message of Japan's supremacy and the constraints of historical specificity in time and space in cinema.

Deleuze defines the close-up as the affection image. On one level, the affect is composed of facial motoricity involving the mobile and immobile aspects of micromovements; a part of a single facial movement taking place on an immobile, sensitive entity of nerve endings is transformed into a series of intensive micromovements of expression. The simultaneous succession of the intensive, expressive micromovements of the face accompanies a shift in quality, giving a "qualitative leap" to the dramatic intensity of the moment of the shot.[43] The intensive, reflexive face carries "a pure Power" and "a pure Quality" per se.[44] In other words, the affect exists for and in itself and does not need to give rise to anything else. The affect goes beyond the reference system, the "firstness," which Deleuze notes "is not a sensation, a feeling, an idea, but the quality of a possible sensation, feeling or idea. Firstness is thus the category of the Possible: it gives a proper consistency to the possible, it expresses the possible without actualizing it, whilst making it a quality of power."[45] Thus, the affect (i.e., the expressed) maintains its quality without changing and produces "the virtual conjunction" with a pure potential that is not actualized, identified, or determined in particular ways.[46] In this way, the affect is a spiritual entity and comes into any-space-whatsoever, "the pure locus of the possible," without linkage to a determinate space.[47]

Referring back to the medium and close-up shots of Maria when Ueno sings, these facial images, on the surface, are nothing but expressions of feelings and actions predicated on the narrative conditions the film sets up. On another level, the close-up shots of her face become "the intensive expressive," the pure possible, constituting a tactile space with feelings not actualized at each moment.[48] Additionally, Ueno's and Maria's singing shows how affection images of the face are presented in close-ups and medium close-ups and how these shots involve voices that express a pure potentiality and a spiritual entity for and in themselves. Deleuze notes that once one leaves face-centered close-up shots, a more nuanced system of emotion, not easy to identify, opens up.[49] The subtle yet highly expressive movements of Maria's face as she sings eloquently render the singing body's feelings, pathos, and pure potential per se, composing a space not determined but "identical to the power of the spirit" with both human and non-human affects.[50] The non-human affects spring from Maria's extremely expressive facial movements without respect to her association with the nightingale, a cultural symbol of a virtuoso singing subject. Her facial movements are independent of the system of reference.

In short, on the one hand, the film unfolds a coherent storyline revolving around Japanese hospitality toward Russian émigrés through the placement of sound and music. On the other hand, it subtly reveals how the movement images and the audiovisual images work together in a relationship that is independent yet produces a complex but creative topography of cinema without being limited to a definite and closed dimension of the regime of image. The significance of the film and its cinematic force reside in co-relational workings of audiovisual and (micro)movement images across speech acts and singing, producing fissure and instability out of simultaneous (re)presentation of those images wherein the new potential forged by creative ways of seeing cinema is delicately inscribed but not wholly defined.

Conclusion

From the moment *My Nightingale* was conceived, it stood at the nexus of an unstable tension seesawing between adopting "European-American" elements and creating a more advanced form of musical film during the war period. The film at first glance is exemplary of this historical moment. The culture of Harbin is identified with the Russian Orthodox churches, the new amphitheater constructed by Russian émigrés connected with the railroad, Western classical music, and refined urban fashions. Just as White Russians are perceived as racially white, Russian culture in Harbin as a whole is identified with the West. Furthermore, by presenting images of the Russian churches that were closely related to the foundation of the Russian community, the film serves as a staunch advocate of Russian efforts to develop Harbin, which in the narrative were allegedly made possible by Japanese hospitality toward Russian exiles. Russian culture as a whole, as represented by classical music and the amphitheater where Maria and the White Russian musicians perform, was utilized to signify the cultural advancement of Manchukuo, thereby promoting the formation and fortification of Japan's cultural hegemony and imperial power backed up by racial ideology through the hierarchical management of space and culture.

In terms of cinematography, however, the film employs diverse noises and sound effects along with music and singing to make audio-sonic settings more realistic and authentic, an amplification of audiovisual effects. The sound effects inserted at intervals function as musical elements and indicate the malleability of time and space in cinema. They multiply the viewer's responses to the images and allow spectators to develop a particular way of viewing audio-visuality within the images, enhancing their appreciation of them. Furthermore, scenes of discord between the sources of sound, speech acts, and subtitles defer the audience's identification of all of the above sources. Consequently, the incongruity between image and sound renders the direct relation of the two more ambiguous and creates a cinematic, hermeneutic space with multilayered signifiers that does not produce any designated center for the viewers.

The existence of diverse multivalent images of movement evinces the fleeting and mobile moments when the relationship between image and speech acts is indirect, irresolute, unidentifiable, and even unlocatable. Thus, the boundary between the real and the imaginary becomes fluid and permeable, floating in a status of constant creative flux without settling definitely and fully into one particular realm. The simultaneous presentation of interrelated images subtly reveals unstable and elusive topographies of cinematography and multifaceted sensory and spatiotemporal worlds within and for them. From the viewers' perspective, the images eventually bring forth momentary yet fecund potential threads of cinematic creativity as cinematic affect, even if the images are transiently glimpsed and constantly changing. The significance of the film consequently resides in the dynamic junctures wherein actualizing, identifying forces and transitory, mobile forces in images work together at once, highlighting the nebulous nature and unbounded meanings of the cinematic topography as opposed to any homogenous and consistent filmic stratum.

Notes

Research for this chapter was supported in part by the Cornell East Asia Program at Cornell University. I thank Michael Raine for sharing his translation of the Japanese subtitles into English.

1. This chapter studies the version of the film reproduced in 1986 by Tōhō Eiga Kabushiki Kaisha, the same company that produced the original version in 1943. *Watashi no uguisu* (My nightingale), directed by Shimazu Yasujirō (1943; Tokyo: Tōhō Eiga Kabushiki Kaisha, 1986).

2. Anne Rutherford, *What Makes a Film Tick? Cinematic Affect, Materiality and Mimetic Innervation* (New York: Peter Lang, 2011), 53.

3. Gilles Deleuze and Félix Guattari, *A Thousand Plateaus: Capitalism and Schizophrenia,* trans. Brian Massumi (Minneapolis: University of Minnesota Press, 1987), xvi.

4. Gilles Deleuze, *Cinema 1: The Movement-Image,* trans. Hugh Tomlinson and Barbara Habberjam (Minneapolis: University of Minnesota Press, 1986), 87.

5. On the diverse religious communities in Harbin, including Jews fleeing from Nazi Germany, and their relation to ethnic identity, see Elena Chernolutskaya, "Religious Communities in Harbin and Ethnic Identity of Russian Émigrés," trans. Julia Trubikhina, *South Atlantic Quarterly* 99, no. 1 (Winter 2000): 79–94.

6. James Carter, *Creating a Chinese Harbin: Nationalism in an International City, 1916–1932* (Ithaca, NY: Cornell University Press, 2002), 3–30.

7. See Michel Chion, *Audio-Vision: Sound on Screen,* trans. Claudia Gorbman (New York: Columbia University Press, 1990), 75.

8. Carter, *Creating a Chinese Harbin,* 12, 17–19.

9. Shi Fang, Liu Shuang, and Gao Ling, *Harbin E qiaoshi* (A history of Russian émigrés in Harbin) (Harbin, China: Heilongjiang renmin chubanshe, 2003), 475–476.

10. Akira Koshizawa, *Harupin no toshikeikaku, 1898–1945* (City planning of Harbin, 1898–1945) (Tokyo: Sōwasha, 1989), 50.

11. This building was constructed in 1916 and is currently home to the Shanghai Municipal Institute of Architectural Design. Nobuyuki Yoshida, *Beijing Shanghai Architecture Guide, Peking, Shanhai kenchiku gaido bukku* (Tokyo: A+U, 2005), 113.

12. Judith Strong, *Theatre Buildings: A Design Guide* (New York: Routledge, 2010), 68.

13. George C. Izenour, *The Theater Design* (New York: McGraw-Hill, 1977), 260.

14. Strong, *Theatre Buildings,* 66.

15. The MMPA was established by the Japanese government on August 2, 1937; its origins lie in a proposal formulated in July 1936 by the Department of Public Relations of the Southern Manchurian Railway Company regarding national film policy. Hu Chang and Gu Quan, *Manying: Guoce dianying de mianmianguan* (Manchurian Motion Picture Association: Observations on national films of Manchukuo) (Beijing: Zhonghuashuju, 1990), 20–29. Ri mentions that *My Nightingale* was considered a Man'ei film but in fact was produced by the Toho Film Company. See Thomas Lahusen, "Dr. Fu Manchu in Harbin: Cinema and Moviegoers of the 1930s," *South Atlantic Quarterly* 99, no. 1 (Winter 2000): 156; and Yamaguchi Yoshiko, *Ri Kōran: Watakushi no hansei* (Half my life as Ri Kōran) (Tokyo: Shichōsha, 1987), 269. The film's cast information substantiates the claim that the production was a collaborative work by both agencies.

16. Yamaguchi, *Ri Kōran,* 275.

17. Michael Baskett, *The Attractive Empire: Transnational Film Culture in Imperial Japan* (Honolulu: University of Hawai'i Press, 2008), 52–53.

18. Sasagawa Keiko, "Ongaku eiga no yukue: Nitchū sensō kara daitōa sensōe" (Situations of musical film from the [second] Sino-Japanese War to the Greater East Asian War), in *Nihon eiga to nashonarizumu: 1931–1945* (Japanese film and nationalism: 1931–1945), ed. Iwamoto Kenji (Tokyo: Shinwasha, 2004), 326–328.

19. Monma Takashi, "Iwasaki Akira no shinwa: *Watashi no uguisu* e no michi" (The myth of Iwasaki Akira: A path to *My Nightingale*), in *Posuto Manshū eigaron: Nitchū eiga ōkan* (Discourses of post-Manchurian films: The interchanges in Sino-Japanese films), ed. Yomota Inuhiko and An Ni (Kyōto, Japan: Jinbun Shoin, 2010), 30.

20. Hu Chang and Gu Quan, *Manying,* 88–98.

21. Amakasu Masahiko, "Kessen shita no Man'ei" (*Man'ei* during the war), *Eiga junpō* 74 (March 1943): 24. *My Nightingale* was completed on March 24, 1944, after sixteen months' filmmaking. Yamaguchi, *Ri Kōran,* 274. Thus, Amakasu announced his guidelines for filmmaking before the film was shot.

22. Baskett, *Attractive Empire,* 28–33.

23. Monma, "Iwasaki Akira no shinwa," 36.

24. Yamaguchi mentions that the Harbin Opera played one of the main roles in the film. Yamaguchi, *Ri Kōran,* 269.

25. Chion points out that "audio-visual analysis does not involve clear entities or essences like the shot, but only 'effects,' something considerably less noble." Chion, *Audio-Vision,* 185–186.

26. Ibid., 5. Added value refers to "the expressive and informative value with which a sound enriches a given image so as to create the definite impression."

27. Ibid., 16.

28. Ibid., 176.

29. Ibid., 61–62.

30. Ibid., 87.

31. David Bordwell and Kristin Thompson, *Film Art: An Introduction* (Boston: McGraw-Hill, 2004), 365. In the sound era, "sound effect and dialogue became tied very strongly to images . . . it became extremely rare that a noticeable visual event, such as moving lips or, say, a glass being placed on a table, was not rendered with synchronized sound." James Buhler, David Neumeyer, and Rob Dememer, *Hearing the Movies: Music and Sound in Film History* (New York: Oxford University Press, 2010), 301. In addition, music and sound effects were usually added in postproduction to ensure the clarity of dialogue (ibid., 325, 335). In China, the technology of talkies was adopted in 1931. Nianlu Li, *Zhongguo dianying zhuanyeshi yanjiu, jishujuan* (Special topics in the history of Chinese film: Cinema technology) (Beijing: Zhongguo dianying chubanshe, 2006), 48. The MMPA had separate studios for synchronized recording, dialogue, music, and mixing sounds in postproduction. Xu Qianlin, *Zhongguo dianying jishu fazhan jianshi* (A history of the development of Chinese cinema technology) (Beijing: Zhongguo dianying chubanshe, 2005), 32–33. Thus, it can be inferred that the mismatch of sound and image in this scene was indeed a technical glitch.

32. Michel Chion, *The Voice in Cinema,* trans. Claudia Gorbman (New York: Columbia University Press, 1999), 52.

33. Ibid.

34. Ibid., 52–53.

35. Ibid., 53.

36. Chion states that the internal voice is "sound, which, although situated in the present action, corresponds to the physical and mental interior of a character. These include physiological sounds of breathing, moans or heartbeats, all of which could be named *objective-internal* sounds." Chion, *Audio-Vision*, 76.

37. Leslie C. Dunn, "Ophelia's Songs in Hamlet," in *Embodied Voices: Representing Female Vocality in Western Culture*, ed. Leslie C. Dunn (Cambridge: Cambridge University Press, 1994), 52–53.

38. Dunn, "Ophelia's Songs in *Hamlet*," 53, quoted in Roland Barthes, *Image, Music, Text*, trans. Stephen Heath (New York: Hill and Wang, 1977), 181, 188.

39. Ibid., 188.

40. Ibid.

41. Gregory J. Seigworth and Melissa Gregg, "An Inventory of Shimmers," in *The Affect Theory Reader*, ed. Melissa Gregg (Durham, NC: Duke University Press, 2010), 3, 9.

42. Brian L. Ott, "The Visceral Politics of *V for Vendetta:* On Political Affect in Cinema," *Critical Studies in Media Communication* 27, no. 1 (March 2010): 49.

43. Deleuze, *Cinema I*, 87–89.

44. Ibid., 90.

45. Ibid., 98.

46. Ibid., 102, 109, 112.

47. Ibid., 87–111.

48. Ibid., 90–98.

49. Ibid., 109–110.

50. Ibid., 117.

Chang Hyŏkchu and the Short Twentieth Century

[Affective responses] are the primitive gods within the individual.
—Silvan S. Tomkins, quoted in David Palumbo-Liu, *The Deliverance of Others*

Seeking the gods, I went to Ise. But there were no gods.
—Chang Hyŏkchu, *Korea and Japan*

Fredric Jameson reassured us long ago that ours is a time of the "waning of affect," since our postmodern age has already dispensed with the "autonomous bourgeois monad."[1] But in fact we continue to find affect everywhere, if perhaps only as a lingering historical aura. From the perspective of the twenty-first century, the twentieth now seems replete with it, and I will demonstrate this by examining a writer whose life spanned nearly the entire centenary. Chang Hyŏkchu (1905–1997), a Korean who halfway through his life took Japanese citizenship, came of age during the imperial interregnum on the Korean peninsula and survived long into a postwar era ruled by its Cold War aftermath. The decades after World War II were immaterial to Chang's destined literary theme, which was also the announced project of the empire: the assimilation of the Korean people into the Japanese. He was prolific after the war, as he was before and during it, but his readers then would be as absent as the retired utopian fantasy of an East Asia homogenized under Japanese rule. Chang's twentieth century was short for no reason other than that its second half abandoned him, and his particular punishment was knowing it full well.

Chang began life as a Korean subject (*shinmin*) and ended it as a Japanese citizen (*kokumin*). The journey in between was his own making but unfolded amid conditions that, like those in Marx' framing of history, were not. He had much company. The writer who migrates from the colony to the metropole, and stays, is a familiar figure who nonetheless troubles modern literary history. Fanon, Naipaul, Rushdie—unlike a Conrad who goes to England or a Beckett to France, the intellectual under occupation who travels to where the occupier springs is not regarded as simply having made a "choice" over where to live or what language to write. Rather, he or she is often charged with betrayal, and so their books, always hybrid, stay suspect as the embarrassing proof of a bastardized miscegenation of modernity's manufacture of "national cultures." That

Chang's companions in this are securely canonical, while he is not, may suggest that East Asian postcoloniality remains troubled with an imperial history perhaps put to rest elsewhere in the world.

Chang Hyŏkchu was born with the given name Ŭnchung in the city of Taegu in southern Korea, the illegitimate son of a landowner who soon abandoned him and his mother. Unusually for her day, she decided to strike out and raise her son on her own. He died as Noguchi Minoru in Japan in 1997. His life was both archetypal and extraordinary. A modern writer under imperialism taken to extremes, he remains controversial in those rare literary histories in Japan and Korea (both of them, North and South) that struggle to accommodate him. Despite the appearance of several new studies of him in South Korea, a leading authority on Chang could write in 2008 that he was "essentially obliterated" (*hotondo massatsu*) from the history of modern Korean literature.[2] The "problem" with Chang is often articulated in the charged rhetoric of political collaboration, the crime of which history has mostly concluded him guilty. But his "conversion" from Korean to Japanese, understood secularly, is the larger conundrum Chang's life presents to anyone who wishes to map the imbricated histories of modern Japanese and Korean literatures and the wider problematics of modern nationhood looming behind them. The story he tells in a long series of works variously faithful to the facts of his life is how he came to naturalize from Korean to Japanese and mold his personal trajectory for what was his ultimate work of docu-art: the person known last in life as Noguchi Minoru, crafted by both desire and necessity over nearly the entire length of the twentieth century—long for some but short, I think, for a writer such as Chang who never succeeded in telling us quite all he wanted to say.

Chang Hyŏkchu (known better in Japan as Noguchi Kakuchū, the pen name he assumed in 1955) became the first Korean to attract wide notice in Tokyo literary circles with the 1932 publication in the soon-to-be-banned journal *Kaizō* of his Japanese-language short story "Hell of the Starving" (Gakidō). It describes the impoverished Korean countryside from the point of view of a teacher; its theme fit well into the thematic parameters of Japanese proletarian literature in its declining years. Chang went on to become what Tak Fujitani calls "one of the Japanese empire's most prolific writers."[3] Chang fretted for years over the fluency of his Japanese, even if he immodestly compared his fluency to Conrad's English and Wilde's French as "not quite perfect."[4] But he certainly possessed impressive linguistic and stylistic skills honed in provincial Korea thanks to the colonial education system imposed on the peninsula in 1911. As a boy Chang was, he tells us, always entranced by the Japanese language; its sounds and its cadences. He heard it from infancy thanks to a young Japanese man who boarded with him and his mother; he dates his attraction to Japan itself from his childhood encounter with the fourteenth-century Japanese classic *Essays in Idleness* (*Tsurezuregusa*).[5] In his 1954 autobiographical novel *Record of a Pilgrim* (*Henreki no chōsho*), he wrote that he felt a kind of nostalgia (*kyōshū*) for the language even as a child.[6] The Japanese principal of his elementary school, Ōsaka Kintarō, inspired him to become an archaeologist, an ambition never fulfilled but never wholly abandoned. His lengthy 1977 meditation on the shared ethnic origins not only of the Koreans, Manchus, and the Japanese but also of native Americans, *The Koreans and the Japanese: Where Did the People of Heaven Come From?* (*Kara to wa: Tenson minzoku wa doko kara kita ka*) proved this interest to be lifelong.[7]

In the Japanese-language classrooms of Taegu, Chang soon fell under the far sway of Kikuchi Kan and other prominent Tokyo writers, especially the proletarian ones then being read enthusiastically in the colonial periphery as well as Japan. When he finally managed a three-month stay in Tokyo in 1932, leveraging his early success with "Hell of the Starving," he was embraced, if at arm's length, by those left-wing partisans of the literary establishment (*bundan*) who, in the face of the suppression of proletarian writings then underway, welcomed a provocative "colonial literature" such as Chang's as the next best thing. Chang's story confronted Japanese readers (who read the work as an ethnic *repōto* "documentary"[8]) with the brutal reality of a southern Korean countryside impoverished by imperial design. Left-wing critics' reviews were laudatory, if often patronizing. By 1936 Chang had published thirty Japanese-language works, one of which—"Oppressed People" (Owareru hitobito, 1932)—was banned in Korea, which only boosted his reputation among the Japanese left. But as he would note in the 1932 essay "My Unique Perspective" (Tokushū no tachiba), he always felt excluded from the literary world in Japan (*bundangai*). Since having "discarded his mother tongue and trying to write in Japanese," he had to exert double the effort (*nijū no doryoku*) of the other aspiring writers of his day, and the struggle took its toll on him personally and professionally. Afflicted by both melancholy (*yūutsu*) and anxiety (*fuan*), Chang wrote as if his mixture of self-doubt and resentment of others were overwhelming his career just as it had begun.[9]

In time Chang would come to be regarded as one of the least savory of all pro-Japanese writers (*ch'inil munin*). Samuel Perry notes in his work on Northeast Asian proletarian literature that "Chang . . . is better known for reproducing stereotypes than for his countering them."[10] Critics note he is typically cast as the ethical opposite of Kim Saryang, whose collaborationist reputation was rescued by his reported death during the Korean War while embedded as a journalist with Democratic People's Republic of Korea forces. Chang's stories and novels would deal less with the disaster of rural Korea under occupation (often his native Kyŏngsang Province) and more with the Japanese literary pursuit of the drama of the alienated individual (*kojin*) in society. He was sensitive to the criticism that he had come late to proletarian literature, just as Korean literature was said to be coming late to modernity—a disparagement that Chang, in fact, would echo. Korean literature, he would write in "The Future of Korean Writers" (Chōsen bundan no shōrai, 1935), inspired a bitter hatred (*hidoi ken'o*) in him.[11] Chang's frequent attacks on other Korean critics and writers never helped his reputation—he wrote, for example, that Yi Kwangsu, as highly regarded a writer as twentieth-century Korea would produce, was afflicted with an "unnatural psychology"[12]—and went on to lambast his fellow Korean writers, critics, and readers as simply inadequate to the task of producing or appreciating literary masterpieces (*kessaku*).

Some literary historians take Chang's 1933 story "A Man Named Kwon" (Gon to iu otoko) as a turning point. Reworked after it was originally banned, it draws on his personal background, as do so many of his stories. Kim Dong'il, the narrator, is a middle-aged teacher with dashed youthful ambitions and a disappointing, languishing career in a poverty-stricken countryside. He becomes entangled with Kwon, a bootlegging bar owner in town with his own murky activist past. But as Hayashi Kōji has pointed out, "'A Man Named Kwon' aims to be high literature [*jun-bungaku*]" describing "the struggle of the individual ego, distinct from social or national [*minzokuteki*] themes."[13] A year later in the essay "My Aspirations" (Waga hōfu) Chang declared that in describing "the individual he conceived his desire for life," which was a "'higher' artistic realm" (*'yori kōdo' na geijutsu sekai)* than any of "the various phenomena arising from the circumstances of the race I belong to."[14] "A Man Named Kwon" was his first work devoted to what he called his God-given (*sententeki*) literary instincts; the 1934 novella *Prostitute* (Garubō) was his second. But both of these works, well received by critics, include critiques of the Korean national character that permitted some Japanese to cite them as proof of what improvements colonial modernity was bestowing upon a backward Korea. In *Prostitute,* for example, Chang's narrator reflects that "my race knows well how indolent it can be, and how given to arrogance we are at the smallest success."[15]

Later, when Japanese fascism discouraged attention on the "individual" as decadent, Chang switched course again by taking the war effort as his principal theme. When he did return to the particular account of Koreans in the empire, he would speak of "them" rather than "we." In a 1935 letter to his proletarian literary mentor Tokunaga Sunao, he expresses exasperation at the Japanese considering him to be a Korean or "colonial" writer at all—"Why don't you see Chang Hyŏkchu as just one ordinary [*atarimae*] writer?" "Isn't it an insult to be noticed because I'm a Korean?" No one, he goes on, patronizes Joyce or Tagore that way—I'm an individual, he insists, gifted with an artistic sensibility (*geijutsukan*).[16]

For a few more years Chang would continue to publish in the Korean language as well as the Japanese, but his Korean-language novels were not well received. They tend to meander, a problem he would always have—and by 1939 he abandoned any notion of spanning both. Two years earlier he noted that, in Korean, he wrote with an entirely different attitude (*taido o mattaku koto ni shite iru)* than he did in works intended for a Japanophone readership. Elsewhere, he admitted that even when working with the same material, his choice of language (*hyōgen gengo*) produced different results. The leading authority on Chang in Japan, Shirakawa Yutaka, finds that his Japanese-language and Korean-language works were "wholly detached within the author" (*sakka no naibu ni oite bekko no mono*).[17] While Chang himself did not elaborate on the distinction between his use of both languages, we might wonder if here is where Chang was conscious of the semiopaque machinery of "affect" behind how he both wrote and expected to be read among two mutually unintelligible audiences. If, as Gregory J. Seigworth and Melissa Gregg claim, "Affect is in many ways synonymous with *force* or *forces of encounter*,"[18] then a Chang Hyŏkchu straddling the idioms of two always potentially hostile readerships would have felt its brunt.

After 1942 he abandoned Korean entirely. Always sensitive to changes in the wind, he had written as early as 1935 that he could not bear to be away from Tokyo, the "center of culture" (*bunka no chūshinchi*).[19] That same year he wrote in a short piece "Sadness upon Leaving the Capital" (Rikyō no kanashimi) that "as my train passes through Shinagawa Station, and then departs Yokohama, I think sadly of myself as an outcast [*rakugosha*]."[20] In 1936 he relocated to Tokyo with the intent to settle there permanently; in 1937 he would express bitterness at ever having been born a Korean in the first place. Chang was not unique in this regard. For Chang, Tokyo was always where history happened: it was a place he yearned for continually but never felt fully comfortable in. As he intimated in his brief note "In Tokyo, Feeling Its Emptiness" (Tōkyō e kite kyomu o kanzuru), he resented the city for exactly that.[21] Everything about Chang seemed of two minds: at least his early work implies he meant to deploy the native language of his colonizer against him. "Hell of the Starving," for example, first appeared heavily censored because of its candid descriptions of what Japanese agricultural policies in Korea had wrought. But even at that time such tactics backfired. In a postscript to "Hell of the Starving" penned by *Kaizō*'s editors, they boasted, "This may be the first Korean writer to become a star in our nation's literary scene, and more importantly it announces the existence of Korean writers to the entire world."[22] Nearly a decade before Kim Saryang would be shortlisted for the prestigious Akutagawa Prize, Chang Hyŏkchu was already having his work cited as an achievement of Japanese colonial largesse.

In order to remain useful to his Japanese patrons, Chang would be tempted to take evermore explicit and even bizarrely pro-Japanese views as the war on the continent and the Pacific expanded, a shift spectacularly evident in his unfinished novel *Katō Kiyomasa,* in which he portrays a sixteenth-century Japanese invader of Korea as a hero. That same year he denounced his earlier "Hell of the Starving" as having only "borrowed the clothes" of left-wing cant.[23] Shirakawa, a friend until the end of Chang's life, candidly declared Chang's role in Japanese literary circles as that of a clown (*piero-yaku*) whose worth to the war effort had expired over a year before the 1945 surrender.[24] The more fanatical Chang Hyŏkchu became, ironically, the less valuable he was to the empire.

Chang did little to resist his coerced march toward Nihonism (Nihonshugi), though we remember that many Japanese colleagues went down this same road, namely from proletarian author to state-sanctioned writer (*goyō sakka*). Two years after the publication of "Hell of the Starving," Chang would write in the journal *Bungei,* "Every time I think, I think in Japanese. It is natural for me to do so. I may not be proud of that, but neither am I ashamed of slighting [*karonzuru*] my native tongue." One of the most notorious pro-Japanese essays written by any Korean during the colonial period was Chang's 1939 polemic "An Appeal to Korea's Intellectuals" (Chōsen no chishikijin ni uttau), a reprise of the similarly controversial Korean-language essay "Mundan ŭi p'esŭt'o kyun" in *Samch'ŏlli* four years earlier. It especially galled Korean writers because his once internecine attacks were now delivered, in the Japanese language, to the enemy camp with which Chang had now fully enlisted. In both pieces he accuses Korea's intelligentsia of being intrinsically prone to violent emotion (*gekijōsei*—perhaps because they are descended from peoples who came from the "north"—like the French, Chang declares).[25] He adds envy (*shitto*) to his list of Korean vices and declares his countrymen temperamentally disinclined to create works of genius. He compares modern Korean literature unfavorably to modern Chinese literature despite the latter's shorter history and accuses its writers, citing bête noire critic Kim Munjip as an example, to be hopelessly given to malicious gossip. While Chang does blame a "colonial psychology" for these faults, his suggested remedy is not for Koreans to throw off the yoke of Japanese domination but rather to surrender entirely to it and become Japanese (Naichika) in every way. "If we were to become thoroughly Japanese," he writes, "we would become a race at peace with ourselves and one 'without perversion [*hinekure no nai*].'" Chang's volte-face was now essentially complete.

In the conclusion to his groundbreaking study of literary collaborators in Korea, *Pro-Japanese Literature* (*Ch'inil munhangnon*, 1966), Im Chongguk divided Korean writers under Japanese rule into several gradations of collaborator, but he granted Chang Hyŏkchu a category all his own. Chang, Im points out, ventured down the pro-Japanese road even before Minami Jirō became governor-general and the screws were tightened on all the intelligentsia. As a boy, Im goes on to say, Chang "had already shown a personal affinity for Japan, and therefore was 'pro-Japanese' in a sense somewhat different from the one I've employed in this study."[26] Others were not so generous in their assessment of Chang, however, and after liberation he was specifically faulted for campaigning actively on behalf of two Japanese colonial polices. The first was the planned abolition of the Korean language. In "Appeal" Chang had noted with approbation that what took the English three hundred years to accomplish in Ireland—namely the near-total elimination of Gaelic—the Japanese could do to Korean in a third of the time. And the sooner the better, Chang insisted. Yeats, he claimed, would never have become a world-renowned writer if he had not written in English, and so Koreans must adopt Japanese because it is the only "international language of Asia."[27]

The second issue was over the entry of Korea youth, first as volunteers and then conscripts, into the Imperial Army. Chang staked out a radical, pro-Japanese position on this policy with his 1943 *Army Volunteer Iwamoto Shiganhei*, which I will discuss presently. But first I need to outline Chang's postwar defense of his wartime servility. A year after the end of the war, Chang started a work, *Race* (Minzoku), with the intent of defending his collaboration with the empire. He never finished it. The best apology he left us was, in my view, the much later novel *Poem in a Storm* (*Arashi no uta*, 1975), in which three decades after the empire's defeat he recalls in semiautobiographical fashion the story of a person conscious of his predisposition to all things Japanese but wary of his choice to accede to that treacherous allure. *Poem in a Storm* tells the life of a Korean writer named Yong (J. Ryū) from his birth in 1905, the year Japan was ceded effective control of the peninsula, until the end of Tokyo's rule in August 1945 and Yong's concurrent decision to remain in Japan. Unlike the earlier but also autobiographical *Record of a Pilgrim,* where he cast his resolve to convert his citizenship (*kika*) to Japanese as a matter of course and wrote, "I had forgotten I was a naturalized Japanese who had come from a foreign people. Japan is my country,"[28] in *Poem in a Storm* his conversion is examined as critical self-refashioning. While most of the unsavory scandals involving author Chang's more virulent attacks on the Korean national character—attacks that if launched by Japanese, Chang was quick to dismiss as the categorical error of mistaking history for national character[29]—are omitted in this ipso facto account. Enough of the account is parallel to Chang's life to suggest that *Poem in a Storm* serves as his ambivalent defense of how he was born a Korean only to become, at precisely the moment he was free of further coercion, a Japanese.

Yong's earliest memory as an infant living on the southern coast of Korea is that of the boarder in his home: Uchiyama Ken, the village's Japanese teacher. His older cousin Myŏngdal takes little Yong with him to Uchiyama's classes, and he grows up hearing Japanese as well as Korean all around him. Uchiyama tells visitors from Japan that his students are especially adept at mastering Japanese because so much of the local population carries the genes of Japanese who intermingled with Koreans during the time of Hideyoshi's invasions. Little Yong believes what he hears. Halfway through the novel, it is 1910, Korea has been ignominiously annexed, and the precocious five-year-old wants to attend a Japanese-run school and quit the old-fashioned Korean one in Kwangju to which he has been sent. Myŏngdal, now a member of the military police, arranges this for him, but once there Yong encounters faculty and students, both Korean and Japanese, who are variously patriotic and sycophantic, bigoted and solicitous. Yong has very mixed feelings. He is sensitive to any slight of being treated differently as a Korean, but at the same time he is drawn to his Japanese lessons, his Japanese teachers, and even ordinary Japanese things. (He wonders, for example, why Koreans cannot make school stationery as fine as the Japanese do.) One of his schoolmates warns him that the colonial staff is only trying to turn them into little Japanese subjects, but Yong is confused—just what is at the heart of being a Korean? Or being a Japanese?

Nonetheless, Yong is an exceptional student and the rare Korean allowed to advance from elementary education to secondary. But unlike other talented Korean boys—yet like the real-life Chang Hyŏkchu—his education will not occur in Japan itself but only within the colonial school system, where he is warned in manifold ways that Japanese ambitions for Koreans have limits. A classmate at another school he attends tells him, yes, we are being taught about everything Japanese at the expense of learning nothing of our own country, but that does not mean we will ever be treated as equal to the Japanese. We are destined to be their crack lackeys (*yūshū na dorei*). But Yong cannot help but admire Japan, especially its literature, as his education progresses. He spends time at a lending library, where he reads Kikuchi Kan, Akutagawa Ryūnosuke, and other celebrated Japanese writers of the day. More important for how he perceives himself, he yearns for friendship with the Japanese boys. Still, his classmate's admonition rings true, and Yong knows that blood (*minzoku*) will always come between him and those potential friends. He does succeed in making a good Japanese acquaintance, an aspiring poet who excitedly speaks to Yong about Japan's Masamune Hakuchō as well as the West's Lord Byron. Finally, Yong is pleased to think that just this once, in his chats with this fellow aesthete, "Here, there was no race" (*Soko ni wa minzoku wa nakatta*).[30]

In time Yong relocates to Tokyo and achieves a modicum of literary stardom when he publishes a story about Korean rural poverty in *"Magazine K"* (surely a reference to *Kaizō*) and marries a Japanese girl named Ai. He is patronized by the Japanese in both senses of the word when his literary success as a writer is praised by critics for being so "fresh" and "continental"; so "authentic" when compared to the stylized mannerisms of Japanese writers. One critic, modeled on the real-life Ōya Sōichi, says, "What wonderful work. Here is something that finally doesn't blame *everything* on the Japanese and breaks new ground by looking at 'colonial complicity.'" Yong is subjected to the classic conundrum of the colonial intellectual who is at home neither in his own country nor that of its colonizers. His second story in *Magazine K* garners more accolades, but when it veers close to blaming Japan for Korea's worsening duress, it is banned in the peninsula. He feels very Japanese at times—spoiled by Ai's Japanese cooking, he can no longer remember the taste of Korean garlic and chili pepper. But without mastering the soul (*kokoro*) of the Japanese, he frets his writings will always be ersatz. Yet, just what that soul is continues to eludes him.

Nonetheless, Yong resolves to naturalize on the same day his homeland is liberated and his adopted country, in turn, is to surrender its sovereignty to the United States. The novel's ending is counterintuitive at first—Yong's discomfort with being Korean in Japan does not change with his decision to stay. Perhaps the nagging ill ease he feels at having shown too much affection for Japan means that returning to a Korea unrestrained by its former Japanese rulers is too perilous a thought to entertain. But in some of his other autobiographical writings, Chang insists that his early passion for things Japanese was never a matter of wanting to *be* Japanese. Rather, it was simply a matter of desiring an education and, above all, modernity—as if a world war and Japan's deployment of Korea in waging it were irrelevant to this naïve set of desires. This runs counter to the popular view of Chang as impaired with, as Im Chŏnhye put it, "a racial complex he wanted to do away with" (*minzokuteki konpurekkusu o fusshoku*) by becoming a Japanese.[31] But perhaps we should take Chang at his word. Even when he argued that Korea had best discard its culture and even its language as soon as possible and, like the Welsh and the Irish, dissolve itself in the culture of the adjacent dominant nation, his Celtic examples of why Koreans should do so are Yeats and Joyce, whom Chang saw as great writers (in English) precisely because they were not great Irishmen. (Somehow their famous espousals of the Irish cause escaped Chang's notice.)

It is conceivable, for such people do exist, that Chang lacked not only patriotism but *any* sense of a national identity other than as a liability, if in his view being "Korean" meant little more than subordination in the metropole for which he wrote and where he chose to live all his adult life. His was, in other words, a conscionable existentialist choice. Throughout *Poem in a Storm,* Chang insists that his partiality for Japan and the Japanese was never forced upon him but resulted from a willed selection inspired by a deeper longing to be cosmopolitan. As Nan Bujin has generalized of colonial-era writers in Chang's generation who likewise favored the Japanese language, it is not enough to say they were either "pro-Japanese" or coerced to use it; it was a "consequence of literary ambition and a craving for what Japanese language could express."[32] Though some might reasonably accuse Chang of bad faith (in Sartre's writings on collaborators, for example, no Frenchman during the war is allowed to "choose" being a German), he did seem to accept that though born a Korean and destined to die a Japanese, he was free to fashion his life between those two inalterable poles as a "Japanese" even if others never fully accepted him as one and even if his own celebrity ironically depended entirely on *not* being wholly assimilated. Whether we allow history to judge him a traitor or our moral precepts to award him the free election of national-cultural-ethnic identities are linked questions we need to resolve, or at least bracket, before a nuanced literary history can proceed further.

Lauren Berlant's characterization of any "object of desire" as a "cluster of promises" is a tempting starting point for understanding Chang's perhaps uniquely twentieth-century dilemma. With no little irony for Chang, we can take Berlant at her word: "All attachments are optimistic."[33] Or at least, let us tentatively posit that this is the case and nominate other words ("drive," "impulse") for those desires and attachments that tend elsewhere. But to call Chang's *desire* to be(come) Japanese "optimistic" must not suppress the lexical fact that optimism usually portends failure as well as success. Berlant cautions that "'cruel optimism' names a relation of attachment to compromised conditions of possibility whose realization is discovered either to be *im*possible, sheer fantasy, or *too* possible, and toxic."[34]

From the very start of his writing career, if not earlier, Chang knew that becoming a Japanese was both his fate and his impossible assignment. *Poem in a Storm*'s Yong's inner thoughts establish the first condition; his Korean classmate's cynical admonishments, the second. In other words he is consigned to be optimistic, just as we in our own present century are left to be optimistic about climate change, peace between Israel and Palestine, or a cure for cancer: we are primed to be disappointed and perhaps even count on it to render our "affect" of sanguinity over world affairs the inevitable "cruel optimism" that Berlant brilliantly, I think, understands as "the condition of maintaining an attachment to a problematic object *in advance* of its loss."[35] By 1975 and *Poem in a Storm,* Chang had to have been aware of how history displaced his ambitions, even if some part of him stubbornly remained in denial; when his protagonist Yong "realizes only years later that there is no greater misery [*fukō*] than human beings holding each other in contempt," Chang is telling the reader that even while adverse passions may have ruled his feelings, the very awareness that they did so is the affect that trumped all others.

Chang spent his entire long life in his short century (short not least because it effectively ended for him mid-point), tortured by his realization that his object of desire (erstwhile Japanese-ness) would have to elude him but could never be yielded. Why? Because, as Berlant again says, "The fear that the loss of the object or scene of promising itself will defeat the capacity to have any hope about anything,"[36] and Chang was not about to be a man without hope—even if he was the author of a literature that chronicled continual disappointment. The reader who follows Berlant up to this point will be tempted to continue her line of reasoning and psychoanalyze this conflict to let it play out on a field of powerful, "unconscious" imperatives in competition with each other. I am not so tempted, but I will allow myself to be "psychological." William James' musings on the mind of the religious convert are suggestive here. "The psychological basis of the twice-born character," he wrote in *Varieties of Religious Experience,* "seems to be a certain discordancy or heterogeneity in the native temperament of the subject, an incompletely unified moral and intellectual constitution." James identifies the "heterogeneous personality" as one naturally occurring in some of us—and says that it "may make havoc of the subject's life," even while it can, in some instances (James' example is Saint Augustine), produce saints.[37] Chang Hyŏkchu was not one of them, and returning to Berlant we see why: that conversion from imperial subject (*shinmin*) to national citizen (*kokumin*), which was never more than a "cluster of promises," was destined to wreak not mere havoc, but abjection. What other word should we use to describe Yong as he stands before his little Japanese house, now in ruins?

I now turn to Chang's 1943 *Army Volunteer Iwamoto.* Inspired by his visit to a training camp and serialized widely in both Korea's and Japan's newspapers, this novel was intended to bolster the morale of Koreans then being conscripted into the Japanese military. The story of a delinquent Korean youth turned good via his indoctrination into Japanese imperial ideology and the virtues of soldierly discipline, it also taught that racially and linguistically the Japanese and the Koreans descend from common stock. The program of forced assimilation under conditions of total war marked, in other words, a just return to ancient and heroic times for both peoples. With the door now open for Koreans to serve as equals in the Imperial Army, they can only rejoice at the proud "equal" future that awaits them and Japanese youth alike. As Tak Fujitani notes, the novel "reveals how nationalism worked through the constitution of subjects who have the freedom to choose their own subjection to the national community."[38]

For Chang's Iwamoto, the army was the means to become Japanese at the root. Fujitani concludes that Iwamoto's self-determination (and by extension, Korea's) "results in self-subjectification to the nation of Japan."[39] For Chang himself, the analogue would have to have been the world of Tokyo writers, a world where he would be a *hantō shusshin no Nihon bungakusha*—a Japanese writer from the peninsula and no Korean at all. *Army Volunteer Iwamoto* is clearly a work of propaganda, though as in so much of Chang's work, it is not without its ideological ambiguities. Surely intended as a catechism for all Koreans, it was written from the pedagogic construct of a wayward young man seeking his moral reconstruction by becoming an imperial soldier. In recent years younger historians have suggested that Japanese propaganda was more effective than previously believed,[40] and *Army Volunteer Iwamoto* was, according to Shirakawa, widely disseminated—ten thousand copies were initially printed, two or three times a novel's usual run.[41]

Cultural geographer Ben Anderson, in his essay "Modulating the Excess of Affect: Morale in a State of 'Total War,'" looks at the issue of morale among American servicemen in World War II, but we can apply his observations to Korea, where morale was no less paramount under similar conditions of total war (defined as the mobilization of all civilian as well as military personnel for the war effort). Anderson quotes American psychologist Harry Sullivan, who said in 1941 that "the circumstances of modern warfare require the *collaboration* [italics mine] of practically everyone. Ineffectual personals in the social organization are a menace to the whole."[42] Anderson's work explores, fortuitously for us in thinking about Chang via affect, "how morale emerged as an object for specific techniques of power as part of changing relations between the state and the population at the start of the Second World War."[43]

Why morale, when something we could call patriotism or duty might have sufficed? Because morale is more than a pledge or obligation; it is a bodily mode of being and one that "exceeds attempts to establish it as a thing in itself":[44]

> Morale is the basis to action because it exceeds present diminishing affections of the body. . . . Morale promises . . . to enable bodies to keep going *despite the present,* a present in which morale is either targeted directly or threatens to break given the conditions of "total war." And what threatens is an unpredictable, uncertain, future "crisis" in which morale suddenly breaks or shatters, bodies are exposed to the conditions of the present, and the movement of "total" mobilization fails or ends.[45]

By the time Chang serialized *Army Volunteer Iwamoto,* the war was not going well for Japan, and surely he knew it. The sacrifices his Korean youth were called to make were all "despite the present" and threatened by "an unpredictable, uncertain, future 'crisis'" that demanded morale even as it promised to destroy it. It is tempting to compare the "morale" Chang urged upon the young soldiers with the "collaboration" counseled him as a writer at the same age by his elders: both had their tactical goals, but both relied on a set of "affects" evermore emotional in inverse proportion to their effectiveness at the end of the war.

Near the beginning of his 1977 *Korea and Japan,* Chang relates an anecdote of how his own morale failed him during the war. The signs of imminent defeat all around, a Chang "in the depths of despair" (*zetsubō no soko ni ita watakushi*) visited the Ise Shrine in search of the Japanese gods in whose names the war had been advertised. He found none—though when wandering the Yamato Plain, he did hear the voices of ancient compatriots "from Paekche, from Koguryo, from Shilla" (*Kodara ga ari Kōkuri ga ari Shiragi ga atta*).[46] His properly twentieth-century morale dashed, Chang thought his ancestors still spoke to him, but importantly *he does not report what they said.* Perhaps it was only bodies' murmuring that never rose to the level of sensible speech; sounds from extinct throats devoid of meaning but with uncanny physical presence. Decades later they would inspire him to write his polemic *Korea and Japan* with a resurrected morale—but unlike the morale, Anderson says, that "becomes linked to 'world-making' in part, then, because it is assumed to be inseparable from the affections of the body and, somehow, to exceed them."[47] Japan's imperial conceit of a Northeast Asian Ur-Race long discredited, Chang retrofits it for his pseudoanthropological divine (*tenson*) race (*minzoku*) whose DNA traveled from west of the Urals to east of the Rockies: organic and "world-making," if now quite incapable of "the affections of the human body."

Chang's *Poem in a Storm,* written around the same time as *Korea and Japan,* revisits the theme of wartime military morale. On his way home after yet another army-sponsored trip to Manchuria, Yong stops in Seoul, curious to see if young Koreans volunteering for the Imperial Army really were doing so of their own volition. At first glance everything looks fine, but on a closer look he finds questionable logic on the soldiers' part. Why did you volunteer? he asks. For Korea, is the answer. If we volunteer the Japanese cannot hold us in contempt any longer. Yong counters: No, you must fight for your *okuni* (country), and your *okuni* is Japan as well as Korea. The question is one of community and it boundaries, and Yong needs his young countrymen to extend morale to the "affections of the [national] body." So Yong delivers a rousing speech that touches on the Japanese classics, the Japanese emperor, and the Japanese spirit (Nihon seishin). It is your spirit too, he instructs the assembled recruits. Japanese blood runs in your veins, and ours in theirs.

Of course, Yong only half believes his own words. That night, back in his hotel room, he receives a threatening phone call. Yong thinks his speech that day was right, but so is the harassing caller's accusation of treason. But Yong cannot abandon his Berlantian cruel optimism, and to the extent that Chang insisted holding on to his aspirations, that optimism was crueler still once "the very pleasures of being inside a relation have become sustaining regardless of the content of the relation, such that a person or a world finds itself bound to a situation of a profound threat that is, at the same time, profoundly confirming."[48]

Poem in a Storm consequently concludes with both a climax and an anticlimax. On his final trip to Manchuria, the protagonist is invited to meet a local legislator of Korean ethnicity named Kim. Kim starts their meeting praising Yong as a hero for his writings, but then he frankly warns him: you are too partial to Japan (*Anta wa Nihon ni katayorisugi da*), a charge that Yong admits to himself is true. "You love Japan," Kim says to Yong, "Does that mean you love Japan's military, its police, all its power?" [49] At the end of their talk, Kim warns Yong that his life may be in danger—a threat that leads to the novel's abject anticlimax. Yong rushes home to Tokyo when he receives a telegram from Ai telling him their home has been destroyed in an air raid. His ship docks in Japan on August 9 as Nagasaki is destroyed by a "new kind of weapon." It is already August 15 when he finally makes it back to Tokyo just as the emperor's capitulation is broadcast on the radio. As he reaches the ruins of his home, Yong resolves, "I am going to become a person of this country [*Boku wa kono kuni no hito ni naru*]. It was as if this were prearranged to happen to me. I suddenly felt destined to always remain joined to an occupied country."[50]

Shirakawa Yutaka has said that Chang's career was long, straddled several languages, and is hard to grasp as a whole.[51] What Taiwanese postcolonial scholar Wang Hui Zhen calls Chang's use value (*riyō kachi*) to the Japanese state ended with the publication of *Army Volunteer Iwamoto.*[52] He attracted little notice after publishing his long 1952 novel about the Korean War, *Aa Chōsen* (Oh Korea!), in which a young student in Seoul, Pak Sŏng'il, finds himself swept up into both sides of the conflict (as in real life were Chang's first wife and their children). Pak's ethical quandary is perhaps not unlike Chang's own during the previous colonial period: the novel readily reads as an analogy for his own dilemma of being caught between Korea and the Japanese empire.

Chang Hyŏkchu left a record of sycophantic writings that earned him little in return, and his efforts to bury them under new themes after the war were the stuff of pathos. Even when he wrote novels that had nothing to do with Korea or the war, such as his 1957 melodrama *A Beautiful Protest* (*Utsukushii teikō*), his protagonists are affected with feelings of irrepressible abjection (*jiko ken'o*).[53] In his last years, he turned to the history of the Incas and the Mayans, to the life of the historical Buddha, and even to the first Gulf War. He began to write in English, his third language, not counting an Esperanto interlude. His grandson, Chang Jiho, told me in Seoul in 2012 that surviving family members found many unpublished English manuscripts in his home. After abandoning first the Korean of his homeland and then the Japanese of an empire, in his last years Chang strove to become—with the affect of cruel optimism?—what Wang calls a "world author beyond the fetters of race" (*minzoku no shigarami o koeta sekai sakka*).[54] But in fact he squirreled himself away in the Saitama town of Hidaka, a place made home by Korean refugees from Koguryo after its defeat by Tang and Shilla in the seventh century and later immigrants from many regions of the peninsula. Its Koma Shrine, the site of Iwamoto's spiritual catharsis in Chang's eponymous novel, is a tourist attraction today, not just for Japanese but for growing numbers of tourists from Korea and China. There, "Noguchi Minoru" spurned visitors (I was one of them) and nursed his resentments. Even his kindest critics recalled his personal and professional faults. When Chang/Chō/Noguchi surfaces in accounts today, it is as a figure out of a tragedy—not dead as in Shakespeare's plays but bitterly disappointed as in Chekov's. The twentieth century might have been short, but he lived too long in it.

In her essay "Imperial Debris: Reflections on Ruins and Ruination," Ann Stoler cites V. S. Naipaul's lament in his *Enigma of Arrival* that he had arrived in the English metropole too late, when it was no more "the heart of empire, which (like a provincial from a far corner of the empire) I had created in my fantasy."[55] Historians of the British or the French Empires have scores of such latecomers to select among, but Chang Hyŏkchu is my choice of a writer who, overstaying his welcome in another empire well-rid of its ideology, was left with little but the pure "intensity" that affect is held by some to be.[56] Chang's smoldering *ressentiment* and Naipaul's withering pique are both what remain, perhaps, when the body is left to deal with what minds have already abandoned.

"All attachments," Lauren Berlant tells us, "are optimistic," but the word here has strayed from common parlance. Looking back over Chang Hyŏkchu's stories and novels, one is convinced he never abandoned his Berlantian optimism—"another definition of desire," Berlant adds, making the word inevitably disenchanting[57]—in coupling himself with the historical and the abstract Japan in both its victories and its defeat. This yearning may not rise to the level of that touted "affect" empowered to psychically structure the world, but it certainly empowered the intimate possession of his world, and until the very end of his life.

Notes

Epigraph. David Palumbo-Liu, *The Deliverance of Others: Reading Literature in a Global Age* (Durham, NC: Duke University Press, 2012), 148.

Epigraph. Noguchi Kakuchū [Chang Hyŏkchu], *Kara to Wa—Tenson minzoku wa doko kara kita ka* (Tokyo: Kōdansha, 1977), 9.

1. Quoted in Rei Terada, *Feeling in Theory: Emotion after the "Death of the Subject"* (Cambridge, MA: Harvard University Press, 2001), 1.

2. Shirakawa Yutaka, *Chōsen kindai no shinnichiha sakka, kutō no kiseki* (Tokyo: Bensei Shuppan, 2008), 37.

3. Takashi Fujitani, *Race for Empire: Koreans as Japanese and Japanese as Americans during World War II* (Berkeley: University of California Press, 2011), 27.

4. Chō Kakuchū [Chang Hyŏkchu], "Waga hōfu," in *Chō Kakuchū Nihongo sakuhin sen,* ed. Nan Bujin and Shirakawa Yutaka (Tokyo: Bensei Shuppan, 2003), 291.

5. Chō, "Waga hōfu," 300.

6. Noguchi Kakuchū [Chang Hyŏkchu], *Henreki no chōsho* (Tokyo: Shinchōsha, 1954), 34.

7. In *Kara to Wa* (244), Chang refers his readers to more of his writings on a shared racial identity between Northeast Asians and indigenous peoples in North America in his serialized essay "Amerika indian no, kodai Nihonjin genryū o saguru," in the popular magazine *Rekishi to tabi,* but I have not been able to find it.

8. Nakane Takayuki, "Bungaku ni okeru shokuminchishugi," in *Shokuminchishugi to Ajia no hyōshō,* ed. Tsukuba Daigaku Bunka Hihyō Kenkyūkai (Tokyo: Tsukuba Daigaku Shuppankai, 1999), 160–161.

9. Chō, "Tokushū no tachiba," *Bungei shuto* 1, no. 2 (February 1933): 66–67.

10. Samuel Emerson Perry, "Aesthetics for Justice: Proletarian Literature in Japan and Colonial Korea" (PhD diss., University of Michigan, 2007), 235.

11. Chō, "Chōsen bundan no shōrai," *Bungaku annai* 1, no. 5 (November 1935): 94.

12. Chō, "Chōsen bundan no genjō hōkoku," *Bungaku annai* 1, no. 4 (October 1935): 63–64.

13. Hayashi Kōji, *Zainichi Chōsenjin Nihongo bungakuron* (Tokyo: Shinhansha, 1991), 224–225.

14. Chō, "Waga hōfu," 294.
15. Chō, *Garubō, Bungei* 2, no. 3 (March 1934): 12–13.
16. Chō, "Watashi ni taibō suru hitobito e: Tokunaga Sunao-shi ni okuru tegami," in Nan and Shirakawa, *Chō Kakuchū Nihongo sakuhin sen,* 299.
17. Shirakawa Yutaka, "Chō Kakuchū no Chōsengo sakuhin kō," *Chōsen gakuhō,* nos. 199–220 (July 1986): 655.
18. Gregory J. Seigworth and Melissa Gregg, "An Inventory of Shimmers," in *The Affect Theory Reader,* ed. Melissa Gregg and Gregory J. Seigworth (Durham, NC: Duke University Press, 2010), 2.
19. Hayashi, *Zainichi Chōsenjin Nihongo bungakuron,* 229.
20. Nakane Takayuki,*"Chōsen" hyōshō no bunkashi* (Tokyo: Shin'yōsha, 2004), 229.
21. Chō, "Tōkyō e kite kyomu o kanzuru," *Bungaku annai* 2, no. 8 (August 1936): 33.
22. Im Chŏnhye [Nin Tenkei], *Nihon ni okeru Chōsenjin no bungaku no rekishi: 1945-nen made* (Tokyo: Hōsei Daigaku Shuppankyoku, 1994), 202.
23. Shibuya Kaori, "Chō Kakuchū ron (1)—debyū toki no san sakuhin o megutte," *Kanazawa Joshi Tanki Daigaku kenkyū kiyō* no. 28 (March 1995): 30.
24. Shirakawa Yutaka, *Shokuminchiki Chōsen no sakka to Nihon* (Tokyo: Daigaku Kyōiku Shuppan, 1995), 188.
25. Chō, "Chōsen no chishikijin ni uttau," *Bungei* 6, no. 2 (February 1939): 227.
26. Im Chongguk, *Ch'inil munhangnon* (Seoul: P'yŏnghwa Ch'ulp'ansa, 1966), 46.
27. Chō, "Chōsen no chishikijin ni uttau," 239.
28. Noguchi Kakuchū, *Henreki no chōsho* (Tokyo: Shinchōsha, 1954), 248.
29. Chō, "Boku no bungaku," 288.
30. Noguchi Kakuchū, *Arashi no uta* (Tokyo: Kōdansha, 1975), 125.
31. Im Chŏnhye, *Nihon ni okeru Chōsenjin no bungaku no rekishi,* 209.
32. Nan Bujin, "Kaisetsu—Nihongo e no yokubō to kindai e no hōkō," in Nan and Shirakawa, *Chō Kakuchū Nihongo sakuhin sen,* 322.
33. Lauren Berlant, "Cruel Optimism," in Gregg and Seigworth, *Affect Theory Reader,* 93.
34. Ibid., 94.
35. Ibid.
36. Ibid.
37. William James, *Varieties of Religious Experience* (London: Routledge, 2002), 133–136.
38. Fujitani, *Race for Empire,* 325.
39. Ibid., 333.
40. Barak Kushner, *The Thought War: Japanese Imperial Propaganda* (Honolulu: University of Hawai'i Press, 2006), 118. I thank Paul Barclay for this reference.
41. Shirakawa Yutaka, "Chō Kakuchū *Iwamoto shiganhei* ni tsuite (kaisetsu)," in *Iwamoto shiganhei Nihon shokuminchi bungaku seisenshū (Chōsenhen 12),* ed. Chan Hyokuchu [Chang Hyŏkchu] (Tokyo: Yumani Shobō, 2001), 1–2.
42. Harry Sullivan, quoted in Ben Anderson, "Morale and the Affective Geographies of the 'War on Terror,'" *Cultural Geographies* 17, no. 219 (2010): 171.
43. Ibid., 163.
44. Ibid., 176.
45. Ibid., 173.
46. Noguchi, *Kara to Wa,* 9.
47. Anderson, *Morale and the Affective Geographies,* 177.
48. Lauren Berlant, *Cruel Optimism* (Durham, NC: Duke University Press, 2011), 2.
49. Noguchi, *Arashi no uta,* 263–264.
50. Ibid., 270.

and social backgrounds varied.[11] It was reported in 1951, for example, that an unnamed male member of the imperial family had just undergone a double-eyelid operation in preparation for a trip to South America, where he was afraid that his "classically Mongolian single-lidded eyes" would be thought "too Asian." The same article also cited the example of a Tokyo University professor who had his nose enlarged, also in preparation for travel abroad (to the United States).[12]

Of course, there were some *pan pan*, or female sex workers, as well as others relying on the patronage of foreign soldiers, who underwent plastic surgery to improve business. Yet it was almost never suggested that *pan pan* or "strip girls" (strippers) or cabaret workers represented more than a minority of all those who crowded into the waiting rooms of clinics in Tokyo and Osaka, and that percentage appears to have decreased markedly over the course of the 1950s. Instead, as was regularly noted in the press, the boom in cosmetic surgery—including breast enlargement—was fed by a wide variety of needs and desires. The vast majority of recipients simply wished to look better, or younger, or just "like everyone else" (*hitonami ni*), according to the standards that prevailed within their own communities.

As reported in the popular press, a typical candidate for cosmetic surgery was an "ordinary girl" in her teens or early twenties who was anxious to find a husband in what was considered to be a highly competitive marriage market. She and very often her parents were convinced that some physical feature, such as a birthmark or freckles or the shape of her eyes or nose, was an impediment to the successful conduct of marriage negotiations. Surgeons were regularly quoted expressing their special satisfaction at being able to help these patients become brides. Another group often associated with cosmetic surgery were young women who worked in clerical and sales positions throughout the towns and cities of Japan. In their case, motivations were said to include a mix of husband-seeking, professional ambition, and fashion or peer emulation. As the distinguished plastic surgeon Ōmori Seiichi commented in 1957, "Many of those who want double eyelids and nose surgery are department store salesgirls and so on. A gets it, and then B hears about it and she gets it too."[13] A third category of patient often mentioned in the mass media was the type that famously comprised the majority of North American cosmetic surgery consumers: the middle-class, middle-aged woman worried about losing her looks and with them, the affections of her husband. This sort of patient was usually most interested in wrinkle removal (*shiwatori*) and cheek plumping, but also purchased the more common treatments for eyelids and noses.

While there was general agreement that most of those obtaining cosmetic surgery were women, men seem to have represented a sizeable minority of patients from the beginning. By the late 1950s and the early 1960s the number of boys and men seeking double eyelids, larger noses, thicker and more masculine eyebrows, and even deeper voices (by means of injections into the throat) had become the subject of general comment. Men's motivations were usually explained in terms of the search for employment or conditions at the workplace. One 1958 story stated that 10 percent *more* of the patients at one well-known Tokyo clinic were men rather than women, and that their "quite practical and realistic" reasons included "among recent graduates and other job-hunters, wanting to do well in interviews—and also there are elementary schoolteachers who wish to produce a pleasing effect on children."[14] A 1961 article about the "quiet boom in men's cosmetic surgery" concurred and quoted several surgeons to the effect that young men tended to want double eyelids, to make them look more intelligent, whereas middle-aged men wanted bigger noses, to give them more authority. As Jujin Hospital's Umezawa Fumio, a well-known plastic surgeon, explained, "When men reach middle age and have achieved some social position, it bothers them to have a nose inappropriate to that position, vis-à-vis women and their underlings."[15] Yet there was also some acknowledgment that men too were motivated by such things as fashion, the wish to be more attractive to sexual partners, or the simple gratification of knowing themselves to be better looking.[16]

The question remains: What defined "better looking" in postwar Japan, and to what extent was that definition influenced by a white Euroamerican physical ideal? Even if the typical recipient of cosmetic surgery in 1950s Japan had no intention of trying to look "Western" or "American" or of seeking to gain the approval of Westerners or Americans, can we conclude that the popularity of cosmetic surgery was unrelated to the global as well as local effects of European and American power? It is surely no coincidence that the two most-requested surgical procedures modified just those features—the "narrow" or "slit" eyes and the "flat" nose—that were (and still are) thought most obviously to distinguish Asian from Caucasian faces. Moreover, the specific modifications sought—to create a fold in the upper eyelid or to build a larger nose—were those generally agreed to make eyes and noses resemble more closely those of white Europeans.[17] The point here is that the desire for eyelid and nose jobs, and the technology to satisfy it, did not come about solely or even mostly as a result of mid-twentieth-century American hegemony. Instead, the popularity of cosmetic surgery in 1950s Japan must be understood as part of the much longer, broader process that began in the 1800s, whereby the great powers of Western Europe and later the United States established a manifold, global dominance, and societies all over the world came to associate "the West" with progress and modernity.

Modernizing the Semifeudal Body

In 1950s Japan, cosmetic surgery and beauty culture in general were informed by the hierarchical taxonomies of race and social evolution first developed by European theorists in the eighteenth and nineteenth centuries. Beauty ideology and practice were also shaped, however, by the history of efforts to negotiate the significance of those taxonomies within a Japanese and East Asian context. Older schemes of racial classification associated with European colonialism—and reinforced by neocolonial American power—continued to assign greatest value to features thought to be characteristic of the Nordic-style white body, such as lighter skin and hair, relatively long legs, prominent noses, and double-lidded eyes. Twentieth-century interpreters were creative, however, in finding ways to locate and maneuver Japanese bodies advantageously along the racial-evolutionary ladder. During the early postwar period, one influential strategy was to draw on developmental, materialist models of history to posit rapid Japanese progress toward bodily modernity: a newly expressive, dimensional, mobile, and individualistic beauty.

The connections between postwar beauty culture and earlier forms of European anthropological knowledge are especially clear in the writings of plastic surgeons and other authorities on the Japanese body. Umezawa Fumio, for example, regularly claimed that the measurements and proportions of the Japanese skull—especially in the region of the jaw, mouth, and nose—located it squarely between those of "primitive peoples" and Westerners. Citing the Dutch physician and anatomist Petrus Camper, who developed a theory about facial angles in the eighteenth century, Umezawa wrote in 1953 that the tendency in Japanese to have mouths and teeth that project too far in front "places them between primitive peoples [*mikaijin*] and Euroamericans [Ōbeijin]." The corresponding racial and developmental categories were made explicit in a 1961 article, in which Umezawa stated, "The Japanese nose, in terms of its height, is precisely in between that of white and black people, which is to say between civilization [*bunmei*] and the primitive [*genshi*]. . . ." Umezawa's debt to the racial—and racist—classifications of the previous century was underscored in visual terms in a lavish book on "beauty medicine" he published in the same year; a drawing comparing the profiles of an anthropoid ape (*ruijin-en*), a "barbarian" (*banjin*), and "cultured man" (*bunkajin*) evoked the older European taxonomies locating black Africans between primates and modern men. Umezawa's

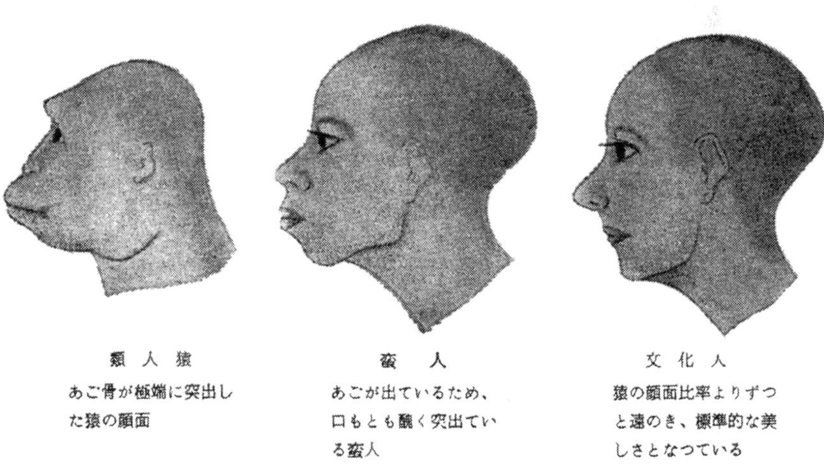

類人猿
あご骨が極端に突出した猿の顔面
蠻人
あごが出ているため、口もとも醜く突出ている蛮人
文化人
猿の顔面比率よりずつと遠のき、標準的な美しさとなつている
口もとの個性は、あご骨とか歯の出来具合によつて大きく左右される

Figure 12.1. Umezawa Fumio, *Utsukushiku naru igaku*. The caption to the illustration reads, "The individuality of the mouth shape is greatly affected by the formation of the jawbone and teeth."

caption to the beaky profile identified with "cultured man" stated that his was the "beauty norm, the farthest from the facial angle of the ape."[18]

Although many scientists had become skeptical of the anthropometric tradition in physical anthropology by the end of the nineteenth century, the idea that measurements of the body could reveal essential truths about racial difference and identity continued to be influential in Japan and elsewhere well into the middle of the twentieth century.[19] The year 1954, for example, saw the respectful publication of a Japanese translation of Carl Heinrich Stratz' 1904 *Die Körperformen in Kunst und Leben der Japaner* (The Japanese body in art and life). A German gynecologist who wrote extensively about female physical beauty, Stratz lived for a time in both Java and Japan and was considered an expert on Asian women's bodies.[20] In the book's fourth edition, which was published just after his death in 1924, Stratz drew heavily on nineteenth- and early twentieth-century scholarship on race, including anthropometric research, to characterize the Japanese, whom he pronounced a unique mixture of the white and yellow races.

One of Stratz' central preoccupations concerned a theory about the mixing of "Mongolian" (yellow) and Ainu (white or near-white) blood as it had produced, over the centuries, several normative Japanese "types:" Ainu, Chōshū, Satsuma, and Mongolian. Stratz judged that of these, the "Chōshū type," in which he claimed that Ainu or Caucasian racial characteristics were strongly evident, was aesthetically superior, as well as most representative of "pure" and original Japanese. Citing the anatomical research in Japan of the German physician Erwin Baelz, along with publications by various anthropologists and anatomists such as Koganei Yoshikiyo and Adachi Buntarō, Stratz asserted that the true (that is, presumably, the Chōshū type) Japanese body showed some Mongolian characteristics, such as the narrow and slanting eye and yellow skin, but was notable for other "better" features that resembled those of the Caucasian: a "high nose," cheekbones that do not project excessively, relatively long legs and arms, and so on.[21]

By the 1950s, half a century after its original publication, Stratz' book had a decidedly antique flavor. Many of his claims were no longer credible by the standards of mid-twentieth century scientific knowledge.[22] Nevertheless, important aspects of Stratz' commentary on the Japanese body resonated with an ongoing common sense about race, developmental hierarchies, and aesthetics. In particular, Stratz' unequivocal statements about the superiority of a certain version of the white European body—his praise of the "straight and narrow nose," large eyes, and orthognathic skulls he claimed were characteristic of the Caucasian race—were consistent with the physical ideals that were touted in a rapidly growing mass media and increasingly admired by the Japanese public. At the same time, Stratz' insistence on the high nose and rounder, double-lidded eye as quasi-Caucasian characteristics found in the "original," "pure" Japanese type is suggestive of the way many surgeons as well as patients understood cosmetic surgery on the nose and the eye. That is, the goal for many was to alter bodily features so as to approximate a physical ideal thought to be indigenous to the Japanese population, *as well as* characteristic of a particular type of white Euroamerican body.

Mid-century discussions of Japanese eyes, especially of upper eyelids, also drew on earlier European thought. As Michael Keevak notes, European accounts of East Asian peoples had long emphasized the distinctive appearance of their eyes: "small," "narrow," "long," "squinting," and "blinking." By the late 1800s, an anatomical term—the epicanthal (or Mongolian) fold—had arisen to designate what was understood as the peculiarity of upper-eyelid formation among many Mongolians or East Asians. For some Western European observers, it even made sense to link the idea of "excessive" or "superfluous" eyelid flesh above the East Asian eye to schemes of racial evolution: the Mongolian eye, which could be seen in some white children and also in persons with "Mongolism" or what is now called Down syndrome, was said to be a racial trait representing incomplete human development toward the higher, Caucasian type.[23]

The views of Japanese commentators varied, and most avoided describing the eye with a "single lid" (*hitoe mabuta*) as defective or blemished, much less as evidence of racial immaturity. A few, such as the plastic surgeon Ōmori Seiichi and the art anatomy scholar Nishida Masaaki, even disapproved of the fad for surgically altering the single-lidded eye and claimed that the results often looked unnatural and unappealing. As Ōmori put it in his 1955 book on cosmetic surgery, "Nowadays it has become fashionable to make one's eyes double-lidded, and many people around us have had this sort of surgery done, but looking at the results, I don't think that it has turned out well for more than two out of ten persons." Nishida wrote, further, that when the Mongolian type of eyelid was shaped well, it made the face look "clear and plump" (*meiryō na hōman na*), while the European style of upper-eye configuration could look "harsh and wasted" (*dogitsui shōmō shita*), as might suit a witch or someone very ill.[24]

Nevertheless, the general consensus was in favor of the double-lidded eye, which was understood to be a larger eye. Occasionally, it was suggested that the epicanthal fold (i.e., the single lid) was an impediment to the physical functioning of the eye, but most commentary focused on other effects—aesthetic, and also social and affective. The cosmetic surgeon Uchida wrote in 1955, "The double-lidded eye is bright, big, and replete with modern beauty, whereas the single-lidded eye is narrow, lacking in expression, and gives the observer a feeling of insufficiency." Or as Umezawa elaborated in a 1956 essay on cosmetic surgery:

> As for why the single lid is disliked, it goes without saying that when the upper lid is too long and drooping, not only does the eye become narrow, but it appears cold, lacking in charm and kindness, and deficient in cheer and vitality, and does not have the attractiveness of the double-lidded eye, which is big and bright and warm, filled with charm, and rich with an atmosphere of intelligence.[25]

In sum, descriptions of the double-lidded eye commonly stressed the way it expressed or communicated to others certain desirable mental and emotional

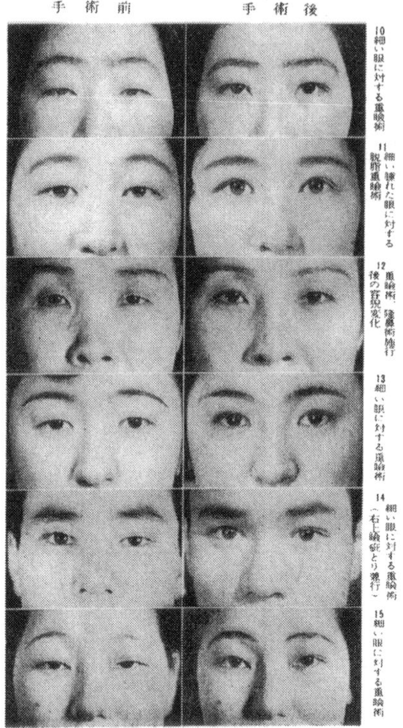

Figure 12.2. From Uchida Jun'ichi's 1955 book on cosmetic surgery, *Biyō seikei*. The "before" column (left) shows a series of patients afflicted with "narrow eyes" (*hosoi me*). Photographs in the "after" column (right) document the results of double-eyelid surgery. In one case, third from the top, the patient has also received a nose job. The surgery performed on the patient fifth from the top (who appears to be a man) is said to have addressed a flaw in his right upper eyelid, in addition to giving him double eyelids.

qualities of its bearer—such as intelligence, vitality, cheerfulness, and emotional warmth. The single-lidded eye, by contrast, was considered to express little.

It was regularly claimed, further, that the larger, more expressive double-lidded eye—and the qualities or affects that it expressed—were more modern. The question of when and how a Japanese modernity might be fully achieved was debated widely in the early postwar years. The tumult of the previous several decades, and especially the enormous task of rebuilding the nation after 1945, set the stage for an almost obsessive effort by many intellectuals to identify what had gone wrong with the modernizing project in the past and how to right it for the future. Any and all aspects of Japanese society and culture were subject to critical study and analysis along these lines—and perhaps particularly those aspects, such as the way people dressed and thought about their bodies, that permeated daily life at the most intimate, fundamental level. For a number of commentators, dramatic recent changes in the way women looked, especially, provoked efforts to make sense of Japanese beauty culture as part of a larger historical progression.

Perhaps the most fully developed analysis of this type was offered by Yamato Yūzō in 1950. Yamato, a senior journalist and editor at a major newspaper, drew attention in that year for his book *Face: A Cultural History of Expression and*

Make Up, in which he proposed a sweeping historical-materialist argument to explain changes in beauty culture through the ages.[26] His discussion began with an account of the face in ancient times around the world and went on to dwell at length on the "feudal face" in Japan as well as Europe. As he argued, "The face is a social phenomenon in a concrete, and not merely abstract, sense" and is shaped first and foremost by the economic conditions of daily life. Furthermore, Yamato insisted, facial ideals along with faces change in a direction reflecting the history of social development, although in a manner complicated by regional unevenness and the survivals of older social forms.[27] Yamato's debt to Marxist historiography is especially clear in his analysis of the modern Japanese face, which he called semifeudal. According to him, from the late nineteenth century through the 1940s, Japanese continued to cultivate a peculiar, mask-like expressionlessness in their faces, mostly as a consequence of the anomalous survival of feudal social and cultural forms within an industrializing, capitalist society. The militarism of World War II only served to exacerbate the semifeudal tendency to suppress emotion and also individuality from the modern Japanese face.[28]

Yamato conceded that race and anatomy play some role, but his emphasis was on the environmental influence of social change: "Of course, considered physically and anthropologically, the Japanese face is flat and has small eyes and protruding cheekbones; however there is an apathy in the face that cannot be explained solely by biology or anthropology."[29] Despite the distortions and delay caused by feudal remnants and total war, Yamato concluded that the Japanese face was finally becoming truly modern, in the sense defined universally by industrial capitalism and epitomized by the United States. The modern face, which first began to appear among intellectuals in urban Japan during the 1910s and 1920s and then spread throughout society in the postwar era, is characterized primarily by individuality and expressiveness. The change was to be found, Yamato claimed, in the eyes above all. Unlike the "doll-like" eyes of the feudal and semifeudal face, modern eyes are highly mobile, have a sharp and penetrating glance, and are full of depth and light. They express the complex interior life and ratiocination produced in individuals by increasingly specialized, mechanized forms of labor; the modern educational system; and other features of industrial society.[30]

Although somewhat idiosyncratic, Yamato's analysis reflected a more general consensus that the rapid changes in the way postwar men and especially women looked—and wanted to look—belonged to a single evolutionary process of modernization. Japan's progress on the path defined by Euroamerican development could be measured, in other words, by changes to Japanese bodies. The conspicuously expressive eye was paramount, but the nose was also important—as a feature capable of giving the face what was widely considered to be another requisite of modernity: dimensionality. Yamato himself wrote later, in an article for the women's magazine *Fujin kōron,* that modern beauty as it first began to emerge among educated women in the Taishō period, later developing into the mainstream, was notable not only for "a gaze with depth" (*fukami no aru manazashi*) but also for "sharply defined features" (*hori no fukai eikakuteki yōbō*).[31]

Nishida Masaaki, another authority on the modernization of the Japanese body, developed a theory in his 1954 book, *New Women's Beauty* (*Shin josei bi*), about dimensionality (*rittaikan*) as the major factor distinguishing Japanese and Western body ideals and practices. Prominent noses, eyes, foreheads, and—in women—breasts and even fingernails were emphasized in Western bodily aesthetics, whereas Japanese tradition valued one-dimensionality or flatness (*heimenkan*). Although Nishida, the originator of a field of study derived from European art anatomy that he called human body aesthetics (*jintai bigaku*), tried to be evenhanded in his assessment of the relative merits of dimensional and flat aesthetics, it was difficult for him to avoid concluding that dimensionality was modern, as well as Western, and therefore Japanese ideas about the body were changing, and should change, accordingly. He wrote, "At present culture is gradually becoming global ('universal'), and because Euroamerican culture is the leader, we—a later-developing country [*kōshinkoku*]—must follow and imitate it." Nishida wrote his book in part to ensure that such followership was as intelligently selective as possible, but his position was ultimately one of advocacy for a judiciously Japanese form of modern, or Western-style, physical beauty: dimensional, expressive, mobile, symmetrical, and healthy.[32]

Here again, for Nishida and others, the assumption was that all societies could be located at different points on a single process of development; Japan, in its

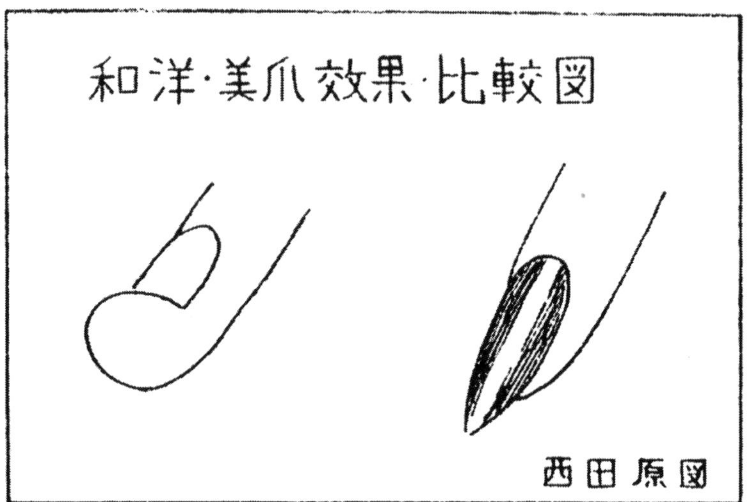

Figure 12.3. Nishida Masaaki, *Shin josei bi.* This illustration is titled "Comparison of the Effects of the Beautiful Japanese and Western Fingernail." The ideal Western fingernail, *right,* achieves an effect that is more "dimensional" (*rittaiteki*) than that of the short, unvarnished Japanese fingernail, *left.*

intermediate position between barbarous backwardness and civilized modernity, was finally catching up. Maruo Chōken, another authority on women's bodies, gave this idea his own spin in a 1957 article in which he proposed a three-part evolutionary scheme. He claimed that primitive peoples such as "Hottentots" (an early modern Dutch name for the natives of Southwestern Africa) have a primitive aesthetic sensibility closely tied to sexual reproduction, and for this reason female beauty is defined by the body, especially by large buttocks and breasts. In a second, more advanced stage, attention shifts to the female face—but only "idiotically submissive" faces that seem to promise subservience to men (such as the faces to be seen in medieval paintings and *ukiyo-e*) are valued. Finally, Maruo concluded, modernity is the age of the "whole body," not merely the face. He cited the French movie star Brigitte Bardot as a good example of the most advanced standard of beauty, in which both face and body are necessary as the means of expressing a woman's individuality. Maruo noted that Japanese women might be worried about the new importance of the body since their bodies are comparatively "meager," but in fact they should realize that now they have at their disposal greater means—no longer only the face—with which to express themselves (*jiko hyōgen*).[33]

"Everyone Can Become Beautiful"

The ideas of beauty authorities were influential in early postwar Japanese society because they reached a mass audience, thanks to the enormous expansion of publishing and other forms of popular media, and because they resonated with key themes and concepts already circulating within the larger culture. By identifying the post-1945 proliferation of larger eyes and noses as a legitimate aspect of rapid Japanese progress toward true modernity, for example, beauty doctors and theorists confirmed the narrative of Japan's Western-style modernization that was reasserted widely after World War II. Similarly, the beauty ideals they urged—of individuality (*kosei*), expressiveness, dimensionality, and mobility—were closely connected to the new, post-1945 orthodoxies of a U.S.-sponsored capitalist democracy. Women, in particular, were the focus of a new discourse of emancipation promoted as much by liberal Japanese intellectuals and activists as by the American reformers who busied themselves with "democratizing Japan" during the years of Allied occupation. The new beauty culture, which encouraged women to assert themselves as individuals, to express themselves freely, to become physically larger, and to move their faces and bodies more vigorously, translated occupation-era reforms into the intimate planes and gestures of daily life.

At the same time, the 1950s beauty project for individual women and men was consonant with a reviving nationalism. Even as postwar beauty culture in Japan was shaped by older Euroamerican ideologies of race and development according to which the Asian body was deficient and backward, it worked to adapt those ideologies to the transwar vision of an upwardly mobile Japan capable of regional and even global supremacy. The postwar theories of many beauty scientists and intellectuals, and the assumptions underpinning much of the beauty discussion in the mass media, accordingly emphasized the malleability of the body and the relative weakness of biological and genetic determinants of physical appearance. Race was less important, according to this way of thought, than social progress and advances in technology. There was a critical, emancipatory potential to the 1950s impulse to reject racial determinism, just as there had been within Japanese imperialism before 1945, but in both cases that potential was mitigated by adherence to ideas about beauty—and the world—that continued to rely upon established racist hierarchies.[34]

By the early 1950s, even so staid a publication as *Housewife's Companion* (*Shufu no tomo*), one of the largest and most influential women's magazines, was running articles on the importance of developing one's own individual beauty. In the September 1954 issue, for example, a beautician and a dress researcher explained the "secrets" of "beauty for the new age": "The requirement for the new beauty is to emphasize your individuality, the goodness that is yours alone." "Tricks" (*kotsu*) included having the confidence to take "little risks" with new colors and hairstyles, affirming yourself "even if your nose is flat," and finding ways to "make your eyes say something."[35] While long-established, respected women's magazines such as *Shufu no tomo* and the higher-brow *Fujin kōron* approached the topic of cosmetic surgery more cautiously than many other periodicals, both regularly ran articles promoting the new ideals and acquainting readers with the surgical methods for achieving them. The well-known cosmetic surgeon Sakurai Rin wrote several articles for *Fujin kōron* during the 1950s. In 1952 he pointed out, in a piece on "the new beauty medicine," that the key to the effective use of cosmetic surgery and other techniques was "to know one's own so-called individuality." In particular, the eyes, "which express a person's individuality so directly that they are called windows to the soul," should be considered with special care.[36] The pervasiveness of "individualism" as a beauty concept is suggested, additionally, by the ubiquity of the term *kosei* in advertising directed at women. Even a weight-loss technique could be touted as a means of "bringing out youth and individuality" (*wakasa to kosei o ikasu*).[37]

Individuality was connected to expressiveness and mobility or animation. It was through movement, rather than stillness, that one's individuality was most fully and engagingly expressed. The participants in a round-table discussion of women's beauty published in the November 1954 issue of *Fujin kōron*, for example, agreed on a basic distinction between "still beauty and active beauty" and complained of the tendency in Japan to value only still or "static" (*sutateikku*) facial beauty. Satta Kotoji, a Tokyo University professor of phonetics, observed that Japanese failed to move their mouths enough when speaking, causing their faces to lack expression. "Even Japanese movie actresses, however beautiful, lack facial expression, because they enunciate in such a restrained way," he said. The American actress Audrey Hepburn was truly beautiful in spite of her many physical flaws, he opined, precisely because of her animation and expressiveness. The link between new beauty ideals and new social ideals for women was made clear at the close of the discussion, when the participants agreed that confidence, pride, and self-respect—such as that felt by active, working women—ensured the right sort of dynamic beauty.[38]

Dimensionality, with mobility and expressiveness, was celebrated in postwar women's bodies as well as faces. One weekly news magazine from 1956 featured an article on the recent transformation of female bodies in which the author emphasized the new "dimensional" (*rittaiteki*) beauty to be seen in the "narrow" and "deeply carved" (*kezuri no fukai*) faces and the taller, more voluptuous bodies of modern Japanese women. Drawing upon the work of Nishida Masaaki, the author attributed most of the changes to the Westernization of daily life, and especially to the "liberation" of women from the confinement of native dress and hairstyles.[39] The idea that women's bodies were becoming dimensional and expressive in a manner linked to their social and psychic emancipation was even more explicit in a 1954 article that focused on the new fashion to "reveal unashamedly the two projections of the breasts." The author of this piece, citing a dress designer on—again—the "still" nature of Japanese clothing as compared to the "movement" of Western-style dress, noted that "Japanese dress has a feudal significance related to the shutting up of women in the home, but also just by looking at it one can see that it is unhealthy in the way it ignores the body 'silhouette.'" By contrast, the natural, visible bulging of breasts and hips is "healthy" and even, a psychologist is quoted as saying, suggests the "expression, in a good sense, of women's desires." In sum, the author declared, "Clothing, as well as the world, is crying out: 'Women! Puff out your chests [*josei yo mune o hare*]!'"[40]

小さいバスト　「ああ、うらやましい！」
鼻と胸　「あの子のは配置をまちがえたんだな。惜しい。」

Figure 12.4. Two cartoons from an article on breasts in *Shūkan josei,* September 1, 1957. The caption to the cartoon on the left, which depicts a small-breasted woman looking at a sumo wrestler, reads, "Small bust [*basuto*] 'Oh, I'm jealous!'" In the cartoon on the right, the woman's nose is shaped like a breast, while her breasts are the shape of ideal noses. The caption reads, "Nose and Chest 'Things are misplaced on that girl. Too bad.'"

Thus, the new beauty culture was, most observers agreed, linked to a more equitable relation between the sexes and to the liberation of women from the oppressive gender norms of a "feudal" past. There was also the suggestion that it resisted older hierarchies of class, as well as gender, and helped to promote a more just and democratic society. For example, the practice of holding beauty contests, which became enormously popular in 1950s Japan as in many other parts of the world, was generally considered to be socially progressive. Again, it seemed to be connected to the emancipation of women, who were asserting themselves, and their bodies, publicly. However, the more generally democratic implications of a competition open to all comers, based upon apparently objective measures applied by a panel of judges (or even, in some cases, by popular vote), were just as striking to contemporary commentators. As one writer began a 1953 magazine article on the fad for beauty contests, "The Greek gods praised Venus, who emerged from the emerald sea, as the goddess of beauty; beauties of the democratic present-day, however, are born from the voices of the people."[41] Even the bathing suit competition impressed some, such as the writer Itō Sei, writing for a 1952 issue of *Fujin kōron,* as laudably egalitarian: "Wearing only a bathing suit, the rich man's daughter is judged by the same standard as the poor man's daughter, and this is something truly humane."[42]

More fundamentally, early postwar beauty culture promised men as well as women that good looks—and the social benefits they conferred—were finally accessible to all, thanks to modern progress. Over and over, the message was repeated that in a truly modern society, it was possible for anyone to make himself or herself beautiful at will, and no one need any longer be condemned by birth to a life of physical and therefore social and psychic inferiority. Cosmetic surgeons were assiduous in promoting the idea that medical advances were bringing about a new age in which women in particular could be "freed from the evil spell of 'facial destiny,'" as Umezawa Fumio put it in 1953. He proposed, further, an analogy to wealth: now, instead of depending on inherited beauty, a woman could create her own assets.[43] The relevance to democratic ideals was clear, as was the emphasis on the importance of individual agency and autonomy in civilized modernity. A 1955 *Shufu no tomo* article instructing readers on the exercises and other beauty techniques used by fashion models used proposed that while beauty was to some extent an accident of birth, "surely, in this civilized world of today, we can remake and beautify our own bodies."[44]

In 1950s Japan it was frequently suggested that to actively cultivate one's own appearance was to participate fully in the enlightened, modern enterprise of self-improvement. To do so by having recourse to modern medicine and technology was only to underscore the point: a modern individual exercised his or her autonomy in a modern, technologically advanced society in order to achieve the happiness promised by modernity.[45] Nor was plastic surgery the only modern technology enlisted in the new projects of self-transformation. For example, women's magazines and even general-interest publications of the mid-1950s eagerly covered the introduction of French beauty technologies, such as new cosmetics like mascara or spa-type water and massage treatments purchased in beauty "salons."[46] Another new technology that attracted much attention during this period was that of exercise science, or physical culture. "Beauty exercises" (*biyō taisō*) were promoted widely, as for example on NHK Radio, which broadcast a popular thirty-minute *biyō taisō* show six mornings a week beginning in 1954.[47] The utopian promise of human happiness through modern science could justify even the use of technologies associated with the atomic bombs. An article in a 1955 issue of the popular weekly *Shûkan yomiuri,* for example, was titled "Nuclear Power Also Creates Beauties: Method of Removing Birthmarks Using Isotopes." After reviewing several success stories involving young women distressed by facial birthmarks, the author concluded by noting that isotope treatment—or the direct application of radioactive substances such as phosphorus-32—could also remove warts and moles and "painlessly" depilate armpits.[48]

The enthusiastic adoption of beauty science in Japan was represented as partly belonging to the larger process of "following" the Western powers, which were further advanced along the path to modernity. Hence, as in the article on isotope treatments, beauty technologies were often identified—and legitimated—by reference to their origins in the West (the isotope treatment, it was noted, had been developed and used in the United States). Yet following other nations could also lead to catching up—and even surpassing. It was possible to accept the European model of linear progress by racial-national entities from barbarity to modernity, and even the premise that Japan was delayed on that trajectory without concluding that backwardness or followership was a permanent condition. Perhaps less obvious is the point that similarly, it was possible to accept European understandings of racial difference and hierarchy without necessarily concluding that the racial characteristics (and inferiority) of a given population were immutably fixed. 1950s beauty culture helped to promote the idea that physical improvement could be undertaken at the national as well as individual level and indeed that Japan was rapidly progressing toward a beautiful bodily modernity comparable and even superior to that of the Western nations.

Thus, Japan's eager and highly organized participation in the major international beauty contests that were founded in the early 1950s—Miss Universe (held in the United States) and Miss World (in England)—should be understood at least in part as a competitive assertion of the national body. The women who were sent each year to compete in London and in Long Beach, California, were atypically tall and full-bodied and invariably sported very light skin, dimensional noses, and double-lidded eyes, but they also tended to be seen as legitimate representatives of a rapidly developing native beauty distinct from that of white Westerners. As national confidence grew over the course of the 1950s, so too did the possibility that difference could be compatible with equality and even superiority.

A 1959 round-table discussion published in *Fujin kōron,* for example, had as its theme the idea of a "five-year plan" to raise the level of women's beauty in time to "astonish foreigners" at the 1964 Olympics, which were to be held in Japan. Although its premise was somewhat jocular, the discussion took seriously the idea that women's bodies were improving rapidly and steadily and also that in aggregate Japanese women compared favorably to women in Euroamerican countries. One participant, the painter Itō Shinsui, stated to general agreement that "I've been abroad, and on the whole Japanese women are prettier; they do have beauties over there, but on average there are more in Japan." There was further agreement on the idea that Japanese female beauty "kept longer"—"foreign women deteriorate after the age of 25, and by 30 they're all fat." All the more reason, then, that Japanese should abandon efforts to emulate foreigners and instead seek to develop their own distinctive look. As the well-known cartoonist Kondō Hidezō concluded, "Instead of pointlessly imitating foreigners, manifest more your own original quality [*dokusōsei*], by choosing to wear things that suit you [such as kimono] because if you just indiscriminately put on their things you will all look ugly to them when they come in five years' time."[49]

The Price of Beauty

In the end, the vision of true, liberating beauty for all was vitiated in several key respects. Whether in its resistance to colonialist ideologies of race or in its stance toward the oppression of social hierarchies of gender and class, postwar Japanese beauty culture was highly ambivalent and even contradictory. By continuing to promote body ideals first shaped by the early industrializing imperialist powers of the West, Japanese beauty culture proved itself to be compatible with renewed Euroamerican global hegemony, even as it held out the possibility of Japanese bodies that might challenge that hegemony. At the same time, the dynamic growth during the 1950s of a commercialized complex of beauty goods, media, and technologies contributed to new forms of Japanese national influence in the region and beyond. Finally, Japan's rise after 1945 as an economic and "cultural" power was based to a large degree, like the military-political power of the pre-1945 imperial state, on the mobilization of a disciplined mass of consumer-workers. The rapid spread of beauty commodities and practices throughout Japanese society played an important role in generating consent to that mobilization and discipline.

At times, for example, the insistence on personal individuality and its expression actually seemed to encourage new forms of physical standardization and regimentation. Articles from the mass-market *Shufu no tomo* offered beauty advice and instruction that were often at odds with the ostensible goal of expressing the self freely. The authors of a 1954 guide to "making the most of your individual beauty" asserted that there are various "types" (*taipu*, given as the reading for the Chinese character ordinarily read *kata*) of individual beauty, such as the "kind type," the "strong," the "cute," the "innocent," the "cheerful," and the "shy." It was necessary to discover which "type" one belonged to, so as to be able to groom and present oneself suitably. Noting that "it is quite difficult to know clearly what type of individuality one has," the authors even recommended that readers look about—"in the street, at the office, in movies"—for people who resembled themselves and then "observe them closely" so as to identify what sorts of dress, makeup, and even walking style were appropriate for the correctly, mimetically individuated self.[50]

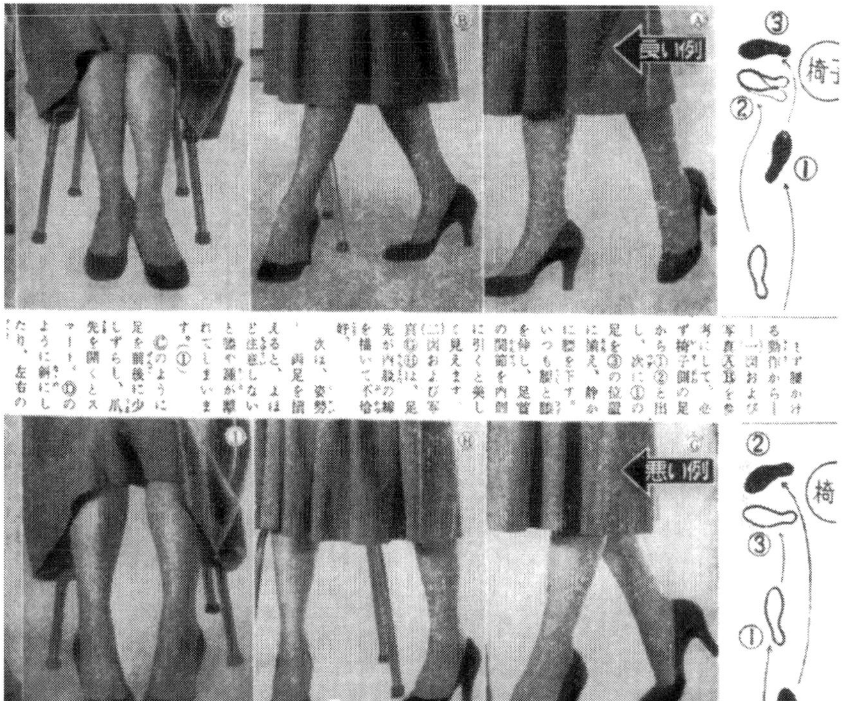

Figure 12.5. From an article on how to sit, in *Shufu no tomo,* April 1956. The three photographs, *top,* along with the diagram, depict a "good example" of sitting. The three photographs, *bottom,* with diagram, depict a "bad example."

The most ordinary gestures of daily life were subject, in this context, to critical scrutiny and discipline. In 1956 *Shufu no tomo* published a three-part series of articles under the general title "Charm Classroom to Make You Beautiful," which instructed readers on how to walk, sit, and talk. Diagrams along with photographs of "dos" and "donts" made clear that even sitting on a bench in Western dress while waiting for a train, for example, was properly—attractively—done in highly choreographed and stylized fashion.[51] Similarly, a Tokyo Charm School that opened in 1957 offered a three-month course promising to "give birth to women full of individual beauty." One journalist's account of the curriculum, which included a segment called Daily Life Performance (*seikatsu no engi*) in which pupils learned how to laugh becomingly and even how to look and behave when jilted by a lover, described the school as "a factory producing a commodity called 'charm.'"[52]

For a number of contemporary observers, accordingly, the new beauty culture suggested less the cultivation of individuality and difference and more the mechanical sameness of American-style mass production. The lead article of a 1954 issue of *Sandee mainichi,* titled "The Age of Mass-Produced Beauties," was largely critical of the standardizing, Americanizing tendency that seemed to be gaining influence in Japan and elsewhere.[53] The application of science and advanced technologies to the problem of beauty creation evoked dystopian possibilities of bodily transformations that might produce estrangement and alienation rather than attraction. In a 1953 novel by the popular writer Hayashi Fusao, for example, one of the main characters is a woman who has made herself unlovably, repellently beautiful by means of cosmetic surgery. Ironically, Hayashi suggested that by altering her features surgically, the character loses the ability to express her true emotions: "My smile is not from the heart. It is the smile of a mask. A smile is a flower that blooms from the bottom of the heart. No matter how ugly a girl is, in her smiling face the beauty of a wildflower blooms. I don't have that anymore." Less dramatically, but in the same vein, commentary on plastic surgery often noted the "coldness" and hardness of the look that was inadvertently caused by a more prominent, surgically reshaped nose.[54]

One suggestive insight by Yamato Yūzō hinted at another type of alienation. In his book *Kao,* Yamato discussed the "face of the object for sale" (*urimono no kao*) as a distinct modern type. Choosing as his example the photograph of a Western model from a fashion magazine, he wrote:

> The eyebrows are drawn up as much as possible. She's looking down her nose. The eyebrows are painted to increase the effect, but it's not just that; the muscles around the eyebrows are pulled up . . . This is the expression of showing oneself to people, of being looked at by people; this is what might be called the advertising expression of commercialism (*hōkokuteki shōgyōshugi no hyōjō*).[55]

Yamato pursued this logic to compare the expression on the fashion model's face to the novelist Mori Ōgai's description of the strangely undifferentiated, even inhuman faces of prostitutes he first observed as a child, in the nineteenth century. While it may be overstating the case to argue that 1950s beauty culture encouraged a project of self-prostituting commodification, Yamato's suggestion points to the way that beauty ideals and beauty practices were increasingly embedded within consumer capitalism and mediated by commodity forms.

In the 1950s world, during the high Cold War era, participation in consumer capitalism was a highly politicized—and contested—act. For a nation struggling to recover from a catastrophic total war and foreign military occupation and located in a strategic hotspot between the United States and the Soviet Union, the question of the role played by commodities in daily life was especially fraught. To develop a mass beauty culture, complete with the American-style postwar trappings of scientific rationality and limited forms of emancipation for women as consumer-citizens, was also to promote and signal allegiance to the U.S.-led capitalist camp in the Cold War. Accordingly, Japanese participation in the Miss Universe and Miss World contests communicated a message of participation in the comity of liberal capitalist nations, even as it encouraged competitive nationalism. At the same time, however, the boom in beauty contests, like the booms in cosmetic surgery and other elements of beauty culture, mobilized ordinary Japanese in new ways that did not necessarily promote individual emancipation, or even wellbeing.

It may be argued that the forms of discipline promoted by postwar beauty culture were less rigorous than those imposed on Japanese bodies—especially female bodies—before 1945. If the girdles and tight dresses, suits and ties, and hard leather shoes of Western-style clothing in the 1950s were confining and uncomfortable, to many people they seemed freer and easier to wear than kimono and obi. Yet the advent of beauty medicine, especially, created and disseminated new practices of bodily discipline that exceeded those of the past in their intensity and even violence. The postwar popularity of cosmetic surgery meant that ever-increasing numbers of people went "under the knife" to achieve the expressive features of face and body that conformed to a modern standard of beauty. Further, although many more men subjected themselves to cosmetic surgery than is usually acknowledged, it is clear that the most aggressive and dangerous forms of beauty medicine were experienced disproportionately by women. The enlargement of breasts by means of injections of silicone and other substances, for example, was something of a Japanese specialty until the late 1960s, when word finally began to get out that liquid silicone was not in fact safely stable or inert within the body.[56] Similarly, the horrific case of one beauty doctor in Osaka, who ordered some strontium-91—a highly radioactive product of nuclear fission—from England in 1956 and began using it improperly to remove freckles and birthmarks, involved many more female than male victims. The story received wide publicity, in part because it seemed to illustrate a larger trend. Accounts of women suffering the consequences of botched unregulated cosmetic procedures became commonplace in the late 1950s popular press.[57]

For some among the many who desired neutrality for Japan among the Cold-Warring nations or who were sympathetic to socialism, the new beauty culture pointed to the costs of "alignment" with the Free World. One critic, the leftist author Ishigaki Ayako, observed in a 1959 article that Japanese cosmetic medicine, for which ordinary people were serving as "guinea pigs," was "distorted by competition, profiteering, and obsessive secrecy." She argued that the wish to make oneself beautiful was natural and proper: "There is nothing wrong with cosmetic surgery, any more than there is with putting on make up, and it is not shameful to want it." However, in capitalist Japan, men and women were driven to alter their appearance by restless, neurotic desires and dissatisfaction.

> Postwar society is apparently stable, but that stability does not have deep roots, and so vulgar human desires are whipped up one after another. Because they cannot sate their desires, people are filled with discontent, and then they think in desperation that at least they can change their bodies, or their eyes or noses, into something magnificent.

Ishigaki claimed that cosmetic surgery was equally popular in the Soviet Union: "In this respect, there is no [difference between] capitalism or socialism." Yet in Russia "people do not seek surgery for neurotic reasons, but rather to make the most of their own beauty and health, and because they seek to live fully."[58]

Ishigaki's somewhat idealized vision of Soviet beauty culture served to emphasize the "darkness" of conditions in Japan, where she noted that racial and national self-hatred was another motivating factor for those seeking cosmetic surgery. The fad for eyelid surgery was caused by "a sense of inferiority as Japanese, having lost the war, and by admiration of foreigners with their double eyelids."[59] For other commentators as well, the spread of new beauty standards and practices was a disquieting sign of Japan's submission to Western, and especially American, hegemony. In his influential 1956 book, *Zasshu bunka* (Hybrid culture), the progressive critic Katō Shūichi wrote, "If Japanese women come to believe that the more they resemble American women the more beautiful they are, and if they then labor to make themselves resemble American women, even resorting to bogus techniques [*inchiki no jutsu*] in order to deceive the eye, and if that trend spreads like a contagion, then the influence on the national sentiment is even greater than that of a military surrender." Because "politically, economically, militarily, and technologically Japan is today nothing more than a satellite of the United States," Katō added, the only hope for national independence is in the realm of aesthetics. To allow American standards of beauty to govern Japan is therefore to give up everything—a true "unconditional surrender."[60]

Conclusion

Despite Katō's fears, postwar beauty culture was not a novel scourge presaging the loss of Japanese national independence or cultural autonomy. Rather, as I have argued, it grew out of prewar beauty culture, in ways that offer insight into the continued layering and interweaving of European, North American, and Japanese power in East Asia. The full scope of the impact of Japanese beauty ideas, practices, and goods in colonial and postcolonial East Asia awaits further research, but there is enough evidence to conclude with a sketch of their transwar persistence and development.

A recent study notes that cosmetic surgery first appeared in China in the 1930s; it was "with the invasion of Japan and other imperialist countries" that Japanese as well as Chinese surgeons began to perform cosmetic procedures such as "double-eyelid blepharoplasty, rhinoplasty, cheek dimple creation, and breast augmentation" in Shanghai and elsewhere.[61] Japanese beauty culture, including cosmetic surgery, certainly became influential throughout an early twentieth-century East Asia dominated by what I have called layered empire and especially by a rising Japanese colonialism. After 1945, cosmetic surgery only continued to grow in popularity—in Japan and also in the region at large.

It seems clear, moreover, that postwar developments in Japan played an important role in promoting cosmetic surgery in East and Southeast Asia.[62] In the late 1950s, the Japanese popular press reported as much, with accounts of Southeast Asian and Chinese patients and doctors flocking to Japanese cosmetic surgeons in order to receive surgeries or learn how to perform them.[63] Of course, Japanese sources announcing the leadership of Japanese culture in Asia must be read with caution. But there is corroborating evidence that a growing audience, and

49. "Orinpikku made no josei bi gokanen keikaku," *Fujin kōron*, supplement, August 1959, 130–134. The discussion also dwelled at some length on the idea that Japanese women look best in a kimono and that their improved postwar bodies were creating a new sort of kimono-clad beauty.

50. Nanbu Aki and Ushiyama Kikuko, "Dare de mo bijin ni nareru," *Shufu no tomo*, September 1954, 352–353.

51. Noguchi Michizō and Miyakawa Mutsuko, "Anata o utsukushiku suru miryoku kyōshitsu: Kakekata," *Shufu no tomo*, April 1956, 216–217. The first of the series, on walking, appeared in the February issue and the third, on talking, in the May issue.

52. "Tōkyō chiyāmu sukūru," *Shūkan shinchō*, May 19, 1958, 36–41.

53. "Bijin ryōsan jidai," *Sandee mainichi*, January 10, 1954, 3–11.

54. Hayashi Fusao, *Musuko no endan* (Tokyo: Shinchōsha, 1954), 236. On the coldness of the altered, larger nose, see, for example: "Bijin wa kō shite tsukurareru," *Shufu no tomo*, May 1953, 304; "Utsukushiku naru tame no igaku," *Sandee mainichi*, February 19, 1956, 5; and Ishigaki Ayako, "Biyō seikei no jinsei biron," *Fujin kōron*, August 1959, supplement 37.

55. Yamato, *Kao: kao hyōjō keshō no bunkashi*, 228–229.

56. Haiken, *Venus Envy*, 247–250.

57. "Josei no kyōfu: Sutoronchiumu 90: Yarisokonatta biyō seikei no chiryō?," *Shūkan yomiuri*, June 30, 1957, 20–21; "Seikei biyō wa doko made shinyō dekiru ka?," *Fujin kōron*, June 1957, 238–243; "Watakushi no kao o kaeshite: Bi o meguru isha to josei no arasoi," *Shūkan shinchō*, November 4, 1957, 48–53; "Aru biyō seikei ga maneita wazawai," *Shūkan josei*, October 5, 1958, 12–14.

58. Ishigaki Ayako, "Biyō seikei no jinsei biron," *Fujin kōron*, supplement, August 1959, 36–41.

59. Ibid., 37.

60. Katō Shūichi, *Zasshu bunka: Nihon no chiisa na kibō* (Tokyo: Kōdansha, 1956), 193, 194. The final chapter of the book, from which the quotes are taken, was originally published as an essay titled "Mujōken kōfuku to hattōshin," in the May 1956 issue of the women's magazine *Fujin asahi*.

61. Wen Hua, *Buying Beauty: Cosmetic Surgery in China* (Hong Kong: Hong Kong University Press, 2013), 30. The reference to Japan comes from a source quoted by Hua, who otherwise ignores Japanese influence on Chinese cosmetic surgery almost completely and insists instead on direct transmission from U.S. plastic surgeons. In part this reflects a tendency by established medical practitioners and institutions to marginalize commercial "beauty medicine" and emphasize instead the authority of (Western) science.

62. See, for example, the discussion of plastic surgery in South Korea in John P. DiMoia, *Reconstructing Bodies: Biomedicine, Health, and Nation-Building in South Korea since 1945* (Stanford, CA: Stanford University Press, 2013), 185–190.

63. "Wandafuru Nippon no biyō seikei," *Shūkan josei*, June 1, 1958, 24–25.

64. Khoo Boo-chai, "The Complications of Augmentation Mammaplasty by Silicone Injection," *British Journal of Plastic Surgery* 22, no. 3 (July 1969): 281–285.

65. On the use of the Sakurai formula in the United States, see H. D. Kagan, "Sakurai Injectable Silicone Formula," *Archives of Otolaryngology* 78 (November 1963): 53–58; and Sakurai Rin, "Seikei biyō i no kiroku," *Fujin kōron*, January 1960, 250–255. Sakurai's visits to Thailand are described also in "Wandafuru Nippon no biyō seikei," *Shūkan josei*, June 1, 1958, 24.

66. Sakurai, "Seikei biyō i no kiroku," 254.

67. L. Ayu Saraswati, *Seeing Beauty, Sensing Race in Transnational Indonesia* (Honolulu: University of Hawai'i Press, 2013), 37–59, 62–66, 115.

Implied Promises Betrayed

"Intraracial" Alterity during Japan's Imperial Period

Even as Japan expanded its formal empire through force, it was also engaged in a process of "peaceful expansion" by which the state encouraged, and in some cases subsidized, the migration of its citizens abroad with no intention of challenging the sovereignty of the target nations. The primary destinations of these migration processes were countries in need of unskilled labor, including the United States, Canada, Australia, and from 1908, Brazil. Having recently lost access to its primary source of cheap labor for coffee plantations, Italy, the Brazilian government encouraged immigration from Japan, which was considered a tolerable substitute in the absence of "white" labor. Due in part to the fact that the United States (in particular, but not solely) had begun to curtail immigration from Japan, a large number of individuals migrated to Brazil with coordinated support from both governments. The result was a large-scale population shift that placed Japanese subjects in direct contact with pronounced heterogeneity of various types. This chapter explores the resulting literary representations of alterity against this historical backdrop. What these representations reveal, unsurprisingly, is that "race" is a central concern; perhaps counterintuitively, however, the writers seem to be preoccupied with intraracial, rather than interracial, alterity.[1] This, I suggest, is prompted not merely by a fear of the instability of identity itself but also by a recognition that the implied solidarity of racial identity did not, in fact, vouchsafe preferential treatment.

Within a decade of the arrival of the first migrants in 1908, Japanese-language newspapers had appeared, many of which contained fiction and poetry—some from Japan, others composed in Brazil. With active support from these local newspapers, which encouraged writers to submit works about their new lives in Brazil, literature quickly became one venue in which first-generation immigrants from Japan worked through the ramifications of their dramatically altered circumstances.[2] These works not only represented individuals marked as Other—primarily, but not solely in terms of race—but also reappraised what could be expected from the relationships with individuals thought to be racially identical. This chapter will focus on three works in particular: "The Death of a Certain Settler" (ある開拓者の死, 1932) by Nishioka Kunio (西岡國雄), "An Age of Speculative Farming" (賭博農時代, 1932) by Sonobe Takeo (園部武夫), and "Tumbleweeds" (転蓬, 1940) by Furuno Kikuo (古野菊生).[3] Today, these three texts are among a very small corpus that has been canonized, for want of a better term, as representative literary works produced in Japanese in Brazil prior to World War II. Part of this process has involved reproduction: between 1966 and 1968, in the largest Japanese-language literary journal in Brazil; in 1975, in an anthology that appeared in book form; and in 2008, as part of a DVD-ROM circulated in conjunction with the Centenário, the celebration of the centennial anniversary of Japanese migration to Brazil.[4] They are among the only texts from the period still relatively accessible today.[5]

The stories show a sensitivity to racial, gender, and linguistic alterity; there is also an awareness of an economic alterity that exceeds simple disparity, as the writers describe exceptional degrees of privation and hardship. What perhaps is unexpected is that difference between racial categories and between languages plays a far less significant role in the stories than does intraracial and intralingual difference.[6] The stories show far greater concern with "acquired" alterity (defined below) and "postlapsarian" alterity (resulting from betrayals of bonds thought to be implied by racial filiation) than they do with threats posed by conventional racial alterity. An examination of these representations of alterity, which are often marked by a negative affective valence and an increased affective intensity, reveals a powerful sense of racial betrayal that stands in relief from any normative evaluations of racial Others that appear in the stories.

"The Death of a Certain Settler"

The first story, "The Death of a Certain Settler" by Nishioka Kunio, most closely conforms (at least at first glance) with a stereotypical narrative of the racial Other as both abject and threatening.[7] A settler, having just begun his triumphant return to Japan after achieving financial success in Brazil, is murdered, presumably by a non-Japanese worker. Rather than portraying the murdered settler sympathetically, however, the story depicts him in a highly unflattering light, perhaps even implying that the settler's brutal end was deserved; to the limited extent that the non-Japanese assailant is developed as a character, he is presented as being hard-working, honorable, and worthy of the reader's sympathies.

The story begins with a confrontation between the races: a Japanese landowner, Kaneko Daisuke, faces a man with "gleaming black" skin:[8]

> A man who seemed to be *baiano,* with a face that gleamed black, and a woman who was presumably his wife, with her belly hugely swollen, stood with their shoulders shrugged in front of his [Daisuke's] home. On the ground to their side was one *arroz saco* jammed with all of their worldly possessions and a large child, with a thin, monkey-like face and wide eyes, who sat staring uneasily at Daisuke.[9]

Although we discover later that the "nearly six-foot-tall" black man would be towering over Daisuke, this is not a case of the threatening Other; rather, it is Daisuke who is attempting to intimidate the visitor. The man has come to

Daisuke's home to ask for work so that he and his impoverished family might eat; Daisuke responds with aggression and condescension but in the end agrees to hire the man.

After Daisuke returns from the day working on his *cafezal* (coffee plantation) with the man and three other young Japanese laborers, they all sit down at a table with Daisuke's wife and son to share a meal. When Daisuke sees the man's wife staring in through the window, however, he calls out abusively, referring to her as a beggar (乞食奴), shouting at her to get lost, and asking if there is "any law that says that someone who doesn't work should eat?"[10] This prompts another confrontation with the man, who leaps up from his chair, glaring down at the diminutive Daisuke with his fists clenched. The man, quickly recognizing he can do nothing under the circumstances but defer to his master (支配者), unclenches his fists, collapses back into his chair, and appeals to the charity of his *patrão* (パトロン, boss). His wife, he pleads, has not eaten all day and cannot work because she is in the last month of her pregnancy. The man assures Daisuke that were he to feed her, in return the man would work even harder the next day. Daisuke remains firm but eventually fishes some coins from his purse and casts them on to the table. The man, wearing a markedly saddened expression, stands up and leaves with his family, refusing to acknowledge the coins.

It is interesting to note that in reflecting on these events the next day, Daisuke does not attribute the "unreasonable" demands of the man and his wife to their race; instead, he disparages the man's "womanly" sentimentality and the "impertinence" he believes the man shares with other young people. To the contrary, later in the story Daisuke states that in the future he intends to hire only *baiano* laborers, who while potentially dangerous, are perfect for "taking advantage of"; simultaneously, he differentiates them from "hairy foreigners" (毛唐人), who will pull out a knife without the least provocation, and Japanese, who are not dangerous but are constantly quibbling.

This confrontation is followed by a second, briefer interaction with racial alterity, which in its positioning is implicitly contrasted with the first. Three or four blue-eyed children, "the sort one sees in the *colônia* on the other side of the mountain," come asking to buy oranges from the trees on Daisuke's property.[11] When they produce a one-*mil* coin, Daisuke stands up and gets them a stick, which the tallest uses to knock down the fruit. Chiding them for knocking so many down, Daisuke counts the fruit off one by one as he puts them in their bag. The scene reinforces the idea that Daisuke is motivated not by racial animosity but instead by imperiousness, greed, and parsimony. While the blue eyes mark the children as being either white or *mestiço* (multiracial) children, producing the option of reading this as differential racial treatment, the story does not explore this further.

After these interactions, the story devotes itself to Daisuke's drunken recounting of his life to an audience of young Japanese men as he prepares for his first trip back to his hometown in Japan in twenty-eight years. Throughout the narrative, Daisuke goes to great lengths to establish that his success is the result of his own labors, often explicitly rebutting assertions by other Japanese that it was the result of luck. We learn that Daisuke, born in Hokkaido in the early 1880s (the narrative never exactly establishes the years) to a former samurai turned millet farmer, left home at the age of twenty. After two years in Tokyo, he begins a process of serial migration: first to Manchuria; then to Lima, Peru (where he is a barber to "hairy foreigners"); then to Chile (where he works mining nitratine for fertilizer); and to Buenos Aires before finally moving to Brazil because he had heard it was "friendly to Japanese." After a dramatic change of attitude, when he realizes he needs to think about the future, he begins to save his carpenter's pay diligently and eventually buys land.

Having purchased the land sight-unseen, he, his wife, and his young son head inland to begin their new lives. At that time the existing train line did not yet reach all the way to the property, so the three of them are forced to hike forty kilometers through dense growth while carrying their supplies. Daisuke acknowledges the relief he felt when they encountered the home of "an Italian" thirty kilometers in and describes the man's generosity toward Daisuke and his family. As Daisuke points out to his audience (without any apparent awareness of the hypocrisy), "deep in the mountains, any man you encounter is a brother."[12] Thanks to the chickens and pigs he purchases from the Italian, he and his family are able to survive until the train line is extended. Despite this fact he concludes his story by telling the young men that although people in their *colônia* believe he succeeded through luck, he, like all men, was made through his own efforts. Although it is not a central component of this story, we should note here that the young Japanese laborers to whom he is speaking are explicitly described as "copper-colored"; Daisuke's own face is described as "reddish black," the result of both intoxication and sun exposure. Though this skin color would be a natural effect of prolonged exposure to the sun in the course of agricultural labor, the fact that it warrants mention is our first indication of the importance of a discourse of acquired alterity, which is present in all of the stories under consideration here and which we will turn to in a moment.

On his last day before setting off on his trip to Japan—a trip in which he will achieve the clichéd goal attributed to many migrants to Brazil, that of eventually returning home "wearing a gold brocade" (錦を着て)—Daisuke visits the twenty-four families, including both *colonos* and four-year contract workers, living on his property.[13] It is at this point that Daisuke decides to contract only *baianos* upon his return, as he recalls an incident from the previous year in which an Italian *colono* had come after him with a knife after Daisuke had berated him. The night before his journey back to Japan he sets off for town, where he plans to spend the night in order to catch his early morning train the next day. On the way, however, he is confronted by a man who steps out from the dense growth on the side of the road. The narrative describes how something "flashed like lightning" amid his "crowded memories" as Daisuke sees the man's face. In the 2008 version of this story, it is not clear which of the many wronged men from Daisuke's past it might be. A shot is fired, Daisuke falls to the ground with a groan, and after a few slight shudders, his body lies still. The story closes a few days later, with a brief description of a new grave marker dedicated to Daisuke in the communal cemetery.

As mentioned, "The Death of a Certain Settler" superficially conforms to a narrative of the racial Other as both abject and threatening: the destitute black laborer, his desperate wife, and his silent child are placed in a position of abjection and supplication vis-à-vis the Japanese landowner; when the laborer is refused food for his wife, the men nearly come to blows. Later in the story, the racial Other—be he *baiano,* Italian, or some other "hairy foreigner"—is characterized as inclined to violence, and some abject subject or other (unclear in the 2008 version, though much clearer in the original, as I will argue) finally carries through on this implied threat of violence. Despite this basic narrative, however, the story clearly functions not to demonize the racial Other but rather to vilify the miserly, arrogant, and cruel Daisuke, who despite receiving kindness from others in his time of need—most notably from an Italian—refuses to acknowledge any ethical debt to those in a similar situation. The violence visited upon Daisuke is implicitly presented as a form of retribution for his vanity—in the end, his body lies on the ground clothed portentously in a "gold brocade covered with fresh blood"—for the economic violence to which he has subjected both Japanese and non-Japanese alike.

The editorial staff of the 1975 anthology made a number of changes to the original text of "Aru kaitakusha no shi," though most were attempts to make trivial corrections. Further—and more noteworthy—changes were introduced when the anthology was reproduced for inclusion on the DVD-ROM in 2008. One specific bowdlerization, which was introduced in the 2008 version, should be given particular attention: the removal of the adjective "black" as a descriptor of skin color. Sufficient information remains—the "gleaming black" face, the "black family," and the reference to the worker as a *baiano*—that the racial marking is preserved. The elimination, rather, seems to be a response to shifting normative attitudes about the propriety of terms denoting blackness, with the editors choosing in most cases to avoid them.[14]

In one way, however, the 2008 edition's concern with discriminatory language actually undermines the apparent intentions of its editors. In the final confrontation, when the figure emerges from the dense growth on the side of the road and is described (in the original and revised versions) as merely a "man," the sudden absence of the modifier "black" is very noticeable in early versions; in the 2008 version, where nearly all references to "black" have been excised, the absence is less conspicuous. Furthermore, when Daisuke sees the face of the man and experiences the shock of recognition, his (original) response is "Aah! That *ku . . .*"; the *ku* is removed from the revised version. In discussing this scene previously, I stated that it was ambiguous (in the 2008 version) who the shooter was; in earlier versions, however, something more complex is happening. The *ku,* I would argue, would likely be interpreted by readers as the first syllable of a racial slur for blacks, *kuronbō* (黒ん坊); the fact that the 2008 editors removed it suggests they may have interpreted it similarly.

This fragment, then, marks the shooter as being black, which when combined with the demonstrative "that" creates a strong likelihood that the assailant is the *baiano* who was wronged in the initial scenes of the story. This then makes the idiosyncratic and conspicuous usage of "man" (rather than "black man") all the more interesting; while it may have been an oversight on the part of the author, it is also possible to read the character as having become a stand-in, an instrument of justice who at that moment has transcended his individual race, for all of the individuals wronged by Daisuke. The racial Other becomes a faceless (or, more accurately, nameless) instrument of a cosmic order that punishes transgressions of an ethic that transcends the racial self-same.

"An Age of Speculative Farming"

While "The Death of a Certain Settler" clearly establishes a narratorial perspective of limited sympathy for its protagonist, it lacks the sustained affective intensity in response not only to alterity but also to intraracial betrayal that is present in Sonobe Takeo's "An Age of Speculative Farming."[15] The story was selected as the first-place recipient in the first Colonial Literary Short Fiction Award competition held by the *Burajiru jihō* newspaper. ("The Death of a Certain Settler" received second place.) The competition explicitly sought works that grappled with "the society of Japanese in Brazil today" that possessed "conditions that were completely different from those in Japan." The story certainly addresses contemporary society; it also dwells extensively on two of the same concerns that we have already seen: acquired alterity and intraracial betrayal. To this story is added a preoccupation with female sexuality and the ways in which it is seen as integrally tied to the other dangers lurking in this new, overtly heterogeneous space.

Unlike the preceding story, "An Age of Speculative Farming" is set in the city of São Paulo. The narrative focuses on a "mixed-blood" (混血児, glossed as アーイノコ [*sic*]) prostitute named Hanaoka Ruriko but also involves her wealthy patron, a tomato farmer and parvenu named Ōmura; his rival, the trader Kurose; and a young Japanese man, newly arrived in Brazil, who is kept by Hanaoka. The story opens with an unnamed vagabond (*vagabundo*)—a common term for young Japanese men who abandoned the life of an agricultural laborer in the countryside for the lures of the city—observing Hanaoka as she ignores a group of young thugs who yell out an epithet at her (whore [売笑婦], glossed as *puta* [プータ]). It is a sight, the text tells us, he sees often. The story first tells us a little about her tastes; we are told she likes "men, *sorvete,* cinema, smelling the soiled flesh of farmers, perverted sexual desire, collecting cheap jewelry."[16] We are then shown Hanaoka plying her trade in the center of São Paulo:

> A single seductive Oriental insect, she always weaves her way through the streets that make up this dizzying triangle. She moves constantly as a point on its sides, passing through the streets of Portuguese flesh—its blend of the

> Italian, French, Spanish, German, Russian, the black [*preto*], and more—passing through this entanglement of all the races, garbed in her single-cut dress and snake-skin shoes, exuding the secrets of her flesh through her transparent wrap.[17]

As she walks through this entertainment district, a new-model Ford suddenly pulls up in front of her. It is her lover, Ōmura, who (the text tells us, again) embraces her "with his soiled, farmer's flesh, which she loves."

The disgust in the narrative is palpable, and its objects are many. Even as the text disdains the proximity to (not to mention participation in) manual agricultural labor that is suggested by Ōmura's "soiled flesh," it is also repulsed by his immodest displays of wealth, as visible in its mention of the parvenu's new-model Ford. It evinces discomfort not only at the presence of multiple races but also by the potentially deleterious entangling (錯綜) of them. The text is also critical of the abusive urban youth who form the Conde gang, the beggars it describes populating the streets, and the "movie-crazy *señoritas*" Conrad Nagel woos from the screen of the Odeon Theater.[18]

More than anyone else, though, the story's disgust seems directed at Hanaoka. She has placed her chastity up for sale, the text laments, offering herself to a filthy farmer and perhaps even to the men of assorted and blended races who fill São Paulo's streets; worse yet, she seems to desire them sexually. She indulges in other vices as well, be it ice cream or the jewels that we later learn are her main reason for being with Ōmura—after all, the text reminds us, "even a monstrous love requires certain appurtenances."[19] All the while, she abuses (emotionally, verbally, and physically) the "stray dog"—a youth who has recently immigrated from Japan—who waits for her pathetically in her rooms (her "deviant playground") and lusts for her "lewd figure" even as (or perhaps precisely because) he knows that she has just been with other men. Most fundamentally, the text registers both derision and disbelief toward Hanaoka's body itself: when she finally takes a stand against Ōmura, the narrator opines that the fact "that Japanese blood circulated in Hanaoka Ruriko's rotting flesh was nothing short of a miracle."[20] As a multiracial subject, Hanaoka becomes an extreme embodiment of acquired alterity, in which the ethnic compatriot is only momentarily recognizable as such before its acquired alterity renders that racial affiliation irretrievable.

The text is at its most intense and experimental in the passages that describe Hanaoka and her overt sexuality, yet after the powerful opening section of the story, the narrative's attention is drawn to another object of disgust: the quest for profit at any cost and the concomitant exploitation of Japanese by Japanese. This obsession with profit explains the somewhat awkward title of the story. As Arata Sumu points out, "speculative farming" refers to the growing of crops (including tomatoes, potatoes, and onions) with an eye toward commodity speculation.[21] Contemporary Brazilian society, the title seems to be suggesting, has entered into a period in which agricultural capitalists practice a form of farming that speculates—literally, gambles (賭博)—on the market rather than (one presumes) engage in sustainable methods determined by organic demand. All of the people involved, the text tells us, make up a "band of crooks" (インチキの群); this is exemplified by Ōmura, who owns a vast tomato farm. Employing all manner of techniques—some of dubious ethicality—Ōmura has produced a large, out-of-season crop that he hopes to sell at market for a great profit. It is also a crop that is of little interest, as a food, to the Japanese laborers; instead, this is a "tomato farm operated by the clever *Nipponico* who encamped here and took advantage of the tastes of the meat-loving race."

In its criticisms of Ōmura's strategies, the text shows a nascent environmental conscience, seemingly concerned with practices that do not allow for sustained cultivation by men and women (particularly Japanese men and women) in such a way as to provide them with dignified livelihoods. The story signals this early on through a scene in which laborers encircle a large vat as they make a pesticide known as Bordeaux solution:

> One of the laborers dissolved quicklime into the solution, choking on the cloud of dust that billowed around him as he did. He then combined the dissolved lime with just the right amount of copper sulfate. The Bordeaux solution that resulted from the combination became an extremely faint blue, like that of the autumn sky in the laborer's hometown, making him sentimental. The greedy history of the immigrants who preceded him became an opaque precipitate; the endless exploitative competition swirled in the mixture, disappearing into the Bordeaux solution.[22]

The text describes the tomatoes as unable to excite the appetites of the exhausted workers who "bore the insecticide sprayers on their backs like debt" as they dusted the plants for three straight months. It describes the sprawling farm as one made possible by the "reckless dumping of chemical fertilizers" such as nitratine and potassium chloride. Ōmura's greed has left the soil "impoverished from the immoderate application of artificial fertilizers." Along with the manipulated drop in market price described below, in fact, "the rampancy of the macrosporum bacteria" and "the indignation of the soil" are explicitly given as the three factors that eventually come to determine the fate of the Ōmura farm.

Ōmura's plans are foiled, however, by the machinations of the *comprador* Kurose, who arranges an unusually low price for tomatoes on the day Ōmura brings in his crop. Kurose has conspired with the other buyers at the Mercado Central—the giant wholesale market in São Paulo, now called the Mercado Municipal—to hold their offered price at ten *mil réis* per crate, a price so low that its announcement leaves all of the farmers dazed. This is not simply a matter of collusion; the story informs us that Kurose has paid the buyers in order to secure their compliance, all with the goal of snubbing Ōmura in revenge for his refusal to accede to a deal Kurose had offered him earlier. Ōmura had been offended at Kurose's attempt to manipulate him; it had insulted Ōmura's pride: "It would be one thing if I were one of those wretched tomato farmers, but he needs to think about who he is talking to!"[23] The battle between these two elite egotists not only exacts a cost from each of them but also wreaks havoc on the subsistence tomato farmers caught up in the price manipulations.

The only group not subjected to the narrative's unadulterated disdain—the agricultural laborers who had migrated from Japan, choosing the "frightening customs officers" over the "sounds of gunfire in Manchuria"—is instead subjected to its pity and condescension. These include workers with hands "perpetually stained by tomato juice" and farmers who "live under fear of malnutrition." At one point the narrator laments spontaneously: "The bodies of agricultural laborers, bent by exhaustion!"[24] Some are themselves caught up in greed, including the "swarm of heroic *Nipponicos* who vie with one another, enslaved by their gambling savvy"—an imaginary savvy they begin to believe they too might possess when they see Ōmura's profit. The story explains how "anyone who did not move quickly to seize his portion of the wealth by producing tomatoes soon became the object of derision, as one ignorant of the ways of the world."[25] Despite this disdain toward their greed, the narrative voice finally sees all of these migrants as "merely ants" and thus pathetic rather than villainous. What is missing, the narrator suggests, is common purpose and unity of action: "When will the day finally come that those desultory ants gather and erect a towering anthill?"[26] In despair that to wait for such a day would be in vain despite the steady flow of shiploads of migrants from Japan, the narrative ends with a laborer (perhaps the *vagabundo* from the story's opening) taking in a deep breath and letting out a scream.

As the quotes above suggests, language in the story is marked throughout with value judgments and affective intensity. It is also filled with problematic terminology, almost all of which is maintained through to the DVD-ROM version. What is removed is unsurprising, given the examples from the previous story: while a reference to a "black woman" remains unchanged, the color of a "black doorman" is removed, as is Hanaoka's epithetic reference to him as a *kuronbo-me* when he tries to drive her off. Left unchanged are terms such as "mixed-blood child" (混血児)—though now without its more problematic gloss of "love child" (愛の子)—and "beggars" and "natives" (土人). A derogatory reference to physically impaired movement (ちんば、ちんばして) is removed but not a reference to "slow" (鈍重な) Brazilians. We also have the term *caboclo* (カボクロ), which appears here without any apparent derogatory intent (at one point, the sounds of a *caboclo*'s *bandolim* can be heard in the background), but that has a complex function in Brazilian racial discourse at this time.[27] Finally, we have a non-Japanese gendered epithet, *puta,* which is left unchanged. Perhaps the editors felt that the term loses expressive potency as it crosses language barriers.

The overwhelming sense conveyed by the story is one of disgust and despair: over migrants who are weak of spirit and solidarity, over female bodies that are deviant through both their desires and their descent, and over the willingness of Japanese to exploit other Japanese, in ways that can transcend simple greed and enter into the realm of viciousness, with no concern for collateral damage. Since the implied fictional interiority experiencing the emotional state that leads to this affective intensity is unclear—perhaps it is that of the *vagabundo* and worker characters that frame the story—the disgust and despair cannot be confined to a single character. There is no point of detachment made available by the narrative. The result is a sense that the story itself is a sort of cri de coeur.

"Tumbleweeds"

Furuno Kikuo's "Tumbleweeds" may be the only story written in prewar Brazil that ever reached a significant reading audience in Japan.[28] After having been published in July 1940 in the journal *Shin Burajiru,* it was subsequently republished in the June 1958 issue of the Tokyo literary journal *Bungei shuto.*[29] The story takes place aboard a ship sailing westward from the Americas and focuses on a group of Japanese emigrants who are returning to Japan, most from Brazil but some from other countries, including Argentina and the United States. The story begins as the ship passes south of the Aleutian Islands and concludes just as it enters Japan's territorial waters. In this depiction of bodies in transit, we see the complexity of the process we know as migration: in addition to the serial migration described in "The Death of a Certain Settler," we see diverse destinations of migration, multiple migrations involving trips to and from Japan, and the ill-named return migration of people of Japanese descent who may never have set foot in the country before.

As with earlier stories, while "Tumbleweeds" does present some instances of racial alterity—we know that there are non-Japanese in the first-class spaces above, and we hear about non-Japanese living alongside Japanese in the *colônia* back in Brazil—the story is almost entirely dedicated to the Japanese passengers and crew in the third-class sections of the ship. As with the previous works, the story's attention is firmly focused on acquired alterity and intraracial interactions. Unlike the earlier works, however, "Tumbleweeds" explicitly asserts a positive valence to acquired alterity and valorizes respectful coexistence. There are limits to this, however; while the focal figures valorize alterity produced by familiar exogenous elements, variant acquired alterity resulting from unfamiliar exogenous elements is met with less enthusiasm. That is, while individuals altered by their connection to Brazil are encouraged to embrace that difference, individuals altered by their connection to the United States, for example, are met with critique that, while not particularly hostile, is negative. The story's strongest criticisms, however, seem to be reserved for Japan.

In the course of the story, we meet a number of characters: the siblings João (age seventeen) and Luísa (age eight); Wakabayashi and his wife, Makiko; Tani, a college student from California; an unnamed former gardener for a rich family in Buenos Aires; and Akita, the character who acts as the focal figure for most of the story. While the information we are given about each of the characters is incomplete, the recounting of fragments from their pasts comprises much of the story, which depicts the coincidental gathering of these diverse individuals as they are about to enter a space of symbolic importance to all of them.

We learn that Akita was born in Japan and lived there long enough to receive his education but that he has since lived in Brazil for years. We know from references to her accent that his mother, who emigrated with Akita, is from Kyūshū. We are told that they lived together in rural Parana before he moved to the city of São Paulo. Finally, during the course of the voyage back to Japan we learn that Akita has decided to spend one month settling some affairs before returning permanently to Brazil to become a cowherd (牛飼い) in Sorocobana.[30] Of the Wakabayashi couple, we learn that they spent more than five years in a *colônia* in the interior of the state of São Paulo, where malaria and pneumonia took their young son's life and the husband's capacity to work. Despite wishing to remain in Brazil, where their child is buried, they have no choice but to accept their relative's offer of work in Sapporo.

The descriptions of João and Luísa's parents come from Akita's perspective. The mother is described as "the sort of housewife with her dry, matte hair up, her bare feet caked in mud, her toothless mouth hidden by her sealed lips, who works from dawn until late into the night."[31] In this regard, she resembles women Akita saw frequently in the *colônia:* "She too was one of those women who has worked continuously for decades, like a draft animal, having lost any trace of sentiment, knowing only the world of virgin jungle, cotton fields, and thatched huts."[32] The description of the children's father differs dramatically: when we see him (through Akita's eyes), he is described as having "skin the color of *a roxa* (purplish-brown soil) that is also flushed from alcohol, with a healthy and happy face and a torso like a camouflaged tank."[33] The difference between the husband and the wife is then generalized, with men described as enjoying far different lives than women: "Every harvest, the men come out of the virgin jungle, cross the cotton fields, and race their trucks to town, where alcohol, prostitutes, and dice await. The town, close to many Japanese collectives, is filled with cheap restaurants catering to Japanese. It resembled suppurating, filthy flesh."[34]

Akita treats the couple as representatives of their genders, in a society with distinct roles that are profoundly unfair to women. Here, we have a female body that is not the site of desires that lead to transgressions that in turn threaten the racial community but is rather the worn vessel of a pitiable victim who has consigned herself to suffering through her own virtue; in contrast, the male body is the vehicle of a corrupt agency, which indulges itself regardless of collateral damage. The male's unwillingness to consider the well-being or desires of his family continues even as they leave Brazil: we discover that the family is only going to Tokyo because of the father; neither the children nor their mother wishes to go.

Despite providing us little concrete information about their background, the text does spend significant time on the siblings João and Luísa and the ways in which they differ from the Japanese around them. The children are native Portuguese speakers but have some Japanese competency. They have acquired gestures that mark them as Other: Luísa raises her eyebrows "like a foreigner" and is described by the narrator as a "young Brazilian woman." This latter description appears in quotes in the text itself, problematizing (or denaturalizing) the relation of the descriptor to the descriptee. The country of their birth has left an imprint on Luísa and João that differentiates them from their peers in Japan: Akita, Makiko, and Wakabayashi find the children raised in Brazil to "all be melancholic to the core" and attribute that to the adult responsibilities children are given in the *colônia.* Makiko adds that girls have it even worse than boys, with upbringings stricter than those of children on the outskirts of Tokyo.[35]

At another point in the story, Luísa and João's father also addresses the fundamental differences in character he sees in his children compared to how he remembers children in Japan; in his case, however, he considers his own children to be more "magnanimous" (鷹揚). This word, attributed to the father, is also in quotes, again suggesting some dissatisfaction with the word's precision. The siblings are not the only individuals raised outside Japan to have this sort of acquired alterity. Tani, the university student from California, is frequently judged (from Akita's perspective, primarily) as behaving differently. Wakabayashi sums it up when he says, "Kids raised among Yankees sure are flashy (派手), aren't they?" In Tani's case, this excessiveness extends not only to his clothing (he is earlier described as wearing a flashy green jacket) but also to his physical size (he has to bend his "tall frame" to enter the room they are in).

The one dramatic event in the story, a confrontation between Akita and a (presumably Japanese) waiter, occurs because of the treatment Luísa receives from the people around her, who see her as a suitable target for ridicule. The waiter convinces Luísa, who is seeing snow for the first time in her life, that if she puts a snowball in her pocket and is careful with it, she will be able to take it to Japan. He then coaxes her over to the stove, in front of the first-class passengers. When she touches her pocket and discovers that the snowball has melted, she breaks into tears; the waiter and the passengers, both Japanese and non-Japanese, laugh at her ignorance. Upon hearing of this, Akita tracks down the waiter, takes him down to the third-class rooms, and slaps him hard across the face. Once he recovers his composure, Akita is angry with himself for his reaction, which he considers childish and excessive. This eruption of affect—a moment in which an emotional response prompts the body to act—is then interpreted by Akita himself, as he speculates about the source of the sentiment that had welled up in him: "I felt, perhaps out of some sense of inferiority, as though all of us emigrants to Brazil were being ridiculed."[36] It is clear that Akita feels protective of Luísa and João, but this is more than mere sympathy; there is some process of identification occurring as well. The identification, I would argue, is not as "Japanese Brazilians"; Akita is clear about the difference he perceives between himself and these children. Instead, the identification seems to be between subjects similarly thrust into specific peripheral, hardship positions vis-à-vis a normative center by forces beyond their control.

When we learn that João has never used chopsticks before, the narrator speculates on what awaits him (and his sister) in Japan:

> The bridge to their life in Brazil had already crumbled when they boarded the Japanese ship. Around them was in all ways Japan. For the individuals whose eyes poured over this dual-citizenship-holding youth of 17, there was not the slightest handicap. The ceaseless, severe training that this child of nature, of that vast continent, would receive in Japan had already begun

> during this sea crossing, which should otherwise have been pleasurable. He could not use chopsticks, nor did he know conversational Japanese. The dim-wit! The cold glares that poured over João at the table frightened him, making him feel as though he were some sort of thief, and forced him to speak, timidly and with a lisp, the heavily accented language of his parents' homeland. Luísa was there too, behind her brother.[37]

Akita rejects the position of abjection that he feels they are forced into vis-à-vis a normative notion of what it is to be Japanese. The action he urges upon them bears some similarity to the one he took in response to the waiter: an aggressive assertion of the value of their nonnormative positionality. Akita urges the children to feel pride in their history and to resist the self-hatred that this normative vision would cultivate within them:

> Thrust your chests out with pride, João and Luísa! Throw away those chopsticks and eat proudly with your forks. Speak to any you encounter loudly in the language of your birthplace, Brazil. If you shrink before them like that, once in Japan you will have people convincing you to put snowballs in your pockets every day!

The story presents Japan, in fact, as a difficult place for more than just these children. Makiko, Wakabayashi's wife, describes her birthplace of Japan as an "unforgiving" country where she "feels that she will not be able to let down her guard."

Wakabayashi envies Akita's decision to return to Brazil and settle there permanently. In contrast he describes his and his wife's situation using the Latin phrase *"va [sic] victus"* (*vae victus*, Woe to the vanquished!); he doubts that happiness awaits them in Sapporo. Akita reminds him, though, that Brazil is not necessarily a solution, either:

> My decision to live in Brazil permanently—no, not just me, sometimes I think every *issei*'s decision to live in Brazil permanently—represents the sad final stop on the journey of an individual who has tired of the search for a meaningful life. I think that it is impossible to choose permanent residence abroad without some tragic resignation.[38]

As with the earlier stories, a few changes have been made over the history of the text's reproduction. Unsurprisingly, the editor's primary concern seems to have been with terms involving blackness. The fairly strong Portuguese epithet *puta merda* (プータ・メルダ) remains in the text, whereas "half-black" (半黒) women become "mulattoes" (ムラト) in one spot in the 2008 version and "mixed-bloods" (混血) in another. It is interesting to note the different value judgments conveyed by the terms in this story compared to those conveyed in "An Age of Speculative Farming." Akita describes the legs of the mulatto women and those of women with "the blood of the people of the Iberian Peninsula" in the more descriptive colors of chestnut and barley, respectively. While noting difference, his gaze seems positive, desiring; more important, those individuals are not mere objects but subjects who interact with him in a way he describes as playful (perhaps flirtatious). In "Tumbleweeds," racial Others are not merely potential romantic partners; they are also members of a functioning heterogeneous community. At the funeral for Wakabayashi and Makiko's child, "black, white, and mixed children of the *colônia* brought flowers" that ended up covering the grave. While we might wonder what category Japanese would join here, it is more important to note the image of a compassionate (though certainly not utopian) multiracial community, mourning the tragic loss of a child.

Conclusions

We may speculate that the process of migrating from Japan to Brazil would have brought at least an amorphous notion of "Japanese-ness" to the forefront of many of the first-generation migrants' consciousnesses. The very idea of emigration would have likely been framed within a rhetoric of departure that implied spatial changes thought not merely quantitative but also qualitative in nature; many described the nearly two-month-long sea voyage as a strange state of suspension and anxiety marking just such a transition.[39] If one's first sight of the port city of Santos did not sufficiently signal alterity, the bureaucratic procedures of migration surely would have. One's travel documents, including many individuals' first passports, would have highlighted "Japanese-ness" as a legal status of citizenship that suddenly rendered them a minority population. Interaction with immigration officials once in Brazil, not to mention with non-Japanese-language speakers during the voyage, would also have reinforced a sense of Japanese-ness in terms of membership in a linguistic community. Once on the streets of Santos or São Paulo, migrants would have soon encountered an unprecedented level of variation in physical appearance, which many would have processed using racializing logic. Given the representations examined here, many migrants also had their own sense of Japanese-ness, this time as racial category, reinforced by this experience. This seems to be the one common element within these amorphous and multiple interpretations of Japanese-ness: a sense of shared biological descent. This experience of migration was surely experienced in radically diverse ways, but we should not be surprised if those undergoing it shared a heightened sense of themselves as Japanese, however defined, when surrounded by many who were not.

Yet these authors chose to concentrate upon neither the differences of those they marked as non-Japanese nor the similarities of those they marked as Japanese. Instead, they focus on the alterity they perceived in individuals they identified as racially self-same. The first form this takes is acquired alterity, in which a once-possessed selfsame-ness is lost through exposure to alien factors ranging from intense exposure to the sun to the introduction of non-Japanese blood. The reactions to this acquired alterity vary here from apathy ("Settler") to dismay ("Farming") to valorization ("Tumbleweeds"). In all three cases, however, the changes are not to the implied alternate subject position with which the narrator beckons the reader to identify (one distanced from the depicted behavior, which the reader is invited to gaze upon critically, alongside the narrator) that is, to the one whose identity has not itself been destabilized. It is possible, then, that acquired alterity here may function to reassure such a reader of his or her own stability amid circumstances that invite anxiety.

The second, more common form of alterity among the racially self-same explored by these writers involves a deviation from a normative expectation for that group, an imagined racial solidarity. Each of the three stories revolves around one or more moments of shock at the behavior of a "Japanese" character toward his or her own kind: Kurose betrays Ōmura, who in turn has systemically exploited his Japanese workers. Ruriko betrays her young lover in order to enter into a mutually exploitative relationship with Ōmura. Daisuke, who was sold undesirable land (by a Japanese broker?), now exploits his Japanese workers relentlessly. The waiter who mocks Luísa is only the first of many Japanese who will persecute them for (nonracial, as both their parents are apparently first-generation immigrants from Japan) deviations for which they cannot reasonably be held accountable.

The shock at these examples of inhumane or unethical behavior seems always to exceed the sin of commission itself; perhaps this is due to the shock being amplified by the sense that an ideal (which up until that point may not have been consciously held) has been betrayed. Emigrants would likely have left Japan prepared for ill-treatment at the hands of the racial Other. Yet what the writers describe time and again is that *identity* fails to guarantee more ethical or compassionate treatment than one would have been led to expect from *alterity.* These literary representations of this unpleasant discovery suggest that the betrayal of expectations of racial solidarity may have left an impression as powerful as, if not more powerful than, interactions with more conventional forms of alterity. It is unclear why this was the case, though one might imagine that writers may have felt freer to express frustration toward their "fellow Japanese" than that which must have arisen in response to other forms of institutionalized racism. Or perhaps they felt, at the very least, that such criticisms had a greater likelihood of being heard.

Notes

1. This chapter takes "race" to refer to the subjective grouping of individuals based on perceived notions of commonality or difference that are linked, sometimes only semiconsciously, to an ambiguous amalgam of phenotype, language, culture, and citizenship but that always presumes some biological basis produced by common descent. It does not presume that any consensus on the precise nature of race would be shared nor that individuals would have a clear or coherent vision of their own beliefs, which would have been developed under the influence of multiple, diverse discourses and need not be consistent over time. As such, "race" should be understood throughout this chapter as "relational and contingent," rather than essential. See Livio Sansone, *Blackness without Ethnicity: Constructing Race in Brazil* (New York: Palgrave MacMillan, 2003), 11. For more on perceptions of Japanese identity among contemporaneous immigrants to the Americas, see Eiichiro Azuma, *Between Two Empires: Race, History, and Transnationalism in Japanese America* (Oxford: Oxford University Press,

2005), particularly 61–85. For the sake of readability, the term will not henceforth appear in quotes. These caveats apply as well to specific racial designations, such as "blackness," used here to indicate some hybrid of the discursive Portuguese category *preto* and the ersatz logic behind the color-inspired slur *kuronbō* rather than as some sort of essentialized biological marking.

2. Although most (if not all) of the Japanese-language writers in Brazil during this period were born in Japan, some had come at a young-enough age to be considered *jun-nisei* (proto-second-generation immigrants). See Zelideth Maria Rivas, "*Jun-nisei* Literature in Brazil: Memory, Victimization, and Adaptation" (PhD diss., University of California, Berkeley, 2009).

3. Since most readers will not be familiar with these texts, summaries of the key elements of the plot have been included. This is necessary not only to acquaint the readers with the stories but also to highlight changes that are introduced from version to version.

4. The literary journal *Koronia bungaku* republished them as part of an ongoing effort to preserve important older works, which would have been largely inaccessible to a postwar readership. The anthology *Koronia shōsetsu senshū,* vol. 1 (São Paulo: Paurisuta Bijutsu Insatsu Kabushiki Kaisha, 1975) was edited by the organization behind the journal, the Koronia Bungakukai. Three additional volumes of later works have been published in this series. The DVD-ROM was produced by the Burajiru Imin 100 Shūnen Kinen Kyōkai, and its contents are now available online. See http://www.brasiliminbunko.com.br/.

5. Of all the works thus anthologized, only ten (these three among them) were written before World War II. Despite this centrality today, the question of the generalizability of the conclusions drawn about these texts—that is, what these works tell us about contemporaneous literary representations, much less popular attitudes—must remain open, given that these works were selected by editors with agendas of their own.

6. In such a situation, racial, linguistic, and economic alterity can be (and historically have been) imagined in ways that reinforce a single imagined group ("Japanese"); gender alterity, of course, would have worked in a more complicated fashion. Space does not allow this chapter to explore this important distinction sufficiently.

7. "Aru kaitakusha no shi" first appeared in six weekly installments in the pages of the newspaper *Burajiru jihō* between May 19 and June 30, 1932. The text also appeared in the May 1967 issue of *Koronia bungaku,* no. 4, on pages 42–48. When it was republished, it was attributed to Tanabe Shigeyuki (田辺重之), the author's real name.

8. This chapter will refer to characters as they are referred to in the stories, that is, sometimes by given name and sometimes by family name. Full names are given in Japanese order. It is uncertain whether the contempt in the description should be attributed to Daisuke. Attribution of narrative passages to individual characters or to a separate narratorial voice is a challenge, as there is often a blurring between the nominally distinct narratorial voice and the focal figure. While I argue later that the overall narratorial stance of this story is antagonistic to (and thus differentiated from) Daisuke, there are also cases of narrative as free indirect discourse, presumably associated with him.

9. See *Burajiru jihō,* May 19, 1932. *Baiano,* which literally denotes a person from the state of Bahia, is in fact a common racialized term that equates the state/region and blackness. Such Portuguese terms that appear in the original without a gloss are left untranslated here and below. The ungrammatical *arroz saco* here matches the form presented (in Japanese transliteration) in the original. Neither Japanese orthography nor grammar would have prevented the author from using the more grammatical *saco de arroz.*

10. Ibid.

11. *Burajiru jihō,* June 2, 1932. Here, the term refers to a group of *colonos* (workers on coffee plantations) who are not Japanese. When used in conjunction with Japanese immigrants, the

term *colônia* (コロニア) in its narrow sense refers to the rural communities of agricultural workers, where efforts were made to preserve Japanese language and cultural practices; in its broad sense, the term can also refer to the community of persons of Japanese descent in Brazil as a whole. This broader sense has fallen out of favor in recent decades. See Jeffrey Lesser, *Immigration, Ethnicity, and National Identity in Brazil, 1808 to the Present* (Cambridge: Cambridge University Press, 2013), 83–84; and Edward Mack, "Ōtake Wasaburō's Dictionaries and the Japanese 'Colonization' of Brazil," *Dictionaries: The Journal of the Dictionary Society of North America* 31 (2010): 46–68.

12. *Burajiru jihō,* June 16, 1932.

13. *Colonos* too were contract workers, but by the 1930s their contracts were usually only for one year (though they were renewable.) Burajiru Nihon Imin 80-nenshi Hensan Iinkai, ed., *Burajiru Nihon imin 80-nen shi* (São Paulo: Imin 80-nen Saiten Iinkai, 1991), 105. See also Lesser, *Immigration,* 39–44.

14. That is not to say that all pejoratives indicating racial categories were edited out. The most conspicuous example is "hairy foreigners," a pejorative originally used to indicate Chinese, which was adapted to refer to individuals of European descent in the nineteenth century. Both instances of this term, however, appear in direct discourse attributed to Daisuke, whereas the uses of "black" mentioned above appear in narrative passages. Given the antagonistic relationship established between the narrative perspective and Daisuke, the text would then not necessarily be perceived as endorsing the character's usage in the same way it would the narrative's usage; it could also be that the term "hairy foreigner" is so out of date that the 2008 editors may have felt that it had lost its capacity to offend the story's contemporary audience.

15. Sonobe Takeo [Inoue Tetsurō (井上哲朗)]'s "Tobaku-nō jidai" appeared in four weekly installments in the *Burajiru jihō* newspaper, from April 21–May 12, 1932. It then appeared in the second issue of *Koronia bungaku,* September 1966, 56–60.

16. *Burajiru jihō,* April 21, 1932.

17. Ibid.

18. Conrad Nagel (1897–1970) was a film star and a founding member of both the Academy of Motion Picture Arts and Sciences and the Screen Actors Guild. As for the Conde gang, this name, if it derives from the name of the street Rua Conde de Sarzedas, might imply that its members are Japanese. The street runs roughly east to west on the northern edge of the Liberdade neighborhood, which was (and remains) the center of the Japanese-Brazilian community in the city of São Paulo.

19. *Burajiru jihō,* April 29, 1932.

20. *Burajiru jihō,* May 12, 1932.

21. Arata Sumu, *Burajiru Nikkei koronia bungei,* gekan (São Paulo: Centro de Estudos Nipo-Brasileiros, 2008), 24.

22. *Burajiru jihō,* April 21, 1932.

23. *Burajiru jihō,* April 29, 1932.

24. *Burajiru jihō,* May 12, 1932.

25. *Burajiru jihō,* April 21, 1932.

26. *Burajiru jihō,* May 12, 1932.

27. See Nishi Masahiko, "Burajiru Nihonjin bungaku to 'kabokuro' mondai," *<Ima> o yomikaeru: 'Kono jidai' no owari* (Tokyo: Inpakuto Shuppankai, 2007), 69–89.

28. This statement of course involves exempting Ishikawa Tatsuzō's *Sōbō* from consideration. His novel is conventionally not counted among the number of Japanese-language works produced in Brazil, though Ishikawa did spend some time in the country.

29. *Bungei shuto* 27, no. 6 (June 1958): 31–40. No notifications of its provenance immediately precede or follow the story. It subsequently appeared in the July 1968 issue of *Koronia bungaku,*

no. 7, as part of their series reprinting older works. I have not seen the 1940 version, so the 1958 text will be treated as authoritative.

30. Hosokawa Shūhei speculates that Akita might be returning the remains of his mother, now deceased, to Japan. This seems very plausible, despite the absence of conclusive textual evidence. Hosokawa, *Nikkei Burajiru imin bungaku II* (Tokyo: Misuzu Shobō, 2013), 316.

31. Furuno Kikuo, "Tenpō," *Bungei shuto* 27, no. 6 (June 1958): 38.

32. Ibid.

33. Ibid.

34. Ibid.

35. It is interesting that Makiko mentions the outskirts (場末) of Tokyo, perhaps suggesting an awareness that Japan itself is not homogeneous in the experiences of children. The question that I cannot answer is why specify the outskirts of Tokyo, seemingly stressing a space less than completely urban while certainly distinct from the rural spaces that make up much of the rest of country.

36. Ibid., 34.

37. Ibid.

38. Ibid., 40.

39. See Hosokawa, *Nikkei Burajiru,* 308–330; and Hibi Yoshitaka, "Fune no bungaku—*Amerika monogatari* 'Senshitsu yawa,'" *Bungaku* 10, no. 2 (March 2009): 41–49.

The Sun Never Sets on Little Black Sambo

Circuits of Affection and the Cultural Hermeneutics of *Chibikuro Sambo*—A Transpacific Approach

In 1952, psychologist M. E. Goodman published a treatise on what she called the "race awareness" of four-year-old American children. By the age of four, Goodman contended, children can perceive and interpret race, assign aesthetic value to skin color, and mobilize these assignments in their own ongoing process of self-identity formation. Children, Goodman concluded, both tell and are told racial stories, and it is through the interpretation of such stories that they create their racial selves. No story, she wrote, was more instrumental to the 1950s construction of children's race awareness than Helen Bannerman's (1862–1946) *Little Black Sambo* (1899); through the mirror of *Little Black Sambo,* Goodman claimed, black children saw reflections of themselves as racialized objects and thereby initiated one of the darker mechanisms of racial identity formation—racial self-loathing.[1]

In 1954, two years after the publication of Goodman's assessment of Sambo's role in the construction of American children's race awareness, Miyahara Seiichi, a social education (*shakai kyōikugaku*) specialist and a member of the University of Tokyo's Department of Education during its founding years, turned a psychoanalytical eye toward the Iwanami translation of *Little Black Sambo* and its reception among Japanese children. Miyahara's target demographic was analogous to Goodman's—he claimed that children begin to show interest in *Chibikuro Sambo* (the Japanese translation of *Little Black Sambo,* hereafter *Chibikuro*) "around the age of three."[2] Contrary to Goodman's study, which comments on the deleterious effects of *Sambo* on black children's notion of race-based beauty and African American parents' vitriolic response to the text, Miyahara suggests that *Chibikuro* "exemplifies the kind of book that pleases children" and that it is "only natural that the book has many fans, particularly among first and second graders."[3] Moreover, Miyahara's rendition of Japanese children's response to Sambo is conspicuously free of any references to race or racism. Japanese juvenile readers—Miyahara tells us—situate themselves vis-à-vis Sambo not by seeing him as a racialized object but by projecting themselves onto Sambo and "becoming" the protagonist-hero of Bannerman's tale.[4]

Even given the brevity of these synopses of Goodman's and Miyahara's respective commentaries, one cannot help but wonder: Did Goodman and Miyahara read the same book? Indeed, *Little Black Sambo* is a text that is both literally and figuratively open to interpretation: since its 1899 publication, *Sambo* has been accompanied by dozens of pirated editions, adaptations, and translations. And for every pirated version and adaptation of *Sambo,* there are an equal number of dissenting voices chiming in on the "proper" interpretation of the text.

This chapter deals with the publication, translation, reception, and cultural history of *Little Black Sambo* and its problematic double on the other side of the Pacific, *Chibikuro Sambo.* I rehearse the history of Sambo's odyssey through the Middle Passage and the birth of Sambo as American cultural icon; Sambo's journey to and subsequent rebirth in India as *Little Black Sambo;* the character's return to America as *Sambo;* and finally, the text's transpacific flight to Japan via the United States. My primary objective is to analyze the cultural hermeneutics of *Chibikuro Sambo* in Japan from the text's groundbreaking 1953 Iwanami rendition to the 1988 *Chibikuro Sambo ronsō* (Little Black Sambo controversy), which culminated in Iwanami and ten other major publishing houses voluntarily halting publication of *Chibikuro* due to a desire to "eliminate discrimination."

Those familiar with scholarship on the 1988 *Chibikuro Sambo ronsō* will also know of its alternative moniker: the *issei zeppan mondai,* or the controversy surrounding the "sudden halted printing" of *Chibikuro.* I argue that, placed in historical context, there was little that was "sudden" about the cessation of publication as these debates are the fifth in a series of skirmishes around this text. This chapter excavates that history. In the first portion, I trace the development of Sambo before *Sambo,* that is, Sambo as a figment of the Western popular imagination; a racial stereotype rooted in the transatlantic slave trade, which functioned as a representative of mid-nineteenth to early twentieth-century black masculinity. It is from this milieu that *Little Black Sambo* was born. In the second portion of this chapter, I focus on the Japanese reception and publication history of *Little Black Sambo,* in particular on the four moments that preceded and informed the debates of 1988: the "child's mind" debate of the 1950s and the 1960s, the "counterfeit texts" debates of 1965, the "racial ideology and children's literature" discussion that haunted the Japanese children's literary scene from the mid-1960s to the mid-1970s, and the period of reconstruction and reevaluation of *Chibikuro Sambo* that occurred from the mid-1970s and throughout the 1980s. I privilege these four moments over the much more publicized debate of 1988 to highlight the fact that the events of 1988 were not stand-alone occurrences. Rather, they were simply the next iteration in a series of discussions of *Chibikuro* in postwar Japan.

The stakes of these discussions—that is to say, one explanation for postwar Japan's fixation on and constant visiting and revisiting of *Little Black Sambo*—are the configuration of what I call circuits of affection. As for the circuitry, the *Oxford English Dictionary* (*OED*) gives us several definitions of "circuit," including: (1) "the line, real or imaginary, described in going round any area," (2) "the visitation of the judges for holding assizes," and (3) "the path of a voltaic current." As for the "affection," one would be hard-pressed to read through the reception history of *Little Black Sambo* in Japan and not notice the way the language of affect dominates Japanese responses to the text, even—or perhaps, especially—when members of the Japanese intelligentsia and literati engage in "analytical" critiques. *Chibikuro Sambo* is at times an a-racial object of love and admiration (i.e., the postwar period), at other times an object of righteous disgust and scorn (criticism from the 1960s and the 1970s), and at other times the trigger for bittersweet nostalgia (the 1990s and beyond).

Insofar as affect "may be thought of as a fundamental response system in its own right, one that feeds into higher mental processes and provides essential input for social action,"[5] circuits of affection include cognitive, evaluative, ethical, and sociopolitical values such that affective thinking evokes effective judgments; "how we feel" slips ever so easily into "how we *ought* to feel"; and the weight of affective ethics has a kind of constitutive, galvanizing power that begins and reinforces discussions of how X affects us versus how it affects *them.*[6] Circuits of affection, then, are—to return to the *OED*—the jolts of voltaic affect that run from text to reader, the assizing that inevitably follows such affective shock, and the lines—real or imaginary—that are described around communities based on shared affective currents. As such, Japan's overwhelmingly affective response to *Chibikuro Sambo* cannot be lightly dismissed; affective responses to *Chibikuro* speak to the thinking, judgment, ethics, and sociopolitics of race, blackness, and minority at a given moment in the history of postwar Japan.

At the same time, the four facets of affective response identified here—cognition, evaluation, ethics, and sociopolitics—are not exhaustive nor do they manifest equally in every affective response. Indeed, it is the *inequality* of their manifestation that interests us: the series of debates that define the cultural hermeneutics of *Chibikuro* and the "proper" interpretation of his blackness in postwar Japan can be read as the power struggle between competing configurations of hypercharged circuits of affection. Following Steven Mailloux's suggestion that we consider "the tropes, arguments, and narratives constituting the interpretations of texts at specific times and places," the second portion of this chapter is interested in reading for affect in the rhetoric of Japan's scholarship and criticism of *Little Black Sambo,* rather than reading for affect in the fiction of *Little Black Sambo* itself.[7]

Finally, I take a transpacific approach to the story's publication and cultural history to remain faithful to the motion and migration that is embedded in the very fibers of Sambo (the cultural icon) and *Sambo* (the text), a motion and migration engendered by the age of empire and colonialism that gave birth to "little black" Sambo/*Sambo.* To consider the cultural hermeneutics of *Chibikuro Sambo* from 1953 to 1988 is to address a formerly occupied nation with defeated imperial ambitions' (Japan's) interpretation of a text illustrated by the (formerly) occupying nation, the United States, about a "black" boy and written in the British Empire by a Scotswoman stationed in the British colony of India. It is the possibility of reading the vertiginous nexus of imperial roots and textualized race in Japan that makes the history of *Little Black Sambo* in Japan so intriguing and allows us to "use history to do theory."[8] We should add that in the Japanese-language scholarship of *Little Black Sambo,* much has been made of "good intentions"; both Helen Bannerman and Iwanami were, supposedly, unaware of the place of Sambo in Britain's and Japan's respective imperial projects.[9] There is a way, however, that this putative nescience makes the remnant machinery of empire *more,* rather than less, potent—the ghosts of empire haunt in ways that their corporeal manifestations never could. The lingering legacies of interracial and interethnic empires catalyze Sambo's circuits of affection in postwar Japan; this history aims to make those ghosts visible.

Sambo before *Chibikuro Sambo*

The genesis of Sambo—that figure in the American popular imagination that functions as a stereotypical representation of mid-nineteenth to early twentieth-century black masculinity—occurred well in advance of the 1899 birth of Sambo as the eponymous protagonist of Helen Bannerman's *Little Black Sambo.* Etymologically, the source of Sambo remains opaque, though several possibilities are germane to my line of inquiry here. In Foulah, for example, "Sambo" is the word for "uncle," or a term of affection for older males. As such, the term functions in a fashion similar to that of the Japanese *ojisan* insofar as it denotes either an avuncular figure or a social relation in which the uncle-niece/nephew relationship is replicated. In Huasa, "Sambo" refers to the secondborn son. This "Sambo" is analogous with the Foulah "Sambo" insofar as it is a familial position that can be transformed into an appellation.

Given the haunting size and duration of the trade that brought West African slaves to the Americas, it is possible that the term "Sambo" survived the journey through the Middle Passage and was introduced into the English language by virtue of the fact that a considerable number of men were named or referred to as Sambo in the black slave population. Those affiliated with the slave trade would not have been oblivious to this fact. Phyllis Barton argues that "prior to Bannerman's use of the name, it was mentioned in innumerable oral accounts and hundreds of times in travel diaries and literature beginning sometime around 1564."[10]

After this early introduction, "Sambo" underwent a peculiar inversion or appropriation, from being a prominent name among the male slave population to an interpellation that supposedly encapsulated the very notion of the African male slave mentality. "Mars Jeems's Nightmare," a short story by Charles Chesnutt (1858–1932) and a contemporary of *Little Black Sambo,* provides an example of "Sambo" as a sobriquet that beckons all black male slaves en masse:

> Mars [Master] Johnson sez ter dis yer noo man:
>
> "W'at's yo' name, Sambo?"
>
> "My name ain' Sambo," 'spon' de noo nigger.
>
> "Did I ax you w'at yo' name wa'n't?" sez Mars Johnson. "You wants ter be pa'tic'lar how you talks ter me. Now, w'at is yo' name, en whar did you come fum?'

> "I dunno my name," sez de nigger, "en I doan member whar I come fum. My head is all kin'er mix' up."[11]

This excerpt from Chesnutt is a subtle reminder of the most insidious use of "Sambo." The black slave, a commoditized being that was literally substitutable, is identified by way of a one-size-fits-all moniker rather than a "proper" name. Note that the narrator, himself a former plantation worker, duplicates this system by referring to the new slave as "de nigger," yet another empty pronoun-like moniker in lieu of an actual name. "Sambo" and its near synonym—"de nigger"—is to be contrasted with the slave owner, whose status as a human being demands the title "suh." This title both creates and verifies the slave owner's place in the master-slave power dynamic.

Sambo, then, would have been a "John Doe" character, the blank yet overwritten African American everyman in the modern American psyche. "By early in the twentieth century," concomitant with the rise of *Little Black Sambo*, "the term 'Sambo' came to be used as a generic name for any black male, particularly in the United States," especially "in Hollywood in the 1920s and 1930s, as well as . . . a common reference to bartenders and shoe shine boys."[12] One could find "Samboes" in magazines, movies, record labels, and especially minstrel shows. What would Sambo have looked like at the *fin-de-siècle?* As Stanley Elkins succinctly summarizes:

> Sambo, the typical plantation slave, was docile but irresponsible, loyal but lazy, humble but chronically given to lying and stealing; his behavior was full of infantile silliness and his talk inflated with childish exaggeration. His relationship with his master was one of utter dependence and childlike attachment: it was indeed this childlike quality that was the very key to his being.[13]

It is into this preestablished context that *The Story of Little Black Sambo* was published by Grant Richards in 1899. Written during her time in what was then Madras, Bannerman's story of Sambo's pacifistic defeat of four tigers was an immediate success. Following its success in London, Richards sold the rights to the story to Frederick A. Stokes, who published the story in the United States. The American version was just as successful as its British counterpart. As a testament to the popularity of the tale, at least twenty-seven unofficial versions of the text were published between 1905 and 1953.

It is at this juncture that Bannerman's Sambo amalgamated with the Sambo of American popular iconography. The synergy between Bannerman's Sambo, the multitude of pirated editions, and the Sambo of American lore altered the trajectory of the image of Sambo toward the American "ideal," each illustrator adding his or her Samboesque touch to *Sambo.* In the Reilly and Britton figure below, we have a sinister Little Black Sambo and a Black Mumbo replete with the attributes of Aunt Jemima: do-rag, polka dot apron, skillet and pancakes, and one hundred pounds of excess weight. In the 1917 Cupples and Leon rendition of Sambo, we notice a marked change in the stylistics of the illustration. Little Black Sambo and Black Mumbo are presented in blackface a la a minstrel show.

Figure 14.1. Reilly and Britton, 1908.

The 1921 Stoll and Edwards version brings us a Sambo from a simpler time. Sambo appears docile and content, his tea kettle, candle, and starry night seeming to signify nostalgia. In 1931 the McLoughlin version of *Sambo* returns to the blackface paradigm but this time with an Africanized twist.

The reaction to this amalgamated Sambo was complex. The *popularity* of the text was undeniable, and that popularity aged well with time.[14] In 1953, the year that Iwanami published *Chibikuro* in Japan, *Children's Books Too Good to Miss* claimed that *Sambo* was just that—it was "no wonder small children love Sambo. He is just the kind of conquering hero they dream of becoming."[15] Such approval, however, came primarily from *Sambo*'s white readership. As Goodman points out in the study discussed in the introduction, African Americans were peculiarly affected by the text, though initially, the response to *Sambo* among the black intelligentsia was affirmative.

Pre-*Sambo* American children's literature was a fairly whitewashed affair. Hay writes that *Sambo* "was one of the very few books then available which even acknowledged the existence of black people. For generations it gave black Americans

Figure 14.2. Cupples and Leon, 1917.

an image of themselves, and white Americans an image of black Americans."[16] From the late 1930s onward, however, many African Americans reneged on their endorsement of *Sambo.* This shift away from Sambo came at the meridian of the Harlem Renaissance, a period in which children's literature was viewed as a galvanizing site; a discursive space that should imbue black children with the subjectivity of the New Negro.[17] It is against this ideological backdrop that criticism of *Sambo* began to mount in the black community.

As such, by 1953, the year that Iwanami published its Japanese translation of *Sambo,* at least two modes of critique developed regarding *Little Black Sambo.* The two responses, one advocating the literary merits of the text, the other deriding its discriminatory demerits, broke with jagged edges, typically along racial lines, and as such the formation of Sambo-related reading communities overlapped with the formation of racial communities. The story of *Little Black Sambo* in Japan is in large part the story of Japanese readers deciding which of these communities to call home.

Sambo's Odyssey Continued: The Production and Reception of Sambo in Japan, 1953–1965

Founded in 1913, by 1953 Iwanami was known primarily for its Iwanami Bunko (Iwanami Library) series and the publication of works of scholarly, literary, and cultural merit. In 1953, however, Iwanami turned its attention toward children's

Figure 14.3. Stoll and Edwards, 1921.

literature in general and picture books (*ehon*) in particular. Mitsuyoshi Natsuya (1904–1989) and Ishii Momoko (1907–2008) were charged with the task of selecting books for the Iwanami no Kodomo no Hon (Iwanami's Books for Children) series. The inaugural line of picture books for Iwanami no Kodomo no Hon was to include six selections: three texts for first and second graders and three for third and fourth graders.

Little Black Sambo was not only selected as one of the six but was the first published, thereby becoming Iwanami's first venture into the realm of picture books. In a 1973 article titled "Iwanami's Books for Children: Children at the Time of Its Publication," Mitsuyoshi himself explains the rationale behind having Sambo be the front-runner: until that point, variants of *Sambo* had been published in children's magazines (*Akai tori* being one of the more prominent venues of *Sambo* publication) and in texts geared toward language learning but never as stand-alone picture books. Mitsuyoshi owned a copy of the 1927 *The Black Sambo*—an American, Dobias-illustrated, Macmillan version of *Little Black Sambo*—that he presented to the general manager of Iwanami.

Figure 14.4. McLoughlin, 1931.

Figure 14.5. Iwanami, 1953. Macmillan, 1927. Bannerman original. Even with Iwanami's dyscalculia, it is clear that the Iwanami translation is based on the Macmillan edition. As such, it is important to note that the Macmillan illustration and, by proxy, the Iwanami reproduction, are informed by the iconography of the minstrel show.

Silenced Blackness and the Child's Mind, 1954–1966

After its Iwanami publication, Miyahara Seiichi was one of the first Japanese scholars to take up *Chibikuro.* As previously mentioned, Miyahara's observations led him to believe that Japanese children took interest in *Chibikuro* around the age of three. That this was the "proper" age to introduce the text was verified by "American psychologists": "Among American child psychologists as well, *Chibikuro Sambo* is considered to be exemplary of the kind of book that pleases children."[18] Miyahara's concern with child psychology—the child's heart/mind (*kodomo no kokoro*), the child's psyche (*kodomo no shinri*), et cetera—was a motif of children's literature studies in Japan at this time.

Miyahara was convinced that Bannerman had a thorough grasp of the child's psyche; it was this mastery that makes her text affective and effective for its child readers. Bannerman was, according to Miyahara, spectacular in her ability to "capture the psyche of children with her authorial intuition."[19] For Miyahara, Bannerman's stunning success—as well as Japanese children extolling Bannerman's work—verified the fact that Japan was *not* producing "literature of the child's mind" or literature with the child in mind. As Miyahara argued: "The thing that has been deemed the child's mind in our country is . . . *adult's nostalgia for the child's mind* . . . It is a matter of course that these tales are not interesting to children."[20]

Miyahara's conjectures are both indicative of a major paradigm of the discourse on children's literature between the mid-1950s and the mid-1960s and serve as a bellwether for this decade of Japanese criticism of *Chibikuro.* The 1950s would see several salvos fired under the banner of "criticism of traditional children's literature" (*dōwa dentō hihan*). Indeed, 1953 saw the publication of "Shōnen bungaku no hata no moto ni" (Beneath the banner of juvenile literature) in *Shōnen bungaku* (Juvenile literature), the journal of Waseda University's Sōdai dōwa kai (Waseda Children's Fiction Association). "Beneath the Banner," an article that scholars of children's literature have dubbed "The Children's Literature Manifesto," was a declaration of artistic warfare against "traditional" children's literature. In the words of the manifesto, "Juvenile literature envisions the ascendance of traditional children's literature to the heights of true modern literature and as such it means a never-ending battle with all antiquated, with all irrational, unmodern literature."[21] With its feverish prose, the manifesto ignited a debate on the essence (*honshitsu*) of children's literature. One school of thought—and we will give a name and texts to this school momentarily—responded with the suggestion that Japanese children's literature had, to borrow the summation of Torigoe Shin, "forgotten children, forgotten its readers."[22] Reminiscent of Miyahara, remembering the child reader would entail emulation of international precedents in children's literature, that is, writing stories that were free of ideological baggage; comprehensible; and most important, "interesting" and as such, affective, to children.

Japanese critics and authors throughout the mid-1950s and into the 1960s saw *Chibikuro* as the international precedent to emulate. Ishii Momoko, who was responsible in part for the inclusion of *Chibikuro* in the Iwanami series, wrote that "we need to study this book [*Sambo*] a hundred thousand times. The reason I find this story so interesting is, to be sure, because I have read the story with children over the last several years. To me, this story is almost a flawless work. I am shocked that a single person produced such a work."[23] The affective shock Ishii, by that time already an award-winning author of children's literature, experienced upon reading *Chibikuro* with children led her to a greater epiphany: "Children," Ishii continues, "who cannot tell us in words, try to teach adults the secrets of their minds . . . The job of adults is to turn our ears toward children's 'voiceless voices' . . . and see what's in the story that pleases children."[24] There is an undeniable affinity between Ishii's conjecture and Miyahara's. Ishii, a la Miyahara, claimed that she knew from personal experience that children find the story interesting, placed a noticeable emphasis on the "genius" of the author, and suggested that adults listen to children's "voiceless voices" to determine what children find pleasing.

If the Japanese literati were to mimic the success of *Chibikuro,* however, they would need to understand what made it so engaging. In 1960, psychologist Murase Takao set out to do exactly that. We recall that, for Miyahara, writing high-caliber children's literature was a job that—although firmly within the jurisdiction of the author—required the insights of a psychologist. Aiming to furnish those insights, Murase's empirical study of *Chibikuro Sambo* was structured as a round-robin-style tournament. He paired texts from the Iwanami's Books for Children series and asked both child and adult readers to vote for their favorite. Murase coupled this popularity contest, which *Chibikuro Sambo* won handily, with textual analysis, arguing that texts that interest children have a certain alchemy that balances the various features of good children's literature, for example, nonsense, rhythmic language, humor, and more. Texts that achieve the ideal balance speak to children or, to use Murase's term, "commune" with them:

> Communion and communication can be clearly differentiated . . . What the children's literature of our country lacks . . . is free "dialogue" between children and the literati . . . *Chibikuro* appeals to children from any country at any epoch because the text was born from the communion of Mrs. Bannerman and her children.[25]

The conclusion of "Children and the Appeal of *Little Black Sambo*" clearly exemplifies the mid-1950s through 1960s discourse on children's literature in Japan. The task of the (adult) author of children's literature is to hear the voiceless voice of children through mystical intuition. Murase uses the terms "communion" (*kokoro no kayoi*) and "divine revelation" (*keiji*) to denote the nonverbal nature of the ideal relationship between the adult author and the child reader. This affective communion—in which the adult author intuits the kind of literature that will capture the child's mind—is placed over and against the precedent of discursive communication established by the proletarian and didactic children's literature of the prewar period. It seemed that Bannerman, who at this point was synonymous with good "foreign" children's literature, was up to the task and Japanese authors were not.

I promised to put a name and actors to the school of thought that focused on international precedent, accessibility, interestingness, and antididacticism and lauded the virtues of *Chibikuro.* Although these tenets had been a recurring theme throughout the *dōwa dentō hihan* 1950s, it was not until 1960—a few months after the publication of the results of Murase's experiment—that the revolutionary *Kodomo to bungaku* (Children and literature) would be published. Six individuals at the forefront of discussions of children's literature wrote and edited the essays of *Children and Literature.* Spearheaded by Ishii Momoko and Seda Teiji, the collection included the meditations of Inui Tomiko (1924–2002), Suzuki Shinichi (1919–), Matsui Tadashi (1926–), and Watanabe Shigeo (1928–2006).

Typically referred to by the acronym ISWMI, this group was a significant cultural force in the movement to "write children's literature with children in mind." *Children and Literature* both critiqued authors that embodied the antithesis of the world standard (Ogawa Mimei, 1882–1961, took the brunt of the barbs) and lauded those who captured the spirit of children's literature (Miyazawa Kenji, 1896–1933, was the primary beneficiary in this regard.) On the same echelon of no less than Miyazawa Kenji, *Chibikuro* too was upheld as an example of how children's literature ought to be.

> Even after six years [from the publication of the Iwanami translation], *Sambo's* popularity has not declined in the least; just as the characters of Shakespeare are immortal in the world of adult literature, *Sambo* has become an eminent figure no less in stature than the Three Billy Goats Gruff, Cinderella, or Tom Thumb in the world of fairy tales for children of those countries.[26]

Resisting the urge to comment on Sambo's eminent stature being compared to that of Tom Thumb, we can say that Miyahara, Ishii, Murase, and Seda exemplify early critical acclaim of *Chibikuro* in that it fit the burgeoning paradigm of "good" children's literature: it was from abroad, which activated the affirmative discourse surrounding foreign children's literature; (supposedly) free of ideological concerns; and, most important, engaging to children. This discovery of "interesting" children's literature was predicated on the assumption that children lack the eloquence to directly communicate that which they find interesting. As such, it becomes the job of the authors and theorists of children's literature to speak for silent children.

It is important to note, then, that during this phase of *Chibikuro Sambo*'s reception in Japan, the text's racial and ideological undercurrents too are silenced by the search for meritorious literature. Even as the young reader's notion of "blackness" was being formed and informed by *Chibikuro,* whether or not the text was interesting dominated discussions during this child-centered era of children's literary criticism in Japan. What we see here is the formation of a circuit of affection that connects author and critic to child by way of positive affective judgment vis-à-vis *Chibikuro,* with terms such as "interesting" and "charming" at the pinnacle of positive valuation. In this circuit, no voice is given to questions concerning the ethics and politics of reading. This silence would begin to break, however, during the counterfeit texts debates of 1965.

The Counterfeit Texts Debates, 1965

In 1964, as a chorus of critics called for interesting children's literature and upheld *Chibikuro* as an example of such a text, the Monbushō (then known as the Ministry of Education, Science, Sports and Culture) adopted *Chibikuro* as a text for second-grade language arts. The synergy of the variety of pirated editions and *Sambo*'s selection as a state-certified pedagogical tool, however, would lead to the first blemishes in *Chibikuro*'s reception history. Torigoe Shin, Shingū Teruo, and Nasuda Minoru published an article titled "Kodomo no tame no ryōsho no jyōken—saiwa honan shōyaku no mondai ten" (The terms of good children's books—the problems of retellings, adaptations, and abridged translations) in the May 1, 1965, edition of *Tosho shimbun.* As the title of the treatise suggests, Torigoe—whom we will recall as the author of the juvenile literature manifesto—and his colleagues argued that the quality of *Chibikuro* fluctuated depending on the hand of the translator. According to Torigoe, the Iwanami version was the most authentic when compared to Bannerman's original. In the words of Torigoe and his colleagues, the Iwanami version did "a splendid job of capturing the rhythm of the original; of all the editions one can find in Japan today, it is one of the best."[27]

The "splendor" of the Iwanami version was to be compared with the subpar translations of the other six permutations. The Froebel edition received the brunt of Torigoe's critique. After citing the openings of both the Iwanami and the Froebel editions, Torigoe proffered the following no-holds-barred critique: "In comparison to this [Iwanami], how does the Froebel version fare? As one gathers even from just the section cited here, drastic alterations to the content and inconsiderate adaptations have made a *Chibikuro Sambo* of a completely different mold."[28] The article went on to frame the *shingan ronsō* (the authenticity debate or, literally, the real or fake debate—another moniker for the *gansaku ronsō*) within the context of motherly concern with the deleterious impact of "poor" adaptations on the pedagogical and literary value of *Chibikuro.* As Torigoe articulated the dilemma:

> One mother who read the Froebel edition first and believed without a doubt that it was the original version says that she was shocked anew by the brilliance of the original when she read the Iwanami version. Ultimately, this shock became doubt in regard to the nature of the introduction of foreign children's literature in Japan and, moreover, anger in regard to the rampant production of false works.[29]

The shift in affective language—from the "love" of the 1950s to "shock" and "anger"—highlights a burgeoning circuit of affection. We will return to this momentarily. For now, we can follow Torigoe in his conjecture that these new-

むかし　むかし、ちいさ
な　くろんぼの　男の子が
いました。チビクロ・サン
ボと　いう　なまえでした。
おかあさんは　マンボと
いう　なまえでした。
おとうさんは　ジャンボ
と　いう　なまえでした。
おかあさんの　マンボは
きれいな　ちいさな　赤い
うわぎと、きれいな　ちい
さな　あおい　ズボンを
つくって　くださいました。
おとうさんの　ジャンボ
は、まちに　いきました。
そして、きれいな　みどり
いろの　かさと、すてきな
ちいさな　むらさきの　く

Figure 14.6. Japanese Ministry of Education, Culture, Sports, Science and Technology-sanctioned textbook edition of *Chibikuro Sambo,* 1968.

found affects represent "readers' criticism in regard to the condition of contemporary books for children."[30] The Froebel translation became synonymous with the "poor" condition of Japanese children's literature.

Iizawa Tadasu (1909–1994), a playwright and translator of the Froebel version of *Chibikuro Sambo,* was not pleased with this assessment. Apparently irked by the characterization of his translation, Iizawa expressed his ire in a May 15, 1965, *Tosho shimbun* article titled "Ii kagen na kyōdō kenkyū—ganbutsu hantei ni kōgi suru" (Half-baked collaborative research—protesting the counterfeit judgment). For our purposes, two planks of Iizawa's argument are revelatory. First, Iizawa argued that Torigoe privileged fidelity to the original *Sambo* above anything else (*gensaku daiichi shugi*), so much so that Torigoe was myopic to the flaws of the original. Iizawa posited the names of the characters as an example. What was, Iizawa asked, Bannerman's intent when she played with the rhythmically rolling names of Sambo, Mumbo, and Jumbo? The answer lies in the "colonial expansion of the British empire during the Victorian age that is at the roots of this tale."[31] Iizawa read white superiority (*kōetsukan*) in the gaze of Bannerman toward her "colored" subjects. Bannerman's supremacist viewpoint was evinced by the name Jumbo, which Iizawa claimed was Swahili for "good day" and had

Figure 14.7. One of the first postwar variant editions of *Chibikuro,* Kōbunsha's 1956 *Chibikuro Sambo no bōken* (The adventure of Little Black Sambo).

been "generalized" into a man's name.[32] That the specificity of a proper name for Bannerman's black father figure was reduced to the generality of a salutation was linguistic proof of the colonization of Bannerman's mind.

Second, Iizawa claimed that the Iwanami version was irresponsible insofar as it did not rectify the zoologically impossible conflation of Africa and India that occurred in the original. Recall that the illustrations and orthography of the Iwanami version were based on the Macmillan edition, which was set in an imagined American Deep South. Iizawa read the South as Africa. As such, he was flabbergasted by what he saw as Iwanami's fusion of Africa and India.

After being criticized with such gusto, Torigoe would argue his case against the Froebel version in minute detail. Torigoe responded to Iizawa's critique in the May 29, 1965, *Tosho shimbun.* The first section of Torigoe's response, titled "Perilous Racial Discrimination?" (Kiken na jinshu sabetsu?) ripostes the claim of racial insensitivity in startling fashion, asserting that *Little Black Sambo*'s ideological "backdrop of the colonialism of the English empire" was "a fact" (*jijitsu de atte*) that "anyone who is a scholar of children's literature knows."[33] Moreover, Torigoe posits that the text's imperial production engenders "repeated arguments [that] have surrounded the treatment of this text—particularly in America, where the black problem (*kokujin mondai*) is clamorously discussed."[34]

We should take note of Torigoe's introduction of the colonialist historical milieu of the composition of *Sambo,* as well as the gesture toward the text's place in American discourse of the "black problem," as "facts" with which any scholar of children's literature would be conversant. This "commonplace fact" had not been commonly mentioned in critical discussions until this point. As such, Torigoe's comments mark a dramatic shift in the hermeneutics of *Chibikuro* in Japan; pace the 1950s discussion and its emphasis on Japanese children's identification with Sambo, Sambo has now become a sign in the discourse of race and colonialism. After the introduction of these facts, Torigoe would articulate what he saw as the proper paradigm for evaluating the text: one in which "whether or not this work runs the risk of implanting feelings of contempt for black people in the children of Japan" is secondary to "the superb points this work has as a story for children."[35] For Torigoe, then, determining whether or not a text with questionable ideological intimations should be given to a child was a matter of placing the text on a kind of scale, with the literary merits of the text on one side and the possibility of questionable ethics on the other.

The rhetoric of Torigoe's argument suggests that a text can have both literary merit and questionable ethics and that one can win out over the other. As such, the counterfeit texts debates opened a space for another kind of affective reader of *Chibikuro Sambo.* Insofar as this reader regards the literary merit of *Chibikuro* as paramount, she is in the mold of the ISWMI reading circle. Unlike ISWMI, however, Torigoe's reader is torn: this reader acknowledges the racially charged affective ethics (how should we feel about representations of oppressed peoples?) of *Chibikuro* only to override them with the aesthetic affects produced by "superb" literary works.

The Aftermath of the Counterfeit Texts Debates and the Transition to Ideology—Racial Discrimination Debates, 1965–1974

Following the publication of the articles that constituted the *gansaku ronsō,* there was an uptick in popular interest in the vacillating quality of several *Chibikuro* editions. This popularization was evinced by the 1972 publication of *Chibikuro Sambo no kenkyū* (Little Black Sambo studies), a special edition of the serial the *Little Library.* The collection is noteworthy in part because of its composers: the General Education Reading Club of the Tanashi Kodai Elementary School PTA, an organization made up primarily of housewives. The research was prompted by the following constellation of concerns: the explosive popularity of *Chibikuro* among children, the rampancy of pirated versions (the count was now at twelve), and the fact that more and more Monbushō-sponsored language-arts textbooks were including some version of *Chibikuro.*

Building on the authenticity debate, the imprecise "some" of "some version" was deemed particularly problematic. The reading club addressed this problem by compiling information on the varying editions and conducting a comparative analysis. The results of their study pointed in two directions. First, it was the Poplar version, not the Iwanami edition, that was "truest to the original edition"[36] despite the fact that the Iwanami version had "up until now been deemed the authoritative version of the *Little Black Samboes* in Japan."[37] The club also broached the issue of the ideological occasion of the text. The club noted that one textbook edition of *Chibikuro* described Sambo as from a "country of the south" (*minami no kuni*). This addition comes in spite of the fact that Bannerman does not use the word "south" in the original text. The circle worried that a textbook sponsored by a governmental institution was facilitating and cultivating racialist sentiment in children via language-arts textbooks. If the text enabled dark pedagogy such as this, the club asked, what exactly was the ideology of *Chibikuro,* a story that had made its way into the hands and minds of so many children?

This inquiry—the ideology, or *shisō,* of *Chibikuro*—was the central focus of the second skein. Teramura Terao, author-scholar of children's literature and husband of one of the members of the reading club, responded to the ISWMI-style charges of *Chibikuro* as ideology-less in an article published as an addendum to the reading club's research. In "*Chibikuro Sambo* no ryōmen" (The two faces of *Little Black Sambo*), Teramura presented two Samboes—the one seen by the juvenile reader and the one excavated by the discerning adult reader. Although "adults may see these as base pleasures," *Chibikuro* was undeniably interesting and gave the child a sense of satisfaction.[38] Interestingness in and of itself, however, is insufficient: "Interestingness is an indispensable condition of children's tales, but when valuating [works] as literature, we frequently run into the question: isn't this *just* interesting? *Sambo* is no exception."[39] Teramura argued that a book is meaningless (*muimi*) if we cannot glean, "the author's position and ideology vis-à-vis life."[40] To Teramura, *Chibikuro* did indeed have an ideological agenda:

> There are many who claim that *Chibikuro* is ideology-less literature, but this is an egregious misunderstanding; the ideology here is "racial discrimination" (*jinshu sabetsu*). Most [of the variant editions] use the word "*kurombō*" [blackie/nigger] as an equivalent term [for "little black"]. At this point in time, Japanese people are too ignorant concerning just how many people in Asia, Africa, and America have been humiliated beneath the connotation of the word nigger . . . we could say that this story is Bannerman's—an Englishwoman who came to colonial India—interesting representation of niggers with a low standard of living who were interesting precisely because they were niggers with a low standard of living.[41]

Teramura's argument marked a dramatic shift from previous critiques of Sambo. First, contrary to critiques that deemed *Chibikuro* an exemplar of what children's literature should be, Teramura claimed that *Chibikuro* could not be called literature at all. The rationale behind the text's demotion was its appalling ideological stance; this is effectively the inverse of Torigoe's argument, which posited that *Chibikuro*'s literary greatness outweighed any potential ideological shortcomings. We see here, then, a connection to the circuit of affection founded by Iizawa during the counterfeit texts debates; a circuit in which the ethical vectors of affective response—how postwar Japanese readers should feel about the representation of the colonized by the colonizer—override the others.

The Reevaluation and Reconstruction of *Chibikuro,* 1974–1987

Clearly cognizant of the ideology and rhetoric of the civil rights movement, scholars who took up Teramura's mantle did so with eyes turned both toward their own racialized identity and toward identification with black Americans, and nowhere was this dual gaze more acutely accentuated than in a 1974 special edition of *Ehon* magazine titled "How Should We See *Little Black Sambo*?" The ten articles that composed the special edition were preceded by a collection of photographs by Yoshida Ruiko (1938–). Yoshida, a Fulbright recipient and award-winning photographer, spent ten years in Harlem. Upon her return to Japan, Yoshida displayed her photography of Harlem at an exhibit titled *Harlem—Black Is Beautiful.* Yoshida was known in particular for her pictures of the children of Harlem. Yoshida photographed the children, whom she affectionately dubbed Haaremu-ko (Harlem babies), from an angle and proximity that gives the viewer the impression that the children are literally and figuratively looking up to her.[42] These photographs, which lock the viewers' gaze with that of the children of Harlem, flanked the articles of the *Ehon* special editions.

Of the ten articles, nine vociferously affirmed the beauty of blackness and condemned *Chibikuro,* a text that did not accurately represent said beauty.[43] The articles shared undercurrents of: (1) anti-*Sambo* (due to its racist connotations and amateurish illustrations) and anti-Bannerman (due to her status as a jewel of the empire) sentiment; (2) familiarity with and mobilization of the *mots d'ordre* of the civil rights movement; (3) self-reference to the Japaneseness of the essay contributors—that is, positing the contributors as "colored" critics; (4) privileging of lived experience and "actual contact" with black culture and black people; (5) criticism of the effacement of the possibility of ideology in nonsensical texts; (6) construction and emphasis of a discriminated/discriminator or colonizer/colonized dichotomy; and (7) criticism of children's literature specialist Watanabe Shigeo's positing of an Archimedean, neutral position from which Japanese critics might read American literature without evaluating its racial overtones.

In concert, these seven points of continuity are an articulation of the bona fides of a burgeoning reading community. This concert sounds the (attempted) creation of a circuit of affection that connects the affective ethics of reading *Chibikuro*—we ought, to answer Teramura's question, to feel disgusted by Bannerman's Sambo—to a transracial, transpacific circuit of like-hearted readers. As Takuma Hideo, one of the contributors to the *Ehon* special edition, concludes: "Can we sit by . . . and say with a careless face that it is like this in America and like that in England? . . . I want people to know the reality of the masses of Japanese people like us who suffer at the hands of groundless discrimination, and that this is a problem that connects with the foundation of Japan's democracy . . . I truly hope that by discussing *Chibikuro Sambo* our inner circle broadens."[44]

The special edition of *Ehon* was both a bellwether and an accelerant of the shifting reception of *Chibikuro* in 1970s Japan. Pace the "raceless" affirmation of the text's literary value that occurred in the 1950s and the 1960s, the post-*Ehon* critique of *Chibikuro* showed affinity with the (predominately) African American critique of the text. Mobilizing the logical, rhetorical, and affective strategies of the black power and the black arts movements, Japanese critics began to question the colonial context of the production of *Chibikuro* as well as the relationship between modes of literary representation and racism/power.

In 1978—five years after the *Ehon* articles—Iwanami released the twenty-eighth printing of *Chibikuro Sambo,* a printing that underwent some thirty-seven edits. The majority of these were geared toward enhancing the rhythm and readability of the text and increasing the fidelity of the Iwanami translation to Bannerman's original. Two of the edits, however, seem to constitute Iwanami's response to the growing maelstrom of anti-*Chibikuro* sentiment. Since its 1953 debut and through twenty-six reprints, the narrator of the Iwanami version had introduced *Chibikuro* as a "cute nigger boy" (*kawaii kurombō no otoko no ko*). In the twenty-eighth edition, however, Sambo received a new epithet: "cute *black* boy" (*kawaii kuroi otoko no ko*). In addition to this substitution of the racial epithet for the (neutral?) color black, this updated version also included Bannerman's parenthetical translation of *ghi.* The sanitization of "nigger" and the insertion of *ghi* can be seen as Iwanami's attempt to distance itself from the claim of racial discrimination that plagued *Little Black Sambo.*

By the 1980s, the onus was now on *Chibikuro* advocates: *Chibikuro* was guilty of racism until proven innocent. Arguing for—rather than against—*Chibikuro* had become anathema. Watanabe Shigeo, the W of ISWMI, was a case in point. In 1980, Watanabe published *Yonen bungaku no sekai* (The world of juvenile literature), a compilation of the essays he had written on children's literature over the years. Watanabe concluded *The World* by recounting his 1977 exchange with the American Library Association (ALA). Watanabe was invited to be a guest speaker at an ALA convention. Upon reviewing a draft of his speech—which had numerous references to how much black people enjoyed *Little Black Sambo* during the 1950s—the ALA informed Watanabe both of his "right" to leave the speech as it was and of the changing popular sentiment regarding Sambo. Americans in the 1970s, the ALA reminded Watanabe, were more cognizant of inequalities that were ignored in the past. Watanabe removed the sections in question from his lecture.

What is interesting about Watanabe's ordeal is that he would face the very same critique on the other side of the Pacific. Miyake Okiko, one of the contributors to the *Ehon* collection, suggested that Watanabe's commentary on *Chibikuro* "didn't give the reader much to chew on" insofar as, when charged with the task of determining which books would be placed on the shelves of the children's library and which would not, Watanabe's Archimedian cry of "not belonging to either side" is an impossibility.[45] Analogous to the ALA admonition, Miyake deemed Watanabe's words tone deaf, naïve, and representative of apathy vis-à-vis discrimination. The affinity between Miyake and the ALA is indicative of the 1980s *Ehon*-styled transpacific circuit of affection.

Conclusion: Toward a Transoceanic *Little Black Sambo* Debate

The popularity of *Little Black Sambo* in Japan was maintained long after scholars such as Miyake rang its death knell. The numbers are telling: twenty-two publishing houses combined to produce forty-nine versions of *Chibikuro* between the years 1953 (when publishing giant Iwanami published the story as a part of the inaugural line of its children's book series) and 1988 (when the outbreak of the *Chibikuro Sambo ronsō* erupted). The Iwanami version alone sold more than 1.2 million copies of the text in the aforementioned time period. More impressive than the quantitative aspect of the proliferation of Sambo, however, is its remarkable cultural reach. From Emperor Showa's childhood fascination with the tale (he would play Little Black Sambo with his English tutor), to bewildered librarians' accounts of the book being so popular that it was literally torn to shreds, to literary scholars arguing that *Sambo* is the paragon of children's literature, to the Japanese Ministry of Education and Technology-sanctioned versions of *Chibikuro,* to parents forming concerned citizens committees, by 1988, *Chibikuro* had, to borrow the words of Ochiai Akiko, "permeated Japanese society."[46]

On July 22, 1988, the *Washington Post* ran an article titled "Old Black Stereotypes Find New Lives in Japan; Marketers Defend Sambo Toys." Margaret Shapiro, an editor and foreign correspondent for the *Post* stationed in Tokyo, argued vehemently that "Little Black Sambo, the racist caricature that most Americans thought had died a well-deserved death years ago, has been resurrected across the Pacific as the mascot of a hot-selling line of Japanese toys and beachwear." The toys and beachwear in question were manufactured by Sanrio and featured Sambo—drawn in the minstrel mode—making color(ed) commentary such as: "When I'm Hungry there's no stoppin' me. I'll be up a palm pickin' coconuts before you can count to three. (An' I can count way past three, too!)."[47]

Starting with the work of scholars such as John Russell, a substantial amount of research exists on the debates that erupted after the publication of the 1988 *Post* article. Indeed, this moment—in which actors ranging from nine-year-old Arita Hajime and his Association to Stop Racism against Blacks to the United States Congressional Black Caucus pressured Japan (which was eager to appear cosmopolitan before and during its bid for the Winter Olympics), its public libraries, and eleven major publishing houses to cease printing and lending *Little Black Sambo*—lends itself to the kind of analysis done here. What I have tried to add to that conversation by moving the 1988 debate to the margins, however, is that which might be lost in the rush to critique *the* Japanese reading of *Little Black Sambo* or uphold *the* American (read: correct) reading. What is lost in the fervent dichotomous rhetoric of us-versus-them is analysis of the hermeneutic apparatuses and affective knowledge that have accompanied and informed interpretations of *Little Black Sambo* since its 1899 birth.

Rhetorical hermeneutic analysis of *Sambo* on both sides of the Pacific reminds us that literature that crosses racial, ethnic, and national borders inevitably and perpetually engenders new localized readings. In an age when words proliferate miles beyond the borders of their point of origin, we must, in the words of Rey Chow, "insist on the careful analyses of texts, on responsibly engaged rather than facilely dismissive judgments, and on deconstructing the ideological assumptions in discourses of 'opposition' and 'resistance' as well as in discourse of mainstream power."[48] I would add to Chow's suggestion that, in the case of the text that is racialized identity, our "responsible engagement" should extend beyond evaluative accounts of fictional texts to accounts of the affective judgments that charge through the circuitry of our reading processes themselves. The need for this extension, moreover, becomes acute when the proliferating stories we are reading retrace the very routes of former imperial power(s). For *Sambo* in postwar Japan, this means recalibrating our methodology so that we can consider the currents of affective knowledge and the historical ebb and flow of the affect of reading race.

Notes

1. See Mary Ellen Goodman, *Race Awareness in Young Children* (New York: Collier Books, 1952), 190.

2. Seiichi Miyahara, "'Chibikuro Sambo' no omoshirosa" (The appeal of Little Black Sambo), *Bungaku* 22 (1954): 54.

3. Ibid.

4. Ibid.

5. "Hearts and Minds: An Introduction to the Role of Affect in Social Cognition and Behavior," in *Affect in Social Thinking and Behavior*, ed. Joseph Forgas (New York: Psychology Press, 2006), 4.

6. Ibid.

7. Stephen Mailloux, "Re-making Slave Bodies: Rhetoric as Production and Reception," *Philosophy and Rhetoric* 35 (2002): 98.

8. My methodology builds on what Steven Mailloux calls rhetorical-hermeneutical analysis, "a version of cultural rhetorical studies that focuses on the tropes, arguments, and narratives constituting the interpretations of texts at specific times and places." Such focus "encourages a practical and theoretical preoccupation with making sense of the political dynamics of cultural conversations at specific historical moments"—a process that Mailloux refers to as "the use of rhetoric to practice theory by doing history." See Mailloux, "Re-making Slave Bodies."

9. The sheer proliferation of Sambo imagery in the years that preceded the initial publication of *Sambo* and its translation into Japanese make such nescience unlikely. Textual analysis of *Little Black Sambo*—particularly when paired with Phyllis Yuill's reconstruction of Bannerman's personal library—suggests that her text is informed by racial encounters with the Sambo prototypes seen in works such as Hoffman's *Der Struwwelpeter*, Thackeray's *Vanity Fair*, and Park's *Travels in the Interior Districts of Africa*. As for Japan, scholars such as Karl Chua, John Russell, and Shana Redmond have documented imperial Japan's Sambo-style, minstrel-like representation of both Southeast Asians and African Americans. For accounts of the history of Sambo in Japanese, see Sugio Toshiaki, *Yakareta "Chibikuro Sambo": Jinshu sabetsu to hyōgen, kyōiku no jiyū* (Burnt Little Black Sambo: Racial discrimination and free expression/education) (Tokyo: Aoki shoten, 1992); and John Russell, *Nihonjin no kokujinkan: Mondai wa "Chibikuro Sambo" dake de wa nai* (The Japanese view of blacks: The problem goes beyond Little Black Sambo) (Tokyo: Shinhyōron, 1991). For an English-language introduction, see Karl Chua, *Gai-*

jin: Cultural Representations through Manga, 1930s–1950s (PhD diss., Hitotsubashi University, 2010).

10. See Phyllis Barton, *The Pictus Orbis Sambo* (Sun City, CA: Pictus Orbis Press, 1998), 67.

11. Charles W. Chesnutt, "Mars Jeems's Nightmare," in *Chesnutt: Stories, Novels, and Essays* (New York: Penguin Putnam, 2002), 36–37.

12. Nina Mikkelsen, "Little Black Sambo Revisited," *Children's Literature* 29 (2001): 261.

13. Stanley Elkins, *Slavery: A Problem in American Institutional and Intellectual Life* (Chicago: University of Chicago Press, 1976), 82.

14. *Little Black Sambo* was often included in anthologies of children's literature and bibliographies of recommended reading for children composed by librarians and scholars of children's literature. In 1909, Gertrude Arnold's *A Mother's List of Books for Children* asserted that "written and illustrated by an Englishwoman in India for her two small daughters, Little Black Sambo, with its absurd story, and funny crude pictures in color, will delight young children of all lands." Gertrude Arnold, *A Mother's List of Books for Children* (Chicago: A. C. McClurg, 1909), 23. The text's public sanctioning spanned the decades; in 1940, the U.S. Department of Interior's book list, *500 Books for Children,* endorsed Sambo, calling him "the beloved heir of the jungle." Nora Buest, *500 Books for Children* (Washington, DC: U.S. Government Printing Office, 1940).

15. May Arbuthnot, *Children's Books Too Good to Miss* (Cleveland: Western Reserve University Press, 1953), 14.

16. Elizabeth Hay, *Sambo Sahib: The Story of Little Black Sambo and Helen Bannerman* (Totowa, NJ: Barnes and Noble, 1981), 159.

17. In 1922, for example, Alice Dunbar-Nelson wrote in "Negro Literature for Negro Pupils" that: "the ancient Greeks, wishing to impress upon their children the greatness of Hellas, made the schoolboys memorize Homer... The Romans saturated their youth with Roman literature... The Chinese child learns volumes of Confucius... The French child recites La Fontaine, even before he can read... All this is by way of reminding ourselves that for two generations we have given brown and black children a blonde ideal of beauty to worship, a milk-white literature to assimilate, and a pearly Paradise to anticipate, in which their dark faces would be hopelessly out of place... There is a manifest remedy to this condition... We will give the children the poems and stories and folklore and songs *of their own people.*" See Dunbar, "Negro Literature for Negro Pupils," in *The Harlem Renaissance 1920–1940: The Emergence of the Harlem Renaissance,* ed. Cary Wintz (New York: Garland Press, 1996), 17–18.

18. Miyahara, "Chibikuro Sanbo," 54.

19. Ibid.

20. Ibid., 56 (my emphasis).

21. As quoted in Shin Torigoe, *Nihon jidō bungaku* (Children's literature in Japan) (Tokyo: Kenpakusha, 1995), 136.

22. Ibid., 139.

23. Momoko Ishii, *Kodomo no toshokan* (The children's library) (Tokyo: Iwanami shoten, 1965), 149.

24. Ibid.

25. Takao Murase, "'Chibikuro Sambo' no miryoku to kodomo," *Bungaku* 28 (January 1960): 38.

26. Momoko Ishii, *Kodomo to bungaku* (Children and literature) (Tokyo: Chuō kōron, 1960), 165–166.

27. Shin Torigoe et al., "Kodomo no tame no ryōsho no jyōken—saiwa honan shōyaku no mondai ten" (The terms of good children's books—The problems of retellings, adaptations, and abridged translations), *Tosho shimbun,* May 1, 1965, 8.

28. Ibid.

29. Ibid.

30. Ibid.

31. Tadasu Iizawa, "Ii kagen na kyōdō kenkyū—ganbutsu hantei ni kōgi suru" (Half-baked collaborative research—protesting the counterfeit judgment), *Tosho shimbun,* May 15, 1965, 6.

32. Iizawa also claimed that an elephant that had been given as a gift from an English zoo to an American zoo had also gone by the moniker Sambo. That Bannerman's black father figure shared a name with an animal was, for Iizawa, further proof of her imperial, colonial mindset.

33. Shin Torigoe, "Chibikuro sambo shingaron ni tsuite, Iizawa Tadazu-shi ni kotaeru" (On the Little Black Sambo counterfeit texts debate—a response to Mr. Iizawa Tadazu), *Tosho shimbun,* May 29, 1965, 7.

34. Ibid.

35. Ibid.

36. Introduction to *Chiisa na toshokan* 14 (Tokyo: Akane shobō, 1972), 8.

37. Ibid., 14.

38. See Teruo Teramura, "*Chibikuro Sambo* no ryōmen" (The two faces of Little Black Sambo), *Chiisa na toshokan* 14, 18. Citing the results of Murase's study that had been conducted some fifteen years earlier, Teramura also contended that *Chibikuro,* in addition to being interesting, had structural rhythm, a plot with unexpected developments, and allowed children to identify with *Chibikuro.*

39. Ibid.

40. Ibid.

41. Ibid., 19.

42. The suffix *ko* (child), when attached to a place name, denotes one who was "born and bred" and therefore representative of a given place. It is often attached to places that hold cultural gravitas, i.e., Edokko, a "Child of Edo/Tokyoite," or Hama-ko (beach baby, one born and raised in the Yokohama area). As such, Harlem-ko is a kind of linguistic inclusion of Harlem in a Japanese practice of identification.

43. The critical undercurrent of these nine articles may be juxtaposed with the tenth entry of the special edition, an interview with Ann Herring. Herring, an Oregon native who received her academic training at the University of Washington and Stanford, was a children's literature specialist who lived in Japan and taught at Japanese universities. Herring's interview was a kind of apologia that responded to the other essays' criticism of Bannerman's text and argued that the problem was not in the text itself but in the Japanese translation and attempted to offset the "racist" facets of the text by situating the work within its "proper" intertextual matrix: Indian folklore. Moreover, Herring effectively inverted the logic of the special edition by proffering that the proliferation of "black is beautiful" rhetoric should mitigate the problems associated with a "little black" protagonist. Herring's contribution takes on a peculiar shape when viewed in the context of the special edition. In a collection of essays that critique *Sambo* to the point of Hitler references, Herring's is the only interview, the only work accompanied by photographs of the author, and the only pro-*Sambo* treatise. It does not seem too speculative to suggest that Herring—a simulacrum of Bannerman whose whiteness was literally shown to the reader but shown between (or interviewed) the critique of white superiority that took place throughout the collection—was presented as a paragon of the lack of the previously noted *bona fides*: (white) Herring cannot intuit the racism of the text, but *we* (colored Japanese) can—Herring is not a member of *our* community.

44. Hideo Takuma, "Chibikuro Sambo de kangaeru koto" (Thinking through little black Sambo), *Ehon,* 1974, 27.

45. Miyake, Okiko. "Watanabe Shigeo *Yōnen bungaku no sekai*—Jidō toshokan no hitsuyōsei ni settokuryoku/hagire no warui *Chibikuro Sambo* ron" (On Watanabe Shigeo's *The World of Children's Literature*—the persuasive need for children's libraries, or inarticulate arguments for *Little Black Sambo*), *Shūkan dokushojin* (November 24, 1980).

46. Akiko Ochiai, "Nihon ni okeru 'Chibikuro Sambo' ronsō no tenkai: Bei-ei to no hikaku kara saguru jinshu mondai to nihonjin" (The development of the "Little Black Sambo" debate in Japan: Investigating the race problem in Japan through comparison with England and America), *Jinbun ronshū* 39 (2004): 35.

47. Margaret Shapiro, "Old Black Stereotypes Find New Lives in Japan; Marketers Defend Sambo Toys," *Washington Post*, July 22, 1988.

48. See Rey Chow, "Theory, Area Studies, Cultural Studies: Issues of Pedagogy in Multiculturalism," in *Learning Places: The Afterlives of Area Studies*, ed. Harry Harootunian and Masao Miyoshi (Durham, NC: Duke University Press, 2002), 115.

Delivering Lu Xun to the Empire

The Afterlife of Lu Xun in the Works of Takeuchi Yoshimi, Dazai Osamu, and Inoue Hisashi

> Boss, Had another unexpected attack of asthma in the middle of the night.
> Won't be able to keep my promise to see you at ten—really sorry about that.
> Just one favor, call Dr. Sudō for me. As quickly as possible . . . Humbly, L.
>
> —Lu Xun

Lu Xun (1881–1936) lamented that he had never been able to write a full-length novel, and yet despite that perceived failure, no other twentieth-century Chinese writer has enjoyed a more legendary afterlife in Japan. Apart from having spent nearly seven years (1902–1909) studying in Japan, his works address questions that resonate deeply in the spiritual and intellectual consciousness of Chinese and Japanese—questions of modernity, urbanization, loneliness, resistance, race, ethnicity, ideology, politics, and war. However, the lingering aura of Lu Xun in Japan is also the product of interpretations that scholars and writers in biographies and fiction have generated about him. Such interpretations deliver images and representations of a Lu Xun whose race and nationality made him different but whose education and deep personal, intellectual, aesthetic, and social commitments in Japan lessened the sense of difference.

Although harsh and unsettled disputes persist between China and Japan, anyone will find it difficult to reject interpretations so sincerely and intelligently packed with sympathy for a tortured artist and intellectual leader who bore the pain of internal political chaos and international war and conflicts. Japanese representations of Lu Xun embody anger, grief, and above all a longing for reconciliation. Such sentiments made it possible to admire the opponent even as the empire was about to implode, and Sino-Japanese relations were teetering toward total collapse. That possibility continues to engender hope in subsequent historical moments, including the current one in which the lingering wounds of territorial disputes and war crimes were recently reopened.

This chapter will focus on representations of Lu Xun in Takeuchi Yoshimi's (1910–1977) *Rojin* (Lu Xun, 1944), Dazai Osamu's (1909–1948) *Sekibetsu* (Farewell,

1945), and Inoue Hisashi's (1934–2010) *Shanhai muun* (Shanghai moon, 1991). There are many other works on Lu Xun by Japanese scholars and writers, but I have selected these three very different writers working in three different genres—biographies, fiction, plays—for their efficacy in creating a figure that crosses national, racial, and ideological borders; that is, a Lu Xun who embodies humanity's frailties and greatness while enduring the trials of a modernizing Asia. None of these writers met Lu Xun in person, and they draw from existing historical records and literary works to compose an afterlife for Lu Xun. However, they would not have been able to deliver a sympathetic Lu Xun, unbound by space and time, had they only relied on historical facts and objective reality. They dig deep into the modes of their being to construct a life that speaks eloquently of their own personal dreams and losses. Their works aim less to defend Lu Xun and more to deliver him in his full presence to the reader. All three writers are seduced by Lu Xun, and they reconfigure him to seduce others, in a subtle, affective, and deeply personal language. They narrate their own stories through the ghost of Lu Xun. Lu Xun, *c'est moi,* they speak quietly yet persistently, and in those whispers one detects the writers' personal struggles with their relationship to the Japanese Empire. It was not simply a matter of whose side they took but whether there was an identifiable side to begin with. Sympathy for Lu Xun evokes a necessary reflection on difference and empire. A combination of sympathy and intellectual reflection augments the human capacity to translate abstract and seemingly larger-than-life issues, such as empire, war, territorial disputes, and political and ideological differences, into simultaneously rational and affective expressions and, in doing so, foster a better state of mutual understanding and tolerance.

Takeuchi's *Lu Xun* and Dazai's *Farewell* were published in the last two years of the Fifteen-Year War, when Sino-Japanese relationships had reached a state of crisis, and signs of the imminent collapse of Japan's Asian Empire were everywhere. Inoue's play *Shanghai Moon* was written nearly half a century later, when the postwar Japanese economic empire was about to implode in 1991 and plunge Japan into a prolonged state of recession that would compel it to enter a soul-searching reassessment of its relations with the United States and its Asian neighbors. In that sense, all three works serve to deliver a thought-provoking Lu Xun who forces a degenerating empire to think about its place vis-à-vis others and, above all, to reflect on its role in an Asian community rife with racial, ethnic, and cultural differences.

Takeuchi's *Lu Xun*

Takeuchi's publication of *Lu Xun* was preceded by an essay submitted to the magazine *Kaizō* (1931) by Masuda Wataru (1903–1977) titled "Rojinden" (A life of Lu Xun)[1] and Oda Takeo's (1900–1979) full-length study by the same title (1941). Masuda had actually studied under Lu Xun in Shanghai in 1931 and was in charge of the *Dai Rojin zenshū* (Collected works of Lu Xun) planned by Kaizōsha soon after Lu Xun's death in 1936, while Oda Takeo's exhaustive biography covered Lu Xun's life from cradle to grave. It was Takeuchi, however, who created the image of Lu Xun as one who shared with the Japanese the burden and exhilaration of modernity as well as the grief and loss of war. Indeed, Lu Xun in Japan is always Takeuchi no Rojin (Takeuchi's Lu Xun), a fact that raises the question of how he was able to produce a figure that found such a widespread sympathetic reception.

Takeuchi entered the Chinese department at the Tokyo Imperial University in April 1931. On September 18, the Manchurian Incident that marked the beginning of the Fifteen-Year War broke out. In 1932, Takeuchi joined the Chōsen-Manshū (Korea-Manchuria) student study tour organized by the Foreign Ministry, visited Changchun and Dalian, and then used personal funds to extend his study for two months in Beijing. The literary scene in China in the 1930s was vibrant. Over ten years had passed since Lu Xun had published the landmark political satire "Kuangren riji" (Diary of a madman, 1918), a story noted for its shocking metaphor of a cannibalistic China, and the literary scene was bubbling with literary societies and politically oriented magazines vying for a place to shape modern Chinese literature. These include Chen Duxiu's Xinqingnian She (New Youth Society), which advocated literary revolution; Zhou Zuoren and Mao Dun's Wenxue Yanjiuhui (Literary Studies Society), whose *Xiaoshuo yuebao* (Fiction monthly) promoted the idea of "literature for the sake of daily life"; and Yu Dafu and Guo Muoro's Chuangzaoshe (Creation Society), whose *Chuangzao jikan* (Creation quarterly) championed romanticism in twentieth-century literature. The young Takeuchi could not tell one magazine from the other, but he was enraptured with all the feverish activities. Upon returning to Japan, he persuaded his college friend Takeda Taijun (1912–1976), as well as Okazaki Toshio (1909–1959), Matsue Shigeo (1905–1995), and Masuda Wataru to start the Chūgoku Bungaku Kenkyūkai (Society for the Study of Chinese Literature) and establish the monthly newsletter *Chūgoku bungaku geppō* (Chinese literature monthly). In 1937, roughly three months after the Marco Polo Bridge Incident that led to an all-out war between China and Japan, Takeuchi left for Beijing to study Chinese literature. What he encountered in a Beijing occupied by the Japanese military was hostility and mistrust from the Chinese and an immense loneliness for a young Japanese scholar irrevocably drawn to Chinese literature.[2]

The realization of loneliness as a modern condition enabled Takeuchi to find a critical voice to create an afterlife for Lu Xun. It spoke for Takeuchi's own shame, loss, anger, and above all, loneliness, as well as that of an entire generation of people on both shores living through the expansion and collapse of Japan's Asian Empire. To Takeuchi, writing about Lu Xun was to write about himself. He confessed an absolute and willing surrender to the power of Lu Xun's afterlife: "I was one of those possessed by Lu Xun. My own life happened to intersect with his at a certain point and I became obsessed with him, and up to this day I am still inextricably bound to him. I am afraid his shadow will be with me all my life. I cannot live without an awareness of him, and the more I am aware of him, the more deeply he dwells within me."[3] While Oda's biography of Lu Xun started with his birth, as biographies usually do, Takeuchi began his at the opposite end—Lu Xun's death—and proceeded with the narrative strategy of constructing, indeed, a ghost and a spirit, instead of a life. On his impulse in writing about Lu Xun, Takeuchi explained, "What I want to write about is the human image of Lu Xun that lives in my imagination."[4] As the testimony of time has revealed, it was not Lu Xun's life but his ghost who took hold of an imagination beyond the confines of nationality and race.

To deliver Lu Xun to the empire in 1944, and to do so in such a way that evoked sympathy and admiration, Takeuchi presented three images of the man: the revolutionary, the loner, and the exile. The reader also sees in those images the shadow of Sun Yatsen (1866–1925), Natsume Sōseki (1867–1916), and Takeuchi himself. He distilled a man's life into a few remarkable qualities to regenerate its intellectual, aesthetic, or philosophical essence. In doing so, what is recognizably heroic, tragic, and sympathetic passes from one body to another and becomes seamlessly incorporated in the collective consciousness of the readers. Takeuchi's Lu Xun was fashioned and delivered with the characteristics of familiar modern heroes that are bound to find resonance in readers no matter where they are situated in the empire. In other words, Takeuchi fashioned a language and a strategy to create a transnational hero in Lu Xun. While Masuda's or Oda's Lu Xun was informative, factual, and even appealing within the confines of given historical and geographical domains, Takeuchi's Lu Xun haunts the modern imagination like a ghost; ubiquitous, regenerative, global—a composition of transnational modern consciousness that crosses borders.

Borrowing from Sun Yatsen's image to construct Lu Xun's came naturally to Takeuchi. In his first visit to China as a student in 1931, he was enthralled with Sun's Three Principles of the People: *minzhu* (the people's rule = populism), *minquan* (the people's power = democracy), and *minsheng* (the people's livelihood). Sun seemed to be Lu Xun's double in many ways—his indefatigable revolutionary spirit, his constant political struggle and exile to Japan and other countries, his lasting achievement of destroying the old regime, the transitory glory before falling out of power—all these matched what Takeuchi identified in Lu Xun's literary protest against a tyrannical regime that "consumed its own people."[5] Lu Xun indeed wrote a year after Sun's death that "he was everything. He was an eternal revolutionary. Every deed of his was a revolution. No matter how much people criticized his shortcomings, he was to the very end revolution itself."[6]

Takeuchi seized upon Lu Xun's admiration of Sun and established the affinity between the two. "Lu Xun admired Sun, and everything that he stood for," wrote Takeuchi. "He adored Sun . . . He considered Sun a real revolutionary. And what is a real revolutionary? It is someone who, in the face of death, cried 'the revolution is not complete.'"[7] In pairing Sun with Lu Xun, Takeuchi delivered the image of Lu Xun as a revolutionary to the empire. That Lu Xun was transformed into a national hero in his death did not detract from his transnational image as an eternal fighter whose war, a war for humanity that transcended borders and barriers, remained unfinished.[8] Takeuchi suggested strongly that Lu Xun's death was a loss not only for the Chinese but for all humanity. The testimony of time revealed that Takeuchi's narrative strategy was on the mark. Like Sun, Lu Xun is one of the very few political and cultural figures in the twentieth century still admired on both sides of the Taiwan Strait and who continues to hold a place in the Asian imagination.

The key to capturing a Lu Xun as a loner came from words that Lu Xun himself provided: loneliness (Ch. *jimuo,* J. *sekibaku* 寂寞) and sadness (Ch. *beiai,* J. *hiai* 悲哀). In the much quoted preface to the anthology *Nahan* (Outcry, 1923), Lu Xun wrote about his own setback in using literature as a tool to modernize China.

> This loneliness grew bigger and bigger each day. Like a poisonous snake, it wound around my soul.

> I felt no anger even though I experienced boundless sadness, since this setback forced me to reflect on myself. I am not a hero who can gather crowds with a simple call.[9]

It is significant that these affective terms bear the same meaning in the Sinophone sphere, and Takeuchi constructed a Lu Xun around those words. Despite Lu Xun's multiple roles as teacher, political leader, and national hero, Takeuchi argued that he was a literary man to the marrow, a loner, and an aborted *Übermensch* (superman) wandering in darkness and despair.[10] Takeuchi painted a portrait of a Lu Xun tormented by the helplessness of literature yet obstinately attached to it. He quoted from Lu Xun's lecture at the Huangpu Military Academy, "Geming shidai de wenxue" (Literature in the time of revolution, 1926):[11]

> We make a fuss about literature precisely because it is powerless and serves no purpose. Those in power kill people without making a sound. If those under duress would speak and write just a tiny bit, they will be killed. As for those who are fortunate enough to escape death, if they were to express their suffering and injustice, they will be tortured and murdered by those in power. There's nothing they can do about it. What's the use of that kind of literature.[12]

Despite his skepticism of the efficacy of literature as a political tool, Lu Xun continued to write, and Takeuchi called Lu Xun's literature "the literature of atonement."

> Whenever I read his works, I always come across something like a shadow. It's always in the same place. The shadow itself does not really exist and disappears when there is light, but it is like a point of darkness that makes one think about existence. . . . Lu Xun bore that shadow on his back his entire life. That's why I call his work the literature of atonement.[13]

Takeuchi did not make a direct reference to Japan's own national writer Sōseki in his portrait of Lu Xun, but the keywords—loneliness, sadness, *Übermensch,* darkness, shadow, skepticism, atonement—suggest a comparison. Sōseki and his characters continued to have a strong hold on the romantic and intellectual imagination on both shores in the course of the rise and decline of Japan's

Asian Empire, and to recast Lu Xun as Sōseki's spiritual brother without spelling it out is an astute deliverance of difference and sameness to the empire. Takeuchi seemed to suggest that Lu Xun is different but also familiar to the Japanese reader.

Finally, the image of Lu Xun as the exile, of one perpetually drawn to the other side despite deteriorating Sino-Japanese relations, reveals an intimate sympathy and reflection inseparable from Takeuchi's own life. In 1939, after spending two years in Beijing in the midst of the intensification of hostility between the two countries, Takeuchi returned to Japan and published an essay titled "Shina to Chūgoku" (Shina and Chūgoku, 1940). "I feel intuitively that the word Shina suits me. Shina belongs to me."[14] In saying so, Takeuchi bade farewell to the modern state of Chūgoku (Ch. Zhongguo), with which Japan was at war, and turned to the term "Shina" with longing and affection, removing from the word the derogative racist connotation associated with China's repeated defeat and humiliation at the hands of Japan and the West since the First Sino-Japanese War (1895) and resuscitating its association with civilization, literature, culture, and refinement. Other aficionados of China—Akutagawa Ryūnosuke, Tanizaki Jun'ichirō, and Satō Haruo—were called Shinatsū (connoisseurs of China) and their China-related works are a testimony to the shared cultural and linguistic heritage of East Asia and to the indelible place China held in the Japanese intellectual and aesthetic consciousness even after the tide of Westernization and modernization washed over Meiji Japan. By making this affectionate identification with an idealized Shina rather than the nation Chūgoku, Takeuchi tapped into the deep cultural and linguistic bond among countries in the Sinophone sphere.

Takeuchi's declaration of his affinity with Shina was preceded by the words, "I have no way to rid myself of this penetrating loneliness," the same *jimuo* that wound around Lu Xun's soul like a serpent. The empire continued to test him during the war years. A Sinologist coping with thought control and censorship in an increasingly desperate and despotic empire, Takeuchi drafted (without signing) the declaration "Daitōa sensō to warera no ketsui" (The great East Asia war and our determination, 1942) and printed it in the January issue of *Chūgoku bungaku* (Chinese literature). May 26 saw the establishment of the Nihon Bungaku Hōkokukai (Japanese Literature Patriotic Association [JLPA]), and Takeuchi's Society for the Study of Chinese Literature (SSCL) promptly became a member to avoid persecution and disbandment. On November 3, the first Daitōa Bungakusha Kaigi (Great East Asia Literary Conference) took place in Tokyo, and the SSCL did not participate. In January 1943, Takeuchi decided to dissolve the SSCL and terminate the publication of *Chinese Literature.* He finished the manuscript *Lu Xun* and sent it to the publisher in November. On December 1, he was conscripted to serve as part of a railroad patrol in the Hubei Province of China. He was sent to Hankou after Japan's unconditional surrender in 1945, and even though he had wanted to stay in China, he was repatriated in June 1946 because of the intensification of the civil war there.[15]

There is no doubt that Takeuchi drew inspiration from Lu Xun's life to sustain himself through his own trials and tribulations during the war and postwar years. Lu Xun's sense of alienation from his own government and his deep relationship with Japan would continue to intrigue Takeuchi. In the last years of his life during the 1930s, Lu Xun lived underground in Shanghai to avoid persecution from political and literary foes both Left and Right, and he came to rely on the good services of Uchiyama Kanzō (1885–1959), the owner of Uchiyama Bookshop. That such trust and mutual reliance were possible between people on opposite sides of a war showed how the intellectual, moral, and aesthetic imagination fostered bonds that transcended the confines of state and ideology and allowed the like-minded to form an affiliation across the barriers of time and space. Kawanishi Masaaki notes, "In *Lu Xun,* Takeuchi's loneliness resonates with Lu Xun's. . . . That loneliness echoes across the wall between China and Japan."[16] Takeuchi invested his intellect and emotion in delivering Lu Xun to the empire and thereby delivered himself from the clutches of thought control and censorship.

Dazai's *Farewell*

Dazai's story was commissioned by the aforementioned JLPA, founded in 1942 under the wartime Cabinet Information Bureau (Naikaku Jōhō Kyoku [CIB]). Its goal was "to gather the strength of all writers to establish a Japanese literature that expresses the tradition and ideal of a nation under the Emperor system, and to spread the culture of the Emperor system through literature."[17] The commission was the JLPA's response to the *Great East Asia Joint Manifesto* (*Dai Tōa kyōdō sengen,* November 6, 1943) issued by the Great East Asia Conference (Dai Tōa Kaigi, November 5–6, 1943), with representatives from China, the Philippines, Burma, Thailand, and India. The manifesto consists of five central themes: coprosperity (*kyōson kyōei*), independence (from the West) and affinity with Japan (*dokuritsu shinwa*), cultural elevation (*bunka kōyō*), economic prosperity (*keizai han'ei*), and contribution to world progress (*sekai shin'un kōken*). The JLPA appointed individual writers to be in charge of fiction and drama written according to those themes, and Dazai was made responsible for "independence and affinity with Japan." Dazai's *Farewell* was one of the two commissioned stories to be published.[18]

In the afterword to *Farewell,* Dazai wrote, "Even if those two divisions (CIB and JLPA) had not approached me, I would have attempted to write the story at some point, so I have gathered materials and planned it for a long time."[19] Moreover, he emphasized, "This work was the free expression by the Japanese writer Dazai, who holds ultimate responsibility for it. Neither the CIB nor the JLPA issued any warning to censor my writing. Furthermore, after I finished the piece and submitted it to the JLPA, it approved the work as it was without changing a single word or phrase. I wonder if I should call this 'government and people one in spirit' (*chōya isshin*), but in any case, I am certainly not the only one to be happy about it."[20]

Was Dazai honest in his statements about the work? According to the critic Okuno Takeo, *Farewell* was a disappointment to Takeuchi Yoshimi, Takeda Taijun, and Tsurumi Shunsuke, who until then were enthusiastic and avid supporters of Dazai's work.[21] Was Dazai a sellout to wartime propaganda, and is *Farewell* an aberration, given Dazai's antiestablishment, Burai-ha (Decadent School) reputation? It would be naïve to think that Dazai was not working under the patriotic demands of his time or to expect him to be entirely free from patriotic sentiment when Tokuda Shūsei (1872–1943), Satō Haruo (1892–1964), Mushakōji Saneatsu (1885–1976), and many others were involved in the JLPA. This is not to excuse any of these writers for their nationalistic and at times vitriolic rhetoric, but the point is that Dazai's involvement was not an exception among the generation of literary figures active during the war. Rather than dwelling on the irresolvable question of Dazai's complicity in the general patriotic demands of his time, I will focus on Dazai's aesthetic strategy in making a sympathetic deliverance of Lu Xun to the empire.

Dazai's Lu Xun was always referred to as Shū-san—for Zhou Shuren (Shū Jujin)—the way Lu Xun was called in his student's days in Japan before his pen name gathered fame. Dazai focused on the unknown writer-to-be, creating a portrait of the artist as a young man, and the story emphasizes the period of his life in Sendai, where he decided to abandon medicine for writing. In a statement titled "The Intention of *Farewell*" (Sekibetsu no ito), submitted as a proposal to the CIB, Dazai wrote:

> I plan to write about the young Shū Jujin with fairness and tenderness, without looking down on the Chinese nor fanning feelings of contempt, in the pure and innocent attitude of "Independence and Affinity with Japan." When young Chinese intellectuals read this, *they will feel that there are sympathizers (of China) in Japan,* and I intend this to be a more effective means to promote general peace between Japan and China than a hundred bullets.[22]

The lip service paid to "independence and affinity" notwithstanding, in the italicized phrase one can detect Dazai's intention to rely on an affective appeal to the *sensibilities* (*kanjō o dakashime*) of Chinese intellectuals and to propagate the idea that there are sympathizers (*rikaisha*) of China in Japan.

Dazai's image of Shū Jujin was entirely text-based. He consulted Oda Takeo's *Rojinden* and Takeuchi's *Rojin;* the former he considered "sweet as spring blossoms" and the latter "harsh as autumn frost."[23] Since the story focused on Lu Xun's student life in Sendai, Dazai also consulted Matsue Shigeo's translation of Lu Xun's *Tengye xianshen* (*Fujino sensei,* 1926), an essay about his mentor Fujino and his experience as a foreign student in Sendai. Still, even though Dazai created a portrait of young Lu Xun from existing sources, the central reference for Lu Xun was Dazai himself, who fashioned the textual Shū-san in his own image and spirit.

Dazai's story is told through the notebook of a fictitious old country doctor in the Tohoku region who studied with Shū Jujin in Sendai in 1904–1906. In response to a request from an unkempt middle-aged newspaper reporter, whose alleged intention is to promote "mutual peace among East Asian people," the old doctor agrees to record the image of Shū deep in his mind and let the local newspaper run it in a New Year series under the title of "Spearheading Sino-Japanese Friendship."[24] Skeptical of the uncouth reporter and the slogans of the time, he remarks, "As a senile country doctor nostalgic about my mentor and old friend, my writing has more to do with the wish to capture his image faithfully rather than express any social and political intentions."[25] Thus from the beginning, Dazai used the doctor as a stand-in to deride the hypocritical slogans of his time and announce his attitude and feelings in writing about Lu Xun.

Unlike the frosty intellectual with a piercing gaze in Takeuchi's *Lu Xun,* Dazai's Shū-san is an ordinary, lonely young Chinese student who speaks Japanese with a foreign accent, breaks into German when Japanese proves inadequate to express his thoughts, sings as one who is tone-deaf, struggles with note taking in Japanese and peer relationships in school, hungers for food and friendship, suffers from chills, and sneezes incessantly in the cold. In short, it is the portrait of an awkward young man struggling with commonplace problems at an extraordinary moment in a euphoric and pompous Japan on the cusp of victory in the Russo-Japanese War.

Dazai's narrative strategy lies in aligning the narrator, Shū, and Fujino sensei on the plane of linguistic awkwardness, which immediately marks all three as outsiders in Japan. Raised in Tohoku and moving to the capital, Dazai would be familiar with the feeling of being a stranger in his own country. In his freshman class, students form a Tokyo cohort, or an Osaka cohort, isolating the inarticulate narrator with his heavy country accent. On their first encounter in a trip to Matsushima, the narrator writes, "Only when I talked to Shū-san was I completely liberated from my melancholy as a country folk. When I was with him, my country accent did not trouble me, and to my own amazement, I was capable of making puns and jokes lightly and fluently. Sometimes I got carried away and imitated the Edokko way of talking. Fellow Japanese would no doubt look disgusted and laugh at a country bumpkin rolling his tongue to imitate an Edokko, but this foreign friend did not notice anything untoward."[26] In response to the narrator's description of himself as "a solitary crow" in a mixture of German and Japanese (*einsam no karasu*), Shū reiterates the German word *einsam* and adds that he is a *Wandervogel,* "a lone migrating bird without a home."[27] In addition to sharing the sense of loneliness as outsiders, they are the only two freshmen who refuse to wear the uniform cap in the entrance ceremony, challenging authority from the start.

To these two loners and outsiders, Dazai added the mentor Fujino Gengorō, who is slack in appearance, wears no necktie and an overcoat too short to cover his knees, and speaks with a heavy Kansai accent. "That Fujino sensei, Shū-san, and I became so close was nothing more than a bond based on our mutual ineptitude in Japanese, it seemed, and I can't help but feel sorry about that. . . . But it also felt as though there was something larger that went beyond our 'mutual ineptitude in Japanese' or our 'hitting it off well' . . . something that we believed in and strived for. As for what that was, I really could not tell."[28] The narrator goes on to speculate about a few possibilities, including "mutual respect," "love for one's neighbors," "justice," or "the original way of the East," but none of those provide the key to the bond. That indefinable feeling, that something that eludes verbal explanation, lies at the heart of Dazai's narrative strategy and allowed him to transcend national barriers and deliver Shū Jujin as an outsider whose voice resonates with other outsiders within Japan.

In addition to forging a bond among the three outsiders, Dazai created a contrast in the Tokyoite character Tsuda Kenji, whose given name means "rule by constitution." Tsuda is a caricature of all that is superficial, hypocritical, snobbish, power-hungry, farcical, stingy, and sycophantic about a slogan-toting Tokyoite. In many ways he is a parody and a reduced version of a Red Shirt in Sōseki's *Botchan.* With his premature false teeth and bad breath, Tsuda is a typical mouthpiece of the so-called patriotic youth of his days: xenophobic, doctrinaire, and high-strung. Tsuda tells the narrator, who maintains a close relationship with Shū, "You're unpatriotic. During a war, any person from a third country can be a spy, especially students from Qing Dynasty China. Every single one of them is a revolutionary. To carry out the revolution, they may ask help from the Russians, so we've got to keep an eye on them. You know, kindness on the surface, and surveillance underneath."[29] Tsuda uses words such as *hikokumin* (literally, a nonnational, to indicate someone who is unpatriotic) and *daisankokujin* (a third-country person), contemptuous and derogative terms that surface occasionally even in today's right-wing rhetoric. Tsuda's caricature helps to seal the bond among the three outsiders and provides an obvious opponent on whom to exercise their resistance.

As the critic Okuno Takeo points out, Dazai is not free from a certain "in praise of Japan" (Nihon *sanbi*) rhetoric in the story. This is most obvious in Shū's incredibly long soliloquy (spanning fifteen pages) in the Matsushima inn where he spends a night with the narrator. Using Shū as a vehicle to stress that real patriots are those capable of criticizing their own country, Dazai compared China and Japan, but the comparisons are overwhelmingly in praise of Japan and critical of China. For example, Shū praises Japan for harnessing Western scientific knowledge for modernization and national defense, for being the most intelligent and independent country in Asia, for combining the philosophy and aesthetics of *yūgen* (mysterious darkness) and the sword of science to become an ideal country, for order and cleanliness, for the Meiji Restoration, and for challenging Russia.[30] In contrast, Shū speaks vehemently about China's scientific (especially medical) backwardness, superstition, imposture, self-satisfaction, indolence, and even the unsightly hairstyle of men wearing queues. Knowing that it is Dazai speaking though Shū, one cannot help but feel uncomfortable about his glib patriotic and patronizing tone and his eagerness to slip his opinions by the censors. Yet objectively, except for the hyperbole about Japan being an ideal country, those were comparisons that sprang from an inevitable gap in development between a country that opted for rapid modernization and one that did not. Dazai's guilt lay more in his "sin of omission," that is, in failing to criticize Japan's shortcomings and wrongs as a rising monolithic and military state. In an attempt to beat the censorship and package an appealing Lu Xun to a desperately belligerent Japan in a long-drawn-out war, Dazai substantially toned down his critical voice.

Okuno has an even more sympathetic reading of Dazai's strategy: "Shū's radical anger toward toadyism and hypocrisy, and his suspicion and loathing of those pretending to be hot-blooded revolution, were all Dazai's own feelings."[31] He also observes that "despite the fact that its language betrays a certain degree of enslavement to its time, *Farewell* captures what lies at the foundation of Sino-Japanese relationship."[32] Dazai's achievement in creating an enduring (if not factual or authentic) image of Lu Xun in *Farewell* depended upon the total transformation of the genre of biography into a coming-of-age story (*seishun shōsetsu*) in which Lu Xun's struggle becomes Dazai's own. He delivered Lu Xun to the empire as another Dazai, complete with the anxiety, comicality, and darkness familiar to those grappling with Japan's own modernity. Lu Xun in *Farewell* receives an afterlife as Dazai's double, which in many ways is more appealing and endearing than the many stately and heroic images invented on both sides of the Taiwan Strait to remake him after his death.

Inoue's *Shanghai Moon*

Inoue's play focuses on Lu Xun's last few years of underground life in Shanghai, when he was dodging the attacks from the Rightist government under Chiang Kai-shek and the vitriolic accusations from Leftists who did not share his political and literary opinions.[33] Lu Xun did not believe writing should be harnessed as political propaganda and found himself under attack from the Nationalist government and increasingly isolated from the Left. He lived in Shanghai for a total of nine years from 1927 to his death, and according to his diary, he went underground to avoid persecution four times during those years (1930, 1931, 1932, and 1934).[34] Inoue condensed those four separate occasions to a single instance of underground hiding to intensify the drama. The play is set between August 23 and September 16, 1934; the place is the second floor storage of the Uchiyama Bookshop in North Sichuan Alley (a blind alley in Shanghai); the characters include Lu Xun (53), his second wife Shu Guangping (36), the bookshop owner Uchiyama Kanzō (49) and his wife Uchiyama Miki (41), Lu Xun's physician Sudō Iozō (50), and the dentist Okuda Aizō (39).

Some historical background is in order to contextualize the relationship between Lu Xun and his Japanese friends. Uchiyama Kanzō opened the Uchiyama Bookshop in Shanghai in 1917, carrying books written by progressive writers and serving as a salon for leading Chinese intellectuals well versed in Japanese. Lu Xun, Guo Moruo (1892–1978), and Yu Dafu (1896–1945) frequented the bookstore, and Japanese intellectuals from Kobayashi Hideo (1902–1983) to Mushakōji Saneatsu would also visit when they were in Shanghai. Lu Xun met Uchiyama on October 5, 1927, and began a lifelong friendship of trust and shared ideals. Uchiyama provided a refuge for Lu Xun during his repeated persecutions in the 1930s, and in 1932 his bookstore began serving as the distributor for Lu Xun's works. Lu Xun called Uchiyama "Laoban" (boss), acknowledging with fondness not only Uchiyama's status as the owner of the bookshop but also as Lu Xun's benefactor.[35] Sudō Iozō (1876–1959) was a retired military doctor who opened a clinic in Shanghai in 1919. He served as Lu Xun's main physician in his last years and paid frequent home visits to him and his family. For over three years until Lu Xun's death, Sudō's name was mentioned over 150 times in Lu Xun's diary.[36] Finally, Okuda Aizō (dates unclear), also known as Okuda Anka, was a dentist and an artist who had a dental clinic near Uchiyama Bookstore. He was at Lu Xun's deathbed and made his death mask, which is on display in the Lu Xun Memorial Museum in Shanghai.[37]

The title *Shanghai Moon* refers to a story that the fictitious Lu Xun plans to write if he were to escape to Kamakura with the dentist Okuda. It is a story about the lack of communication among people dwelling in close proximity and Lu Xun's vision of what the world would be like if people's hearts were to meet. In a tone characteristic of Inoue's picturesque urban scene making, Lu Xun talks about the novel that he will write:

> One day in Shanghai. The time was near moonrise. On the first floor, a young mother lulled her baby to sleep. On the second floor, a dancer put on a jazz record. The third floor attic had no electricity. In the pale moonlight, an ailing young man was on the verge of death. In the house next door, the boisterous laughter of the stockbrokers was mixed with the sound of mahjong. Next to it was a ditch. A boat appeared like an animal skeleton in the moonlight, and in it, a little girl clung to her dead mother, crying. Scattered here and there, our sadness, suffering, happiness simply don't meet. People live and die as sand in the wind. Why don't our hearts meet? How do we change ourselves to make our hearts meet? This will be the theme of this novel. I will call it *Shanghai Moon,* and this will be the first thing I'll write in Kamakura. Thanks! I feel I can write one novel after another! (He scribbles a memo on a notepad with a blunt pencil from his pocket). I'm sure I can do it![38]

Even though the story was never written and the historical Lu Xun did not escape to Kamakura, Inoue delivered to 1991 Japan, now an economic empire on the verge of decline, a Lu Xun who dreams about the meeting of hearts and minds among neighbors; a kind and gentle Lu Xun.[39]

Inoue's work is largely based on information gleaned from Masuda, Oda, Takeuchi, and Dazai, but his portrait of Lu Xun is warmly sympathetic and humorous. By temperament, Inoue was an artist who valued comedy and humor and despised idolization and hero-worship. His most astute political drama and fiction always contain a mixture of piercing political criticism, satire, compassion, and a dose of laughter.[40] His representation of Lu Xun to an economic Japanese Empire struggling with establishing rapport and trust with fellow Asian countries, especially China, conveys Inoue's wish for true reconciliation and understanding. In 1991, when Inoue published the play, some might have taken friendship between China and Japan for granted. Nearly twenty years had passed since the signing of the Joint Communiqué of the Government of Japan and the Government of the People's Republic of China (1972) that reestablished diplomatic relations, and thirteen years had passed from the signing of the Treaty of Peace and Friendship (1978). Yet historical differences and ongoing territorial disputes between China and Japan over the Senkaku Islands (Ch. Diaoyudao), most recently resulting in the cancellation of celebrations on both shores of the fortieth anniversary of the Joint Communiqué, continue to feed into the animosity and distrust between the two countries. These disputes have revealed that the lesson of true reconciliation has neither been learned nor put into practice. Inoue revived Lu Xun in 1991 neither as a national hero nor as an ideological icon but as a compassionate artist who asked these simple questions as he was nearing death: "Why don't our hearts meet? How do we change ourselves to make our hearts meet?"[41]

Inoue's play emphasizes Lu Xun's ailments and frailties in his final years and his deep friendship with the Japanese. However, true to Inoue's comic spirit, Lu Xun's physical impairments and the various methods devised to examine or cure him are delivered in a slapstick comic mode. The play consists of two acts, six scenes, a prologue, and an epilogue. Five of the six scenes center on Lu Xun's illness. The six scenes are titled, respectively, "Arrhythmia," "Tooth ache," "Pathological Suicidal Wish," "Letter and Postcard," "Aphasia," and "Recovery." Not included in the title but included in the play were detailed descriptions of pathological paranoia, decay, nervous conditions, dementia, slurred speech, and hemorrhage that plagued the ailing Lu Xun, all of which are graphically depicted yet rendered as a dark comedy. Inoue uses "aphasia" as a metaphor for Lu Xun's inability to produce literary work and "pathological suicidal wish" to indicate his final desperation. The last scene, "Recovery," is not so much about Lu Xun's actual recovery but the reconfiguration of Lu Xun's final vision as a conscientious writer, an image of Lu Xun that Inoue invents according to his own ideals. Lu Xun's speech, muddled until a moment earlier with aphasia, bursts into lines of great clarity and insight.

> Shanghai is the heart of this country. This is where I will stay. I may not be able to write the novel *Shanghai Moon* anymore, but that doesn't matter. I will write essays to point out the follies of the world. I will not stop writing. That's my responsibility toward the world to come. I will shoulder the burden of my time and place as long as I live.[42]

The epilogue, like the prologue, consists of soliloquies in the form of letters read by the individual characters after Lu Xun's death. His common-law wife, Shu Guangping, utters the last words, which summarize the mystery of Sino-Japanese relationships in 1936.

> Finally, I will list the people who were present at Lu Xun's deathbed. Zhu An,[43] you will be surprised to hear that they are all Japanese. Uchimura Kanzō and his wife Miki, the dentist Dr. Okuda Aizō, who took Lu Xun's death mask, and Dr. Sudō Iozō, his chief physician.[44]

What image of Lu Xun did Inoue intend to deliver in *Shanghai Moon*? In 1936, on the eve of full-fledged war between China and Japan, the man who was later hailed as a national writer and hero by political leaders who used his reputation to their advantage[45] was living in hiding, surrounded by Japanese sympathizers, to escape the hounding of Leftists and Rightists who suspected his loyalty. Lu Xun was resilient and unyielding, but he was no longer capable of producing stories of piercing insight and deep compassion as he had in his most productive years. As an artist he was practically dead already during his final years. Yet Inoue used Lu Xun and his unlikely and unusual sympathy with Japanese friends at a moment of intensifying belligerence between China and Japan as a metaphor to evoke the possibility of human understanding and trust that transcends war and eliminates borders. Inoue emphasized a true reconciliation that can never be taken for granted because it is rarely accomplished or complete. He was a pacifist and an idealist, and his image of Lu Xun conveys a vision of peace that transcends difference and boundaries.

Conclusion

It is difficult to write about Lu Xun without referring to the long process in which I became acquainted with the different versions of him. Growing up bilingual in Chinese and English in the former British colony of Hong Kong and acquiring Japanese in college in the United States, I first encountered the textual Lu Xun in his own writings in Chinese when I was a child. I then studied critical works about him in Chinese and English as a college student and finally, read Japanese works on Lu Xun from the time I was a graduate student to recent years. In this long process of getting to know Lu Xun, I realized Lu Xun was packaged and delivered in different ways, and I also found myself reacting differently to the many versions of Lu Xun, even though there is no final proof that one version is more authentic than another.

My first glimpse of Lu Xun the writer writing about Lu Xun the persona was through the stories *Fengzheng* (The kite, 1925) and *Guxiang* (My old home, 1921), stories incorporated into the elementary and junior high school curriculum in the 1970s. Both stories are replete with loss and regrets; the adult Lu Xun persona in *The Kite* regrets the power abuse over his little brother in his youth and the lost opportunity of apology and forgiveness, while the grown-up protagonist in *My Old Home* mourns the unbridgeable gap that has opened up between himself, now a well-educated man, and his childhood companion, who remains a down-to-earth servant of his family. In addition to these narrative personae, two other Lu Xun personae stand out in my memory. One is the Lu Xun who traces his own decision to abandon medicine for writing to the shame and anger triggered by a slideshow he saw in a Sendai classroom. It showed a group of bemused or nonchalant Chinese witnessing the imminent decapitation of a Chinese man caught by the Japanese as a Russian spy during the Russo-Japanese War.[46] The other is the Lu Xun who captures his own pride and humility in two lines of a poem, "With furrowed eyebrows I withstand the criticisms of a thousand men / Lowering my head I willingly offer my back for a child to ride."[47] These images reveal an extremely self-conscious Lu Xun who continues to cultivate an affective and appealing persona for his reader. The Lu Xun delivered by Lu Xun is deeply affective not because he was always correct, compassionate, or eloquent; on the contrary, the Lu Xun persona tends to be obstinate and unforgiving. Yet he remains appealing to the modern reader because he is always remorseful, critical, skeptical, flawed, and human. In delivering himself to generations of readers, Lu Xun was good at what Brian Massumi called "self-affectation," that is, "the artificial construction of a self and of the suffusing of that self with affect."[48] As a child, not equipped with a critical language to analyze Lu Xun's narrative strategies, I was deeply drawn to his multiple personae.

I must confess that I prefer Lu Xun's delivery of Lu Xun to the national hero packaged by the governments on both sides of the Taiwan Strait after his death. The national hero Lu Xun was placed on stamps and currency and delivered as gigantic statues in alabaster and bronze. I have no interest in Lu Xun placed on a pedestal, but the textual Lu Xun continues to have a strong hold on my imagination and intellect.

In the 1960s and the 1970s, Chinese scholars working outside the Communist regime, such as C. T. Hsia in U.S. academia and Sima Changfeng in Hong Kong, had a tendency to deliver Lu Xun as a quarrelsome polemicist and express disappointment at the lack of creative writing in the last decade of his life. Encountering such critical judgment in my college years, I, too, experienced a deep sense of loss and grief, as though the creative Lu Xun I knew as a child had made a conscious decision to abandon literary art and engage in bitter quarrels with his ideological and political opponents. It was not until the recent encounter with Davies' *Lu Xun's Revolution: Writing in a Time of Violence* (2013) that I came to understand that Lu Xun the polemicist was in fact Lu Xun the artist, since in an age of political and ideological tyranny and savagery, Lu Xun's culminating artistic performance was to argue vehemently in public. Davies has effectively argued that in the last ten years of his life, Lu Xun took polemics to a new height as an art form for the expression of justice.

Another recent scholarly work on Lu Xun, Eileen J. Cheng's *Literary Remains: Death, Trauma, and Lu Xun's Refusal to Mourn* (2013), reevaluates eight short stories collected in *Old Tales Retold*, written in the supposedly parched years of his creative life. Cheng delivers a Lu Xun who refuses to accept the conventional treatment of heroes and sages as superhuman but "humanizes them" in his rewriting of old stories.[49] Thus, it is tremendously stimulating and redeeming that recent critical assessments of Lu Xun break away from the standard judgment and deliver a polemicist who retains his creativity and artistic resilience in an increasingly violent and explosive time both within China and in the Sino-Japanese relationship.

My encounter with Lu Xun in Japanese writings, the focus of this paper, was an important discovery. It was preceded by my earlier encounters with Lu Xun in Chinese and English and came as a belated and pleasant surprise. Lu Xun was liberated from his assigned roles as national writer or hero to become a vehicle and a metaphor for the reader, regardless of nationality, to contemplate modernity and

Sino-Japanese relations. It was refreshing that none of the three writers—Takeuchi, Dazai, and Inoue—attempted to hide Lu Xun's otherness as they deliver him to a system and a historical context that abhors excessive difference.

In thinking about my three encounters with Lu Xun over the years in three different languages, I realize that each encounter fulfills a different need in me to understand him and his work better. The original Lu Xun—that is, Lu Xun on Lu Xun in Chinese—is endearing, intimate, and unmediated in that it has appealed directly to generations of Chinese in the twentieth century who have lost their homes or were born without a sense of home or country. The Lu Xun in critical academic writing in languages accessible to me fulfills an intellectual quest to locate Lu Xun's literary, historical, and political legacy in East Asia and the world. Finally, the Japanese writings on Lu Xun in my selection prove to be a moving and memorable encounter for me—born, raised, and academically trained in the space between languages and cultures and engaged on a personal and intellectual level in understanding and processing the differences and sameness between China and Japan. In the end, Takeuchi's, Dazai's, and Inoue's writings are memorable not because they are factual but because they are so invested in the intellectual, political, and affective import of the figure they create. They deliver a Lu Xun who embodies otherness but with whom one desires connection and dialogue and with them, hope for genuine reconciliation in East Asia.

Notes

Epigraph. Lu Xun's last written words in a note scribbled in Japanese to the owner of the Uchiyama Bookshop in Shanghai, Uchiyama Kanzō, whom Lu Xun fondly addressed as "Boss" (Ch. *laoban*), October 18, 1936. See Oda Takeo, *Rojinden* (Tokyo: Daiwa shobō, 1966), 175.

1. See Masuda Wataru, "Rojinden," *Kaizō* 14, no. 4 (April 1932): 1.
2. See Kawanishi Masaaki's commentary, quoted in Takeuchi Yoshimi, *Rojin* (Tokyo: Kōdansha, 1994), 227–230.
3. Ibid., 226.
4. Ibid., 234.
5. This refers to the central metaphor of cannibalism in *Diary of a Madman,* 1918.
6. See Takeuchi, *Rojin,* 150.
7. Ibid., 151.
8. Ibid., 22.
9. This refers to the failure in starting the coterie magazine *Xinsheng* (New life). See preface to Lu Xun's *Nahan* (Taipei, Taiwan: Fengyun chubanshe, 2011), 11.
10. See Takeuchi, *Rojin,* 52, 133, 134, and 142, respectively.
11. Lu Xun delivered a lecture on April 8, 1926, at Huangpu Military Academy in Guangchou. For Takeuchi's comments, see *Rojin,* 172–184.
12. Quoted in ibid., 174–175.
13. Ibid., 61.
14. Ibid., 232.
15. Ibid., 244–245.
16. Ibid., 237.
17. Yoshino Takao, *Bungaku hōkokukai no jidai* (Tokyo: Kawade shobō shinsha, 2008), 79.

18. The other one is a play by Morimoto Kaoru, *Onna no isshō* (A woman's life, 1945), in *Nihon no kindai gikyoku* (Modern Japanese plays), ed. Nihon kindai engekishi kenkyūkai (Tokyo: Kanrin shobō, 1999).

19. Dazai Osamu, *Dazai Osamu Zenshū 7* (1999; repr. Tokyo: Chikuma shobō, 2008), 320.

20. Ibid., 321–322.

21. See Okuno Takeo's commentary in Dazai Osamu, *Sekibetsu* (Tokyo: Shinchō bunko), 388.

22. See Okuno, ibid., 386 (my emphasis).

23. See Okuno, ibid., 386.

24. Ibid., 222.

25. Ibid., 222.

26. Ibid., 238.

27. Ibid., 239.

28. Ibid., 281.

29. Ibid., 291–292.

30. Ibid., 248.

31. Okuno, ibid., 387.

32. Okuno, ibid., 388.

33. According to C. T. Hsia, in 1927, "Chiang Kai-shek had decisively launched an anti-Communist campaign in Shanghai . . . In 1928 two major Communist groups, the Creation Society and the Sun Society, started a concerted attack on Lu Hsun in retaliation for his jeering attitude toward revolutionary literature." See Hsia, *A History of Modern Chinese Fiction: Third Edition* (Bloomington: Indiana University Press, 1999), 49.

34. Events and incidents that sent Lu Xun underground included the following: in 1930, the Ziyou Datongmeng, the Freedom Alliance, which later became the League of Left-Wing Chinese Writers, was under attack; in 1931, the left-wing writer Rou Shi was arrested and secretly executed; in 1932, the Shanghai incident (January 28–March 3), a battle between the armies of China and Japan, took place in the extraterritorial Shanghai International Settlement; in 1933, a fellow member of the Chinese Alliance for the Protection of Civil Rights, Yang Quan, was killed by the Nationalist secret police; in 1934, a leading left-wing writer and Lu Xun's close friend, Qu Qiubai, was arrested by the Nationalist troops and executed in 1935 in Changting, Fujian Province. See "Chronology of Events," in Takeuchi, *Rojin*, 219–220. Also see "Guide and Chronology," in Gloria Davies, *Lu Xun's Revolution: Writing in a Time of Violence* (Cambridge, MA: Harvard University Press, 2013), xviii–xxiii.

35. For information about Uchiyama Kanzō, see Ōta Naoki, *Densetsu no Nicchū bunka saron Shanhai Uchiyama shoten* (The legendary Sino-Japanese salon Uchiyama bookstore in Shanghai) (Tokyo: Heibonsha, 2008); and Yoshida Kōji, *Rojin no tomo Uchiyama Kanzō no shōzō* (Tokyo: Shinkyō shuppansha, 1994). See also "Uchiyama Kanzō," *Nippon daihyakka zenshū (Nipponica): Japan Knowledge*, accessed August 10, 2013, https://ccvpn10.cc.sophia.ac.jp/. For information about the Uchiyama Bookshop, see also Davies, *Lu Xun's Revolution*, 114.

36. For information about Sudō Iozō, see Zhou Guowei, *Lu Xun yu Riben youren* (Shanghai: Shanghai shudian chubanshe, 2006). Also see "Sudō yiyuan" (Sudō clinic), Shanghai Historical Map, accessed August 10, 2013, http://historicalmap2010shanghai.com/category/commentary/hongkou/page/3. Lu Xun's only son, Zhou Haiying, who was seven at the time of Lu Xun's death, wrote about his suspicion of a murder conspiracy and accused Sudō of negligence that resulted in Lu Xun's death. See Zhou Haiying, *Lu Xun yuwo qishinian* (Taipei, Taiwan: Lianjing, 2002), 66–74. The suspicion remains unsubstantiated.

37. Lu Xun's son, Zhou Haiying, recorded the making of the death mask in detail. See Zhou Haiying, *Lu Xun yuwo qishinian*, 64. Also see Watanabe Takashi, "Rojin to Nitchū jūgonen sensō" (Lu Xun and the Fifteen-Year War between China and Japan), in *Jūgonen sensō to Nihon*

no igakuiryō kenkyūkai kaishi (Journal of the Research Society for the Fifteen-Year War and Japanese Medical Science and Service) 3, no. 1 (2002): 42–49.

38. See Inoue Hisashi, *Shanhai muun* (Shanghai moon) (Tokyo: Shūeisha), 199, 163–164.

39. This image of Lu Xun is very different from the harsh and vitriolic polemicist gleaned from critical assessments of American and Chinese scholars. C. T. Hsia, for instance, portrays Lu Xun in his last years as an embittered old man deprived of literary inspiration; despicable and mistrustful of both the Leftists and Rightists around him; eager to pick fights with old friends and new foes; and devoted, in his last years, to endless ideological battles instead of literary creation. See Hsia, *History of Modern Chinese Fiction,* 51–52. The Chinese scholar Sima Changfeng is slightly more sympathetic in his portrayal. Lu Xun is presented as a stubborn individualist caught in the crossfire between the Rightists and the Leftists, with no choice but to resist. Sima quoted Lu Xun, "What I attack is the various forms of darkness in society. My attack is not aimed only at the Nationalist party. The roots of darkness are deep: some stemmed from one or two thousand years in the past, some several hundred years, some several decades, yet the Nationalist party refused to eradicate the roots. They want to silence me in order to cover up for all the darkness in these thousands of years." Quoted from Cao Juren, *Lu Xun Pingzhuan* (A critical biography of Lu Xun) (Hong Kong: Xinwenhua chubanshe, 1956), 108. Sima commented, "Lu Xun was a stubborn man. The more they wanted to silence him, the more he resisted. The Nationalist party had the upper hand on the Communist party at that time, and even though Lu Xun did not fully agree with the Communist party, he shared with them the sense of persecution. Thus one can say it was the Nationalist party that compelled Lu Xun to join the League of Left-Wing Writers." See Sima Changfeng, *Zhongguo xinwenxue shi,* vol. 1 (Hong Kong: Jaoming chubanshe, 1980), 241.

40. These include the political satire *Kirikirijin,* 1981; the antinuclear weapon play *Chichi to kuraseba,* 1994 (*The Face of Jizō,* 2004); and the play *Ningen gōkaku* (Qualified to be human), 1990, a parody of Dazai's *Ningen shikkaku,* 1948 (*No Longer Human,* 1958).

41. See Inoue, *Shanhai muun,* 163.

42. Ibid., 201.

43. Zhu An was Lu Xun's first wife.

44. Ibid., 211.

45. For instance, Mao Zedong claimed Lu Xun for the Communist Party in a hyperbolic language of praise. "Lu Hsün was the representative of the large majority of the nation and the most correct, courageous, resolute, loyal, and sincere fighter against the enemy, indeed an unprecedented national hero. The direction of Lu Hsün is the direction of the new Chinese culture." See Mao's *The New Democracy,* 1940, quoted in Hsia, *History of Modern Chinese Fiction,* 29.

46. See Lu Xun, *Nahan,* 10. See also Hsia, *History of Modern Chinese Fiction,* 30.

47. This is taken from the poem *Zichao* (Self-mockery), written in 1932 for Liu Yazi.

48. See Brian Massumi, *Parables for the Virtual: Movement, Affect, Sensation* (Durham, NC: Duke University Press, 2002), 63.

49. See Eileen Cheng, *Literary Remains: Death, Trauma, and Lu Xun's Refusal to Mourn* (Honolulu: University of Hawai'i Press, 2013), 180.

CONTRIBUTORS

Paul D. Barclay is associate professor of history at Lafayette College. His research focuses on the history of visual culture in the Japanese Empire. In addition to publishing numerous articles on Taiwan's Japanese-indigenous frontier, he currently serves as general editor for the East Asian Image Collection Digital Archive at Lafayette College. He has received grants from the Taiwan Ministry of Foreign Affairs, the National Endowment for the Humanities and the Japan Society for the Promotion of Science Research to support both his scholarship and archival work.

InYoung Bong studies modern Chinese literature. Her research focuses on colonialism and racial and social formation in cultural production in East Asia. Her most recent articles, on White Russians and the cultural politics of fear, appeared in *Modern Chinese Literature and Culture* (2014) and *Journal of Modern Chinese Literature* (2015), respectively.

Kim Brandt is a historian of modern Japan. Her written work includes *Kingdom of Beauty: Mingei and the Politics of Folk Art in Imperial Japan* (Duke University Press, 2007) and *Japan's Cultural Miracle: Rethinking the Rise of a World Power, 1945–1965* (Columbia University Press, forthcoming).

William H. Bridges IV is assistant professor of Japanese at the University of California, Irvine. After completing a BA in Japanese and English literature at the University of Texas at Austin, he received a PhD in Japanese literature from Princeton University. His teaching interests include the Japanese language, modern and classical literature, and popular culture. His research considers questions at the intersection of race and literature. He is coeditor of *Traveling Texts and the Work of Afro-Japanese Cultural Production* (2015).

Christopher P. Hanscom is associate professor in the Department of Asian Languages and Cultures at the University of California, Los Angeles. He is the author of *The Real Modern: Literary Modernism and the Crisis of Representation in Colonial Korea* (2013) and coeditor of *Imperatives of Culture: Selected Essays on Korean History, Literature, and Society from the Japanese Colonial Era* (2013).

Todd A. Henry is associate professor of history and director of the Program in Transnational Korean Studies at the University of California, San Diego. He specializes in modern Korea, with a focus on the period of Japanese rule (1910–1945). He is also interested in social and cultural formations linking post–Asia-Pacific War South Korea, North Korea, and Japan within the geopolitical contexts of American militarism and the Cold War. He is the author of *Assimilating Seoul: Japanese Rule and the Politics of Public Space in Colonial Korea, 1910–1945* (University of California Press, 2014) and is currently working on a comparative and transnational study of queerness in contemporary South Korea (1953–1993) focusing on authoritarian development, sexualized labor, and the entertainment industry.

Ji Hee Jung is a research assistant professor for the Humanities Korea Project at the Institute for Japanese Studies, Seoul National University. She received her PhD in history from the University of California, San Diego. Her research centers on the social and cultural history of modern and contemporary Japan, with a particular focus on the intersections of the culture and the subjectivity of nonelite and marginalized people, mass media, nationalism, imperialism, liberalism, fascism, and the Cold War. She is currently writing a book based on her dissertation, tentatively titled *Japanese Radio Culture and the Politics of Subjectivity, 1920s–1950s.*

Chul Kim is a professor in the Department of Korean Literature at Yonsei University in Seoul, Korea. His work, which includes *Overcoming the Nation* (2001), *The Slave Called "National Subject"* (2005), *The Ventriloquists* (2008), and *Embracing Colony* (2009), analyzes modern Korean literature through the problematic alignment of colonialism, nationalism, and imperialism. He has also edited several volumes, including *Fascism in Literature* (2001) and *Rethinking the History of before or after the Liberation* (2006).

Gyewon Kim is a visiting professor in the Department of Fine Arts at Sungkyunkwan University, South Korea. Her research interests include landscape photography, the politics of knowledge, documentation, and the archive, and questions of subjectivity within the context of visual culture in East Asia. Recent publications appear in *positions: east asia cultures critique* (March 2010), *Representations* (November 2012), and *History of Photography* (November, 2015).

ann-elise lewallen is assistant professor in modern Japanese cultural studies and anthropology at the University of California, Santa Barbara. She is coeditor of *Beyond Ainu Studies: Changing Academic and Public Perspectives* (University of Hawai'i Press, 2014), and her monograph, *The Fabric of Ainu Indigeneity: Contemporary Identity and Gender in Colonial Japan,* is forthcoming (University of New Mexico Press and School for Advanced Research Press). Her research focuses on indigenous movements in Japan and Asia; environmental justice; the intersections between gender, ethnicity, and race; and multiculturalism in contemporary Japan.

Edward Mack is associate professor of modern Japanese literature and culture at the University of Washington. Author of *Manufacturing Modern Japanese Literature: Publishing, Prizes, and the Ascription of Literary Value,* he currently focuses his research on Japanese-language literary creation and reception in Brazil during the twentieth century.

Kate McDonald is assistant professor of history at the University of California, Santa Barbara. Her research focuses on the cultural and technological history of mobility. She is currently at work on a history of travel and the spatial politics of the Japanese Empire. Her most recent article, a history of the global transportation network in early twentieth-century East Asia, appears in the January 2015 issue of the journal *Technology and Culture.*

Kari Shepherdson-Scott is assistant professor of art history at Macalester College. She specializes in Japanese visual culture from the nineteenth and twentieth centuries, focusing on the visual expression of national identity and empire. Her publications have examined how Japanese media and exhibitions during the 1930s and the early 1940s idealistically imagined occupied Manchuria as part of public relations campaigns at home and abroad. She is currently researching the relationship between wartime mobilization, spectacle, and representation during the late 1930s.

John Whittier Treat is professor emeritus at Yale. He is the author of *Writing Ground Zero: Japanese Literature and the Atomic Bomb* (Chicago, 1995) and is now working on a study of pro-Japanese Korean intellectuals under Japanese occupation. His novel *The Rise and Fall of the Yellow House* was published by Big Table Publishing in 2015, and his history of modern Japanese literature is forthcoming from the University of Chicago Press.

Dennis Washburn is the Jane and Raphael Bernstein Professor in Asian Studies in the Comparative Literature Program at Dartmouth College. Author of *The Dilemma of the Modern in Japanese Fiction* and *Translating Mount Fuji,* he has also edited several volumes, including *Word and Image in Japanese Cinema* and *Converting Cultures.* His translations of fiction include Yokomitsu Riichi's *Shanghai,* Minakami Tsutomu's *Temple of the Wild Geese,* Tsushima Yuko's *Laughing Wolf,* and *The Tale of Genji.*

Angela Yiu is professor of modern Japanese literature at Sophia University. She studied comparative literature as an undergraduate at Hong Kong University and Cornell University and completed her PhD at Yale University. Her publications include *Chaos and Order in the Works of Natsume Sōseki* (University of Hawai'i Press, 1999) and *Three-Dimensional Reading: Stories of Time and Space in Japanese Modernist Fiction, 1911–1932* (University of Hawai'i Press, 2013). Her current research interests include modernism, utopian studies, postwar literature, urban studies, and women writers.

INDEX

Page numbers for figures are in bold face.